HIROSHIMA

THE MAKING OF THE MODERN WORLD

This group of narrative histories focuses on key moments and events in the twentieth century to explore their wider significance for the development of the modern world.

PUBLISHED:
The Fall of France: The Nazi Invasion of 1940, Julian Jackson
A Bitter Revolution: China's Struggle with the Modern World, Rana Mitter
Dynamic of Destruction: Culture and Mass Killing in the First World War, Alan Kramer

FORTHCOMING:
The Vietnam Wars: A Global History, Mark Bradley
Algeria: The Undeclared War, Martin Evans

SERIES ADVISERS:
PROFESSOR CHRIS BAYLY, University of Cambridge
PROFESSOR RICHARD J. EVANS, University of Cambridge
PROFESSOR DAVID REYNOLDS, University of Cambridge

HIROSHIMA

THE WORLD'S BOMB

ANDREW J. ROTTER

OXFORD
UNIVERSITY PRESS

OXFORD

UNIVERSITY PRESS

Great Clarendon Street, Oxford OX2 6DP

Oxford University Press is a department of the University of Oxford.
It furthers the University's objective of excellence in research, scholarship,
and education by publishing worldwide in

Oxford New York

Auckland Cape Town Dar es Salaam Hong Kong Karachi
Kuala Lumpur Madrid Melbourne Mexico City Nairobi
New Delhi Shanghai Taipei Toronto

With offices in

Argentina Austria Brazil Chile Czech Republic France Greece
Guatemala Hungary Italy Japan Poland Portugal Singapore
South Korea Switzerland Thailand Turkey Ukraine Vietnam

Oxford is a registered trademark of Oxford University Press
in the UK and in certain other countries

Published in the United States
by Oxford University Press Inc., New York

British Library Cataloguing in Publication Data

Data available

Library of Congress Cataloging in Publication Data

Rotter, Andrew Jon.
Hiroshima: the world's bomb / Andrew J. Rotter.
p. cm.
Includes bibliographical references and index.
ISBN 978-0-19-280437-2
1. Atomic bomb—History. I. Title.
QC773.R67 2008
355.8'251190904—dc22   2007045146

Typeset by SPI Publisher Services, Pondicherry, India
Printed in Great Britain
on acid-free paper by
Clays Ltd, St Ives plc

ISBN 978-0-19-280437-2

1 3 5 7 9 10 8 6 4 2

To my daughters, Sophie and Phoebe Rotter.

Praise for Hiroshima

'An engaging and exceptionally skillful combination of the scientific, technological, military, diplomatic, political, and cultural history of the atomic bomb in an international context. By any standard, a terrific book.'

J. Samuel Walker, author of *Prompt and Utter Destruction: Truman and the Use of Atomic Bombs against Japan*

'In a smart, useful, and beautifully written book, Rotter treats the atomic bombing of Japan in its multinational context. Synthesizing a huge literature, he concisely shows in how many ways this truly was the world's bomb.'

Laura Hein, Northwestern University, and author of *Living with the Bomb*

'A profound look at one of mankind's most significant (and tragic) events . . . diplomats and their politician bosses should read this work for an understanding of the dire outcomes that diplomacy—and a lack thereof—can reap.'

Thomas W. Zeiler, University of Colorado, and author of *Unconditional Defeat: Japan, America, and the End of World War II*

Acknowledgements

I never intended to write a book on the atomic bomb, but when David Reynolds emailed out of the blue, as it were, in the summer of 2001 and asked me to write one for a new Oxford series, I could not resist his invitation. I have appreciated his support and advice throughout the protracted writing process. Katherine Reeve was my first editor and got me started; Luciana O'Flaherty took over and prodded me to finish during my sabbatical leave in London in 2006. Luciana's able and helpful assistant, Matthew Cotton, and my Oxford production editor Kate Hind, brought the book home. Hilary Walford copyedited the manuscript, even as the water rose around her house in Gloucester during the summer of 2007. Zoe Spilberg hunted down the photographs and negotiated permission for their use. Carolyn McAndrew handled the proofreading and eliminated the last of my sincere but, as it turned out, unnecessary attempts to spell in British.

I got interested in the atomic bomb because of my Stanford University graduate adviser Barton J. Bernstein, whose deep research on the subject I only gloss here. At Colgate University, my home institution, I was lucky enough to teach a course on the bomb with my colleague from across the Quad, Charles Holbrow. Since Charlie was responsible for doing the physics part of the course, I was fortunate that Robin Marshall, a physicist at the University of Manchester, read the manuscript and saved me from a number of errors. Laura Hein offered suggestions throughout, and Sam Walker bravely read the entire manuscript and said nice things about the writing. Conversations with friends and colleagues, including Carl Guarneri, David Robinson, Karen Harpp, Walter LaFeber, Frank Costigliola, and Jeremi Suri, helped to keep me on task, more or less. I am grateful to them all. I also thank audiences at the University of Minnesota, the University of Wisconsin, Fitchburg State College, Nanzan University, Kitakyushu University, and the Hiroshima Peace Institute, for questions, comments, and corrections following my lectures at these places. Students and colleagues at Colgate helped enormously. Thanks especially to my four terrific research assistants: Sarah Hillick, Alexander Whitehurst, Adam Florek, and Casey Graziani.

My parents, Roy and Muriel Rotter, and my in-laws, Chandran and Lorraine Kaimal, supported me unswervingly, which they seem to think is their job. My daughters, to whom the book is dedicated, have become young women in the course of my writing it. In the acknowledgements in my last book I characterized them as "naughty"; they are that no longer, but smart and beautiful and my proudest work ever. As always, my greatest debt is to my wife, Padma. Writing about the atomic bomb is not the most cheerful of pursuits. She kept me going, and much more.

Contents

Plates

Introduction
The World's Bomb

The atomic bombing of Hiroshima, Japan, on 6 August 1945, seems in many ways an event characterized by clarity and even simplicity. From a clear blue sky on a radiantly hot summer morning came a single American B-29 bomber (warily flanked by two observation planes), carrying a single bomb. The plane was called the *Enola Gay*, after its pilot's mother; the bomb bore the innocent nickname 'Little Boy'. There were no Japanese fighter planes to challenge the *Enola Gay*, no airbursts of flak in its way. Japanese civil defense, evidently having been fooled by a lone American reconnaissance plane over the city an hour before, now did not bother to sound the alert that would have sent people in Hiroshima to air-raid shelters. The target of the bomb was the Aioi Bridge, which spanned the Ōta River at the heart of the city. At 8.15 Hiroshima time the crew of the *Enola Gay* released the bomb. Forty-three seconds later, at an altitude of about 1,900 feet, Little Boy exploded.

One plane, one city, one morning in August, one atomic bomb: simple. The commander of the *Enola Gay*, a 29-year-old air-force colonel named Paul W. Tibbets, had practiced many times during the preceding weeks and months dropping mock equivalents of atomic bombs, filled with concrete and high explosives, on an isolated patch of the Utah desert and in the Pacific Ocean. The way his plane bounced upwards once the bomb had been dropped and then detonated was no surprise to him. That the bomb worked, creating an awesome cloud of fire and smoke and dirt and buffeting the *Enola Gay* with its shock wave, was testimony to the technological competence of an American-based team of scientists, who had solved many (though hardly all) of the scientific problems the Second World War had presented. And there seemed to the crew of the plane that bright morning a moral simplicity to what they had done. The criminality of the Japanese—all Japanese, without distinction—was to them unquestionable.

The Japanese had treacherously attacked Pearl Harbor. They had murdered civilians in China and Southeast Asia, tortured and starved their prisoners, and fought remorselessly for their island conquests in the South Pacific. If dropping an atomic bomb above the center of Hiroshima would end the war sooner, the men of the *Enola Gay* would simply do it, without hesitation and untroubled by pangs of conscience.

Over sixty years after the atomic bombing of Hiroshima (and Nagasaki, bombed three days later), we remember the event with much of the same stark simplicity with which it was regarded at the time. The atomic bomb, many claim, was an appropriate punishment for a people who had visited war and misery on the world, a punishment commensurate with Japanese malfeasance in Asia and throughout the Pacific. The Japanese deserved the bomb. Moreover, the bomb was essential to end the war. The Japanese war cabinet, or influential members of it, had vowed to sacrifice multitudes of their fellow citizens in defending their homeland against an anticipated invasion by the United States. The devastating firebombings of Japanese cities, including Tokyo, had not caused military officials to waver. Only a shock as powerful as the one the atomic bombs administered was sufficient to convince Japan's leaders, including the Emperor Hirohito, to quit the war on reasonable terms. The bombs thus saved hundreds of thousands of Japanese and American lives.

Or: The atomic bomb was a weapon so heinous in its composition, so willfully indiscriminate, so simply and obviously aimed at ordinary people, that its use was a moral outrage, even if it might in the end have saved lives. No people, regardless of the behavior of their government, deserves annihilation by a weapon as terrible as a nuclear bomb. In its very singularity as an instrument of war the atomic bomb stood condemned. It was the only known weapon to destroy so much by itself, to create such a powerful blast, such a devastating fire, and—perhaps above all— to spread radioactivity throughout its targeted place, with consequences as fearsome as they were at the time poorly understood. And, critics charged, the atomic bombings of Hiroshima and Nagasaki were unnecessary to win the war. Japan was near defeat by the summer of 1945, and some cabinet members, and possibly even the Emperor himself, were frantically looking for a way to surrender to the Americans while saving a measure of face and preserving the imperial system of rule. Had the Americans modified even slightly the terms of surrender, guaranteeing that Hirohito would keep his life and his position, Tokyo would have conceded. The Americans knew this. They used the bombs anyway in order to see what their new weapon—a $2 billion investment—would do to a city, and especially to end the Pacific War before the Soviet Union could enter it fully, and thereby demand a prominent role in the reconstruction of postwar Japan. The use of the bombs would in addition intimidate potential adversaries, serving notice, particularly in Moscow, that the United States had harnessed the power of the nucleus and would not scruple to use it.

But, of course, the atomic bombing of Hiroshima was not so simple, neither in 1945 nor today. That the dispute about its use remains bitter is evidence of that. The questions linger. Were the Japanese on their last legs by the summer of 1945? Did their leaders know it? Did the Americans think the Japanese leaders knew it? Was the bomb necessary to end the war? Were both bombs needed? In their absence, or with a decision not to use them, would it have taken a bloody American invasion of Japan itself to achieve surrender? Or would the war have ended, as the US Strategic Bombing Survey concluded in July 1946, 'certainly' before the end of 1945 'and in all probability prior to 1 November 1945 ... even if the atomic bombs had not been dropped, even if Russia had not entered the war, and even if no invasion had been planned or contemplated'?[1] Would it have been enough for the United States to have modified its demand that Japan surrender unconditionally, perhaps by signaling that the imperial system, the *kokutai*, could be retained? Was the bomb used chiefly not for military reasons but to intimidate the Soviet Union?

And yet, even these difficult and complex questions, along with their fraught and complicated and necessarily qualified answers, frame the argument too simply. For the atomic bombing of Hiroshima was not merely a decision made by US policymakers in order to punish the Japanese, not just an issue in Japan–US relations, but instead the product of years of scientific experimentation, ethical debate within the scientific community, and significant changes in the conduct of war—all undertaken globally. Americans alone did not decide to build the bomb, and neither did they alone actually build it. The science that enabled the bomb was conducted internationally; Hungarian, British, and German scientists and mathematicians, for example, were among the bomb's most important theoretical pioneers. Even after many of the world's leading mathematicians, physicists, and chemists had gathered in the United States and had combined their talents in the top-secret Manhattan Project, other scientists remained in their home countries, contributing to fledgling atomic bomb programs.

Limited by doubting governments and scarce resources, these programs nevertheless sustained the international scope of the pursuit of nuclear power, and internationalized as well the scientific and ethical debates over the atomic bomb that emerged with new intensity after August 1945.

If the making of the atomic bomb and the discussion that surrounded it had international sources, so too did the bomb have implications that stretched beyond the territories of the United States and Japan and well beyond the sensibilities of Americans and Japanese. News of the Hiroshima bombing was greeted with profound shock everywhere. A Mexican newspaper likened it to an earthquake, while a Trinidadian paper chose a comparison to a volcano—both familiar yet potentially catastrophic occurrences that were beyond human responsibility or control. The bomb killed mostly Japanese, of course, but also many Koreans and Chinese, and (indirectly) a few Americans, none of whom was in Hiroshima that dreadful morning by choice. Otto Hahn, one of the Germans who had discovered fission in 1938, was badly shaken by news of Hiroshima and blamed himself for the hundreds of thousands of deaths, while Werner Heisenberg, head of the German atomic-bomb project throughout much of the war, would not believe that the news was true.[2] When the Soviet dictator Josef Stalin heard about Hiroshima, he called in his scientists and declared himself fully for a crash program to build a Soviet atomic bomb. The British, proud of their contribution to the Manhattan Project—there were nineteen British scientists at the laboratory at Los Alamos, New Mexico, where the bomb was designed—decided nonetheless to build their own bombs. So, ultimately, did the governments of France, Israel, China, South Africa, India, Pakistan, North Korea, and possibly Iran.

The atomic-bomb tests that followed the Hiroshima and Nagasaki bombings put into the air radiation that no human-made boundary could contain. The waste products of nuclear reactors, on line for peaceful or warlike purposes, threatened to poison ground water as well. Fear of a nuclear nightmare also transcended nations. The creation of Soviet or (mostly) US military bases that held, or were reputed to hold, nuclear weapons within their gates—bases in the Philippines, Okinawa, Cuba, Turkey, and England—brought home to nearby residents the possibility that they might be the targets of a nuclear attack or victims of a nuclear accident. Resistance to the testing and deployment of nuclear weapons ranged far and wide, from Japan and Oceania to Europe and the United States. Popular culture, including literature, art, music, and even humor, reflected global fears of nuclear war, and just as often a heady defiance of those apparently willing to wage or countenance it.

The uranium-based bomb that was dropped on Hiroshima was thus the world's bomb. While it was an American's hand that released the bomb from the belly of the *Enola Gay*, and while Japanese died in droves that morning as a result, the atomic bomb was in a meaningful sense everyone's offspring and certainly thereafter everyone's problem. Had the Japanese, or the Germans, the British, or the Soviets made the bomb first, they surely would have used it against their enemies; that they did not get the bomb first had nothing to do with any moral qualms about producing it. No one's hands were entirely clean. Otto Frisch, the Austrian who came to Los Alamos and worked on assembling the critical mass essential for a nuclear chain reaction, felt nauseated when his fellow scientists celebrated the destruction of Hiroshima, while the Hungarian scientist Leo Szilard told a correspondent that the bombing was 'one of the greatest blunders in history', eroding as it did 'our own moral position'. Robert Oppenheimer, scientific head of the Manhattan Project, lamented to President Harry S. Truman that he had 'blood on his hands' because of his contribution to the bomb. (According to some accounts, Truman caustically offered Oppenheimer a handkerchief to wipe the blood off.) 'As far as I can see,' said Mahatma Gandhi, 'the atomic bomb has deadened the finest feelings which have sustained mankind for ages'—meaning that everyone, not just the immediate perpetrators of the bomb, had been morally compromised.[3]

This book tells the story of the Hiroshima bomb. It will explore, in layperson's terms, the physics of the bomb, the international crises that led to the Second World War, the creation of a community of scientists, throughout the world and especially in the United States during the 1930s and 1940s, dedicated to developing a weapon that could undo the evil that resided in Nazi Germany, the harnessing of their efforts by the wartime state, the political and strategic decisions that led to the bombing itself, the impact of the bomb on Hiroshima and the endgame of the Pacific War, the largely unavailing attempts to control the spread of nuclear weapons in the war's aftermath and the evolution of the nuclear arms race, the effects of the bombing and the bomb on society and culture, and the state of things nuclear in the early twenty-first-century world. Throughout, the account will contextualize the event—too seldom regarded as the place—we call Hiroshima as an episode in international history, not solely the consequence of wartime hatreds that marked the American–Japanese relationship in 1941–5. The result, I hope, is a serious, readable overview of one of the truly critical moments in the history of the twentieth-century world and all human history. 'The scientists, helped by the engineers, had drawn a line across history so that the centuries before August 6, 1945, were sharply separated from the years to come,' wrote the historian Margaret Gowing. 'And though perhaps they did not contemplate the technical "escalation" of the next fifteen years nor think in terms of megatons and megadeaths, of weapons that could obliterate not a single town but half a country, they knew that the atomic age had only begun.'[4] More than sixty years later, the Cold War is past, the danger of a nation-to-nation exchange of nuclear bombs or warheads seemingly diminished. Yet in an age of stateless terrorism and great power arrogance, where international norms and institutions appear helpless to prevent violence and nuclear materials go ominously missing, where there are no longer one or two nuclear nations but perhaps ten, we may wonder whether the world is safer from nuclear holocaust than it was in the bewildering days following that clear August morning in 1945.

ONE

The World's Atom

'Never believe', wrote the British physicist Jacob Bronowski, 'that the atom is a complex mystery—it is not. The atom is what we find when we look for the underlying architecture in nature, whose bricks are as few, as simple and as orderly as possible.' Reassuring words, perhaps, to a beginning student of physics, and logical too, for humans naturally seek to reduce large and complex matters to their essences. But the presence of atoms was neither demonstrated nor universally assumed until relatively recently. It is commonly said that the ancient Greeks postulated the existence of the atom, and it is true that the word *atomos* is Greek for 'indivisible', a coinage made by the philosopher Democritus around 430 BCE. Both Plato and Aristotle, however, disparaged the notion of the atom, Plato contending that the highest forms of human society, including truth and beauty, could not be explained with reference to unseen bits of apparently inert matter. The Platonic–Aristotelean view largely held the field for centuries. In 1704, Sir Isaac Newton wrote (in *Optics*): 'It seems probable to me that God in the beginning formed Matter in solid, massy, hard, impenetrable moveable Particles,' which made the case for something like atoms, however 'massy' they might prove. A century later, the English chemist John Dalton posited the existence of atoms as hard and round as billiard balls, though these were particular to chemical elements and not, as Democritus had claimed, all like each other in composition.[1]

1. Dissecting the atom

Undoing the atom was fundamentally the atomic inheritance of Ernest Rutherford, a New Zealander who came to study physics at Newton's university, Cambridge, and its Cavendish laboratory, in 1895. 'I was brought up to look at the atom as a nice hard fellow, red or gray in colour, according to taste,' he would write. For a time, Rutherford found no cause to change his mind. He worked on radio waves at the Cavendish, then spent nine years at McGill University in Montreal, tracing atomic 'emanations' but not yet investigating the atomic structure itself. In the meantime, however, J. J. Thomson, one of Rutherford's mentors, found in a closed glass tube evidence of particles with negative electrical charges that were themselves tinier than atoms; these would be called electrons, a name already long devised by the Irish physicist George Johnstone Stoney, who had posited though not demonstrated their existence. Using a similar tube, W. C. Röntgen, working at the University of Würzburg in Germany, produced an electrical discharge that yielded an odd glow. When he covered the tube with black paper and placed his hand between the tube and a screen, he could see faintly projected the bones of his hand. Röntgen called the phenomenon 'X-rays'. (A startled and righteous assemblyman in New Jersey, apprised of the discovery, introduced legislation 'prohibiting the use of X-rays in opera glasses'.) In 1896, the French physicist Henri Becquerel, inspired by Röntgen's finding, decided to look for X-rays in materials that fluoresced—that is, absorbed light from one part of the spectrum and emitted light from another part. He wrapped a photographic plate in black paper, dusted it with a uranium compound, then left the plate in the sun. After a few hours, he wrote: 'I saw the silhouette of the phosphorescent substance in black on the negative.' Becquerel tried the experiment again, but, discouraged by a succession of cloudy days in Paris, and assuming the sun had caused the tracing on the negative, he closed the plate in a drawer. He was surprised, several days later, when he looked at the plate, to find that the silhouette effect had occurred even in the dark. It was not the sun, but something in the uranium, that had penetrated the black paper and left its ghostly image. Two years later, the French wife–husband team Marie and Pierre Curie discovered two new elements, polonium and radium, that gave off Becquerel's mysterious discharge. They dubbed it 'radioactivity'.[2]

Something was coming off, or out of, atoms. They were not themselves the smallest things, nor were they as solid and 'massy' as billiard balls. Thomson's tiny electrons and the presence of radioactive emission demonstrated that. (Scientists would ultimately identify three types of radiations— alpha, beta, and gamma rays—with the betas being streams of electrons.) Over the first two decades of the twentieth century, Rutherford, who moved from Montreal to Manchester in 1910, 'systematically dissected the atom', as Richard Rhodes has written. He found that atoms, far from stable, might change themselves into another form of the same element they comprised (called an isotope) or another element altogether. He calculated that an enormous amount of energy came with radiation; if things went badly wrong, he said, 'some fool in a laboratory might blow up the universe unawares'. And, on 7 March 1911, speaking before a general audience in Manchester, Rutherford announced that he had revised his notion of the atom's structure: it had a central mass, or nucleus, around which spun electrons. Since electrons carried negative electric charges, the atomic nucleus must be charged positive. The force exerted by the electrons must be equal to that of the nucleus for the atom to remain stable.[3]

Rutherford did not work alone. At McGill he had teamed with Frederick Soddy, a chemist who, like Rutherford, would win a Nobel Prize, and also with the German Otto Hahn, who conjured with isotopes and would go on to do revolutionary experiments with the nucleus during the 1930s. In Manchester there was another German, Hans Geiger, builder of an electrical machine that detected radiation and clicked in its presence. He helped train James Chadwick, the Australian Marcus Oliphant, the Russian Peter Kapitsa, and the Japanese Yoshio Nishina—the latter two of whom would play leading roles in their nations' nuclear-weapons programs. The great Danish physicist Niels Bohr considered himself Rutherford's student, though he was Rutherford's equal at refining ideas about the structure of the atom. (Curiously, a Japanese scientist named Hantarō Nagaoka suggested in 1903 that an atom resembled the planet Saturn, with the planet itself as a nucleus and the rings representing electrons orbiting it. Rutherford seems not too have known of Nagaoka's vision, despite the two men having met in Manchester.)[4]

Rutherford concluded in 1919 that the nucleus of hydrogen, the first element in the periodic table, was a single, positively charged particle he called a proton. More complicated elements had more protons, and every nucleus of a single element had the same number of protons, which figure gives the element its atomic number. Rutherford and others, however, suspected that there was something more to the nucleus, for nuclei were evidently too heavy to consist only of protons. Suspicion was one thing, detection another. The other nuclear particles (to be called neutrons) were hard to find, as Laura Fermi wrote, because, unlike protons and electrons, they lack electrical charge, and because they 'stay very much at home inside atomic nuclei, and it is very difficult to get them to leave'. It was James

Chadwick who found the neutron, in experiments at the Cavendish in 1932. He reported his discovery before a group of physicists on 17 February, then said: 'Now I want to be chloroformed and put to bed for a fortnight.'[5]

While a neutron likes to stay put, it is, as a result of its electrical neutrality, an ideal projectile with which to enter and explore the nucleus. Probing the nucleus with a neutron, especially the large nucleus of one of the heavier and less stable elements, instantly destabilizes it. This nucleus busting, this breaking of atoms, is called fission. It was first observed by Otto Hahn and Fritz Strassmann in a laboratory in suburban Berlin in late 1938, properly interpreted by Lise Meitner and her physicist nephew Otto Frisch at the year's end (Hahn was inclined to resist the implications of his own experiment), confirmed experimentally by Frisch, then published in the February 1939 issue of the journal *Nature*, and even before that disclosed by Bohr at a meeting of the American Physical Society in Washington— from which excited physicists departed early in order to try the experiment themselves, and on which more later.

Holding together the protons and neutrons (the nucleons) is the strong nuclear force, which means that large amounts of energy are locked up inside the atom's nucleus. When a projectile neutron strikes a target nucleus, the nucleus breaks apart, yielding two nearly equal halves, a burst of energy, and some its own neutrons. 'These fly through the rest of the material,' Bronowski explains, 'and if the piece is large enough each neutron is certain to strike another nucleus and thus set off another burst of energy—and fire off still other neutrons to carry on the reaction.' The materials most likely to sustain such a chain reaction (as it is called) are those with heavy, unstable, neutron-rich nuclei, particularly uranium and human-made plutonium. A gram of uranium, fully fissioned through such a chain reaction, produces enough energy to light 20,000 light bulbs for ten hours. A similarly fissioned pound of uranium makes as much energy as millions of pounds of coal. Near the culmination of this process comes the release of radiation in the form of beta particles and gamma rays.[6]

Certainly Ernest Rutherford, the nucleus around whom buzzed an electron cloud of other scientists, had not, despite his puckish comment about a fool in a laboratory blowing up the universe, set out to make a powerful explosive. Anyone claiming that the day of atomic power was dawning was 'talking moonshine', he wrote dismissively in 1933. The excitement of discovery was thus not tied to some cataclysmic result, and for this reason not circumscribed by the nation. Even during the First World War, Rutherford had stayed in touch with scientists throughout Europe, including those in Germany. When the war ended, cooperation redoubled; what the American J. Robert Oppenheimer called the 'heroic' days of atomic physics, the time of 'great synthesis and resolutions', occurred during the 1920s, when the world was at peace. In the great centers of interwar physics—Cambridge, Paris, Copenhagen, Göttingen—there was excitement about theory, tiny particles of matter and their puzzling behavior, and how to reconcile the evidence recorded on machines and with the eyes with what one knew, or thought one knew, about the way atoms worked. In 1914, the writer H. G. Wells published a novel called *The World Set Free*, in which the earth, forty years hence, was a place of atomic-powered cars and radioactive bombs made of an element Wells called 'Carolinum', which bored deep into the soil and fired off 'puffs of heavy incandescent vapour and fragments of viciously punitive rock and mud, saturated with Carolinum, and even a center of scorching and blistering energy'. Leo Szilard, the Hungarian scientist who would become the Cassandra of the nuclear physics community during the 1930s and 1940s, at first regarded the book as entertaining fiction.[7]

2. The republic of science

The scientists had faith that, whatever they were conjuring with, whatever danger inhered in the explosive potential of the nucleus, they would, as a group, never allow their discoveries to be used by nation states against humanity. For they had their higher allegiances, whose purposes transcended those of petty polities shaped by the whims of nationalism or politics and susceptible to abuse by despots. They were part of what the philosopher of science Michael Polanyi would call 'the republic of science'. The republic had its own rules, cultures, practices. New initiates served as apprentices to elder masters, were taught how to do their work and evaluate the work of their colleagues. The point was, as Rhodes describes it, to create a 'political network among men and women of differing backgrounds and differing values', by establishing conventions of judgment and trust. The scientific republic did not replace the nation state but rested in consolidating fashion atop all such states.[8]

Above all, the republic must allow its constituents to work alongside each other, if not literally then with full knowledge of what all its other members are doing. Polanyi likened the process to assembling a jigsaw puzzle: while each person involved in the assembly contributes his or her skills to matching colors and shapes to make the pieces fit, in the end the puzzle must be a group enterprise, wherein skills, and puzzle components, are merged to form a whole. Each scientist (to depart from the metaphor) must see the entire problem laid out, and must contribute to its solution. There was no real hierarchy among scientists: 'The authority of scientific opinion remains *essentially mutual*; it is established *between* scientists, not *above* them.' That discoveries concerning the atom would be shared, through journal articles, at conferences, in coffee houses and taverns and labs, was a matter of faith among the world's physicists before the Second World War. One could not patent or nationalize the atom.[9]

James Chadwick was caught in Germany at the onset of the First World War and interned at a prison camp outside Berlin. A number of German scientists supplied him with enough equipment to set up a small laboratory, in which he worked with other scientist prisoners. In the midst of the war's carnage in May 1918, Chadwick wrote reassuringly to Rutherford that he was about to start work 'on the formation of carbonyl chloride in light'—scientist language for phosgene gas. The pace of scientific exchange quickened considerably with the end of the war, during Oppenheimer's 'heroic time'. ('It involved', Oppenheimer wrote, 'the collaboration of scores of scientists from many different lands . . . It was a time of earnest correspondence and hurried conferences, of debate, criticism and brilliant mathematical improvisation.') In Munich's cafés, students of the physicist Arnold Sommerfeld scrawled formulas on the marble tabletops; waiters at the Café Lutz were told never to wipe the tables without permission. Oppenheimer was one of many young American scientists who came to Göttingen during the 1920s (he was there nicknamed 'Oppie', or 'Opje', which he had difficulty getting used to). A group of remarkable Hungarian Jews—Polanyi, Edward Teller, Eugene Wigner, John von Neumann, Theodor von Kármán, Leo Szilard—left their home country during the 1920s and 1930s, driven out by political instability, state violence, and a rising tide of anti-Semitism. The Japanese physicist Nishina, who would be the first scientist contacted by the Japanese government to explain what had happened at Hiroshima, worked with Rutherford and Bohr, and in 1927 hosted Albert Einstein in Tokyo.[10]

Like Nishina, many came to study with Bohr in Copenhagen, and Bohr
himself frequently seemed to be in several places at once. He consulted
men who would stay and work in Nazi Germany, most famously Carl
Friedrich von Weizsäcker and Werner Heisenberg. He also welcomed those
escaping the oppressions of dictators and helped hundreds get safely off
the Continent as Hitler's darkness fell. (He himself would escape, first to
Sweden, then to Britain and the United States, in late 1943.) In Polanyi's
scientific republic, Bohr was *primus inter pares*. He embodied the ideal of a
scientific community, offering by example a model of integrity and probity,
encouraging others in their work, sharing, with his wife, Margrethe, his
hospitality, and most of all failing, in the most admirable ways, to respect
political and national boundaries that stood in the way of scientific progress.

Bohr's supreme cosmopolitanism would bring him to understand that a
terrible explosive based on the energy of the atom was no more susceptible
to monopoly than the atom itself. More than anyone else, Bohr would
grasp the ultimate unity of the world's scientific community. The secret
of the atomic bomb was in his judgment no secret at all, since intelligent
men and women across the globe had come together to understand the
forces that made it work. Borders between nations, hardened by mistrust
and war, were finally ineffective against the spread of scientific knowledge.
'The chain of scientific events that led to the threshold of the bomb',
wrote Laura Fermi, had gone 'zigzagging without interruption from one
country to another'. In 1943, Bohr felt that the republic of science, looming
transcendently over the artificial collection of nation states, would be the
final arbiter of the bomb. He knew the Russian scientists, including Peter
Kapitsa, and he knew that they would figure out how to build a bomb. Why
not admit that secrets were impossible to keep in a polity based on sharing,
and acknowledge the scientific republic by letting the Soviets know that an
international group of scientists was making a bomb in the United States?[11]

Bohr's teacher, colleague, and friend Ernest Rutherford was gone by
then; he would never see his 'moonshine' made horribly manifest at
Hiroshima. Rutherford apparently once claimed that he could do his
research at the North Pole, provided he had a lab and the right equipment.
Rudolf Peierls, a German who came to work in England in 1933 and later
helped to develop the bomb in Los Alamos, knew Rutherford (and Bohr)
well, and doubted either could have worked successfully in isolation. 'The
Rutherford and Bohr types thrive on contacts,' he wrote. 'They are kept
going by their own initiative, but they must share their knowledge and their

discoveries with friends and colleagues.' Both men were too much part of the scientific republic to have left it for a smaller, more parochial place.[12]

3. The republic threatened: the advent of poisonous gas

Despite the creation of Chadwick's prison camp lab, despite the determination of Bohr and Rutherford to maintain the flow of scientific information across national boundaries, the First World War challenged international cooperation and threatened republican scientific loyalties. It did so in part because many scientists in the belligerent nations went to work for their governments and helped develop weapons that destroyed men in the name of national honor, security, or purpose. Probably the most notorious of these, and a sobering harbinger of nuclear arms, were chemical weapons, often (though not always) dispensed in the form of poisonous gas. Near the Belgian town of Ypres, at 5.00 in the afternoon on 22 April 1915, the air was suddenly filled with 'thick yellow smoke...issuing from the German trenches'. 'What follows', reported the British Field Marshall Sir John French, 'almost defies description. The effect of these poisonous gases was so virulent as to render the whole of the line held by the French...practically incapable of any action at all...Hundreds of men were thrown into a comatose or dying condition, and within an hour the whole position had to be abandoned, together with about fifty guns.' There were estimates that 5,000 soldiers died in the attack, and twice that number were injured, their throats and eyes and lungs left burning and their memories haunted. 'It was', wrote a British clergyman who observed the retreat, 'the most fiendish, wicked thing I have ever seen.'[13]

The Germans had been thinking about chemical weapons since at least the previous year. From the first, German military officials had involved academic and industry chemists in the quest for an agent that would disorient and damage enemies dug into trenches on both fronts. They experimented in the fall of 1914 with a compound that caused violent fits of sneezing, pouring it into howitzer shells and launching them at the French at Neuve Chapelle in October. The compound dispersed poorly and had no apparent effect on the battle, and the shortage of shells and launchers made continued experiments unattractive. The eminent chemist

Fritz Haber found a solution: disperse chlorine gas from metal cylinders, creating a toxic cloud that would settle over enemy positions. The German command agreed to try this. The generals recruited scientists and soldiers to serve as forward observers—that is, to find the most favorable positions from which to launch the gas cloud. Six thousand cylinders were opened simultaneously that April afternoon. The cloud at first looked white, then intensified to yellow and green as the amount of chlorine in it rose, drifting higher and moving south and west over French and Algerian posts. The affected soldiers broke and ran.[14]

Among those Germans sent to plan the attack was Otto Hahn, already well known for his work on radiation with Ernest Rutherford in Montreal. Haber pressed Hahn into service in the name of science and loyalty to the German state. By his own account, Hahn was not so sure, objecting that the use of gas would violate the Hague Convention of 1899, which proscribed the use of projectiles to diffuse 'asphyxiating or deleterious gas'. Haber responded, first, that the French had already started it, having filled rifle cartridges with tear gas (a dubious claim when Haber made it, in January 1915), and, more important, that the use of gas would ultimately save lives on all sides because it would end the war sooner. It was also technically true that the release of a gas cloud did not involve launching projectiles. Hahn evidently accepted this logic. 'I let myself be converted', he remembered, 'and threw myself into the work wholeheartedly.' He remained involved in chemical warfare, and was called a 'gas pioneer', until the armistice—even after Haber had confided to him that he thought the war was lost.[15]

The Germans continued to develop new chemical compounds and new ways to deliver them. Shells came largely to replace clouds released from cylinders; chlorine was succeeded by phosgene and chloropicrin, harder than chlorine to detect and more destructive. In the summer of 1917 they fired at Ypres shells marked with a yellow cross and filled with mustard gas, which smelled like horseradish and was, according to one commentator, 'the war gas *par excellence* for the purpose of causing casualties'. Men were blinded, in some cases permanently, about seven hours after exposure to it. German use of gas increased especially on the Eastern Front, where prevailing winds favored the emissions and where the Russians were slower than the Western Entente combatants to develop effective gas masks. Hahn helped to coordinate a chlorine and phosgene attack against Russians in Galicia in June 1915. The Russians were taken by surprise, and, as Hahn advanced with German troops, he found their enemies *in extremis*. 'We tried to use our own respirators to help some of them, to ease their breathing, but they were past saving,' Hahn wrote. His conscience prickled. But he and Haber were hardly alone in the work: they were joined by several noted chemists and the physicist James Franck, who would later join the Manhattan Project and urge that atomic bombs not be dropped on Japan. Some 2,000 German scientists all told were involved in chemical warfare in 1914–18.[16]

Neither were the Germans alone in the work. The French, as Haber seems to have anticipated, were at the time of the chlorine cloud attack at Ypres at work on tear-gas bullets and grenades. Prominent Britons condemned the use of gas—Arthur Conan Doyle charged that the Germans had 'sold their souls as soldiers', and Lord Kitchener insisted that 'these methods show to what depths of infamy our enemies will go'—but the British quickly set to the task of manufacturing chemical weapons and masks to protect their solders against their use. The Allied response-in-kind to the German attacks was uncoordinated and fitful. The British worked hard at developing chemicals, but their way to success was slowed by bureaucratic competition, panic-induced haste, and an official willingness to entertain, at least, crackpot suggestions by amateurs that the British set fire to the atmosphere or spray German lines with amyl nitrate, an inflammable liquid. Hand grenades filled with what were described as 'annoyers' were rushed to France in May 1915, and the Scottish physiologist J. S. Haldane devised defenses against gas that involved breathing through a bottle loosely filled with dirt or a urine-soaked sock. French military headquarters, as L. F. Haber (Fritz Haber's son) has described it, 'was all energy and valorous sentiments', but was unable to produce much: the French lacked chlorine to make that gas, and plans to retaliate against the Germans with gas-cloud attacks foundered on command's decisions to build gas squads largely from wounded soldiers. The French did manage to fill some 50,000 shells with a tear gas that dispersed so rapidly that the targeted Germans appeared not to notice they had been gassed. Even the Russians blustered about making gas clouds—threats, as Haber notes, that were never taken seriously by anyone.[17]

The US president Woodrow Wilson entreated the European belligerents not to use chemical weapons in May 1915. But the United States itself had not signed the 1899 Hague Convention; its delegate, Admiral Alfred Thayer Mahan, said then that he could see no distinction between killing unsuspecting men by explosive or gas. The United States did ultimately agree to an international ban on the use of poison (codified in Hague II, 1907, and signed by the United States soon after), but, like the other signatories, the Americans found ways to evade the ban, and, once the United States had entered the war in April 1917, the Wilson administration, as Haber writes, 'took gas very seriously indeed'. Responsibility for developing chemical weapons and protection against them was at first given to the US Bureau of Mines, though in June 1918 it was taken on by the Chemical Warfare Service, which undertook both research into and the production of chemicals. American University in Washington DC became in mid-1917 the center of chemical investigation, absorbing work done previously at other universities, though retaining branch laboratories at several. In marshland 20 miles east of Baltimore, the Americans built an enormous chemical manufacturing complex called 'Gunpowder Reservation', later the Edgewood Arsenal. The plant employed thousands of men and women, and produced chlorine, phosgene, chloropicrin (which caused weeping and vomiting and which defeated then-existing gas masks), mustard, and several others. By the summer of 1918, Edgewood was contributing heavily to gas warfare on the Western Front. As the Armistice neared that fall, an American observer could not conceal his dismay: 'Here is a mammoth plant', he wrote of Edgewood, 'constructed in record time, efficiently manned, capable of an enormous output of toxic material, and just reaching its full possibilities of death-dealing at the moment when news is hourly expected of the signing of the Armistice. What a pity we did not possess this great engine of war from the day American troops first sailed for France.'[18]

Casualty figures for those gassed during the First World War are elusive. Estimates made during the two decades following the war ranged from 560,000 to nearly 1.3 million dead or injured. L. F. Haber refuses to try to count Russian casualties—the figures are wholly unreliable, he says—and estimates about half a million gas casualties. While many more men were killed or wounded by explosives or bullets, these are nevertheless substantial numbers, and use of gas later caused reflection and remorse among some of the chemists who had participated in its manufacture. Otto Hahn struggled to absorb the sight of Russians killed by his chlorine cloud in Galicia in 1915. One of Hahn's contemporaries, Hermann Staudinger, argued that scientists ought to renounce the use of chemical weapons and work to educate their fellow citizens about the special horrors of gas. (Staudinger's suggestion brought a sharp rebuke from Fritz Haber.) Some American scientists expressed disgust with gas; in France, an eminent chemist urged that chemistry not be used for destructive purposes. Two weeks after the Armistice, a group of British medical researchers, in a letter to *The Times* of London, criticized the use of gas because (they said) it could not be contained to military targets and because it killed in a particularly heinous way. Sir Edward Thorpe decried 'the degradation of science' that resulted from the battlefield use of gas. For scientists to contribute to the death of innocents at the behest of the state was wrong. The critics of gas were to some extent vindicated by future decisions: chemical weapons were evidently not used in the Second World War, and only in a few other instances—by the British against Bolsheviks in 1919, by the Italians against Abyssians in 1935, and by the government of Iraq, against Iran and its own citizens, in the 1980s and 1990s—during the twentieth century.[19]

4. The ethics of battlefield gas

What was it about chemical weapons, and gas in particular, that made it the subject of special opprobrium by scientists and others after the war? It was not that gas killed more men more efficiently than other weapons, as the First World War casualty figures indicate. Gas-protection technology advanced quickly beyond Haldane's urine-soaked sock, so that with enough warning and proper discipline soldiers in gassed trenches could remain undamaged. But there lingered what was called the 'subjective effect' of gas. In an English test of a lachrymator abbreviated SK in early 1915, an officer standing well upwind of a burst shell later complained of weakness and illness, despite his having done no more than observe the explosion. Haber explains the man's fear as the product of an overactive imagination. That is precisely the problem with gas, or part of the problem: it insinuates itself into the atmosphere that people must breathe to live, thus destroying any idea of a boundary between what brings death and what sustains life. Unlike a bullet or a bomb, it kills quietly, insidiously, masquerading as something innocuous or even pleasant. 'The English gas is almost odorless and can only be seen by the practised eye on escaping from the shell,' recalled a German infantry officer. 'The gas steals slowly over the ground in a blueish haze and kills anyone who does not draw his mask over his face as quick as lightning before taking a breath.' Mustard gas smells like horseradish, though the Germans would later mask it with the scent of lilac. Phosgene bears a faint odor of cut grass and may not immediately affect those who breathe it; twelve hours later its victims' lungs fail.[20]

Not only does gas refuse to acknowledge the elemental boundary between life and death: it also resists containment, and it is thus inherently indiscriminate. Infantry soldiers hated it when their own side attacked with gas, since a change in wind direction could reverse the direction of the cloud and envelop them. (A few of their officers thought the use of gas unsporting.) Civilians near the Western Front were increasingly subject to the vagaries of gas during 1916–18. Distribution of gas protection and information to local residents was haphazard in Belgium and France; during one particularly heavy German attack with mustard near Armentières in July 1917, 86 civilians died and nearly 600 others were injured. Haber estimates conservatively—his figures include no Germans—that 5,200 civilians were poison-gas casualties during the First World War. By the war's end, technicians were experimenting with a variety of ways to deliver gas so as to achieve the greatest and quickest effect, including the use of long-range artillery shells filled with gas and chemicals disbursed from airplanes. That the latter innovation was a likely feature of the next war was little disputed by scientists, novelists, and strategists of battle. American planners imagined attaching gas sprayers to the wings of aircraft. Others pictured gas bombs. Amos A. Fries, head of the US Chemical Warfare Service during and after the war, meant to reassure when he wrote (with Major C. J. West) in 1921: 'As to noncombatants, certainly we do not contemplate using poisonous gas against them, no more at least than we propose to use high explosives in long range guns or aeroplanes against them.' The nature of gas as a substance able to drift over distance and penetrate standard defenses of populations made it a terrible, logical weapon to envision as useful against civilians.[21]

There is also the matter of how gas kills. While burning and blinding are common injuries resulting from gas attacks, death from gas is most often caused by suffocation. Chlorine and phosgene are lung irritants. They inflame respiratory tissue, causing in it lesions and drawing fluid from elsewhere in the bloodstream, thus overwhelming the lungs with congestion. 'In severe cases,' writes Edward Spiers, 'the victims die from asphyxiation, drowning in the plasma of their own blood.' A British sergeant recalled seeing a dozen men gassed with chlorine in May 1915: 'Their colour was black, green, and blue, tongues hanging out and eyes staring—one or two were dead, and others beyond human aid, some were coughing up green froth from their lungs. It is a hateful and terrible sensation to be *choked* and suffocated and unable to get breath: a casualty from gun fire may be dying from his wounds, but they don't give him the sensation that his life is being strangled out of him.' To be sure, dismemberment by explosive, multiple gunshot wounds, or burns from incendiary bombs are awful too, and horribly painful. But the thought of suffocation, slow and uncontrollable, touches the deepest place of human fear. It is a primal, helpless death, one of betrayal by the silent unbreathable air; it is slow, unheroic, panic-inducing, ugly. It is not unlike death by radiation.[22]

The scientists and soldiers who developed chemical weapons for their belligerent nations during the First World War seemed to establish a camaraderie one finds in those who come together for a noble cause. An interviewer once told Otto Hahn that he was surprised so many noted German chemists had joined the war effort in such dangerous work as gas provided. 'Why?', asked Hahn. 'We volunteered, we offered our services.' A British chemist recalled that 'we were, with one or two exceptions, a band of brothers', and French planners met frequently, if not always effectively, to coordinate offensive and defensive chemical strategy. They were professionals, called upon by their government to help protect soldiers and civilians. They were doing patriotic service, an argument that may have been especially meaningful to Fritz Haber, a Jew who was, according to his son, 'well aware that his Jewish origin was both obstacle and spur' to his loyalty. They could tell themselves—some did—that gas was far more likely to disable enemies than kill them, so it was an oddly humane weapon.[23]

What the chemists and users of gas told themselves above all was that their weapon worked best if men and women perceived it to be horrible, because the graver the apparent threat from the weapon, the more likely an early concession by its victims. Leaders of warring nations, behaving rationally, like scientists, would seek to avoid national annihilation. Great danger of annihilation meant a shorter war. Amos Fries told a Senate committee just after the war that, the more 'deadly' the weapons, 'the sooner . . . we will quit all fighting'. Make war terrible enough, and men would never start it. Haber had persuaded Hahn to work on gas—indeed, to throw himself 'wholeheartedly' into the work—by insisting that chemical weapons would end the war quickly. The use of gas would finally save lives.[24]

This was bold justification of weapons' work, and probably believable on some level to those who advanced it. But most men cannot read about the results of their research crippling and killing other men without feeling remorse. Otto Hahn, who, unusually for a scientist, came face to face with Russian victims of a gas attack, confessed to feeling shame for his role in their deaths, but in the end ascribed them to 'the senselessness of war', not to human agency (and certainly not to his own). His boss, Fritz Haber, was confronted by his chemist wife, Clara, about the 'barbarism' of poison gas; it was, she insisted, 'a perversion of science'. Not so, Haber remonstrated, rehashing arguments he had used earlier with Hahn. The night after their argument, Clara Haber took her life. After the war, Hahn related, Haber feared trial as a war criminal. He dropped out of sight for awhile, then reappeared having grown a beard, in the hope of avoiding recognition.[25]

There are many ways in which the development of chemical weapons differed significantly from the manufacture of an atomic bomb. The chemistry of gas was easier to master than the physics of the nucleus. Gas carries no powerful blast or searing fire, it is fickle when it is blown or burst into the air, and most of all it can be protected against, provided a targeted group has adequate notice and equipment. But the similarities between chemicals and nuclear weapons are sufficiently arresting to justify the lengthy consideration of gas offered here. Chemicals and atom bombs were in their times new weapons, understood by those who made them as things unprecedented and possibly decisive in war. Both chemicals and chain-reacting neutrons put weapons into a sinister dimension virtually beyond sight and sound: in trenches men blundered into undetectable pockets of gas, while radiation (following a blast that Hiroshimans, of course, saw and heard) worked its deadly way undetected into people who had apparently escaped harm. And both weapons, even in their preparation, killed scientists hideously, much as they would kill many others with their use on battlefields and over cities. In December 1914, Dr Otto Sackur, an associate of Fritz Haber, died when a tear-gas compound he was working on exploded. Marie Sklowdowska Curie, discoverer of the radioactive elements polonium and radium, died in 1934 of leukemia. She was by then nearly blind, and her fingers were twisted and burned from the radiation to which she had exposed herself in the laboratory. Sackur and Curie were early casualties of weapons once fanciful, then dreadful, and harbingers of far greater harm that would be visited on the world.[26]

5. Scientists and states: the Soviet Union and the United States

There is one more way in which gas production resembled the making of the atomic bomb: both enterprises called academic science into wartime service to the state, on an enormous scale and in several countries at once. This observation raises the important question of how, or whether, the scientific republic can survive the harnessing of science to a nation's foray into war. Scientists need cooperation to do their work. They also need the freedom to pursue mysteries, wherever they might reside, and without regard for the possible political consequences of their discoveries. The mythical scientist is both sustained by colleagues and freed by the beneficence of the scientific republic. In the lab he seeks only truth. Values, in theory, do not interest the scientist, nor do political agendas, righteous or unrighteous causes, or the concerns of statesmen and -women. The mythical scientist is not, of course, without political feeling or ambition; it is simply that she would separate these things from the pursuit of results in the lab.

In reality, though, scientists at nearly all times and in all places have depended not only on colleagues but on support from the institutions they serve, including governments. The scientific republic is necessarily circumscribed by the requirement that scientists live in one or another country, whatever their feeling about nationalism. One can claim to practice value-free science and to serve no political master. But, whatever the scientist's indifference to the state, the state is likely to be interested in him, especially if he is a chemist or physicist working on some form of military apparatus. The level of state interest and the degree to which the state might act on it depend on the state's institutions and relations between political, economic, and scientific elites. Etel Solingen has proposed what she terms 'a crude fourfold typology' to describe twentieth-century states and predict how they would treat their scientists. Her political axis includes 'pluralist' and 'noncompetitive' (that is, 'autocratic'), her economic axis 'market-oriented' and 'centrally planned.' Let us choose one pre-Second World War example from the two opposite ends of Solingen's four categories and in this way examine the influence of state form on scientific communities.[27]

We can begin with the Soviet Union, a 'noncompetitive centrally planned' state. The Russian tsars mistrusted science, discerning in it the impulse toward free enquiry, modernization, and democracy, all of which they regarded with suspicion. The Bolsheviks, who took power in 1917, had a different view. Marxism itself purported to be scientific, and the Bolsheviks' tenuous hold on authority through the early 1920s made pragmatists of them—after signing the humiliating Treaty of Brest–Litovsk with the Germans in 1918, Lenin said grimly that 'it is necessary to master the highest technology or be crushed'. That did not mean that the new government had a policy toward science in mind. And, despite their ideological and practical embrace of science, the Bolsheviks were wary of 'bourgeois' scientists themselves, which feeling was mutual. Through the 1920s, with the Communists preoccupied with fending off their enemies and building the economy, scientists enjoyed reasonable autonomy, and their numbers and organizations and status grew.[28]

This began to change at the end of Bolshevism's first decade in power, as Josef Stalin solidified his control of the Soviet state. Scientists were told to submit five-year research plans that could grow to hundreds of anxious pages of self-explanation. Scientific professional societies, which had proliferated during the 1920s, were now increasingly absorbed by the scientific apparatus of the state and subsequently eliminated altogether. The Party insisted that scientific research have as its object the improvement of industry. Basic research was starved out, or at least left hungry, leaving only 'applied science' as having some obvious benefit to the nation's political economy. The Party also reined in scientists' travel to international conferences, prevented to some extent their receipt of scientific journals published abroad, and impeded generally contacts between Soviet scientists and their counterparts elsewhere. Those with foreign training or monied backgrounds were isolated, harried from their posts, or shunted off to Stalin's Gulag. Certain kinds of science were condemned as anti-proletariat; 'pure science' was deemed effete, and thus useless, or worse, to the purposes of the revolution. (This 'Proletkultist' movement would win its greatest victory after the Second World War, when the pseudoscientist Trofim Lysenko eliminated the serious study of genetics in the Soviet Union. This 'rejection of the gene', as Paul R. Josephson has called it, lasted until 1965.)[29]

The development of the 'noncompetitive centrally planned' state in the Soviet Union had particular impact on the physics community. During the First World War the physicist Abram Ioffe created, in Petrograd (soon to be renamed Leningrad), the State Physiotechnical X-Ray Institute. Ioffe's institute would become the 'forge' of Soviet nuclear physics. The first chair of its nuclear department was Igor Kurchatov, a bearish and humorous scientist who in the early 1930s immersed himself in the growing scholarship on nuclear physics and thereafter built a proton accelerator at the institute—though he changed course when he read about the Italian Enrico Fermi's revolutionary work with neutrons. By the middle of the decade, a British physicist pointed to four international centers for nuclear research: the Cavendish, Fermi's lab in Rome, Paris (wherein worked Marie Curie's daughter Irène and her husband, Frédéric Joliot), and 'Kurchatov and his people', who were 'not far behind us considering the time difference in receiving journals'. The institute physicists would eventually be awarded by the People's Commissariat of Heavy Industry a cyclotron, a magnetic, circular accelerator of subatomic particles.[30]

How much faster Kurchatov and his colleagues might have gone had they not been restricted by their government's rigidity and suspicion is difficult to say. Travel to the West was curtailed: Peter Kapitsa was prevented from returning to the Cavendish in 1934, and Kurchatov was not allowed to accept an invitation to Berkeley, where Ernest Lawrence was pioneering particle acceleration techniques, in the winter of 1934–5. Soviet travel restrictions worked in the other direction, too. David Holloway has noted that, at the annual Soviet nuclear conference in 1933, half the papers were presented by non-Soviet scientists. Four years later, just five of the twenty-eight papers were given by non-Soviets, and by 1938 no one from abroad participated in the meeting at all. The extraordinary sensitivity of nuclear physics saved the physics community from the utter devastation that would be suffered by the biologists under Lysenko. But these conditions were not enough to keep scores of the most talented physicists from being arrested, sent to the Gulag, or shot. Research nevertheless went on. In David Holloway's judgment, 'Soviet physics reached a high standard in the 1930s'—testament to the intelligence and determination of people working under a government both authoritarian and capricious.[31]

The United States during the interwar period represents, following Solingen's typology, a pluralist state with a market-oriented economy—the opposite, in other words, of the Soviet Union. Daniel Kevles has traced the developing relationship between American physicists and the state, and in particular the association made between the scientists' work and national security, beginning during the First World War. This affiliation was by no means inevitable. Like all scientists, American physicists cherish their independence and do not lack for ego. 'The vehemence of conviction, the pride of authorship burn as fiercely among scientists as among any creative workers,' noted the eminent chemist and scientific administrator James Conant. There existed a tension between the physicists' view that, in a free society, they ought to be able to follow whatever scientific paths they chose, and the government's view that resources must go first to those engaged in what it considered to be useful work for the state. In times of national emergency, when US security is threatened, these visions may coincide. In June 1916, prodded by President Woodrow Wilson and its own foreign secretary, the astronomer George Ellery Hale, the National Academy of Sciences formed the National Research Council (NRC), which promised to support scientific research aimed at 'the national security and welfare'. Some scientists objected; one, a pacifist, branded the NRC 'militaristic'. But, when the United States went to war with Germany in April 1917, most physicists resolved to help in the effort. American scientists devised new and more effective ways to detect German submarines, worked with allies' models to develop a system to pinpoint the location of enemy artillery, and, as noted, explored a new generation of chemical weapons, including how to deliver and protect against them. Thomas Edison, notes Kevles, 'fashioned some forty-five devices for the military', all, in Edison's view, 'perfectly good', though none was used. The war, as Hale put it, had 'forced science to the front'.[32]

Not for all time. Democracies are generally quick to demobilize after wars end, their citizens returning to peacetime pursuits and frequently with expressions of regret for time lost to militancy. Scientists determined to do their duty in wartime (and no doubt excited by the quick application of their work) balked after the Armistice at the discipline and secrecy imposed on them by military authorities. American scientists were not shot for alleged ideological crimes, but they had sometimes felt themselves bullied and disrespected by high-handed officers. The generals, for their part, had tired of civilian independence, insubordination, and impracticality. In the military's parlance, the scientists were 'damn professors', useful if paying attention to realities, but too often inclined to loose gossip and head in the clouds theorizing.[33]

Science, including physics, nevertheless proved popular in America during the 1920s. George Hale persuaded philanthropists to finance a science school in Pasadena called the California Institute of Technology. It quickly attracted top physicists—it would share Robert Oppenheimer with Berkeley—and drove other universities to expand their physics programs in response. Exciting discoveries inside the atom raised the visibility and glamor level of the physicists, even if most laypersons failed to grasp the essence of atomic science. The federal government funded research, and state legislatures boosted the budgets of their home universities. Most of all, the market worked to the considerable advantage of scientists generally. 'Science is not a thing apart,' insisted the *Saturday Evening Post* in 1922. 'It is the bedrock of business.' By the latter part of the 1920s, the United States was spending $200 million each year on scientific research, with industry spending three times as much as the government. A cult of admiration, even affection, emerged around Albert Einstein, the exponent of the theory of relativity and German emigré who settled permanently at the Institute for Advanced Study at Princeton in 1933. Einstein was more rumpled than glamorous, but that proved no obstacle to the chemist and scientific popularizer Edwin Slosson, who wrote in 1925 (and apparently not about Einstein) that scientists were as 'cleanshaven, as youthful, and as jazzy as a foregathering of Rotarians'.[34]

What the market provided for American scientists during the 1920s it took away during the 1930s. With the onset of the Great Depression in 1929, funding for physics research, both government and private, dried up. Kevles summarizes the damage: federal government scientists were fired in droves, AT and T sacked 40 percent and General Electric 50 percent of their lab workers; untenured university faculty feared for their jobs and senior faculty had difficulty finding positions for their students; NRC fellowships grew scarce. Along with that, many Americans bizarrely blamed scientists for plunging the nation into penury. Humanist critics decried the nation's over-reliance on science and technology; with efficient machines had come less work for men and women. Religious critics saw in the disaster evidence that science, not God, had gained control of the American mind, with predictably awful results. Across the country rolled a wave of recrimination directed at scientists, in whose hands so many had recently and gratefully placed their fate.[35]

The situation for scientists in the United States would improve dramatically, of course, with the arrival of the Second World War and the end of the depression in the early 1940s. Public esteem for physicists in particular would grow once more, while federal funding would increase with the demand for new weapons and military countermeasures. In Stalin's Soviet Union scientists served at the pleasure of the state, especially after the mid-1930s. In the United States scientists negotiated a system that was at once more benign and complex. They could do whatever research pleased them, as long as they could interest the government, a university, or industry sufficiently to fund their projects. Failure to achieve significant results was disappointing, but it was unlikely to mean arrest. In times of national emergency, and war in particular, scientists' value to the state made their status skyrocket—until such time as their own scruples, or the end of the war, or the generals' suspicion of them, highlighted their desire for independent research and thus their long-term unreliability as agents of a specific national cause. American scientists were subject to the market, the state, and their own ambitions, with all the freedom and uncertainty such relationships implied.

6. The ethical obligations of scientists

Behind the issue of the scientist's relationship to the state there lurk several questions. Does the scientist have a responsibility to serve her nation if she is asked to do so by her government? Is there an obligation for all citizens to put aside other loyalties, including that to the scientific republic, in the event of what is judged by political leaders a situation requiring national service? Or do scientists have the right, or even the obligation, to weigh the ethical or moral import of what they are being asked by the state to do, and to refuse to serve if they find their government's cause or means of attaining it ethically or morally wanting? These are fraught questions that bear, of course, on a scientist's decision to help build a weapon like poison gas or an atomic bomb.

It is possible to suggest that there is no need for individual handwringing over these questions. In an authoritarian state, naturally, citizens have no choice: they can be, and usually are, conscripted into service. In a pluralist state, conscription can occur during time of war, as in Britain in 1916–18 and the United States in 1942–5. More often, and even during war, the pluralist state must ask its citizens for their help. It must persuade them that an emergency exists, or great danger looms, and that their involvement in the war effort is essential to ending the emergency or warding off the danger. Citizens in a democracy must be its defenders; all must do their part as shareholders in a system that protects and rewards them. Young men (and sometimes women) must fight, farmers must grow more food, workers must shoulder the wheel to increase industrial output, and scientists must contribute their expertise to the war effort. Moral considerations do not apply because the state itself, and the international system in which it participates, are amoral. Governments decide what to do based on national interest, not on what is right or just or moral. This is the realist paradigm of government, expressed most extremely by Benedetto Croce (an admirer of Machiavelli), and more plausibly during the twentieth century by the American scholar/diplomat George Kennan. The combination of state coercion or political obligation *and* a belief in the need for realism in international affairs makes the scientist's choice easy: one serves the state because one ought to do so, and because there is no need to make a moral decision when doing so.[36]

But it is precisely during wartime that the realist paradigm falters, for war by definition raises moral issues of the profoundest sort. These start with the justice of the war itself. Scientists in an authoritarian country cannot assume that a war entered into by their government is popularly condoned or based on generally accepted principles of international law: dictators are known to flout these standards of right and wrong. (Authoritarian states are not always in the wrong when it comes to fighting; the Soviet Union was engaged in self-defense after Germany attacked it in June 1941.) Nor is it entirely safe to assume that a nation with a pluralist form of government will embark only on a just war. Wars of empire—the British in India and South Africa, the Americans in the Philippines, the French in Indochina—are morally problematic, and, even after the end of formal empire, adventures from Suez to Saigon suggest that democracies sometimes go to war for the wrong reasons. These are matters concerned with *jus ad bellum*—the justice of war. Equally complicated are issues of *jus in bello*, justice in war. A nation might go to war for good reason: because it is attacked or is in imminent danger of attack, because it wishes to stop aggression, or because it is determined to end a genocide or the terrible suffering of another nation's people. Yet in its just wars it must fight well and fairly, doing only what damage is necessary to defend itself or halt aggressions or stop the slaughter of innocents. In the realm of *jus in bello* lies the real vexation for scientists who serve the state.[37]

There is a scientific counterpart to Crocean realism, as applied to international relations. It is best represented by Percy W. Bridgman, who was Robert Oppenheimer's physics teacher at Harvard. Even after the Second World War, Bridgman claimed that scientists were meant only to seek the truth and then to publicize it. What politicians and policymakers do with the truth thus uncovered is up to them and to the societies they represent, not to the scientists who make the discoveries. To demand scientific responsibility for the terrible things done with their discoveries is to put science in thrall to the state, chilling scientific research by insisting implicitly that it remain safe, free of any possible application to harmful purposes. A biologist might be constrained from working with microbes that, if misused, might cause an epidemic, but if used properly could eradicate a disease. An experiment in genetics could be used by a state to enforce a policy of racist eugenics—or lead to a cure for diabetes or cerebral palsy. It must remain for the scientist, according to Bridgman, to conduct her work without fear that the state will do the wrong thing with its result. Science must be amoral.[38]

Bridgman's 'ethical positivism' became problematic in the extreme for the physicists and chemists who designed and built the atomic bomb. It remained possible to argue, in 1945, that the bomb was, as Irving Langmuir wrote, an 'accident' onto which scientists had stumbled, or that the bomb in essence already existed as a force of nature, which scientists had thus not so much invented as discovered. But most of those involved in the atom bomb project felt differently. Had they not solved the structure of the atom and made its nucleus fission? Had they not *taken it upon themselves* in 1939 or 1940 to stop publicizing their findings in the international republic of science for security reasons, and to entreat the US president Franklin Delano Roosevelt to authorize the building of the bomb? Had they not constructed a graphite-moderated pile to elicit a chain reaction in uranium, fashioned great factories to produce the bomb's nuclear fuel, worked months on end in the New Mexico desert to refine the bomb's shape and design, forge its metal jacket, and fabricate its delicate triggering mechanism? In H. G. Wells's *The World Set Free*, Wells Holsten learns how to make radioactivity. Afterward, he 'felt like an imbecile who has presented a box full of loaded revolvers to a Creche'. 'I am become Death, the shatterer of worlds,' thought Oppenheimer as he watched the mushroom cloud rise over Alamogordo at dawn on 16 July 1945. Another physicist put it more prosaically: 'Now we are all sons of bitches.'[39]

Decent and humane by nearly all accounts, the scientists from many nations delivered to the US military an atomic bomb. They knew that the bomb would be used against an enemy (though some hoped that after Germany surrendered the bomb would not be dropped on Japan, a lesser evil in their view), and they suspected how awesomely destructive it would be. They nevertheless convinced themselves that the bomb should be built and used, not so much because it represented human progress, or because they as scientists were amoral with respect to politics and military strategy, but rather because they believed that using the bomb would defeat the enemy more quickly than not using the bomb and thus save human lives on all sides. In this calculation, considerations of *jus in bello* yielded to *jus ad bellum*: any means can be employed if the cause is represented as just and the aim is to end a combat as soon as possible—which is, presumably, a universal desire. Shorter wars mean fewer people die. There is a logic to that, though hardly an impeccable logic; as Michael Walzer points out, it is not clear why civilians in Hiroshima sacrificed their rights to remain unharmed during the war. Nor would Americans have looked benignly on an atomic bombing of Philadelphia had the Japanese possessed the bomb and felt the need to shorten the war and thus save lives on all sides.[40]

TWO

Great Britain: Refugees, Air Power, and the Possibility of the Bomb

The World Set Free, H. G. Wells's futuristic novel simultaneously dystopian and hopeful, was published as Europe verged on war in 1914. It was dedicated, curiously, not to an intimate, nor even a person, but to another book: *The Interpretation of Radium*, by the University of London chemist Frederick Soddy, which Wells acknowledged as the principal source for his scientific material. In his book, Wells predicts the discovery of nuclear fission. His character Wells Holsten explores the phosphorescence of Italian fireflies, then moves to experiment with heating and cooling gases. Another character—a physics professor at Edinburgh—lectures on radioactivity. He declares that the atom, which 'once we thought hard and impenetrable', was in fact 'a reservoir of immense energy', capable of powering an ocean liner, lighting the city streets for a year, or—and here the professor waved a small bottle of uranium oxide—blowing the lecture hall and everyone in it to fragments. It is, unhappily, to this last purpose that humankind chooses to put nuclear power. World war breaks out in the mid-twentieth century. A plane from the Central European alliance strikes Paris with an atomic bomb. A French pilot vows to retaliate; he flies off to Berlin carrying three atomic bombs made from the radioactive element Carolinum. The moment of truth seems in retrospect almost quaint. As his 'steersman' guides the plane, the pilot ('a dark young man with something negroid about his gleaming face') straddles his box of bombs. Lifting out the first, 'a black sphere two feet in diameter,' he activates it by biting through a celluloid strip between the bomb's handles, then heaves it over the side of the plane in the general direction of Berlin. He repeats the process with the second bomb, but the third one detonates while it is still clutched to his chest, turning pilot, steersman, and plane into 'flying rags and splinters of metal and drops of moisture in the air'. Below, struck by the first two bombs, Berlin is laid waste.

All the atomic bombs dropped during Wells's world war burrow into the earth, where they create a volcano effect, turning soil and rock molten and spewing forth radioactive Carolinum and vapor for weeks or months or years. After Berlin has been obliterated, the Germans punish Holland with atom bombs that 'fell like Lucifer' on Dutch dikes. The East End of London is destroyed, as is Parliament and an additional portion of Westminster. China and Japan bomb Moscow, the United States hits Tokyo, a Japanese attempt on San Francisco falls short but makes the Pacific steam, and, with the bombing of New Delhi—'a pit of fire spouting death and flame'—India falls into anarchy. Everywhere the sky grows dark, blotting out the daylight. The ground fissures. Radioactivity drifts miles from the bombs' targets, rendering nearly every major city and its environs uninhabitable.

In the end, however, Wells offers hope. A few humble statesmen bring their colleagues together in the north Italian countryside. The devastation of the world, the collapse of capitalism, government, and social cohesion, require the abolition of nation states and the advent of a 'World Republic'. The leaders agree to ban atomic weapons and the means by which to make them. A governing council is elected by universal suffrage. (One renegade king tries to secrete away three atomic bombs, but he and his henchmen are discovered, and dispatched, by agents of the newly formed council.) 'The moral shock of the atomic bombs had been a profound one', Wells writes, 'and for awhile the cunning side of the human animal was over-powered by its sincere realisation of the vital necessity for reconstruction.'

All this seems promising. But there remains considerable bleakness in Wells's vision. The man mostly responsible for devising the technology of the bomb, young Holsten who once played with fireflies, is tormented by his discoveries even before they wreck, then set free, the world. Perhaps what is done is done; he is helpless to alter the course of events, for, he says, 'I am a little instrument in the armoury of Change'. Indeed, he despairs, 'if I were to burn all these [scientific] papers, before a score of years had passed some other men would be doing this'. The book ends with the death of a selfless hero named Marcus Karenin. Before his death, Karenin's caretakers at a hospital high in the mountains of Kashmir express optimism that humans have learned their lesson, bitterly taught by atomic bombs. Karenin is doubtful: 'There is a kind of inevitable logic now in the progress of research . . . If there had been no Holsten there would have been some similar man. If atomic energy had not come in one year it would have come in another.' This logic would become familiar to the physicists who, through the 1920s and 1930s, closed in on the awesome and terrible potential of the atom's nucleus.[1]

Wells was hardly the first, of course, to consider the potentially disastrous consequences of science and technology run amok. Mary Shelley's *Frankenstein* (1818) comes readily to mind. Less commonly read is the dystopian novel *The Coming Race*, published in 1871 by Edward Bulwer-Lytton, who is perhaps best remembered for writing the sentence, 'It was a dark and stormy night.' *The Coming Race* concerns the discovery, beneath the surface of the earth, of a people called the Vril-ya, who have harnessed an enormously powerful force called vril. This substance gives the Vril-ya light, the ability to heal the sick, and control over the weather. Because it is at the same time so destructive, it has made war impossible: 'If army met army, and both had command of this agency, it could be but the annihilation of each.' Bulwer-Lytton concludes that a society so fearfully well adjusted must be deadly dull, unable to produce art, culture, or military heroes such as Hannibal or George Washington. Whatever the logic of Bulwer-Lytton's position, it was not *The Coming Race* but *The World Set Free* that captured the imagination of an avid reader named Leo Szilard when he encountered Wells's book nearly two decades after it had been written.[2]

1. Hitler's gifts, Britain's scientists

Szilard was a Hungarian-born physicist. Drafted during the First World War into the Austro-Hungarian army, he had survived only because he was sent home from his unit with what turned out to be Spanish influenza; while he was recovering in Budapest, his regiment was sent to the front and wiped out. After the war he left Hungary to study in Germany, first engineering, then physics at the University of Berlin. Albert Einstein was there, and Max Planck, and the chemist Fritz Haber, who had survived professionally his involvement in manufacturing poison gas and was back at work. Szilard's was a restless mind that settled eventually on nuclear physics. He was also an avid reader, and in 1928 he read Wells's *The Open Conspiracy*, which envisioned a version of Michael Polanyi's scientific republic. The following year Szilard went to London to meet Wells, but only in 1932 did he discover *The World Set Free*. He denied the utility of Wells's atomic vision—'all this moonshine', he wrote dismissively to a friend, echoing Ernest Rutherford—but he nevertheless included with this note a copy of Wells's book, and he added that he had 'reason to believe that in so far as the industrial applications of the present discoveries in physics are concerned, the forecast of the writers may prove to be more accurate than the forecast of the scientists'.[3]

Moonshine, and yet powerful explosions, the prospect of cities destroyed by atomic bombs: denial offset by scientific curiosity and the possibility that the work of physicists like him might bring the world to catastrophe or triumph. There were great scientific brains in the Soviet Union during the 1930s. In the Berlin suburb of Dahlem the Kaiser Wilhelm Institute housed Szilard's brilliant teachers, and Göttingen remained the destination of choice for the brightest young minds in international physics. France had Frédéric Joliot and Irène Curie, Denmark Niels Bohr, and Japan Yoshio Nishina. Despite the ravages of the Great Depression, the United States had potentially the greatest number of human and financial resources in physics. Yet Szilard had come and would later return to Great Britain, now home to Rutherford, James Chadwick, and Frederick Soddy. Many others would join him. Britain would become during the 1930s a place of remarkable scientific fertility, congenial home to a combination of soundly practical lab work and the grandly apocalyptic and finally resurrectionary vision of H. G. Wells.

Physics returned quickly to international status following the First World War. During the 1920s, one prominent physicist likened his professional colleagues to a colony of ants: individual ants carried new particles of information into the anthill, but when they turned away their fragments were snatched up and moved elsewhere by other ants eager to add new information to their own (mutable) piles of knowledge. The ants moved so often and so quickly that it was difficult to follow them. Charles Weiner has called this activity a 'traveling seminar', in which physicists drawn by conferences or long-term fellowships shuttled between Brussels, Copenhagen, Rome, Paris, Leipzig, New York, and Cambridge. The Italians were peripatetic: Emilio Segré spent time in Hamburg and Amsterdam, Franco Rasetti visited Lise Meitner in Berlin and Robert Millikan in Pasadena, Enrico Fermi taught in Ann Arbor. (All three men eventually settled in the United States. Segré and Fermi worked on the Manhattan Project, Rasetti refused to do so.) Hans Bethe joined the traveling seminar with a Rockefeller Foundation fellowship and went to Rome and Cambridge. He began his teaching career at Tübingen, went to Manchester then Bristol, and, in 1935, found a permanent position at Cornell University. Most nuclear physicists were similarly wide ranging.[4]

The Cavendish Lab, writes Weiner, was the physicists' Mecca in the 1920s and 1930s. The best in the field were pulled there to visit, including Albert Einstein, Bohr, Werner Heisenberg, Nishina, and George Gamow. They came to work with Rutherford, of course. But the Cavendish also had the finest instruments in the world. Rutherford himself was by nature frugal, and before 1919 the lab had never exceeded £550 annually in expenditure for apparatus. That figure increased decisively into the 1930s. A variety of wealthy men contributed to the lab, but ultimately the growing needs of the scientists studying the nucleus outstripped private means, and the lab came to rely on assistance from the state. The British government was generous, so the Cavendish stayed ahead of its rivals.

The visitors also came to Cambridge to work with the lab's staff scientists. Rutherford drew to the Cavendish men of extraordinary talent—innovative, painstaking in their methods, and adept with their newfangled instruments. 'His boys,' he called them. 'Having no son himself,' notes Robert Jungk, 'he lavished all the vigilance, help, and affection he had to give on these aspiring young men.' They included F. W. Aston, P. M. S. Blackett (who came originally to take a single course at the lab, then stayed on), the Japanese researchers Shimizu and Ishida, John Cockcroft, Norman Feather, and the Australian Marcus Oliphant, who would later help convince the Americans that an atomic bomb was feasible. Rutherford's favorite, by most accounts, was the Russian Peter Kapitsa, who came first to the Cavendish in 1921 and established himself as a moving spirit there, a man in Rutherford's image. Kapitsa liked driving fast on narrow English roads and plunging nude into English streams. More than once he pushed his lab machinery beyond its capacity, setting fire to cables and blasting overloaded electrical coils. (He wrote to his mother: 'Today a new record was set for magnetic field strength. I would have gone higher but the coil burst. It was an impressive explosion.') To this energy, to this intelligence and instrumental abundance, to this atmosphere charged with scientific excitement, the best physicists in the world were drawn.[5]

The pull was from Cambridge; the push came from the rise of political
and religious oppression in Germany. Kapitsa, it may be recalled, was
prevented by Stalin from returning to England following a visit home in
1934. The Soviets declared that 'they could no longer dispense with his
services, in view of the danger from Hitler.' But the chief effect of Naziism's
advent was to drive scientists out of Central Europe, often first to Great
Britain and then to the United States. Hitler came to power early in 1933.
Almost immediately, groups of Fascist Brown Shirts demonstrated against
university faculty who were Jewish or had married Jews, and within the
first month of the regime orders from Berlin brought the dismissal of seven
prominent scientists at Göttingen. Max Born, director of the Institute for
Theoretical Physics and a later winner of the Nobel Prize, was put on
paid leave; he used his salary to underwrite Jewish friends and relatives
whose circumstances were worse than his. James Franck, who had won his
Nobel in 1925, was initially spared despite his Judaism (recall that Franck
had worked on gas during the First World War), but he soon resigned
to protest that German Jews were being 'treated like aliens and enemies
of our country'. Between 1901 and 1932, one-third of Nobel Prizes had
gone to German scientists. Roughly a quarter of these were Jewish. After
1933, nearly all Jewish scientists who wished to continue their work had no
choice but to leave Germany. And not only Jews: the faculty at Göttingen
was so demoralized that only a third of the mathematicians and physicists
stayed in their jobs.[6]

Hitler looked upon Jews with murderous intent, and he had no particular
use for physics. 'If the dismissal of Jewish scientists means the annihilation
of German science, then we shall do without science for a few years!' he
reportedly declared. He did not altogether mean it, for, as war approached,
scientific and technological work considered by the regime essential to
preparedness went forward without great ideological encumbrance. (Frank
Pfetsch notes that Jewish scientists and those with Jewish spouses were able
to work throughout the war at the Zeiss glass and optical plant in Jena.) But
many scientists understood the attacks on Jews as violations of academic
freedom generally, as evidence that religious intolerance could be readily
transformed into contempt for intellectuals and their work. Science did not
end in Germany between 1933 and 1945, but it was decisively compromised
in the way that academic work always is when racism taints it, when
powerful ideologues insist on selecting its practitioners and commanding its direction. 'National Socialism', wrote Joachim Fest, 'represented a

politically organized contempt for the mind.' A year after the mass dismissals at Göttingen, the mathematician David Hilbert found himself at a banquet seated next to Bernhard Rust, Hitler's minister of education. 'Is it really true, Professor, that your Institute suffered so much from the departure of the Jews and their friends?' asked Rust. Hilbert retorted: 'Suffered? No, it didn't suffer, Herr Minister. It just doesn't exist anymore!'[7]

Dismissed outright, put 'on leave' from their universities and institutes, treated with unspeakable rudeness by colleagues and former friends (the Berlin University physiologist Wilhelm Feldberg was summoned one morning in April 1933 and told, 'Feldberg, you must be out of here by midday, because you are a Jew'), and horrified by portents foretold by widespread book burnings that May, Jewish scientists, a good number of them nuclear physicists, made exodus out of Germany. Many found welcome in Britain. Albert Einstein was in California when Hitler took power and the Reichstag burned. He had long faced anti-Semitism in Germany, including from physicist colleagues, but had nevertheless thrived at the Kaiser Wilhelm Institute in Berlin. The triumph of Naziism, however, made him doubtful of returning. While in New York, he found in a German newspaper a photograph of himself captioned 'not yet hanged'. News that his home near Berlin had been searched and its garden dug up settled the matter: he gave up his German citizenship, stopped briefly in Belgium, then went to Christ Church, Oxford, for a stay. He did some lecturing and appeared, in October 1933, at a Royal Albert Hall rally on behalf of scientific refugees. That same month he sailed for the United States, and the Institute for Advanced Study at Princeton. Max Born, the eminent physicist dismissed from Göttingen, moved first to the Italian Tyrol. There he fielded invitations from, among others, Oxford's Frederick Lindemann, who arrived in a chauffeur-driven Rolls Royce to recruit him, and P. M. S. Blackett of Cambridge, whose offer Born accepted. It was a demotion, from head of a prestigious institute to 'research student' status, but Born found his new post stimulating and enjoyed the experience. In 1935 he was given the Chair of Physics at Edinburgh. Born hated Naziism, but he could not bring himself to work on the atomic bomb; he would shun the path taken by many of his colleagues and spend the war in Scotland.[8]

Fritz Haber had shown his zeal for Germany during the First World War, when he not only pioneered the manufacture of chemical weapons but found a new technique for making ammonia, a vital component of high explosives. After the war, he evaded the Locarno Treaty's ban on

poison gas by experimenting on animals, in the process developing the
pesticide Zyklon B, which would be modified somewhat and used to
murder millions of his fellow Jews in the Nazi extermination camps. This
loyal service was not enough to win him Hitler's favor. Though Haber
was not himself dismissed, his Jewish staff were fired, and his work thus
seriously restricted. Haber had been widely condemned by British scientists
for his work on gas, but in 1933 the scientific republic had grown attentive
to the oppressions of Naziism toward all its members, and what his son
calls 'the old-boy network' secured for Haber a position at Cambridge.
Rutherford, however, refused to meet him, and others in his lab treated him
coldly. On a visit to Switzerland the following year Haber died of a heart
attack.[9]

Franz (later Francis, then Sir Francis) Simon trained at the Kaiser
Wilhelm Institute, specializing in low-temperature physics. He was Professor of Physical Chemistry at Breslau when Hitler came to power in
early 1933. The same Frederick Lindemann who tried to entice Max Born
to Oxford arrived at Simon's door that spring and offered the German a
place in Oxford's Clarendon Lab. 'How would you like to go to England?',
Simon asked his wife, Charlotte, that evening. 'Rather today than tomorrow,' she answered. Managing to take with him not only his family but vital
equipment from his Breslau lab, Simon left for Oxford over the summer.
The salary was low, the lab shockingly primitive, but jobs in wealthier
places, despite Simon's qualifications, were in short supply. The family
found a house in north Oxford that became a refuge for other Jews living
in the city or passing through, and Simon's colleagues and students were
welcoming. By 1938 work had begun on a renovation of the Clarendon,
inspired in part by the promise of Simon's research.

When war came in September 1939, Simon and his Birmingham colleague Rudolf Peierls, not yet naturalized citizens, were forbidden to work
on the top-secret military project, radar. They were shunted instead to the
exploration of an atomic bomb, considered sufficiently fanciful as to allow
research on it by non-citizens. (Naturalized later that year, Simon stayed
with the bomb project, and also spent a good deal of time trying to get
other German-Jewish scientists released from the internment to which the
British government now subjected them.) Simon worked on separating out
the light isotope Uranium 235, which was much more likely to fission than
its more stable, and thus more common cousin U-238. Filtering gaseous
uranium through an extremely fine membrane seemed to Simon the best

way to achieve separation; one day in 1940 he stole the family's metal kitchen strainer, smashed it flat, then used it to capture carbon dioxide from water vapor—a model for his means of filtering uranium. Simon's 'gaseous diffusion' method was ultimately used to produce fissionable uranium for the Hiroshima bomb. Simon was also instrumental in persuading Winston Churchill that a bomb was feasible. Simon himself went to Los Alamos to help in the bomb work, returning to Oxford, and low-temperature physics, once the war was over.[10]

Leo Szilard, the reader and promoter of H. G. Wells, undertook a similar odyssey, from Central Europe to England and, finally, to the United States. He was the conscience and the gadfly of the physics community during the 1930s and after. By turns warmly supportive of colleagues, irascible, impatient unto captiousness, and either absent-minded or callous in his treatment of subordinates—the maids in his hotel complained that he refused to flush the toilet after use—Szilard came early to the conclusion that 'something would go wrong in Germany', as he put it. During the 1920s (it may be recalled) he worked in Germany, at the Kaiser Wilhelm Institute, and on the side invented and applied for patents of devices for home refrigeration. He visited the United States in early 1932, then returned to Berlin, and was there in January 1933 when Hitler assumed the chancellorship. 'I lived in the faculty club of the Kaiser Wilhelm Institute,' he remembered, 'and I had my suitcases packed'; he meant this literally. He left Germany a month after the Reichstag fire. He went first to Vienna, where he met Sir William Beveridge, head of the London School of Economics, who happened to be staying at Szilard's hotel. Szilard prodded Beveridge to help German academics, recently dismissed or soon to be, find jobs at British universities, and Beveridge agreed, establishing, following his return to London, the Academic Assistance Council with Ernest Rutherford at its head. Szilard then came to London in part to help with the placement work. Soon, Szilard noted, 'practically everyone who came to England had a position, except me'.

Szilard's wide variety of interests ill suited him for a single job, and his personal eccentricities made him a difficult colleague. He spent his mornings thinking about physics and other things as he sat in his hotel corridor bathtub; during the afternoons and evenings he walked the streets of London, also thinking. He considered a switch from physics to biology, but by then developments in physics—the exploration of radioactivity and the prospect of a chain reaction, prophesied by H. G. Wells—were too compelling to abandon: 'I decided', he remembered, 'to play around a little bit with physics.' It was summer 1934. He wandered over to St Bartholomew's Hospital, whose physics director he knew slightly, and asked if he might have lab space and the use of some radium that was not otherwise needed over the summer. Working with T. A. Chalmers, a member of St Bartholomew's physics department, Szilard experimented with the splitting-off of neutrons and published two important papers in the journal *Nature* that September. The papers gained him enough recognition to win him a fellowship at Oxford. But he felt the war looming. In 1937 he gave up half his fellowship to spend six months in the United States. The following year, listening to news of Munich on a friend's radio in Urbana, Illinois, Szilard decided to stay in America. Britain had served his purposes, but if war came he might not be considered patriotic enough for war work, given his status as a foreigner. Transplanted once more, this time for good, Szilard would play a crucial role in initiating the Manhattan Project, though his disenchantment with its inevitable result indicated that he had not forgotten the fate of Wells's *World Set Free*.[11]

Max Born met Klaus Fuchs at Edinburgh in 1937. Fuchs was, Born remembered, 'a very nice, quiet fellow with sad eyes'. Dorothy McKibben, whose job it was to greet and help settle the scientists who came to Los Alamos in 1943 and after, thought Fuchs 'one of the kindest and best-natured men I ever met'. Assigned to the British delegation at Los Alamos, Fuchs was cooperative, hardworking, and serious. He spoke infrequently— 'penny-in-the-slot Fuchs', Genia Peierls called him—and willingly babysat other people's children, having none of his own. He was pale and round-shouldered, nearsighted, and a chain smoker.[12]

Fuchs was not Jewish, but he was nevertheless one of Hitler's victims and his gifts. His father was a Lutheran pastor who later cast his lot with Quakerism, a pacifist in a society with limited tolerance for peacemonger-ing. Klaus's mother and sister both committed suicide. At the University of Leipzig, where he studied math and physics, Klaus became a political activist, first as a member of the Socialist Party, then as a Communist sympathizer who openly opposed Fascism and organized left-wing militants to do battle with the Fascist Brown Shirts who descended like plagues on German campuses. He was at the University of Kiel when Hitler took control of the country. One February day in 1933, a group of Brown Shirts arrived to harass professors and intimidate left-wing students. One of them spotted Fuchs, who was known to have informed on the Nazis previously. The Brown Shirts beat Fuchs badly and threw him into the Kiel Canal.[13]

If Fuchs had had doubts about formally associating himself with the German Communist Party, they now dissipated. A few days after he had been beaten in Kiel, he took a train to Berlin and declared himself to the Party leadership there. 'I was ready to accept the philosophy that the Party is right,' Fuchs said later, 'and that in the coming struggle you could not permit yourself any doubts after the Party had made a decision.' The Party decided he should go to England to finish his education. He arrived in Bristol that summer bearing a large bag of dirty laundry; he was housed by a local family with Party ties, and given an assistantship at Bristol University by a physicist there. He moved to Edinburgh, and Max Born's lab, four years later. Fuchs now did solid work for Born and seemed less angry than when he had first come. Still, he was German and a Communist, so he was swept up in the net of British internment in May 1940 and transported to a camp in Canada, where he uncomfortably shared a barracks with Nazis. Released at the year's end, Fuchs returned to Edinburgh, but soon thereafter he received an invitation from Rudolf Peierls at Birmingham, asking that Fuchs join him for work on a secret project. 'We knew what it was,' recalled Born. 'I told him of my attitude to such kind of work and tried to warn him not to involve himself in these things. But he was filled with a tremendous hatred, and accepted.' He was given security clearance to begin work on the atomic bomb in May 1941.[14]

'When I learned the purpose of the work,' said Fuchs later, 'I decided to inform Russia and I established contact through another member of the Communist Party.' Fuchs was given over to a handler named S. D. Kremer (Fuchs knew him as 'Alexander'), who was military attaché at the Soviet embassy in London. Fuchs gave him copies of his reports on isotope separation and critical mass. He would later pass much more information, in London, New York, and New Mexico.[15]

The experiences of physicist refugees in the United Kingdom during the 1930s obviously varied, and so did their responses to being uprooted. Max Born loathed Hitler, but wanted nothing to do with making an atomic weapon. Leo Szilard had no hesitation contributing his expertise to the bomb project, so great was his hatred for Naziism and so avid his interest in solving scientific puzzles, yet he believed that the bomb should belong to the world or to no one; the trick was to arrive at the conclusion of Wells's *The World Set Free* without first living its apocalyptic narrative. Klaus

Fuchs, like Szilard, thought the bomb was no single nation's property, and that the Soviet Union in particular must be told its secrets. Yet the process of exodus might perhaps have had some common influence on those who undertook it. For their departed homelands, they felt anger, sadness, worry, resentment, and affection. Germany had not turned against them, they reasoned: the Nazis had. Their efforts to destroy Hitler, to help Britain win the war, were fueled by a hope of redemption for their land and people. The metaphors they imagined were surgical—cut off the diseased limb that was the regime, excise the rot or infection or tumor, and thus save the patient, without altogether erasing his memory of his illness. Toward the country that took them in they felt gratitude, suspicion, inferiority, confusion, and delight. They were safe, but usually poor. They had places in laboratories, but generally far lower in status than those they had occupied in Germany. The food was wrong, the buildings too, and when they spoke English their accents might be mocked. (Sir Francis Simon, self-mockingly, styled himself 'vice-president of the Broken English-Speaking Union'.) And many of them were interned by the British government as 'enemy aliens' once the war began, and even after their release were forbidden to work on the most sensitive military projects. So, ironically, a good number found themselves working to turn 'moonshine' into a war-winning nuclear weapon.[16]

Above all, the refugee scientists must have felt their identities at least bifurcated, sensing that they were two people at once—or more, if they then went to the United States, as many did. Such a bifurcation can be disorienting. A man's nationality is not the whole of his identity, of course, but when he is removed from his language, his home, his favorite coffee house or beer hall, his tools and his newspaper and the streets where he once walked freely, he cannot help but lose something essential of himself. And yet, is there a better citizen for Polanyi's Republic of Science than a scientist with more than one national loyalty? Belonging no more to just one nation, the refugee has seen the tragedy of nationalism and the potentialities of cosmopolitanism. His perspective is broader, his sensibility more generous. The late Edward Said wrote several times of the twelfth-century Saxon monk Hugo of St Victor, who once said: 'The man who finds his homeland sweet is still a tender beginner; he to whom every soil is as his native one is already strong; but he is perfect to whom the entire world is as a foreign land.' So it was with the refugee scientists who came to Great Britain during the 1930s.[17]

It is not fully clear to what extent, or when, the nuclear physicists understood that their findings might be weaponized. Szilard was at least intrigued at the prospect of an atomic bomb. On receiving the Nobel Prize for discovering radioactivity with his wife, Irène Curie, in 1935, Frédéric Joliot described 'nuclear transformations of an explosive character'—language difficult to misunderstand. Still, even in 1939 many leading physicists remained in denial about the implications of their work, among them Einstein, Niels Bohr, and one of the discoverers of fission, Otto Hahn, who insisted that a nuclear explosive 'would surely be contrary to God's will!'[18]

2. The advent of air power

Among the pioneers of air power, those who designed or flew airplanes or thought about their strategic utility in war, there was less pretending. The experience of the First World War produced true believers in air power to change the nature of combat forever. Through the 1920s and most of the 1930s, the new air-power theorists reckoned without the possibility of an atomic bomb, whatever their understanding of Wells's prediction. They nevertheless had faith that attacking from the air would prove pivotal in future wars, for they could not imagine a way to prevent bombardment from the sky. 'The bomber will always get through,' wrote British Prime Minister Stanley Baldwin in 1932. 'The only defence is offence, which means you have to kill more women and children more quickly than the enemy if you want to save yourselves.' Baldwin thus assumed that the targets of bombers were not enemy armies or enemy factories but enemy towns and cities, where old men, women, and children lived. The use of air power indicated, for Baldwin anyway, not just a new weapon of war and a new way to deliver it, but an ominous definition of who was and was not a combatant.[19]

It is a bit difficult to say when air bombardment began, particularly attacks on noncombatants. On 1 November 1911, an Italian pilot named Giulio Gavotti, whose unit was fighting Turks in Libya, overflew the enemy camp and tossed four grenades on its residents. ('No Turks were injured,' reports Gerard DeGroot, 'but they were mighty angry.') Soon after the First World War began, a German dirigible, designed by Count Ferdinand von Zeppelin, bombed Antwerp, killing six. The British Royal Naval Air

Service promptly retaliated, sending four aircraft from Belgium to bomb Zeppelin sheds in Düsseldorf and Cologne; only one plane reached its target and unloaded its bombs. Sporadic bombing missions by both sides followed, usually aimed at enemy armies or supply depots. But not always: in January 1915, Zeppelins bombed the east coast of England, causing twenty casualties, mostly civilian. These attacks persisted, and, while they were not generally effective, they understandably terrified citizens who might become their targets.[20]

Matters changed in the late spring of 1917. Concerned about the vulnerability of the Zeppelin, the German High Command had ordered production of thirty Gotha bombers. With offset double wings, a range of just over 500 miles, a top speed of 87.5 miles per hour, and an ability to carry a payload of 1,100 pounds (the weight of the Germans' single heaviest bomb), the Gothas looked liked flying breadboxes. But they quickly proved more lethal than their dirigible predecessors. The Gothas first attacked Folkestone, an English coastal town through which thousands of British soldiers passed on their way to France. The raid killed or wounded 300, just over a third of whom were soldiers. Three weeks later, by the light of day, fourteen Gothas appeared over London. Their bombs caused roughly 600 casualties, only a handful of whom were military men, and 46 of whom were children in a nursery school. The Germans considered the London attacks a success, and so they continued. An American serviceman witnessed the impact of one of the raids from a stairway landing in a subway station:

> The air was as foul as the Black Hole of Calcutta and those people certainly were scared. We cheered the girls up and drank the whiskey and felt better . . . I hadn't realized before how successful the raids are. It doesn't matter whether they hit any thing of note as long as they put the wind up the civilian population so thoroughly. Those people wanted peace and they wanted it quickly.[21]

With civilian morale thus shaken, the British War Cabinet, headed by Prime Minister David Lloyd George, summoned from the battle-field in France Hugh Trenchard, commander of the Royal Flying Corps (RFC). Speaking before the Cabinet a week after the Gothas had bombed London, Trenchard urged a forward strategy: capture the coast of Belgium, thereby lengthening the distance German planes would have to fly to reach England, interposing Allied-held territory between German bases and their bombers' English targets, and providing the RFC with airfields closer to German industrial centers. Meanwhile, the RFC and the French air corps should do all they could to strike German air bases behind the front. This would help Allied soldiers fighting in the trenches—Trenchard's first concern—and might also destroy airplanes that could be used to attack London. Flying protective patrols over the English Channel would not, Trenchard thought, do much good, since the number of planes and crews available for such patrols was far fewer than needed to find and stop the Gothas. Lloyd George wanted to bomb the industrial city of Mannheim. Trenchard thought this impossible under current circumstances, though he had no moral objection to attacking such targets. As for raids against undefended cities that were not manufacturing centers, Trenchard declared these 'repugnant', but thought they might ultimately be necessary should other means of reprisal fail. If the government decided to bomb German towns, it must anticipate that the Germans would respond in kind, and, 'unless we are determined and prepared to go one better than the Germans, whatever they may do and whether their reply is in the air or against our prisoners or otherwise, it will be infinitely better not to attempt reprisals at all'. Here was common sense. Here also was an invitation to unlimited escalation and total war against civilian populations. If the government chose to open the door to attacks on German towns, it must not hesitate but rush through with its guns blazing.[22]

The Gothas struck London again just three weeks later, once more by the light of day. Members of the British Air Board watched, shocked, from the balconies of the Hotel Cecil as the bombers unleashed their terror. The capital succumbed once more to an apoplexy of fear, anger, and recrimination. Channel air patrols increased, despite Trenchard's doubts, the Cabinet ordered more war planes, and Lloyd George renewed his demand for the bombing of Mannheim (it went unmet). Trenchard was dismayed that the Germans had again bombed London, but he continued to believe that air support of the army was the most efficient use of limited resources. Lloyd George appointed the South African statesman and War Cabinet member Jan Smuts to investigate the problem. Very quickly Smuts produced two reports, the first an unhappy account of London's air defenses, the second, more significant, a call for the development of a separate Air Ministry. Smuts implied here that air power might have a future distinct from that of the army and navy that it had heretofore served. 'Air power', he wrote, 'can be used as an independent means of war operations . . . As far as can at present be foreseen there is absolutely no limit to the scale of its future independent war use. And the day may not be far off when aerial operations with their devastation of enemy lands and destruction of industrial and populous centers on a vast scale may become the principal operations of war, to which older forms of military operations may become secondary and subordinate.' By such advocacy, and prophecy, would Smuts earn his title as father of the Royal Air Force.[23]

Smuts had other careers in front of him; he established his paternity of the Air Force and moved on. It was Hugh Trenchard who became Britain's pre-eminent air strategist in the years between the wars. Trenchard, nicknamed 'Boom' for the volume and authority of his voice, began his military career during the Boer War. In the Transvaal in October 1900, he was ambushed and shot through the left side of his chest. The bullet creased his lung and then his spine, leaving him susceptible to respiratory problems and temporarily unable to walk without crutches. (He recovered his ability to walk unaided, incredibly, following a toboggan accident in Switzerland early the following year.) Drawn to the air, he learned to fly in 1912. When the war began two years later, Trenchard was assigned to build squadrons of flyers for the RFC at Farnborough, Hampshire. By mid-November 1914 he had been summoned to France to take charge of an operational air wing, one of three, of the Army Corps. Following the first German gas attack at Ypres in April 1915, Trenchard sent his planes over German trenches to do reconnaissance for the forthcoming counterattack. His superiors were pleased with his daring and innovativeness. That August he was named Commander of the RFC.[24]

Unconvinced that Britain could defend its cities and towns against German air assaults, additionally constrained by the limited range of his airplanes based in England and France, Trenchard nevertheless endorsed 'forward action' against German airfields and storage facilities wherever these could be reached. 'The aeroplane is not a defence against the aeroplane,' he wrote in a widely circulated memo in September 1916. 'But the opinion of those most competent to judge is that the aeroplane, as a weapon of attack, cannot be too highly estimated.' In the wake of the Gotha attacks on London the following year, Trenchard unleashed two flights of de Havilland bombers against the Burbach iron foundry, outside Saarbrücken. Unmolested by German opposition, the de Havillands hit several buildings and railway lines, encouraging Trenchard to repeat the performance several more times that fall, and then with renewed intensity once the weather had improved in the spring and summer of 1918. William Weir of the Air Board wrote to Trenchard that September: 'I would very much like if you could start up a really big fire in one of the German towns.' Nor would Weir 'mind a few accidents due to inaccuracy', since 'the German is susceptible to bloodiness'. 'I do not think you need be anxious about our degree of accuracy when bombing stations in the middle of towns,' replied Trenchard. 'The accuracy is not great at present, and all the pilots drop their eggs well into the middle of the town generally.' Under British bombs, a German civilian wrote, 'one feels as if one were no longer a human being. One air-raid after another. In my opinion, this is no longer war, but murder.'[25]

Murder it may have been, but the air war had developed a relentless logic by the time of the Armistice in November. As they had done when the Germans used gas, the British had claimed to be outraged when the Zeppelins and Gothas rained bombs on English cities. Then they had then done their utmost, as before, to retaliate in kind. The justification for bombing was similar, too. Someone else, someone more barbaric, had done it first. There was no choice but to attack the enemy's cities, since technology did not permit of any defense against bombers. (Trenchard likened it to trying to stop submarines from penetrating a naval blockade.) The soldiers on the ground deserved the protection that air strikes could provide. And, of course, the hardiest justification of all: holding civilians hostage in war would inevitably increase the pressure on their government to sue for peace. Bombing cities, like using gas, would end wars more quickly and thus save lives. It was humane to bomb noncombatants.

The 'Trenchard Doctrine' was the name given to the policy of using bombers as offensive weapons following the First World War. But Trenchard was not its only advocate, nor its most emphatic; 'if I had the casting vote,' he said ruefully in 1925, 'I would say, "Abolish the air."' Others, outside and inside Britain, embraced air power. The Italian air commander Giulio Douhet published, in 1921, *The Command of the Air*, in which he claimed that air superiority was the only way to win the wars of the future. Targeting ordinary citizens was essential: 'Mercifully,' Douhet wrote, 'the decision will be quick in this kind of war, since the decisive blows will be directed at civilians... These future wars may yet prove to be more humane than wars in the past in spite of all, because they may in the long run shed less blood.' The American Billy Mitchell met Trenchard in France during the war, and oversaw an attack by Allied planes against German forces in the Saint-Mihiel salient. He later met Douhet. In a July 1921 demonstration, Mitchell and his fliers famously sank off the coast of Virginia several captured German ships in an effort to show the superiority of air over sea power. ('He's a man after my own heart,' Trenchard said of Mitchell. 'If only he can break his habit of trying to convert opponents by killing them, he'll go far.') The British military theorists J. F. C. Fuller and Basil Liddell Hart concurred with the air-power advocates that bombing cities made sense. Fuller did the math, concluding that killing a few thousand civilians would save the lives of millions of soldiers and 'incident[al]ly several thousands of women and children'.[26]

Trenchard's commitment to air power was partly utilitarian: during the relative peace of the 1920s and 1930s, he sought to justify the maintenance of an independent and reasonably well-funded British air force. In this effort he found an ally in Winston Churchill, who was Secretary of War in 1919 when he reminded the Commons that 'we have all those dependencies and possessions in our hands which existed before the war...The first duty of the Royal Air Force is to garrison the British Empire.' Trenchard and others would refer to this function as 'air control' or 'air policing' of those the RAF War Manual of 1928 called 'semi-civilised enemies'. An opportunity to marry Trenchard's faith in air policy to Churchill's concern for the Empire arrived in 1919. At intervals since the beginning of the century, the British in their colony of Somaliland had attempted to subdue Mohammed bin Abdullah Hassan, a radical Muslim who had organized an army in the jagged hills of the Somali interior. The British regarded Abdullah Hassan as a fanatic and dubbed him the 'Mad Mullah', a sobriquet so pithy that few in Britain ever remembered his real name. Put on lean rations by the tight colonial budget, the perceived remoteness of East Africa, and military demands of world war, the British constabulary in Somaliland could not control the Mullah and his followers, who at leisure sortied out of their hilltop fortresses to plunder lowland villages.

In May 1919, the Colonial Secretary, Lord Milner, summoned Trenchard to ask his advice about the Somali situation. 'Why not leave the whole thing to us?' Trenchard asked. 'This is exactly the type of operation which the RAF can tackle on its own.' Milner was not so sure, and others remonstrated too, but, after six months of lobbying and no more success by British land forces in capturing Abdullah Hassan, the government gave its consent.

A bomber squadron of a dozen planes arrived in Somaliland from Cairo in January 1920 and immediately went into battle. The planes bombed and strafed Abdullah Hassan's headquarters and his fort at Jidali. His army broke up under fire; a locally recruited Camel Corps occupied the enemy's strongholds. Abdullah Hassan was tracked to Abyssinia and killed soon after.[27]

Air control had proved itself effective, and the brief Somaliland campaign was, as the new Colonial Secretary Leopold Amery boasted, 'the cheapest war in history'. There were other 'semi-civilised enemies' evidently deserving similar treatment. The RAF flew six squadrons of planes to northwest India, where they could be used to pacify obstreperous villages. The planes would dump leaflets on an offending village, warning its inhabitants to leave, for their homes were about to be bombed. The home of a suspected law breaker would be particularly targeted. After the attack would come an 'air blockade', in which the village and its outskirts would be selectively bombed to keep its residents away, until they agreed to abide by the law. The Emir of Afghanistan was reportedly deterred from attacking India when a 20-pound bomb was dropped on his palace grounds. Similar attacks were administered to rebellious Iraqis in 1921 and 1922. 'The tribesmen and their families were put to confusion, many of whom ran into the lake, making good targets for the machine-guns,' noted the operational report of an attack on Naseriyah—which occasioned an alarmed minute from Churchill, who worried the report would be published. In 1923 Trenchard's airmen stopped a column of Turks intent on invading Iraq (or 'Mespot', as the British called it), and Trenchard's bombers helped put down an incipient rebellion against the compliant King Abdullah of Transjordan.[28]

The executor of the bombing campaigns in India, Afghanistan, and Iraq was Arthur Harris, an air-power enthusiast in the mold of Trenchard, Douhet, and Mitchell. 'Bomber' Harris, he was called, as well as 'The Chief Bomber' (by Churchill), 'Butch' (by his crews), and 'Butcher' (by his critics). His father served in the Public Works Department in India, for which he designed buildings. Arthur spent much of his youth away from his parents in England, where he lived in 'baby farms' provided for the children of the Empire's servants. At the age of 17, and like his future patron Trenchard, Harris went to southern Africa, in his case Rhodesia. He built houses, grew tobacco, and, when the First World War broke out, joined the 1st Rhodesian Regiment to fight the Germans in Southwest

Africa. The campaign victorious, Harris left the regiment for England in August 1915. He was marched out: he wanted, he wrote, 'to find some way of going to war in a sitting posture'. He did not trust horses. He joined the Royal Flying Corps.[29]

Harris was a pioneer of night flying. He served in the air defense of London, and also spent time in France, 'bagging an occasional German fighter with our rear guns and photographing enemy trenches'. When the war ended he 'more or less drifted into the RAF as a regular' and was given command of a squadron. Demobilization loomed, and Harris despaired for the future of the air force. At that juncture, Churchill and Trenchard put forward their vision of air control. Harris was sent to India in 1921, there to take charge of mastering obstreperous villagers and dissuading the Emir of Afghanistan from invading the Northwest Frontier. He was transferred to Mespot in 1922, where he commanded the 45th Squadron of bombers. Harris put men and machines to frequent use, bombing Turks and tribals by day and night. 'You could just imagine', he wrote, 'what they would think if they heard us over them in the darkness—you know, ' "By Allah they can ruddy well see us in the dark too." ' The success of the night raids, undertaken with what Harris called 'baby incendiaries', was of great interest to his superiors.[30]

The possibility that such attacks were unethical tugged only slightly at Harris, for he shared the views of Trenchard and the others that aerial bombing saved lives by ending wars more quickly. Bombing civilians was not illegal. Hague IV, ratified on 18 October 1907, had prohibited 'the attack or bombardment of towns, villages, or buildings which are not defended', but it pertained only to war on land. Hague IX, ratified at the same time, governed naval bombardment. In late 1922, while Harris was planning bombing runs in Mespot, the United States proposed, once more at The Hague, a convention governing aerial bombardment. It would have prohibited attacks from the sky 'for the purpose of terrorizing the civilian population', and declared such bombardment 'legitimate only when directed at a military objective, that is to say, an object of which the destruction or injury would constitute a distinct military advantage to the belligerent'. Planes could not attack cities, towns, or villages unless these were in 'the immediate neighborhood' of land forces. The American proposal was rejected.[31]

Home from his adventures in Asia, Harris stayed in military harness but chafed at what he considered regressive thinking by officials. In 1919 the

Lloyd George Cabinet had established the 'Ten Year Rule', which averred
that Great Britain would not be forced to fight a major war for a decade.
The rule was frequently reinvoked, including by Winston Churchill in
1928, and as such hobbled efforts to prepare the nation for later conflict
and brought the military branches to squabbling with each other over
scarce resources. Harris regarded the government's attitude toward future
war as tantamount to whistling past the graveyard. Meanwhile, he served
as a senior staff officer in Egypt, and commanded a bomber group in
Yorkshire. In 1938 he embarked on a plane-purchasing mission to the
United States. He bought a number of aircraft from a small company
called Lockheed, professing himself delighted with the planes and with
American efficiency and ingenuity, but he voiced disappointment with the
current state of the US air forces. A long-awaited trip to Palestine followed;
Harris was eager to resume air policing, and he did so during the Arab
Revolt in 1936–9. Harris was back in England on holiday on 1 September
1939, when Prime Minister Neville Chamberlain announced that Germany
had invaded Poland. The British declared war on Germany two days
later.[32]

3. War again, and the new doctrine of air bombardment

Chamberlain was clear about his views on the use of air power: it was
illegal, he thought, to bomb civilians, and targets must be chosen with care
to avoid secondary damage to highly populated neighborhoods. Fine sentiments, but ones that would quickly prove untenable, according to Bomber
Command. Air control in the colonies had allowed—had embraced—the
targeting of civilians, albeit men, women, and children of color whose
lives were hardly treasured by British government or military officials. The
Germans had already demonstrated, once again, their contempt for the
distinction between military and civilian targets. Late in the afternoon of
27 April 1937 German air squadrons of the Condor Legion bombed and
strafed Guernica, a Spanish town of 7,000 that was 20 miles from Bilbao and
at least 10 miles from the front line of battle between Republican and Fascist
forces. Some 1,000 people died in the attack, and Guernica was all but
destroyed. Despite widespread condemnation of the assault, the German

air force, the Luftwaffe, found Guernica a useful exercise. When, following the ground attack on Poland in 1939, Warsaw refused to surrender, the Germans unleashed their bombers. The city was not altogether defenseless, and indeed its refusal to capitulate allowed the Germans to claim it as a legitimate target. They blasted the suburbs and finally the city center, using in a series of raids hundreds of tons of bombs and incendiaries to create what the Luftwaffe war diaries called 'a sea of flame' that engulfed and obscured the city. The air attacks began on 8 September; Warsaw surrendered on the 17th.[33]

Chamberlain's distaste for bombing cities may have been eroded after Warsaw, but any residual opposition he may have had was made irrelevant after he was ousted from the prime ministry on 10 May 1940. Winston Churchill, the champion of air control, now took over. Within two months he proclaimed the need for 'an absolutely devastating, exterminating attack' on Germany, and on 25 August 1940 he authorized a bombing raid over Berlin. Sir Charles Portal, who was Commander-in-Chief of Bomber Command until October 1940, when he was promoted to Chief of the Air Staff (CAS), was willing to oblige Churchill. As C-in-C he was directed to attack industrial targets—factories and refineries, especially— by night. To this he objected: such targets, he said, were 'too small to be found with any certainty on moonlit nights by average crews'. He urged instead hitting industrial towns in their totality, with the understanding that civilian morale in these towns was the real target. Once named CAS, Portal pressed his case on his successor, Sir Richard Pierse: the C-in-C, declared Portal, should pick twenty to thirty German cities and subject them to massive bombing attacks every few nights. By the end of October 1940, according to the official historians of the air war against Germany, 'the fiction that the bombers were attacking military objectives was officially abandoned. This was the technique which was to become known as area bombing.' Undertaken after dark (with factories reserved for targeting only if there was a bright moon), the strategy was designed to strike fear into the hearts of German civilians. The Germans, meantime, had seen fit to bomb London during daylight hours starting that September, and in November launched a destructive nighttime terror attack on Coventry.[34]

While Churchill, Portal, and Pierse reshaped British air-war strategy, Arthur Harris waited for orders. When war broke out he was given command of the No. 5 Group at Grantham, a cluster of clumsy and uncomfortable Hampden bombers. He moved, in late 1940, to the Air Ministry, then the following June was posted to Washington as head of an RAF delegation charged quietly to discuss joint strategy and the possibility of more American planes for the British. In February 1942, with the Americans in the war at last but with the Allies reeling from setbacks in Europe, North Africa, the Soviet Union, and Asia, Harris replaced Pierse as Air Command C-in-C. He inherited a new Air Directive that listed a number of German industrial cities, including most of the Ruhr, as legitimate targets for British bombers, which were about to be equipped with a new navigational technology that would make attacks on cities, as well as precision attacks on buildings, more fruitful. Harris's job, according to the 14 February directive, was 'to focus attacks on the morale of the enemy civil population, and, in particular, of the industrial workers'. Explaining his mandate, Harris would also cite an earlier Air Staff paper, which declared that the aim of bombing towns was 'to produce (i) destruction, and (ii) the fear of death'; the production of death itself was, curiously, left off the list. Enabled by these directives, inclined by his instincts, and increasingly equipped with planes numerous and powerful and well flown enough to produce both destruction and fear of death, Harris opened his bomber offensive.[35]

His planes dropped two types of bombs. Most common were high explosive or 'general-purpose' bombs, which were powerful and volatile chemical cocktails encased in metal. Early in the war, the RAF used mainly 250- and 500-pound high explosives, equipped with fins for guidance and fuses that would detonate the explosive on contact with the ground. Later in the war, and particularly after the destruction of Hamburg in July and August 1943, the RAF increasingly used a second type of bomb, the incendiary, to burn German cities and towns. Incendiaries were thermite or magnesium-based weapons that burned at temperatures exceeding 1200° F. In their use the British were urged on by the Americans, whose universities and chemical and oil companies had developed sophisticated versions of the weapons. A Harvard University chemist, working for Standard Oil, devised napalm, a jelly-like substance that was propelled out of the rear of a bomb called the M-69 and burned remorselessly anyone or anything with which it came into contact. If the Trenchard–Harris doctrine of air war was to destroy civilian morale and thereby end the war quickly, a good thing for all remaining alive concerned, it followed that the most terrifying weapons were finally the most humane.[36]

4. The discovery of nuclear fission, and the bomb reimagined

As the doctrine of air power evolved toward the targeting of civilians, and as weapons to be dropped from aircraft became more powerful, so did the refugee scientists, at Cambridge and elsewhere in Great Britain, come to discover that the awesome power of the atomic nucleus might ultimately be of interest to those with seemingly more prosaic strategic and military concerns. Weaponized atomic energy was not, as it turned out, mere 'moonshine' or H. G. Wells's fictional Carolinum. Nuclear research continued throughout the 1930s at an astonishing pace. In 1934 Irène Curie and Frédéric Joliot made radioactive isotopes from ordinary stable elements by blasting them with alpha particles. The same year, Enrico Fermi, in Rome, switched from alphas to recently discovered neutrons and had even better success producing isotopes, and found, mostly by chance and good guessing, that a barrier of paraffin placed between projectile neutrons and target nucleii would slow the neutrons slightly and make them likely to hit more nuclear targets and produce greater radioactivity. In the course of his experiments Fermi split the uranium atom, though it was not clear to him that he had done so. Indeed, when the physical chemists Ida and Walter Noddack, at the University of Freiburg, suggested that he had, Fermi dismissed their suggestion. Instead, he thought, he had found a new element, one higher on the periodic table than uranium.

The mystery of exactly what Fermi had found was taken on by the German radium expert Otto Hahn and the Austrian physicist Lise Meitner, who had collaborated at the Kaiser Wilhelm Institute (KWI) outside Berlin since its opening in 1912. Hahn was the confident and generous German who had worked with Ernest Rutherford in Montreal before returning to Berlin in 1906 and during the First World War had worked on poison gas. Meitner, the daughter of assimilated (even baptized) Viennese Jews, was as shy as Hahn was gregarious, but a hardworking and imaginative scientist. Along with another colleague, Fritz Strassmann, Hahn and Meitner sought to repeat the Curie and Fermi experiments and comprehend their results. But in March 1938 the Anschluss brought Nazi racial laws to bear on Austrians, now citizens of greater Germany, and Meitner was forced to leave Berlin. That July, playing tourist, she bluffed her way across the border with the Netherlands, went next to Copenhagen as a guest of the Bohrs, then came to rest at a physics institute near Stockholm, as arranged by Niels Bohr.

Hahn and Strassmann carried on with the work at KWI. Skeptical especially of the Joilot and Curie findings—it seemed to them implausible that an alpha or a neutron could drive a particle out of a nucleus—they nevertheless pursued the experiment themselves. By bombarding uranium with neutrons, they produced a result that was, in Robert Jungk's words, 'chemically incontrovertible but physically inexplicable': the process yielded small amounts of the element barium, which weighs slightly more than half as much as uranium. Hahn and Strassmann could hardly believe their data. (Neither, for that matter, had Joliot and Curie, Fermi, the Noddacks, or physicists at the Cavendish, who saw energy bursts off a bombarded uranium nucleus as the probable result of equipment malfunction, believed what their eyes told them.) Hahn sent a tentatively worded paper based on the experiment to the journal *Naturwissenschaften*. He sent a copy of the paper to Meitner in Stockholm. She brought it with her to an inn in the Swedish town of Kungälv, where she was spending the Christmas holiday with her nephew, the physicist Otto Frisch.

Together, Meitner and Frisch studied their colleagues' paper and its tremulous conclusions; Frisch skied while Meitner walked briskly beside him. Imagining the nucleus as a drop of liquid, a model suggested by Bohr several years earlier, they decided that the intervention of a neutron projected into a uranium nucleus made the nucleus split into two roughly equal pieces. Each had about half the mass of uranium, hence the surprising production of barium in the Hahn–Strassmann experiment. Along with the large pieces came some neutrons liberated from the target nucleus, and these might then collide with other uranium nucleii, and so on, to create a chain reaction. (This feature of the process they did not immediately understand.) With this splitting came also the release of an enormous quantity of energy. Frisch likened the dividing of the nucleus to the way in which bacteria multiply and so dubbed it 'nuclear fission', terminology that appeared in the article Frisch wrote with his aunt for the journal *Nature* and published in February 1939. When Frisch told Bohr about the revelation a month before the article appeared, Bohr slapped his forehead and groaned, 'How could we have overlooked that so long?' He would disclose the news of fission to scientists in Washington two weeks later.[37]

A quarter century had passed since the publication of *The World Set Free*, Wells's prediction of fission, nuclear power, and atomic bombs. Leo Szilard had enjoyed the book but thought it 'moonshine'; now he thought again. In January 1939, just after reading the Hahn–Strassmann article and having heard about Frisch and Meitner's forthcoming piece in *Nature*, he wrote to Lewis Strauss, a wealthy Jewish-American financier with a longstanding affection for physics and a particular determination to produce radium for treating patients with cancer, from which his parents had recently died. Szilard alerted Strauss to the two revolutionary articles. Their conclusions, he wrote, 'might lead to a large-scale production of energy and radioactive elements, unfortunately also perhaps to atomic bombs'. Thereafter Szilard wrote often to Strauss, whom he viewed, accurately as it turned out, as a potential patron and sufficiently well connected to serve as a conduit between the physics community and the politically powerful.[38]

There is no indication that Szilard had meanwhile encountered another futuristic novel, this one published in 1933 by Harold Nicolson, the husband of Vita Sackville-West and biographer of Tennyson, Lord Byron, and Algernon Charles Swinburne. Nicolson had joined the diplomatic service in 1909 and was a member of the British delegation at Versailles, edited the newspaper of Oswald Mosley's New Party until Mosley announced his Fascism, and stood for election to Parliament in 1931 (a loss) and then in 1935 (a victory). His novel, entitled *Public Faces*, brought together Nicolson's interests in literature, diplomacy, and politics, and the role of gossip in all three. The book pretends that, in the summer of 1935, a geologist from Nottingham named James Livingstone discovered, on the Persian Gulf island of Abu Saad, a strange new ore that he called 'Deposit A'. Livingstone speculated that the ore, if in sufficient quantity and refined to its 'pure state', would immediately 'transmute itself' so violently that it would explode, eradicating everyone and everything 'within a considerable range'. This 'atomic bomb', as scientists in the know had quietly begun to call it, no bigger than a parliamentarian's inkstand, might be powerful enough to destroy a major city.

The liberal members of Prime Minister Spencer Furnivall's Cabinet, including the ineffectual foreign secretary Walter Bullinger, are appalled at this news, but there is far worse to come. As it happens, Sir Charles Pantry—Sir Charles Portal?—the secretary of state for air, has taken it upon himself to arrange, with the government of India, the excavation and removal from Abu Saad of most of Deposit A. It took very little—'some coolie detachments from Bombay and a few tankers', says Pantry offhandedly—to procure this ore, and to leave almost none of it for anyone else. Deposit A was found to be useful for building rocket planes that were light and fast and strong enough to carry Deposit A-based atomic bombs. And, by the way, the Air Ministry had already built eleven rocket planes, and the first test of an atomic bomb to be delivered by one of the planes was scheduled for the upcoming Sunday at dawn.

Pantry is beyond control, or at least Bullinger and rest of the dithering Furnivall Cabinet cannot stop him. Assuming that the circumference of the bomb's explosion will not be wider than 30 miles, Air Ministry officials authorize its release into the North Atlantic, apparently at a safe distance from any ship and all land masses. But they have miscalculated its power. The bomb creates a tidal wave and an enormous bank of white steam so hot that it scalds to death an underdressed observation plane pilot who flies too close. The wave sinks the British aircraft carrier *Albatross*, whence the rocket plane flew, the American cruiser *Omaha*, and SS *Calanares* of the United Fruit Company. And it inundates Charleston and Myrtle Beach, South Carolina, killing 80,000 people. In his explanation of the disaster, the Prime Minister admits that 'the destructive range of this bomb had been seriously underestimated', indeed, by a factor of two and a half. He expresses regret and offers to compensate the Americans. And he proposes to destroy within six months his country's entire stock of atomic bombs—as long as all the other powers would promise to eschew aerial and submarine warfare. If not, the British government would have to 'resort to progressive means of compulsion'.

There existed, of course, the possibility that the other powers would not agree to Britain's conditions. What then? Lady Campbell, the aristocratic mother of Jane Campbell, who was Parliamentary Secretary at the Foreign Office, was not terribly worried, and espoused an early version of nuclear monopoly deterrence that would become popular in Washington in a very few years:

> 'War?' said Lady Campbell, having resumed her knitting. 'War with whom?'
> 'War with everybody,' said Jane, swallowing her coffee in desperation.
> 'But surely, my dear Jane, how ridiculous you are! If the bomb is as bad as all that, and if we have several of them, no one will dare to go to war. Not if we have enough of those bombs. Besides, in any case, darling, you can't dash off like this directly after luncheon.'[39]

Science is experimentation, observation, the careful use of instruments and numbers and applied principles and techniques. It is also imagination, the ability to think beyond received wisdom and to see what the instruments offer the eyes despite what the brain stubbornly insists cannot be true. Not only British scientists, nor those from other places who were welcomed into British laboratories, were capable of imagination, as the work of Joliot and Curie, Fermi, Hahn, Strassmann, Meitner, and Frisch indicates. But it took H. G. Wells and Harold Nicolson to imagine the atomic bomb, and the revelation of Leo Szilard, the Hungarian soaking in his London bathtub, to grasp that the discovery of fission might lead to terrible weapons. Two others transplanted to Britain, Frisch and Rudolf Peierls, would in 1940 crystallize this understanding in a memo of extraordinary consequence. In the end, as Margaret Gowing has written, 'Britain had been the midwife of this bomb.'[40]

THREE
Japan and Germany:
Paths not Taken

There is nothing outwardly remarkable about the ore pitchblende. Samples of it are available in university geology laboratories, where they might be inspected by students or borrowed by school girls masquerading as Marie Curie at science fairs. Pitchblende is brown, gray, and black, with a lustre described in technical manuals as 'greasy', and it sometimes appears in clusters that resemble grapes on a vine. Madame Curie, who got her samples of pitchblende from Europe's geological museums, discovered that the ore held small amounts of radium, which interested and delighted her; she and her husband, Pierre, filled test tubes with radium to show captivated visitors, and Marie kept a glassful of the stuff next to her bed for illumination. Pitchblende is the most common form of the mineral uraninite, which holds traces of radium, thorium, and polonium but is principally constituted of uranium oxide. It yields abundant uranium.

1. Finding uranium

The source of Curie's museum pitchblende, and before the First World War the only known source of uranium anywhere, was Joachimsthal (or Jáchymov) in northwestern Bohemia, then part of Austria-Hungary. The area, known as the Erzgebirge, is wooded and mountainous. It was first known for its silver, discovered there early in the sixteenth century and formed into coins by the local count. He called the coins 'Joachimsthalers', later contracted to 'thalers' and then 'dollars' in English. The silver ore appeared in the upper workings of the mine; cobalt, nickel, and bismuth came further down; at the lowest level, embedded in narrow veins that ran through dolomite and quartz, was pitchblende. The Renaissance scientist Georgius Agricola came to Joachimsthal to study the region's minerals, to write the first serious book that classified minerals according to their properties, and to invest enough in the Gotsgaab (God's Gift) mine to keep his family comfortable for the rest of his life. The German chemist Martin Heinrich Klaproth was the first, in 1789, to derive a grey metal from Joachimsthal pitchblende. He called it uranium, after the recently discovered planet Uranus. Ceramicists found uranium a useful coloring substance for their glazes, for it imparted a yellow, orange, or brown color to the vessels they made. Early in the twentieth century, Joachimsthal and its surrounding area became a destination for Europe's rich, seeking out the nourishing radioactive waters at Carlsbad, Marienbad, and Jáchymov itself, site of the world's first radon spa. A precocious American student named J. Robert Oppenheimer would later write his prep school thesis on the ores of Joachimsthal.[1]

After the First World War Joachimsthal uranium slipped from prominence—several recently found sites were richer—but with the discovery of uranium fission by Otto Hahn and Fritz Strassmann in late 1938 the Czech deposits assumed enormous strategic importance. The Erzgebirge was part of the Sudetenland, given to Hitler following the Munich Conference in September 1938. The German War Office learned in April 1939, a month after the German occupation, in violation of Munich, of all Czechoslovakia, that a nuclear weapon might be feasible. The physical chemist Paul Harteck and his colleague Wilhelm Groth wrote to military officials that 'the newest development in nuclear physics...will probably make it possible to produce an explosive many orders of magnitude more powerful than conventional ones'. The War Office gave the Berlin-based Auer Company a contract for refining Joachimsthal's uranium. The director of Auer's laboratory, Nikolaus Riehl, had been a student of Hahn and Lise Meitner in Berlin. Thereafter, Professor Abraham Esau took charge of the project (though 'project' is perhaps too grand a term to describe it at this stage). By early the following year a good deal of Joachimsthal's uranium was arriving at the War Office. German officials decided that spring to prohibit export of uranium compounds.[2]

The uranium at Joachimsthal gave the Germans a head start on their nuclear reactor, or burner, a machine needed to initiate controlled nuclear chain reactions. But the ore dug from the Erzgebirge was neither as abundant nor as pure as that found near the village of Shinkolobwe, in southern Katanga province of the Belgian Congo. Local people had mined the area for copper long before the Europeans arrived. In 1915 a Briton named Robert R. Sharp came upon a ridge that rose 35 feet above the Katangan countryside. It was speckled with green, yellow, and orange minerals— copper, presumably, in the first instance, but something very different in the second and third. Underneath the topsoil Sharp found a large vein of pitchblende. A bit of digging revealed an extensive web of pitchblende and a colorful variety of other uranium minerals, in shades of yellow and orange. At Sharp's prodding, the Belgians opened a mine on the Shinkolobwe outcrop in 1921.[3]

The Belgian firm Union Minière du Haut-Katanga took charge of mining at Shinkolobwe. No one was yet interested in the uranium compound of pitchblende, but geologists knew that, where there was uranium, there was also radium, Marie Curie's experimental interest and a substance with commercial appeal: manufacturers of wrist watches painted it on timepiece dials to make them glow in the dark, and some scientists hoped it might be used to treat cancer. Hidden away in three tons of uranium was a single gram of radium, 20,000 times more precious than gold. Union Minière hired 200 local Bayeke men to work the mine. Four white company officials gave the orders and handed the Bayeke picks and shovels. The men chopped at the earth, dislodging heavy chunks of the yellow ore, which they placed in cloth sacks. Full sacks went by buffalo cart to the railhead at Kambove, next in British-built train cars to Lobito on the West African coast, and then by ship to Antwerp. Over time, steel drums replaced the inefficient sacks. And the miners went deeper into the earth, revealing ever-richer deposits of uranium and its more exalted constituent. From Antwerp the ore was sent to a newly constructed refinery in the town of Oolen, which processed out of it minute portions of radium. Marie Curie was made a consultant to the process. The radium was carefully encased in lead and sent under guard to hospitals and labs throughout Europe. The spent uranium was dumped in piles outside town, where, as Martin Lynch has written, 'the yellowish waste was left to soak up the rain'. There the piles sat, and grew, for nearly two decades.[4]

2. The Germans advance

Having taken Czechoslovakia virtually by British and French invitation in 1938 and 1939, having then launched the Second World War on 1 September 1939 with an attack on Poland that included the terror bombing of Warsaw, the Germans briefly halted. Some in the West dubbed the winter of 1939–40 the time of the 'phony war'. But the Blitzkrieg started again that spring. On 9 April, three weeks after Italy had entered the war on the side of Germany, the Germans invaded Denmark and Norway. The shocked Danes capitulated almost immediately, though their resistance to Nazi oppression from that moment forward was among the most vigorous in Europe. The Norwegians fought back, and received some poorly organized help from the British. King Haakon escaped his country, the government of Neville Chamberlain fell in part as a result of its blundering efforts in Norway (to be replaced by a Conservative government formed by Winston Churchill), and Norway's resisters finally surrendered in early June. Meanwhile, on 10 May the Germans invaded the Netherlands, Luxembourg, and Belgium. Overwhelmed, the Luxembourgers surrendered almost immediately, the Dutch five days after the German bombing of Rotterdam that killed 30,000. The Belgians held out for nearly three weeks before capitulating; Dunkirk was evacuated in late May and early June. On 5 June the Nazis struck France, which surrendered after seventeen days. Even as Fascist armies moved against North Africa, Eastern Europe, and the Balkans that summer, the Battle of Britain began in earnest. Churchill rallied his people. The American president, Franklin Delano Roosevelt, sent Churchill his sympathy and as much aid as he could muster through his own office or with the limited support of a cautious Congress.

The fall of Norway meant that the great factory at Vemork, owned by the firm Norsk Hydro, was in German hands. Norsk Hydro produced heavy water, in which two atoms of deuterium replace the two hydrogen atoms: D_2O. (Deuterium is an isotope of hydrogen, heavier because it carries one extra neutron.) Heavy water was known to be a moderator of a potential chain reaction—that is, it slows projectile neutrons so as to make them more likely to strike uranium nucleii. Norsk Hydro produced far more heavy water than anyone else in the world, and the Germans quickly commandeered the plant. The previous March, under cover of the phony war but fearing the worst, Frédéric Joliot had instigated the purchase of

185 kilograms of heavy water from Norsk Hydro and brought it to Paris in twelve aluminum canisters. When the Germans breached the French front in June, Joliot spirited the heavy water to Bank of France vaults in the center of the country, thence to a death-row prison cell at Riom (the doomed convicts carried the water into the cell themselves), and finally to a British coal ship called the *Broompark*, which sailed from Bordeaux with the water and a load of industrial diamonds and safely reached England later that summer. It thus followed the many scientists who had left the continent for Britain over the previous seven years—and, as we shall see, it carried two others.[5]

The Shinkolobwe uranium, piled in Oolen, escaped too. In the spring of 1939, the physicist G. P. Thomson, of the Imperial College of Science and Technology in London, asked officials to obtain for him a ton of uranium oxide, for experimental purposes. Thomson's request ultimately reached his rector, Sir Henry Tizard, who also chaired the Research Department of the Royal Air Force. Thomson got his ton of UO_2, while Tizard was concerned enough by the request to call a meeting with the Belgian ambassador to Britain and two officials of the Union Minière du Haut Katanga—the Briton Lord Stonehaven, and Edgar Sengier, the Belgian who managed the Shinkolobwe mine for the company. Tizard asked that the British be granted an option to buy all the uranium ore that would be mined at Shinkolobwe; he evidently did not know about the pile of uranium ore already in Belgium. The Belgians refused. As the meeting broke up, Tizard said to Sengier: 'Be careful, and never forget that you have in your hands something that may mean a catastrophe to your country and mine if this material were to fall into the hands of a possible enemy.'[6]

Several days later, back in Brussels, Sengier heard much the same warning from Joliot. At that point, worried, he packed the Oolen ore, over 1,200 tons worth, into 2,000 steel drums marked 'Uranium Ore, Product of the Belgian Congo', trucked it to port at Antwerp, and placed it on two ships bound for Staten Island, New York. Sengier then tried several times without success to interest the Americans in the ore. (On 18 September 1942, the day after General Leslie Groves took charge of the US atomic bomb project, Groves's deputy, Kenneth Nichols, found Sengier at Union Minière's New York City office. 'I've been waiting for you to come,' Sengier told Nichols. If the Americans wanted his uranium, they could have it. Nichols and Sengier scribbled an agreement on a piece of paper—the ore was sold for the low price of $1.60 per pound—and within the week it was on its way to American laboratories.[7])

Thus did the raw material for a possible atomic bomb come into the hands of Germany, Great Britain, and the United States. To some extent, heavy water and especially uranium followed the best-equipped physics labs and physicists imaginative enough to use them. But not entirely, for Niels Bohr's small country had no uranium, and the Soviet Union at first appeared to lack the ore that Peter Kapitsa and his colleagues might have put to use. Neither did the Japanese have a source of uranium, even as their scientists experimented with fission and their military spread Japanese authority over the East Asian mainland. Whether Japan would have been able to build atomic bombs had it found a Chinese Joachimsthal or a Malayan Shinkolobwe will always remain a matter for speculation; Germany, after all, had uranium and heavy water but did not, as we shall see, come close to making a bomb. There were in fact many reasons why the Japanese failed to acquire an atomic bomb. The story of the Japanese nuclear project is a tale of a road not taken, or several roads, with critical implications for the world during the 1940s and after.[8]

3. Japan's nuclear projects

Japan certainly had able physicists before the Second World War. Yoshio Nishina had worked with Rutherford at the Cavendish and Bohr in Copenhagen for five years during the 1920s, and he was friendly with Ernest Lawrence of the University of California, who advised Nishina on the building of a Japanese cyclotron—a particle accelerator—in 1937 and provided the machine with a 60-inch magnet. Nagaoka Hantarō anticipated by several years Rutherford's description of a 'Saturnian' atom, and Hideki Yukawa predicted an atomic particle called a meson—much heavier than an electron and a carrier of nuclear strong force—in 1934. By that time, the Institute of Physical and Chemical Research, called the Riken, had been open in Tokyo for nearly two decades. Like the Europeans and Americans, the Japanese had been convinced by the experience of the First World War that science must be supported by the government if their nation was to compete economically with the West. Nishina started the Nuclear Research Lab at Riken in 1935. His younger colleagues called him Oyabun, the old man, though he was a sprightly 52. An admirer of the West, Nishina kept *Webster's International Dictionary* on a stand near his desk so he could polish his English.[9]

Japanese physicists also knew what was meant by a chain reaction. Bunsaku Arakatsu, who had been apprenticed to Rutherford and Einstein, built a particle accelerator and by 1936 was bombarding nuclei. In October 1939, less than a year after Hahn and Strassmann had announced their discovery of fission, Arakatsu and a colleague published an article estimating with good accuracy the number of neutrons liberated each time the fissioned nucleus broke apart. Arakatsu understood, as did Nishina and many others, that a successful chain reaction could in theory produce a big explosion. But Japanese scientists in general seem to have been little interested in pursuing a nuclear weapon—or, if they were, their path to its pursuit was so thickly littered with obstacles as to make a Japanese bomb unlikely.[10]

One obstacle was the scientists' own uncertainty that a nuclear bomb could be built. Nishina and the others knew, in the first place, that an atomic bomb was a good deal more than a laboratory exercise in making fissions. It would require close organization, coordination of science and engineering, an enormous commitment of financial resources, a solution to problems like fuses and initiators and fin design, that had not been broached, and a substantial amount—no one knew how much; an educated guess was 100 tons—of fissionable uranium 235, to be derived from uranium ore that Japan appeared not to have. Scientists lacked heavy water and pure graphite, predicted moderators of a chain reaction. Japan at peace was a country whose economic health depended on a vigorous foreign trade and careful management of scarce land, oil, and minerals. Japan at war would have its natural scarcities exaggerated, its priorities recast, and its services stretched to breaking point. Its immediate needs—for fighting the war, and for keeping the population sufficiently well fed to prevent domestic uprising—could not be served by an expensive and probably quixotic quest for a nuclear weapon. Japanese popular fantasies about atomic bombs were certainly no less vivid than European ones. As John Dower has noted, just before Pearl Harbor a Japanese scientist who was a member of the House of Councillors spoke openly of an overwhelmingly powerful bomb the size of a matchbox. (This boast was repeated by another scientist-politician in the House of Peers a year and a half later.) During the war, a magazine for boys ran a story called 'Atomic Bomb'. But these visions of grandeur did not change scientists' skepticism concerning the likelihood of building a nuclear weapon. After the war, one eminent physicist pointed out that the Japanese research effort 'might have looked very well on paper, but [it] really amounted to very little' in practice. The United States would spend $2 billion to build its atomic bombs. The total outlay for nuclear weapons research in Japan during the war was no more than $11.2 million, and perhaps as little as $650,000.[11]

A second obstacle to a successful nuclear weapons program in Japan was a general lack of enthusiasm for it among scientists. It is comforting to believe that Japanese physicists (and German ones) were reluctant for moral reasons to build weapons, especially nuclear weapons. It is also true that after the war scientists in defeated nations had an interest in underplaying their contributions to making weapons viewed with horror by much of the world. It is nevertheless plausible that Japanese scientists held themselves back from developing a weapon about which they had serious practical—not ethical—doubt. The widely held perception that a bomb was beyond Japan's capacity to build would have contributed to a disinclination to work on the project: scientists may have asked themselves whether the bomb *should* be built on the discouraging assumption that it probably *could not be*. Dower has noted that Nishina, ordered by the military to undertake the bomb project, never by his behavior seemed to endorse the task. Nishina often seemed unresponsive to the military's entreaties to work faster, privately expressed doubts about whether Japan could win the war under any circumstance, and ultimately put in charge of the project two scientists who were not among the luminaries in the field of nuclear physics. One of them, Masashi Takeuchi, who was to supervise the delicate task of uranium separation, later described himself as a 'blank page' where atomic research was concerned. There is some evidence that Nishina and Arakatsu requisitioned young scientists for nuclear projects they regarded, not unhappily, as hopeless, with the chief intent of keeping their most prominent charges out of the military and away from the front.[12]

Insofar as the Japanese state took notice of the atomic bomb, it made little effort to mobilize scientists into a cohesive unit to work on it. Here was the third and most important obstacle that stood in the way of a successful program. The military, which held predominant influence in the government, was interested in obtaining any weapon that might prove decisive against the Americans, particularly after confidence waned following the Japanese naval defeat at Midway in June 1942. But the military's effort on this score was hampered (again) by scientists' skepticism that a bomb was a practical possibility, the prospect of other winning weapons—rockets, so-called 'death rays,' and suicide planes or torpedoes—competing with nuclear weapons for budgetary favor, and above all a lack of coordinated thinking by the military branches that might have set the priorities for scientific projects and directed funds to those that seemed most likely to succeed in the shortest possible time. That the Japanese state during the Pacific War was authoritarian did not mean that its scientific and technological planning was fully coordinated. Japan's pursuit, such as it was, of an atomic bomb ran on at least two tracks at once, one sponsored by the army, the other by the navy.

The Japanese program was initiated by the Army Lieutenant General Takeo Yasuda in the spring of 1940. Yasuda, who was trained as an electrical engineer, had read about fission in science journals, and he requested a fellow officer with slightly more expertise in physics than himself to 'explore the possibility of an atomic bomb'. The officer's twenty-page report, which came out that October, expressed optimism that Japan might be able to capture enough uranium to build a bomb. The army contacted the Riken physicists the following April. The institute director handed the problem to Nishina, who, more interested in the performance of his cyclotron than in weapons production, let it languish. Meanwhile the navy, represented by Captain Yōji Itō, whose credentials in physics were somewhat better than those of his army counterparts, opened a discussion of nuclear research, presumably to include work on a bomb. After Midway, Admiral Isoroku Yamamoto ordered his researchers to develop new weapons for the war and provided Itō's committee with $500 (!) to begin its work. Evidently without knowing that Nishina had some fifteen months earlier been asked to assist with the army's nuclear project, the navy committee invited Oyabun to serve as its chair. Each project was top secret, but Nishina was functionally in charge of both. While Nishina seems to have found his bureaucratic home thereafter in the navy committee, fission work continued on parallel and compartmentalized courses.

The Itō Committee met some ten times between July 1942 and March 1943. Itō later summarized its conclusions. While it was 'obviously' possible theoretically to make an atomic bomb, Japan lacked the uranium necessary to do it, and although there may have been deposits in the 'wrinkles in the earth' in Burma, there was no assurance of this. Above all, the committee considered it unlikely that the United States could produce an atomic bomb before the end of the war. This assessment reflected optimism about the limitations of American technology and perhaps pessimism about the duration of the war. Such conclusions discouraged the navy from continued, active pursuit of a nuclear bomb; Yamamoto's decisive weapon would have to be something else. Nishina now focused his efforts on behalf of the army, and on the separation of uranium 235 from the odd shipments of uranium ore his subordinates managed to find. His lab was handicapped by persistent shortages of materials—his Riken colleague Kunihiko Kigoshi had to plead from the army, and finally steal from his mother, enough rationed sugar to conduct a heating experiment—and his own serious miscalculation of the timing of a chain reaction: he was off by a factor of ten.

The army-sponsored program, called the NI (for Nishina) Project, inched forward from May 1943 on. Located in Riken building number 49, put up the previous year in part as a mess hall, it was dedicated almost exclusively to the separation of U-235 through the time-consuming method of gaseous diffusion, such as Francis Simon had explored at Oxford. (The work was now more sophisticated than Simon's experiments with the family kitchen strainer. Researchers were to make hexafluoride gas, then force it through a number of baffles, whose tiny holes were to admit the light 235 isotope while blocking the bulkier U-238.) The gas itself proved difficult to produce: much-qualified triumph came in January 1944, with the emergence of a hexafluoride crystal the size of a grain of rice. The entire process remained on a ludicrously small scale. Riken lacked the space, the money, the isotope separators, and even the electricity needed to create the fissionable uranium necessary for a bomb; Walter Grunden estimates that by early 1945 the lab would have needed 10 percent of the electrical power then available in the entire country to be successful. That February, Nishina placed what distillate his researchers had produced into one of his cyclotrons and blasted it with neutrons. No radioactivity resulted. Then, on 13 April, American bombers struck Tokyo. In the pre-dawn chill, hours after the planes had dropped their bombs and flown off, Building No. 49 suddenly burst into flames and was destroyed. That all but put an end to Japan's atomic quest.

Its destruction was no great surprise, and at the time well down the list of Japanese disappointments and concerns. The Japanese government never expected to have an atomic bomb, and the military branches, working separately from each other, saw nuclear bombs as a prospect more remote than the fabrication of other fantastic weapons. Scientists like Nishina were unenthusiastic about the bomb, and others, including Kigoshi and his colleague Takeuchi, were in over their heads. Theoretical sophistication aside, Japanese scientists lacked the apparatus and materials they needed to do more than dream about an atomic bomb. By 1945, like their countrymen and -women, they were trying desperately to survive. (Dower observes that Kigoshi was finally so weak with hunger that he had trouble holding a test tube steady.) History might have remembered Japan's pursuit of an atomic bomb as simple folly. In the aftermath of Hiroshima and Nagasaki, it seemed equally a grim irony.[13]

4. Germany's nuclear projects

Scientists and statesmen in Europe and the United States were largely unaware of Japanese efforts to build a bomb, and they allowed themselves to be unaware because they were unconcerned at the prospect. The Japanese, the 'little men', were regarded with contempt in the West: they were able imitators of the inventions of others, it was said, but incapable of developing new, large-scale technologies on their own. This was not the view held of the Germans. Despite losing dozens of distinguished scientists as refugees from Naziism, Germany in the 1930s retained some of the best theoretical and experimental physicists in the world. Otto Hahn remained. Kurt Diebner led physics research at the Army Weapons Bureau and in the early years of the war took charge of uranium research at the Kaiser Wilhelm Institute in Dahlem. Paul Harteck, the physical chemist who predicted a powerful nuclear explosive in 1939, was at Hamburg; Carl Friedrich von Weizsäcker, whose father, Ernst, was the second-ranking official in the German Foreign Office, was at KWI, as were Erich Bagge and Horst Korsching (both of whom specialized in isotope separation), and the Nobel Prize winner Max von Laue, famous for his work on X-rays— though, as it turned out, someone who would evade weapons research during the war.[14]

Above all, Germany had Werner Heisenberg. He was one of the world's great theoretical physicists, the man James Chadwick had called 'the most dangerous possible German in the field because of his brain power'. Heisenberg had taken his doctorate at Munich with Arnold Sommerfeld,

finishing the degree in 1923, when he was 22 years old. The previous
year he had heard Niels Bohr speak at Göttingen, and had been captivated by the Dane's depth of understanding, his brilliantly discursive
presentation, even the famous mumbling that rendered his words barely
audible. Heisenberg had asked Bohr a sharp question, and Bohr invited
him for a walk following the lecture. 'My real scientific career began only
that afternoon,' Heisenberg would write. Thus inspired, Heisenberg began
postdoctoral work at Göttingen with Max Born. It was Born who coined,
in 1924, the term 'quantum mechanics' to describe the nature of matter,
especially at the atomic and subatomic levels. It was a way of knowing
that would lead to a new understanding of the structure of atoms: they
were made of particles, and electrons spun in orbits around their nucleii.
Electrons might jump from one orbit to another, gaining (if jumping
away from the nucleus) a quantum, or fixed measure, of energy, losing a
quantum if jumping toward the nucleus. Bohr worked most imaginatively
on the new physics, and it was thus to him that Heisenberg came, in
March 1924, in the hope of extending his own investigations. Within five
days of arriving in Copenhagen, Heisenberg had been invited to stay the
year.[15]

Bohr recognized Heisenberg's quality. The men talked together for hours
each day, often as they walked through the park surrounding Bohr's institute. It was here that Heisenberg devised his uncertainty principle, which
held, broadly speaking, that sure knowledge about a particle's position in
space erased certainty about its momentum, and vice versa. There was
something finally unknowable (even if predictable) about the atom. So
much for direct causation: 'In the strict formulation of the causal law—if
we know the present, we can calculate the future—it is not the conclusion
that is wrong but the premise,' wrote Heisenberg. Bohr was not altogether
convinced, and neither was Albert Einstein—'God does not throw dice,' he
scoffed—but the uncertainty principle came gradually to gain widespread
acceptance and dramatically altered the landscape of quantum mechanics.
Perhaps it also became a metaphor for Heisenberg's life, or more particularly
for his ethical position on serving the German state, come what may. If
the smallest structures in the universe could not be known or understood
in their totality, frozen in time and seen in full as if on a slide under
a microscope, how was it possible for a human being, infinitely more
complex than an atom, to know for sure what was right? If Einstein was
wrong, and God did in fact throw dice, what kind of moral assurance could

one expect from men? In November 1933 Heisenberg learned by telegram that he had won the Nobel Prize for physics. Students at the University of Leipzig, where he was now teaching, honored him with a torchlight march through the streets to his home. Heisenberg also thought it necessary to reassure the local head of the Nazi Students League of his support for the Führer now in charge in Berlin.[16]

By the time Germany attacked Poland in 1939, Heisenberg and the others had taken a strong interest in the release of energy by nuclear fission and knew a good deal about it. Hahn, of course, knew more than practically anyone. Other German scientists grasped at least the rudiments of nuclear science; Harteck and Groth had written to the War Office in April 1939 that a nuclear explosive might be possible. Carl Friedrich von Weizsäcker, at the KWI, was close to Heisenberg and had talked to him about fission. Heisenberg's own path seemed to lead inexorably toward a bomb. He discussed it with colleagues in Germany; outside Germany its presence in his conversation was implicit. In summer 1939 Heisenberg came to the United States for a series of meetings with American and emigré scientists. Heisenberg avoided talking about the prospect of war, though he would do so if others insisted. The Americans avoided talk of atomic bombs. Wherever Heisenberg went—Cal-Berkeley to visit Robert Oppenheimer, the University of Chicago for Arthur H. Compton, to the University of Rochester, Purdue, and Columbia—his friends urged him to stay in the United States. He was pressed especially at the University of Michigan in Ann Arbor, where he arrived in late July. The Dutch physicist Samuel Goudsmit was there, as was Enrico Fermi, and Fermi's former assistant Edoardo Amaldi, who was hoping to get permanently out of Italy, and a graduate student named Max Dresden, who served as bartender at a party one Sunday afternoon. Half a century later, he recalled the conversation. Fermi, Goudsmit, and others doubted that a scientist could 'maintain his scientific integrity and personal self-respect in a country where all standards of decency and humanity had been suspended'. Heisenberg disagreed, arguing that his reputation in Germany would compel even the worst government to see scientific matters his way. Fermi dismissed this as Panglossian: 'These people have no principles,' he said of the Nazis, and 'will kill anybody who might be a threat... You have only the influence they grant you.' In the end, Heisenberg reverted to the argument he made everywhere that summer: he was a loyal German—loyal, that is, to an organic Germany, not some temporary German government—and

German science needed him. He would go back. Things could not be that bad.[17]

Heisenberg's relationship with the Nazi state was complicated. While he had not welcomed Hitler's arrival in early 1933, he was relatively sanguine about the resiliency of the polity in the long run and the continued independence and efficacy of German science. When the eminent physicist Erwin Schrödinger resigned in protest from the University of Berlin in September 1933, Heisenberg got angry with him, 'since he was neither Jewish nor otherwise endangered'. Of the Nazi regime he wrote a month later: 'much that is good is now . . . being tried, and one should recognize good intentions.' In 1938 Heisenberg, assigned to the army, almost went to war over the Sudetenland grab; he was spared by the Allied capitulation at Munich. He was no subversive, no ethical hero. At best, he hoped to temporize with the regime so he could get on with his scientific work.[18]

In fairness—and it is necessary to bend over backwards to find much sympathy for him—Heisenberg had a frightening encounter with the most rabid representatives of the Nazi apparatus. In the late 1920s two disgruntled scientists, Philipp Lenard and Johannes Stark, once well regarded but now increasingly left behind by the new thinking in theoretical physics, began writing and speaking on behalf of what they called *deutsche* physics. They insisted that true physics sprang naturally from Aryan soil and was thus deeply connected with 'purely' German culture. The dangerous opposite of *deutsche* physics was 'Jewish physics', which in the form of relativity theory and quantum mechanics truckled to the devil. Science, proclaimed Lenard, was not international in scope but instead 'conditioned by race, by blood'. One need not, it turned out, be Jewish to be accused of practicing Jewish physics. When in 1935 Heisenberg was being put forward as successor to his old teacher Arnold Sommerfeld at Munich, Stark and Lenard intervened, demanding that Hitler's government prevent the high-level appointment of a scientific heretic. In the summer of 1937, Stark placed an article in the SS newspaper *Das Schwarze Corps*, in which he attacked Heisenberg as one of several *weisse Juden* (white Jews). The appointment to Munich was held up while Heisenberg fought back. Using a faint family connection, he enlisted the help of Heinrich Himmler, head of the SS. Himmler demanded that Heisenberg make his case, and Heisenberg did so, in writing and in several harrowing sessions with Gestapo interrogators in Berlin. In the end, a full year after the publication of Stark's 'white Jews' article, Himmler exonerated Heisenberg 'precisely because you were recommended to me by my family', and because, as Himmler wrote to Gestapo head Reinhard Heydrich, Heisenberg seemed a 'decent person' whom they 'could not afford to lose or to silence decisively'. Heisenberg had to agree not to mention in his classes the names of Jewish scientists, and he gave up the effort to move to Munich, remaining at the University of Leipzig until called to the KWI in 1942.[19]

Thus, along with his dedication to his country and its science, his identification in good part of German science with himself, and his belief that Naziism might not be so terrible in the long run or at least susceptible to his influence, Heisenberg might have felt in a perverse way grateful to Himmler for having exonerated him, or at least for having protected him from the poisons of Lenard and Stark. As David Cassidy has written, for Heisenberg 'remaining in Germany was apparently worth almost any price, as long as he could continue to work and teach'. The pleas of his colleagues in America during the summer of 1939 only made him more determined to return home. While he abhorred the racist parochialism of the *deutsche* physics advocates, their rhapsodizing concerning the uniquely glorious properties of German culture was not entirely without attraction for him. Werner Heisenberg was no Nazi. But in the name of Germany, and for physics itself, he was more than willing to continue his work, even to the benefit of the Third Reich.[20]

His remaining assured that German science would make a serious exploration of the uses of nuclear power. The Germans were quick off the mark. Fission was discovered by Hahn and Strassmann, then confirmed by Meitner and Frisch, in December 1938; Bohr reported on it in Washington in late January. Hahn and Strassmann then further clarified the process leading to a chain reaction ('There could then simultaneously be a number of neutrons emitted,' they wrote in January), and three French physicists, led by Frédéric Joliot, confirmed the news of a chain reaction in uranium in a letter to the journal *Nature* on 7 April. Two weeks later, and two days after the Joliot letter had been published, Harteck and Groth wrote to the Reich War Office about the possibility of a nuclear explosive. And on 29 April, the Reich Education Ministry (REM) convened a meeting of experts at its headquarters in Berlin to discuss the findings to that point. Scientists here spoke mainly of constructing a nuclear reactor, a 'uranium burner' as the Germans liked to call it, out of which discussion came the decision to end the export of uranium, most of it available from the mines at Joachimsthal. (This step, along with an alarming report of the 29 April meeting given to a British scientist by the German chemist Paul Rosbaud, got the attention of British scientists, and ultimately several in the United States.)[21]

For all the loyalty German scientists like Heisenberg felt for the German state, and for all the apparent totality of the Nazi regime, physicists resisted a centralized nuclear project. Or perhaps it simply did not occur to them at first to combine efforts. Though out of the REM meeting there came the Uranium Club, or Uranverein, a group of scientists united in the cause of making fissions, as in the United States the scientific habit of independent research persisted, and as in Japan there was more than one government agency interested in directing the work. The REM, which had called the 29 April meeting, proceeded under the leadership (it will be recalled) of the physicist Abraham Esau to capture as much uranium as it could with an eye toward building a reactor. Meanwhile, Harteck and Groth's provocative letter to the Army Weapons Bureau prompted the bureau's explosives expert, Kurt Diebner, to initiate a parallel course of research, evidently unbeknownst to Esau and the REM. With the invasion of Poland in September, Diebner's project gained the upper hand. When the Uranverein was summoned to the War Office on 16 September, Esau was not on the list of invitees; he learned of the conference, he later sniffed, 'quite by chance'. The scientists in attendance were told that German intelligence had discovered that uranium research existed in other countries. Was it likely to lead to weapons? If so, Germany would need to accelerate its nuclear work. It was too soon to predict outcomes, the scientists replied— more research was needed, and Heisenberg, who was not at the meeting, would have to be enlisted in it.[22]

In the aftermath of the Berlin meeting, the Weapons Bureau ousted Peter Debye, the Dutch-born head of the KWI Physics Institute, and replaced him provisionally with Diebner. (Debye decamped to the United States, where he told journalists of the German military's plans for his former professional home.) Dahlem thereafter became headquarters for German uranium research and strivings toward a burner. But the KWI, as one physicist privately complained, was now full of Nazis, and thus not immediately attractive to every scientist pursuing nuclear physics. Paul Harteck remained in Hamburg, where he built a primitive uranium pile using dry ice as a moderator. He competed for the uranium oxide necessary for the experiment with Heisenberg, who had stayed in Leipzig to work on a reactor of his own. In early 1940 Baron Manfred von Ardenne, not a physicist but an intellectually agile scientific entrepreneur, found a bountiful stream of funds from the Reich Post Office, which was headed by a friend of his father. At Post Office laboratories in Berlin-Lichterfelde, Ardenne designed his own reactor and worked on separating isotopes. Diebner tried in vain to coordinate these efforts.[23]

The researchers lacked neither imagination nor enthusiasm for their task. In the years following the war—in fact, from the moment German physicists learned of the bombing of Hiroshima—Werner Heisenberg, assisted by his colleague Carl Friedrich von Weizsäcker, cultivated a myth that he and others had conspired to subvert research toward a German atomic bomb. Opposed to Hitler's murderous regime and to the moral enormity of nuclear weapons in Hitler's hands or anyone's, Heisenberg had slowed his work deliberately and pointedly failed to pursue leads that he suspected might provide breakthroughs in decoding the science of the bomb. In a September 1941 meeting in Copenhagen with the revered Niels Bohr, Heisenberg claimed he had asked, albeit somewhat clumsily, whether Bohr thought it possible that physicists everywhere might refuse to work on the bomb, as he implied he himself would do. Heisenberg also passed Bohr a drawing of the reactor he was working on. According to Heisenberg's subsequent, rueful account, Bohr misunderstood him to say that he hoped Bohr would use his influence to get the Allies *alone* to cease bomb research. Bohr in any case bridled, concluded that Heisenberg was, wittingly or otherwise, promoting Naziism, and thereafter refused to trust the man who had once been his closest scientific confidant. Heisenberg returned in frustration to Leipzig.[24]

Already *primus inter pares* among German nuclear scientists, Heisenberg was to become even more central after July 1942, when he replaced Diebner as director of the KWI Institute of Physics. Thus, his ethical position on nuclear weapons, and on a German bomb in particular, has undergone exacting historical scrutiny and has generated enormous controversy since 1945. Mark Walker has divided commentators into two camps: the 'apologists', who accept Heisenberg's version of the meeting with Bohr and thus proclaim his innocence, even his nobility in quietly resisting the demands of the Nazi state; and the 'polemicists', who insist that Heisenberg's version whitewashes the truth of his own complicity with Naziism—that the German failure to build an atomic bomb had nothing to do with deliberate subversion and everything to do with Heisenberg's incompetence.

While this is an argument worth having, at least for awhile, certain judgments seem finally irresistible. First, the divisions in the German scientific community, even within the Uranverein, made success in building a bomb problematical. If the most bilious attacks by the advocates for *deutsche* physics had faded by the early 1940s, the various sites of reactor building in particular frustrated any coordination of effort. Scientists competed for limited resources, especially uranium oxide and heavy water. What is lauded as academic freedom and scientific independence in peacetime comes to resemble an unaffordable luxury of disorganization in times of all-out war, as the Americans would discover. To an extent, Heisenberg's appointment to the KWI in mid-1942 focused the effort to build a uranium reactor, and the center of nuclear research overall was the Virus House, built on the grounds of the KWI Institute of Biology and Virus Research. Still, scientific jealousy prevented any synchronization of the investigation. The ousted Kurt Diebner retained funding from the Army and resumed his reactor work in the Berlin suburb of Gottow. Experiments to separate isotopes and create chain reactions also continued in Berlin itself and in Munich.[25]

The lack of coordination among laboratories was never remedied by the German government, which had its own disjointed relationship with nuclear science, and here is a second reason why the German program failed. Some in the regime were suspicious of nuclear physics because of its association with Einstein and other prominent Jews. Hitler wanted weapons, certainly, but he never understood the science and technology that produced them. When the distinguished Max Planck, president of the Kaiser Wilhelm Society, approached the Führer in May 1933 to argue that Jewish scientists could contribute to the state and should not be driven off, Hitler became so apoplectic that Planck simply got up and left. (Einstein reported that Hitler had threatened during his tirade to throw Planck, who was 75, into a concentration camp.) Reichsmarschall Hermann Göring, head of the Reich Research Council, ridiculed the hypothetical scientist who felt he must proclaim 'his discoveries to the world, as though they are too much to hold in his bladder one moment longer'. He complained that 'we can't read the papers that these scientists publish—or at any rate I'm too feeble to'. (Göring soon thereafter relinquished management of the Research Council.) Bernhard Rust, the

Minister of Education involved in the quest for fission since the first meeting of scientists in April 1939, was uninterested in nuclear research, preferring instead to rewrite history textbooks and purge Jews from universities.[26]

Albert Speer, who had once considered mathematics as a career, became the chief architect of the Third Reich and, in 1942, the Minister of Armaments. Only after this second appointment did he learn of the prospect of an atomic bomb. In June 1942 Speer and a trio of military representatives were briefed by Heisenberg, Hahn, and several others on the progress in nuclear research. Heisenberg talked about the 'uranium machine', his favorite nuclear subject, and could not help complaining about the lack of support for nuclear research by Rust's ministry and the probability that the American scientists were by now ahead of the Germans as a result. Speer asked Heisenberg about atomic bombs. 'His answer was by no means encouraging,' Speer remembered. 'He declared, to be sure, that the scientific solution had already been found'—indeed, Heisenberg had believed this as early as September 1941—'and that theoretically nothing stood in the way of building such a bomb'. But the technology was lacking and would remain so for at least years, even if the project suddenly received full government support; Speer subsequently heard a timetable of three to four years. The session left Speer doubtful that a bomb could be built in time to win the war. He was additionally wary of raising Hitler's hopes unduly, acquainted as he was with the Führer's 'tendency to push fantastic projects by making senseless demands', and so reported Heisenberg's news to Hitler 'only very briefly'. Hitler had previously heard more exciting accounts from others, who offered what Speer termed 'Sunday-supplement' versions of the bomb's possibilities. But Hitler did not press Speer for details, and government sustenance for nuclear research remained inconstant, with occasional bursts of enthusiasm failing to overcome a patchwork system of administration and a good deal of official ignorance.[27]

The progress and regress of the war also shaped the German nuclear program. From 1939 until sometime in 1942, most in Germany were confident of victory. The Germans won virtually all the battles, in Europe and Africa, on land and sea. They had invaded the Soviet Union (where the gradual turning of the tide was either not yet fully perceptible or hotly denied) and attacked Great Britain with war planes. Much of the German population celebrated the Third Reich's triumphs; Heisenberg was at worst resigned to them and more likely content, and he especially hoped for the destruction of communism in the East. If what the German military was doing seemed to be working, there was no need to pursue such chimerae as atomic bombs. More ordinary weapons would finish the job. Once the war seemed to turn against the Germans—with the Allied victory at El Alamein in October and November 1942, or more clearly the German surrender at Stalingrad on 2 February 1943—the argument concerning nuclear weapons, oddly, remained much the same: while other new weapons, such as V-1 and V-2 rockets, might be within reach and increasingly necessary as the German military situation grew dire, atomic bombs were beyond German imaginings or budgets.

The deterioration of Germany's military position was brought about in part by the increased ability of Allied bombers and commando teams to strike in German-held territory or inside Germany. High on British and American target lists were weapons research and manufacturing facilities, and prominent among these were sites of nuclear investigation. The British, Norwegians, and Americans attacked the mammoth heavy-water plant at Vemork, Norway, destroying a ton of heavy water through sabotage in February 1943, hitting it with bombers the following November, and finally sending a last shipment of heavy water destined for Germany to the bottom of a deep Norwegian lake on 20 February 1944. RAF attacks on Hamburg and Kiel during July 1943 forced the removal to Freiburg of an ultracentrifuge that was (slowly) enriching fissionable Uranium 235, and raids that November on Frankfurt destroyed the factory responsible for producing uranium metal. In February 1944 the RAF hit Berlin, not for the first time. The Americans had encouraged the attack, unabashedly seeking to kill Heisenberg and Hahn, who were known to work at the KWI. While the raid only broke the windows of the Physics Institute, it burned out the Institute of Chemistry, in which Hahn had been working on fission. The scientists present stayed safe in a bunker built for them by Speer, but the attack was so devastating that one scientist suspected it had been conducted using nuclear weapons and authorized the examination of bomb craters and debris with Geiger counters. Soon the labs were disassembled and moved south.[28]

The relocation, to Hechingen, Tailfingen, and Haigerloch in the southwest not far from Freiburg, offered only temporary respite from Allied harassment. Heisenberg set to work on a new reactor in a Haigerloch cave previously used for storing wine, but supplies of the uranium cubes needed for the machine were very limited; the pile fell well short of criticality. Meanwhile, the Americans, who remained fearful that German science would yet produce a nuclear weapon, took steps to locate and dismember the German program. General Leslie Groves, the man in charge of the American Manhattan Project, working with the Office of Strategic Services, the US intelligence arm during the war, created in the fall of 1943 a special unit to chase down the German secret. 'We had to assume', wrote Groves, 'that the most competent German scientists and engineers were working on an atomic program with the full support of their government and with the full capacity of German industry at their disposal.' The group adopted the codename Alsos—to Groves's horror, for *alsos* is Greek for 'grove'. The work began with a largely unprofitable probe into Italy, then the dispatch to Switzerland of an extraordinary mission by the OSS agent Moe Berg, an enigmatic, multilingual, former baseball catcher with a creditable throwing arm and a deep knowledge of the game. Berg also had a basic understanding of nuclear physics. Berg's assignment—given to him, apparently, by the OSS rather than by Groves directly—was to attend a physics lecture to be given in Zurich by Heisenberg in late December 1944. Berg carried a pistol in his suit pocket. If Heisenberg uttered a single sentence indicating that Germany was close to having an atomic bomb, Berg was to render him 'hors de combat', then and there, with a well-aimed gunshot or two. Heisenberg's lecture proved to be sufficiently general in scope as to save his life.[29]

By that time, Alsos had mounted a systematic effort to uncover German scientific progress. Under the direction of Col. Boris Pash, who had previously tried to demonstrate that Robert Oppenheimer had been associated with communists or was one himself, and Samuel Goudsmit, the well-regarded Dutch physicist who had attended an Ann Arbor garden party with Heisenberg in July 1939, Alsos attached itself to the vanguard of Allied forces that moved into Paris in late August 1944. There they met with Frédéric Joliot, who had disappointingly little information about the German bomb project and made clear his recently found dedication to communism. Mission members sampled river water in Holland as that nation was liberated, reasoning that radiation might be detected in the runoff from a German reactor; the samples were negative. (Goudsmit hurried to The Hague, his boyhood home, hoping for news of his parents, from whom he had had no word since early 1943. Among the broken window glass he found his high-school report cards. He later found an SS murder list revealing that his parents had been gassed at Auschwitz on his father's seventieth birthday.) When Strasbourg fell in mid-1944, Pash and his team discovered at the university's Physics Institute a handful of physicists, who were unforthcoming, and the scientific papers of Carl Friedrich von Weizsäcker, examination of which indicated that the Germans were well behind the Americans in their quest for an atomic bomb.[30]

Having thus far captured no reactors or leading scientists, the Alsos team pressed on. By April 1945, with the outcome of the war no longer in doubt, the French had been given a German occupation zone that included Hechingen and Haigerloch. Neither Pash nor his handlers had any intention of allowing any other nation to grab people who might provide valuable nuclear intelligence, so Pash hastily assembled a flying column including a pair of tanks and a handful of trucks and jeeps and rushed into Haigerloch on the morning of the 22nd. There he found the Germans' uranium burner. Many of its uranium cubes had been taken off to a nearby barn and concealed under the hay—shadows of H. G. Wells—but a German scientist told Pash where they were hidden. Pash had the reactor blown up. On the 23rd, the Americans proceeded to Hechingen, where they found and detained Erich Bagge, Weizsäcker, Max von Laue, and their colleague Karl Wirtz, then went on to Tailfingen and arrested Otto Hahn. ('I have been expecting you,' he said, when they arrived.) Heisenberg, the Americans' 'target number one', remained at large. Worried about his family as the Western Front crumpled, Heisenberg had left Hechingen on 19 April on his bicycle, heading for home in Urfeld, some 150 miles away. Pash and a small contingent of soldiers, having bluffed then shot their way through German lines, caught up with Heisenberg on 3 May. The quantum physics pioneer was sitting on his veranda. He asked the Americans in and introduced them to his wife and children. Pash allowed Heisenberg to collect a few things, then took him, by armored car and jeep, to occupied Heidelberg. Along with the five men taken earlier, and four others including Karl Diebner and Paul Harteck, Heisenberg was detained, from 3 July 1945 until 3 January 1946, at Farm Hall, a British intelligence 'safe house' near Cambridge.[31]

The Alsos mission revealed perhaps the single most important reason why the Germans failed to build an atomic bomb. For all the manifest brilliance of Heisenberg and his fellow scientists, and notwithstanding the limits of German resources and heightened pace of Allied attacks on German facilities after 1942, the Germans lost the first nuclear arms race because they did not fully grasp the science and technology required to build an atomic bomb. It was Heisenberg, the most eminent of the atomic scientists, who made two fundamental miscalculations. First, misunderstanding the fission process, he dramatically overestimated the amount of enriched U-235 needed to sustain a chain reaction, believing it to be a ton or several tons, rather than the 56 kilograms actually needed. As Jeremy Bernstein has demonstrated, even after the Farm Hall Germans got word of the Hiroshima bombing, Heisenberg failed to understand the physics of U-235. Attempts to refine enough uranium to produce its reactable form in the amount Heisenberg thought necessary proved time-consuming and frustrating. Second, the equally frustrating pursuit of many gallons of heavy water was the result of Heisenberg's belief that it was the only possible moderator of a nuclear chain reaction. The Germans had tried experiments using graphite as a moderator; these had proved unavailing. But this was because the Germans had used industrial graphite contaminated with boron, a substance that, as Bernstein puts it, 'soaks up neutrons like a sponge'. The Allies would understand the problem and demand pure graphite from their manufacturers. It was graphite that worked perfectly as a moderator in the atomic pile superintended by Enrico Fermi in a University of Chicago squash court in 1942.[32]

German scientists got a good deal of the bomb's physics right: they experimented, for example, with creating a transuranic element that might be easier to use for a chain reaction than U-235 (plutonium, element 93, would be the basis for the Nagasaki bomb), seemed at times to grasp the proper scale of the bomb (Heisenberg may have told Albert Speer and others, in June 1942, that a bomb the size of a pineapple would be sufficient to destroy a city), and appeared to understand the difference between running a reactor and constructing a bomb (principally the speed of the chain reaction). But the miscalculation of the chain reaction's critical mass and mistakes made in choosing a moderator for the reaction fatally undermined the Germans' bomb project. These errors offer the simplest, and in this case the best, explanation of the German failure.

There is one thing more to be said. The mistakes of the German nuclear physicists during the war were in part the result of the enforced insularity of German physicists, pariahs to most of the rest of the world by their association with a murderous aggressor state. The Germans had left, and had been expelled from, the republic of science. They were expelled, wrote the American physicist Philip Morrison after the war, because, unlike those who planned and built the American bomb, 'they worked for the cause of Himmler and Auschwitz, for the burners of books and the takers of hostages'. Brilliant as they were, Heisenberg, Diebner, Hahn, and the others were trapped inside a hardened, darkened bubble, unable to see or hear what was going on in the scientific community outside Germany, beguiled by the echoes of their own voices bounced back at them by the bubble's inner surface. The community's self-reflexiveness was made worse by the rivalries within it. Heisenberg, Diebner, and Manfred von Ardenne pursued their own nuclear projects and conferred only occasionally, and the separate scientific communities that formed around these men were thus even smaller and more limited in their knowledge than a single Uranverein would have been. At Los Alamos, New Mexico, where scientists from the United States and Europe devised and assembled the world's first atomic bomb, efforts by General Groves to 'compartmentalize' the work process were frustrated by the scientists' need to talk to each other, to solve problems across labs, tasks, and academic disciplines. Groves wanted each scientist to 'know everything he needed to know to do his job and nothing else'; our people, he wrote, must 'stick to their knitting'. Robert Oppenheimer, the scientific leader of the project, placated Groves as much as possible while encouraging his charges to exchange ideas through lectures and seminars. The information-sharing drove Groves wild, but it proved invaluable.[33]

Samuel Goudsmit came to the point another way. Along with Boris Pash, Secretary of War Henry Stimson's aide General George Harrison accompanied Goudsmit and the Alsos team to Hechingen, where together they entered the office of the departed Heisenberg. 'The first thing they saw', Goudsmit recalled, 'was a photo of Heisenberg and myself standing side by side.' The two physicists had a complicated relationship. Once colleagues and friends, they had fallen out, for obvious reasons. At Ann Arbor in the summer of 1939 Goudsmit had futilely urged Heisenberg to stay in the United States, and Heisenberg had in 1943 written a letter to the authorities asking consideration for Goudsmit's parents, who had recently been sent to Auschwitz; the letter was less than forceful. However they felt about each other now, there the two men were in a photograph on Heisenberg's abandoned desk. Harrison was suspicious and wondered if Goudsmit could be trusted. 'I could have helped him out, I suppose,' wrote Goudsmit, 'but that didn't seem quite the moment to explain about the international "lodge" of the physicists.' Carl von Weizsäcker used a different metaphor: 'We physicists formed one family,' he claimed. Perhaps, he said, the family ought to have had 'disciplinary power over its members'—but was 'such a thing really at all practicable in view of the nature of modern science?' Yes, Goudsmit would have said. Weizsäcker had violated family rules, and was therefore cast out.[34]

5. The Americans and British move forward

The German and Central European scientists who remained in the lodge, or the family, were those who had left their country and continued their scientific work in America and Britain. Leo Szilard had professed to the American financier Lewis Strauss his disquiet over the possibility that a bomb might be made: 'All the things that H. G. Wells had predicted appeared suddenly real to me.' He pestered Edward Teller in Washington, Eugene Wigner in Princeton (both fellow Hungarians), and I. I. Rabi at Columbia University, whom Szilard dispatched to warn Enrico Fermi, then also at Columbia. Despite the Hahn–Strassmann finding and Bohr's American preview of it in January 1939, Fermi remained skeptical that a neutron chain reaction might be created and ultimately produce a functional atomic bomb. When Szilard quizzed Rabi about Fermi's response to his warning, Rabi reported dutifully that Fermi had said 'Nuts!' Szilard could not believe it, so he and Rabi bearded Fermi in his office.

> Rabi said to Fermi, 'Look, Fermi, I told you what Szilard thought and you said "Nuts!" and Szilard wants to know why you said "Nuts!"' So Fermi said, 'Well there is the *remote* possibility that neutrons may be emitted in the fission of uranium and then of course that a chain reaction can be made.'

Rabi wanted to know what the man they called 'The Pope' meant by 'remote possibility'. 'Ten percent,' said Fermi. Rabi retorted: 'Ten percent is not a remote possibility if it means that we may die of it. If I have pneumonia and the doctor tells me that there is a remote possibility that I might die, and that it's 10 per cent, I get excited about it.' Fermi reconsidered.[35]

In the aftermath of Szilard and Rabi's confrontation with Fermi, both Szilard (with Walter Zinn) and Fermi, working in Columbia labs, produced fissions; Szilard called Teller in Washington to report, in Hungarian, that he had 'found the neutrons'. It was vital, Szilard thought now, to conceal this information from the Nazis, so he urged a ban on publishing accounts of progress toward creating chain reactions. This was too much to ask, at this point, of the scientific republic, members of which insisted, variously, that the Germans had pioneered fission anyway, that publication of data would spur essential research in American labs, that no one had yet actually produced a chain reaction, and that even a chain reaction would not necessarily lead to the creation of an atomic bomb. In France, Frédéric Joilot and two collaborators replicated the Szilard and Fermi fissions and refused to withhold publication of their results. The world was not yet officially at war, nor had Werner Heisenberg yet declared to American-based interlocutors that he would stay in Germany. Szilard shifted tactics. He called Albert Einstein in Princeton.[36]

It was July 1939, and Einstein had gone north to Peconic, Long Island, to sail and think. On Sunday 16 July Szilard and Wigner—the former never learned to drive—drove to the Long Island house. The conversation came quickly to chain reactions, using uranium, of which Einstein had neither heard nor conceived. He was persuaded that there was grave danger should the Nazis find a way to weaponize atomic energy, so he dictated, in German, a letter to a Belgian Cabinet member he knew, with the understanding that it first be cleared by the US State Department. Several days later, Szilard met Dr Alexander Sachs, a Russian-born economist with the Lehman Corporation who was on good terms with President Franklin D. Roosevelt. Sachs knew the physics literature and recognized the urgency of the issue as Szilard presented it to him, along with Einstein's letter. Sachs wanted Einstein to redraft the letter and address it to the President. He himself would deliver it. Szilard drafted the letter, met Einstein again to discuss it, then rewrote it twice more, with the second redraft receiving Einstein's signature. The final version, given to Sachs to give to Roosevelt, told of the near certainty of achieving a nuclear chain reaction 'in the immediate future'. 'This phenomenon', Einstein/Szilard went on, 'would also lead to the construction of bombs, and it is conceivable—though much less certain—that extremely powerful bombs of a new type may thus be constructed.' (The language is curious here: chain reactions 'would', not could, 'lead to' an atomic bomb, yet such a thing was by no means 'certain'.) The letter closed by noting the German embargo on sales of uranium and the presence of Carl Friedrich von Weizsäcker, son of the high-ranking German Foreign Office man, at the KWI, 'where some of the American work on uranium is now being repeated'. The letter was dated 2 August 1939; Szilard gave it to Sachs on the 15th.[37]

Delay set in. Sachs admitted to Szilard that he was 'still sitting' on the letter. In the realm of nuclear research, Szilard complained, 'things were not moving at all'. Sachs finally moved on 11 October, over a month after the outbreak of war in Europe. Given to prolixity and indirection, Sachs nevertheless managed to hold Roosevelt's attention for nearly an hour, reading to the President from a recent book describing some of the history of nuclear exploration, from his own lengthy memorandum, detailing (as Peter Wyden has described it) 'the roles of Hahn and Meitner and Szilard and Fermi and Wigner and Teller', and finally from a portion of the Einstein/Szilard letter dated more than two months earlier. Roosevelt began to flag, so Sachs cadged an invitation for the following morning. He spent the night rethinking his approach, and, though he still could not avoid rambling, he managed at breakfast to make his point: if the Germans built a bomb first, it would be disastrous for the world. Turning to his aide, General Edwin 'Pa' Watson, Roosevelt said, 'Pa, this requires action.' Action of a sort ensued. Watson set up an Advisory Committee on Uranium, constituted of representatives from the Bureau of Standards, the Army, and the Navy. The committee held its first meeting ten days after Sachs had first met the President. On hand, along with the government representatives, were Sachs, Szilard, Wigner, and Teller. The men sparred about the urgency of nuclear research. In the end, the officials offered the scientists $6,000 to buy graphite. Roosevelt took note of the committee's report coming out of the meeting, and, to Szilard's enormous frustration, matters once more receded into the shadows.[38]

In Great Britain, there was also growing interest in an atomic bomb. Unlike the United States, Britain was from the beginning of the Second World War on the front line, and its refugee scientists had in their new government an ally in their urgency to beat the Germans in the nuclear weapons race. Otto Frisch, the nephew of Lise Meitner who had, with his aunt, worked through the implications of the Hahn–Strassmann fission research in late 1938, was in Birmingham when war broke out, and, rather than return to Copenhagen where he was now based, he decided to remain in Birmingham to work with his fellow refugee Rudolf Peierls. Initially skeptical that a chain reaction could be harnessed for a bomb—it would be 'prohibitively expensive' and probably ineffective, they thought—the scientists changed their minds as they contemplated using not a compound of uranium 235 and 238 but pure 235 at the core of the bomb. Early in 1940 Frisch and Peierls produced a three-page memorandum that laid out, more logically and bluntly than any single document previously written, how to go about building what they called a 'Super-Bomb'. Using U-235 exclusively would mean not having to slow down neutrons, allowing fission to take, as it were, its natural course, and rapidly releasing an enormous amount of energy. They suggested fabricating a bifurcated uranium sphere, its halves to be thrown together at great speed to produce an explosion. In three paragraphs, Frisch and Peierls indicated that thermal diffusion, filtering a gaseous uranium compound through a long series of 'separating units', should produce enough U-235 for an atomic bomb.

The memo ended with a remarkably prescient warning concerning the dispersal of radiation from the bomb:

> Most of it will probably be blown into the air and carried away by the wind. This cloud of radioactive material will kill everybody within a strip estimated to be several miles long. If it rained the danger would become even worse because active material would be carried down to the ground and stick to it, and persons entering the contaminated area would be subjected to dangerous radiations even after days. If 1% of the active material sticks to the debris in the vicinity of the explosion and if the debris is spread over an area of, say, a square mile, any person entering this area would be in serious danger, even several days after the explosion.

Frisch and Peierls added that radiation exposure would not be felt immediately by those subject to it. Like poison gas, it was an insidious killer.[39]

The Frisch–Peierls memorandum, as Margaret Gowing has pointed out, asked (and answered) the right questions. The Japanese and Germans never properly asked them. The Americans had not yet asked them, though the Hungarians in the United States, backed by Einstein, had started to do so. The memorandum made its way through the physics community in Britain during early 1940, as the blitzkrieg paused, ominously; 'interest about the uranium bomb which had been waning now waxed rapidly,' according to Gowing. As in the United States, a committee was formed to consider the feasibility of building a bomb. It included, among others, G. P. Thomson (its chair), whose request for a ton of uranium oxide the year before had stirred the curiosity of Henry Tizard, the chemist and chair of the Committee on the Scientific Survey of Air Defence, who now also joined the group. The committee met first on 10 April to hear from Jacques Allier of the French Ministry of Armament, who reported the Germans' sudden craving for heavy water. At its second meeting two weeks later, the Thomson group discussed the Frisch–Peierls findings concerning the prospect of an atomic bomb. 'The Committee generally was electrified by the possibility,' wrote participant Marcus Oliphant some years later. Across England, the pace of experimentation now picked up. The Americans dithered. The war resumed its fury.[40]

FOUR

The United States I: Imagining and Building the Bomb

The high-level British scientific committee inspired by the Frisch–Peierls memorandum was meeting with regularity by the middle of spring 1940. Its chair, G. P. Thomson, thought it needed a name, so in June 1940 he christened it the MAUD (or Maud) Committee, imagining he was appropriating a fragment of code from a telegram sent to England by Lise Meitner—though in fact Meitner had only wished to contact Niels and Margrethe Bohr's former governess, Maud Ray, who lived in Kent. The MAUD Committee coordinated and encouraged rudimentary bomb research. It employed a good number of so-called 'alien' scientists, or 'exotics' as some called them: Frisch and Peierls, Francis Simon, who did advanced work on isotope separation, Hans von Halban and Lew Kowarski, who had collaborated with Frédéric Joliot in Paris, and methodical Klaus Fuchs. They were not allowed to work on radar or own bicycles without permission. They were permitted to do nuclear research. Under MAUD auspices, there occurred a number of remarkable advances in nuclear physics and chemistry that would be consolidated the following year.[1]

1. The MAUD Committee and the Americans

MAUD's work was closely monitored by Frederick Lindemann, the Oxford physicist, recruiter to Britain of Central European scientists, and confidant of Winston Churchill. The committee and its scientists also cooperated fully with the Americans. John Cockcroft, the Cambridge physicist and an important figure in MAUD, corresponded frequently with American colleagues and visited the United States and Canada in the fall of 1940. British scientists also entertained high-level American visitors. James Conant, eminent chemist, president of Harvard, and head of the National Defense Research Committee (NDRC), established to follow and encourage the work of the American nuclear physics community, crossed the Atlantic in February 1941. He met Halban at Cambridge; the Austrian-born scientist discoursed on heavy water and chain reactions. ('Look,' said an uncomfortable Conant, 'you're not supposed to talk to me about this thing.') But back in London Lindemann raised the issue too, confiding in Conant over lunch that it might be possible to make a powerful explosive by slamming together two pieces of U-235. Conant was followed to England by the nuclear physicist Kenneth Bainbridge. Invited to attend a MAUD meeting, Bainbridge was, like Conant, surprised to learn that British scientists had 'a very good idea of the critical mass and [bomb] assembly', and hoped to 'exchange personnel' and thus information with the Americans. Back home in early June, Bainbridge told the University of Chicago physicist Arthur Holly Compton and a group assembled at Harvard of British achievements and ambitions, including the hope that a nuclear explosive might be ready for use in two years.[2]

Similarly, the NDRC ordnance specialist Charles Lauritsen sat in on a MAUD meeting in early July, at which he heard Thomson give a preliminary survey of what was called, simply, 'MAUD Report'. (The final version came at the end of that month.) The conclusions of the report echoed the optimism and determination previously expressed to Conant and Bainbridge. Building a uranium-based bomb was a project 'of the very highest importance', so the work must move forward 'as rapidly as possible'. There should be more investigation of fission in U-235, an effort to design a fuse for the bomb, and construction of a 'pilot plant' for the separation of the uranium isotope, with the possibility held out that the full-scale plant would be built in Canada. Conant and Vannevar Bush, the inventor and lately scientific administrator who was then director of the government Office of Scientific Research and Development (OSRD), got a copy of the complete draft report in mid-July. It stirred them to nudge the NDRC to negotiate contracts for uranium work.[3]

The MAUD Report came also to Lyman Briggs, the director of the National Bureau of Standards who had in 1939 been designated by the president chair of the new Uranium Committee. Briggs's admirers described him as conservative and methodical; those less inclined to charity found him maddening in his deliberateness and his seeming suspicion of nuclear physics, in which he was not trained. (He had studied soil for the Department of Agriculture.) Briggs mistrusted foreigners and had a mania for secrecy, and he tried to exclude Szilard and Fermi from his committee's sessions. By 1940 he was 66 years old, inattentive at meetings, and worried about the effect on his reputation should his uranium project receive lavish funding yet fail to produce results. So he resisted lavish funding. Prodded by Bush, Roosevelt had in June 1940 placed the Uranium Committee under the control of Bush's newly established NDRC. But the Uranium Committee retained bureaucratic authority over the nuclear program, and Briggs could still mount obstructions if he wished to. When he got his copy of the MAUD Report in July 1941, Briggs promptly put it in his safe without showing it to the other committee members. MAUD's conclusions, Briggs thought, were too sensitive to remain in the light of day.[4]

Marcus Oliphant, the Australian-born Rutherford student who worked on radar and nuclear physics at the University of Birmingham and was a member of the MAUD Committee, was one of those who wondered why the Americans had seemed to respond so tepidly to the MAUD Report's extraordinary conclusions. In late August, just as Adolf Hitler was escalating the air war against Britain, he flew to the United States seeking answers. In Washington he met Briggs, who reassured him that the report was tucked away safe from the prying eyes of other Uranium Committee members. Oliphant registered his dismay. Granted an audience with the committee as a whole, Oliphant pointedly and frequently used the word 'bomb' to describe what MAUD had recommended, and he insisted that the Americans, the only ones able to spare the $25 million he thought the bomb would cost, had a responsibility to build it. Not satisfied with the response, Oliphant flew to California in early September and in Berkeley met the practical-minded physicist Ernest Lawrence. Here, at last, he found someone who shared his sense of urgency about a possible nuclear weapon. Lawrence showed Oliphant around his Berkeley facility and talked of using great machines to separate uranium and create plutonium. Oliphant told him of the MAUD conclusions; Lawrence paced worriedly among the eucalyptus trees as he heard Oliphant out. (Robert Oppenheimer joined the men afterward in Lawrence's office, and there heard, for the first time, about interest in building an atomic bomb.) Lawrence promised to help, and immediately called Bush and Conant and urged them to see Oliphant. Both subsequently did so, though both were coy about how much they already knew about chain reactions and fast neutrons, and Conant was as uncomfortably evasive as he had been in England earlier that year— Oliphant's news was 'gossip among nuclear physicists', he said. Oliphant also saw Enrico Fermi, who seemed to him as skeptical and cautious as Bush and Conant had been. As Richard Rhodes writes: 'Oliphant returned to Birmingham wondering if he had made any impression at all.'[5]

2. The Americans get serious

He had. On a chill September evening, shortly after Oliphant's departure from the United States, Arthur Compton welcomed Lawrence and Conant into his Chicago living room. The visitors had come to the heartland city to receive honorary degrees from the University of Chicago; Compton thought it a propitious moment to engage them in serious conversation. They stood in front of a fire and drank coffee served by Compton's wife, Betty, who then retired discreetly upstairs so the men could talk. Their subject for the evening was the atomic bomb.[6]

Ernest O. Lawrence was a small town boy from South Dakota, with a reputation for probity and decency underscored by his use of expletives no sharper than 'fudge!' Wooed away from Yale by Berkeley in 1928, Lawrence refined his fascination for machines, joined to his acuity for nuclear physics. In the hills behind the Berkeley campus Lawrence built a cyclotron, in which nuclear particles were accelerated at great speed around a magnetized circular racetrack, producing radioactive isotopes of the elements. He also developed a humbly righteous sense of the potentialities of nuclear products. In 1937 Lawrence's mother, Gunda, had been diagnosed with inoperable cancer. Ernest, along with his physician brother John, had bombarded Gunda's tumours with neutrons, far more penetrating and therefore more effective for use on humans than gamma or X-rays, and her amazed doctors pronounced her cured. The rectitude of making radioisotopes was thus to Lawrence beyond question. Whether their use in a possible bomb-building project was equally legitimate was yet to be determined.[7]

Compton's other visitor was Conant. He had worked on mustard gas during the First World War. President of Harvard and head of the NDRC, 'Conant operated at the crossroads of America's power elite—gliding easily among educational, scientific, political, corporate, military, media, diplomatic, nuclear, and intellectual realms', as his biographer James Hershberg has written. Some regarded Conant as aloof—Supreme Court Justice Felix Frankfurter characterized him as 'incurably cold, without radiations'—while others found him capable of humor, spontaneity, and intellectual flexibility. Whatever decision the three men reached that night in Compton's living room would come in some form to Conant's NDRC, as Compton well understood.[8]

The host himself was as widely known and respected as the others. Like Lawrence, he came from a small, Midwestern town: Wooster, Ohio, in his case, where his father was a Presbyterian minister and Professor of Philosophy at the local liberal arts college. His mother was a missionary for religious causes; his sister and her husband were also ministers. Arthur's older brother, Karl, had become a physicist, and was now at MIT. Arthur's own gifts had won him a Nobel Prize (for work on gamma rays), his academic position as Dean of Physical Sciences at Chicago, and chair of the National Academy of Sciences committee formed to advise the government on possible military uses of nuclear energy; he was thus Conant's organizational complement. Compton could seem stiffly pious in his willingness to bring God into his classroom and his social discourse, and his prominent jaw and erect bearing put some off. But there was no doubting his qualities as a physicist. Enrico Fermi, recalled his student Leona Woods, believed that 'tallness and handsomeness usually were inversely proportional to intelligence', but 'he excepted Arthur Compton . . . whose intelligence he respected enormously'. (Fermi was balding and compact.) Compton's religious inclination was to avoid weapons work. His hatred of Naziism pulled him another way.[9]

Lawrence spoke first. His recent conversation in Berkeley with Marcus Oliphant had persuaded him that an atomic bomb might be feasible, and a series of breakthroughs in his own lab and elsewhere in the country convinced him further. Months earlier, using Lawrence's cyclotron, the Berkeley physicist Glenn Seaborg had bombarded U-238 with neutrons and coaxed from it at last a transuranic element with the atomic number 94; Seaborg would call it plutonium. Enough plutonium extracted from common uranium would provide a suitably powerful core for an atomic bomb. It seemed equally likely that enough uranium 235 might be refined, as researchers at Columbia University (John Dunning and Harold Urey) were reporting success with gaseous diffusion, of the type that tempted and beguiled the Germans. Above all, said Lawrence, it was essential now to move forward quickly, because the Nazis were without doubt pushing ahead with a bomb-building program of their own. 'If they succeeded first,' Compton recalled Lawrence saying, 'they would have in their hands the control of the world.'

Conant went next, and appeared to resist Lawrence's logic. With war seemingly imminent—the Americans and Germans were shooting at each other in the North Atlantic, and negotiations with the Japanese in Asia were at a standstill—the scientific community must not waste its time chasing nuclear ghosts. It made better sense, he said, to focus on projects in the realm of the plausible, those that extended known truths and existing knowledge rather than those as yet sustained only by bold theory. Though neither Compton nor Lawrence knew it, Conant was in fact already convinced that an atomic bomb could be built. Having been to England, he was, of course, aware of the Frisch–Peierls memorandum and the MAUD Committee report. Several months before, Conant's Harvard chemistry colleague George Kistiakowsky, having come, like Lawrence, to the idea of a nuclear explosive through an interest in medical radiation, concluded that an atomic bomb might be feasible. 'It can be made to work,' Kistiakowsky told Conant in June 1941. 'I am one hundred percent sold.' Trusting the British and the man he called 'Kisty', Conant was now fully sold too. In September he wanted only to hear Arthur Compton make his own case for the bomb, and he wanted to hear Ernest Lawrence say that he would play a leading role in its development.

That is what he got. Compton made a spirited argument for pressing ahead, rehearsing Lawrence's contentions and emphasizing particularly the need to beat the Nazis. Conant turned to Lawrence. 'Ernest,' he said, 'you say you are convinced of the importance of these fission bombs. Are you ready to devote the next several years of your life to getting them made?' Peter Wyden has Lawrence sitting up 'with a start' at this, his eyes glazing, his mouth dropping open. Perhaps. He replied: 'If you tell me this is my job, I'll do it.' It was decided. Lawrence would return to Berkeley and continue work on plutonium and uranium separation. Compton's NAS Committee would add chemists and engineers to its roster of physicists. Conant would contact Vannevar Bush at the OSRD and ask him to alert 'the highest levels' of the Roosevelt administration to the scientists' new interest in the bomb.

Obligingly, and momentously, Bush met Franklin Roosevelt and Vice President Henry Wallace on 9 October. They decided to replace Briggs's sleepy Uranium Committee, constituted as a result of the Hungarians' importunities concerning atomic power nearly two years earlier, with a high-level group that was to 'advise the president on questions of policy relating to the study of nuclear fission'. That committee included Bush, Conant, Secretary of War Henry L. Stimson, Chief of Staff George C. Marshall, and Wallace, who had a mind for science and would thus serve as Roosevelt's liaison to the group. The committee was called Section-1 of the OSRD, and it would ultimately give its innocuous initials (S-1) to the bomb project itself.[10]

There seems about these decisions, in retrospect anyway, an aura of inevitability. After all, with the descent into the Second World War by the European nations in September 1939, the United States was uniquely positioned to move forward on a bomb project. It had the world's largest collection of first-rate scientists, their ranks having been swelled by the arrival of refugees direct from Central Europe or by way of Great Britain. While the depression lingered, not fully tamed by Roosevelt's New Deal, physics had recovered from the worst of its problems and was entering an era of sophisticated machines and ambitious projects both theoretical and experimental—'big physics', it was called. University and corporate laboratories ranked with the best in the world. The desperate need to focus on the here and now, to defend against air attacks and detect German submarines, to extend existing technologies—all of which characterized Britain, for example—was absent in the United States, for the country was not yet at war. And yet, because the threat of war seemed real enough, to many Americans and certainly to the President, there ought to have been an incentive to build an atomic bomb. Not everyone wanted war, but, beyond Charles Lindbergh and his isolationist America First Committee, few Americans had the illusion that it might be possible to temporize with Naziism or even Japanese militarism.[11]

That the US bomb project was on virtual hiatus from the time of Alexander Sachs's meeting with Roosevelt in October 1939 until the creation of S-1 fully two years later indicates that factors to move ahead with the bomb were less compelling than those that acted as obstacles in its way. If the United States was uniquely qualified to build an atomic bomb after the discovery of fission, it was also uniquely remote from the problems that might have demanded, and would eventually come to demand, an all-out nuclear project. Despite recognition of German and Japanese aggression, there remained wishful thinking that the war would bypass the United States, or end, somehow. If it did, an atomic bomb would not be necessary, and it would be terribly expensive, and it might not work, and how would it be dropped? (Even Einstein, Frisch, and Peierls thought a bomb would be so enormous that it might have to be delivered by ship to an enemy's shores.) Nations not at war and not expecting to initiate war are reluctant to build costly new weapons. Wars seem to catch Americans unprepared, even when it later looks as though they ought to have seen them coming.

Americans, of course, did finally imagine and build and use the atomic bomb. There is no point denying that fact, no point in shifting responsibility for these decisions onto anyone else. President Franklin D. Roosevelt authorized the development of the bomb, its progress was overseen by US government representatives, hundreds of American scientists worked on the bomb, and thousands more Americans staffed the plants that manufactured the components, including fissionable ones, that made the bomb work. American scientists, or rather those working in the United States, saw the bomb successfully tested and knew basically what it would do to a city and its residents. President Harry S. Truman, who succeeded Roosevelt when the latter died in April 1945, authorized the atomic bombings, with the advice and consent of his closest advisers. The United States can be properly credited with having made the decisive weapon in the Pacific War—and it can be rightly blamed for having unleashed upon the world the special destructiveness of nuclear power.

And yet, for all its apparent remoteness and its uniqueness, in fashioning the bomb the United States, and especially its scientific community, remained deeply attached to the rest of the world in all respects of its decision to build a nuclear weapon. Americans alone could not, and would not, have built the bomb. The project required, most obviously, the involvement of scientists who were citizens of other countries, some of whom had arrived so recently in the United States that their thick accents or unusual syntax made them difficult to understand. They were (almost exclusively) men, of a cosmopolitan worldview, deracinated and ironic, and, while convinced that the world was endangered by Nazi aggression, they were frequently dedicated more to abstract principle than to the goals of a particular country, even their adopted one. Disgusted as most were with Werner Heisenberg and the other German scientists who had remained in Germany, they retained a loyalty to the scientific republic and thus a belief that their work transcended any national cause. Impelled as it was by the strategic and economic decisions made by the US government, the bomb project was also the offspring of another polity, one whose members were moved by their desire to subjugate evil and an enormous curiosity to see if their bold ideas would work. And many of them hoped, perhaps naively, that the atomic age ushered in by the presence of the bomb would prove utopian: the world would be set free by the cleansing fire of the bomb and liberated thereafter by a commitment to avoid war forever and to harness the power of the nucleus to peaceful pursuits.

3. To war

The deterioration of US diplomacy created serious additional pressure on the government to prepare for war. Some American scientists knew the work of their Japanese counterparts, Yoshio Nishina and Hideki Yukawa. Few regarded Japanese nuclear physics as a threat to the West. But the Roosevelt administration did worry about the Japanese military challenge in Asia. As early as 1937, when the Japanese had created a pretext for invading China, Roosevelt had urged his fellow citizens to 'quarantine' aggressors, to isolate them diplomatically so as to prevent a contagion of aggression— disease being a prized American metaphor for inimical ideologies borne by war. There followed a series of tit-for-tat measures undertaken by both governments: Japanese aggression followed by a partial US embargo on scrap metal (or, in the Japanese calculus, the encirclement of Japan by Western imperialists in Asia precipitating a Japanese effort to break the confining ring); Japanese designs on the resource-rich European colonies in Southeast Asia responded to by a full US embargo of scrap, along with oil; efforts by Japan's civilian government to achieve a modus vivendi with the United States on the basis of Japan relinquishing any claim in Southeast Asia in return for US acceptance of its position in China and a resumption of metal and oil shipments—and so forth. Roosevelt's secretary of state, Cordell Hull, resisted what he considered the appeasement of the Japanese, and by the time Compton and the others had resolved to move forward with the bomb in September 1941, relations between the nations neared the breaking point. The Japanese civilian government fell in November, supplanted by a military-dominated regime headed by General Hideki Tōjō.

The new government resolved to strike a blow at the US Pacific Fleet, based at Pearl Harbor, Hawaii. Tōjō reasoned that the blow would demoralize the Americans and cripple their capacity to respond to further planned attacks in Asia and the Pacific. On 7 December 1941 scores of Japanese planes—fighters, dive-bombers, and torpedo planes—surprised the Americans just after dawn. In two precisely flown waves they did grievous harm: 2,400 Americans killed, nearly 1,200 more wounded, 8 battleships and 3 each of cruisers and destroyers sunk or damaged, 300 aircraft destroyed or badly damaged. The next day, a somber Roosevelt requested from Congress, and got, a declaration of war against Japan. 'Always we will remember the character of the onslaught against us,' he said. Americans did remember, and they demanded retribution.[12]

The Japanese attack brought the United States into war, and war became the context for the American quest for an atomic bomb and lent urgency to the quest. Some American strategists imagined from the first that the bomb would be used against the Japanese, because of Pearl Harbor and subsequent Japanese maltreatment of American prisoners of war, and because they feared that, if a bomb dropped on an enemy was a dud, the Germans, not the Japanese, might profitably dissect it for their own purposes. Generally speaking, however, the government and especially the scientists involved with S-1 had Germany in mind as the target for their weapon. They thought German aggression even more brazen and threatening than Japanese. They also believed that Naziism was more heinous than Japanese militarism. And they were very much afraid that German scientists were ahead of them, or at least even with them, in the race for the bomb. Fear of German progress toward a working bomb moved Leo Szilard to urge secrecy on the nuclear physics community early in 1939 and to seek help from Einstein to gain the President's notice. The Szilard/Einstein letter that resulted drew pointed attention to the German bomb threat, and Ernest Lawrence and Arthur Compton both made prominent mention of a possible German bomb when they gave their reasons for pushing ahead with the US program. Every German move that portended work on nuclear weapons—the ban on uranium exports, the capture of Norway's heavy-water plant at Vemork, the information from Paul Rosbaud that German physicists were taking a bomb project seriously—brought anxiety to the American scientific community and a renewed determination to forge ahead with its own work on the bomb.[13]

4. Resolving to build and use the bomb

And so, shown the way to fission by Germans, a Dane, a Frenchman, and an Italian, nudged forward by Hungarian and German expatriates, and all but cuffed about the ears by Britons (and an Australian living in England), the Americans finally embraced a project to build an atomic bomb. Or, more precisely, at the 9 October meeting with Roosevelt and Wallace, Bush was authorized to explore the feasibility of the bomb, to determine what research and which resources, natural and financial, would be needed. It was not quite yet a decision to build the bomb, though implicit throughout the detailed conversation the three men had was an understanding that, if the bomb could be built, it should be. The logical extension of this understanding was an assumption even more significant: that if the bomb could be built, it should then be used, against anyone with whom the United States was at war. From the first—that is, from the moment he heard the news about Pearl Harbor—Franklin Roosevelt resolved that the United States must unequivocally (if not yet unconditionally) defeat Japan (and Germany), and must do so at the smallest possible price in American lives. When Alexander Sachs, Vannevar Bush, or anyone talked to the President about the bomb, they emphasized its unprecedented power, but they did so by comparing it to current weapons. It was, after all, a bomb they were seeking, even if it was an 'extremely powerful' one, as Szilard and Einstein had written in 1939. Already in July 1941 Bush had written to Roosevelt of a bomb 'a thousand times more powerful than existing explosives', unparalleled in its magnitude but not its nature, for it was still a bomb. 'Certainly, there was no question in my mind,' wrote Leslie Groves, 'or, as far as I was ever aware, in the mind of either President Roosevelt or President Truman or any other responsible person, but that we were developing a weapon to be employed against the enemies of the United States.' Groves dated this assumption to September 1942, when he assumed control of what had become the Manhattan Project, established a month earlier to build an atomic bomb. Yet there is no reason to think that Roosevelt waited eleven months from the pivotal meeting with Bush to decide that an atomic bomb, if developed and needed to win the war, should be used. Indeed, Winston Churchill wrote later, 'there never was a moment's discussion as to whether the atomic bomb should be used or not'.[14]

Authorized by Roosevelt, who promised Bush money for nuclear research from a secret fund available only to the President, the American bomb quest began, like those in Japan and Germany, on several fronts at once. Fermi, Szilard, John Dunning, and Harold Urey were at Columbia, the first two working chiefly on building a nuclear reactor (or 'pile') to create a chain reaction, the second two experimenting with the gaseous diffusion method of procuring U-235. At Princeton, Eugene Wigner was also working on a pile. Other methods of uranium separation—by centrifuge, and by thermal diffusion—were also under way. On 6 December, Bush, with Conant, summoned Compton and Lawrence to Washington. There it was decided that Compton, at Chicago, would work to design the bomb. Lawrence was to try to make fissionable uranium using his magnetized racetracks; he departed from lunch to get back to Berkeley. Neither Bush nor Conant had much faith in plutonium production at this stage. The following day, Pearl Harbor was attacked. The bomb was now more urgent.[15]

The multiple centers of research and labor frustrated Compton and, in his opinion, prevented the coordination of effort essential to move the project along. In January, though ill with the flu, Compton gathered Szilard, Lawrence, and several others at his home. The time had come, said Compton, to pull together. Work at various locations caused duplication of effort and was unsustainable. The scientists made the case for consolidation in their own laboratories. Compton argued for Chicago. The city was centrally located and unlikely to be bombed, the facilities were good, housing existed despite wartime shortages, and there remained competent scientists available locally. In the end, Compton simply overrode objections. He hoped, he said, that the others would join him. Ernest Lawrence remained a doubter. 'You'll never get the chain reaction going here,' he insisted. 'The whole tempo of the University of Chicago is too slow.' Compton disagreed, and two men ended up betting a cheap cigar on whether it would happen. Feverish, Compton rose with difficulty and went to his study to call Fermi in New York and Wigner in Princeton. Both men agreed to relocate, bringing to Chicago their plans for a reactor. His sights set at this stage mainly on plutonium, despite Bush's and Conant's doubts, Compton engineered the (voluntary) eviction of the university's math department from Eckhart Hall and christened the Chicago project as a whole the Metallurgical Laboratory, or Met Lab.[16]

'Now is the time for faith,' Compton wrote to Conant. 'It isn't faith we need now, Arthur,' Conant replied. 'It's works.' Compton kept reading his Bible, sometimes to his fellow scientists, but he worked, too. To raise morale among the scientists displaced to Chicago, Compton and his staff found housing (Fermi's assistants Herbert Anderson and John Marshall were placed in Compton's son's room), schools for children, and family doctors and dentists. The Fermis found a house near campus. It came furnished with a short-wave radio and included two young Japanese women as tenants upstairs. Fermi was still classified as an 'alien', so both radio and women were removed. Compton set the Met Lab three sequential tasks: first, create a chain reaction, using uranium 238; second, extract from the fissioned uranium the plutonium that would presumably be produced; and, third, extrapolate from this pilot experience the conviction and expertise needed to build a production plant big enough to yield the nuclear fuel for a bomb. He needed a nuclear reactor, and he gave Fermi the task of building it.[17]

In a squash court under the university's Amos Alonzo Stagg Field, the turf largely abandoned since the school had given up varsity football some years earlier, Fermi created his pile. His goal was to induce fission in uranium 235, embedded in U-238 in the ratio of 1:140. To prevent capture of his projectile neutrons by U-238, Fermi needed to slow his bullets down, thereby increasing his chances of hitting U-235, and for that a moderator would be essential. Lacking heavy water—recall that the Germans relied on this substance, which had its absorptive hydrogen replaced by more cooperative deuterium—and at the urging especially of Szilard, Fermi settled on graphite. The German reactor would founder in part because the graphite its builders obtained was impacted with boron and thus insufficiently 'clean'. In the United States, the National Carbon Company provided graphite made pure by its well-chosen coke base and extra time in the furnace. Supplies of the moderator—enough, figured Laura Fermi, to provide everyone on earth with a standard pencil—began arriving in Chicago in September 1942. Physicists, technicians, and a crop of local high-school dropouts unloaded the graphite, planed and shaped and smoothed it with saws and a lathe into bricks 16.5 inches long and weighing 19 pounds, then drilled into some of the bricks channels that would hold slugs of uranium oxide, the fission source. They worked at close quarters in the squash court, the surfaces of which became black and slippery with graphite powder: 'Hell's Kitchen,' thought Laura Fermi. Her husband had planned a roughly spherical pile 26 feet in diameter, but he ran out of room at the ceiling, so the finished reactor was flat on top.

On 2 December 1942, the first day of Chanukah and also a day of mourning for Jews, an estimated two million of whom had already been murdered by the Nazis, Fermi was ready to test his strange machine. Over forty people squeezed onto the balcony of the squash court, among them the head of research for the Du Pont Company, whom Leslie Groves was hoping to attract to the bomb-building project. The pile was punctured at various points by control rods made with cadmium, an absorber of neutrons. A young physicist named George Weil, the only person on the floor next to the pile, was responsible for manipulating these. Three young men stood atop the pile wielding buckets of cadmium salts; the physicist Norman Hilberg held an axe that could cut a rope holding a master safety rod should it be necessary to halt a runaway reaction. Just after 10.30 a.m., on Fermi's order, Weil pulled the last safety rod, 13 feet in height, out 1 foot. Radiation-measuring instruments clicked audibly. A graph confirmed the presence of radiation. Fermi checked his calculations against the readings and told Weil to withdraw the rod another 6 inches. As if alarmed by the subsequent rise in neutron activity, the safety rod, on its own volition, slammed down into place. 'I'm hungry,' Fermi said. 'Let's go to lunch.'

The experiment resumed at 2.00 p.m. The last control rod was withdrawn another 6 inches and the meters showed another jump in activity. 'The clicks came more and more rapidly,' wrote Fermi's colleague Herbert Anderson, 'and after a while they began to merge into a roar; the counter couldn't follow anymore.' Technicians changed the scale of the recording devices, trying to keep up with the pile's intensity. Fermi proclaimed that the pile had gone critical. He let it run for twenty-eight minutes altogether as the neutron counter continued to click and the stylus on the chart recorder swung upward. 'When do we become scared?' the physicist Leona Woods asked Fermi. Finally, as the instruments showed that radiation levels in the balcony were becoming worrisome, Fermi ordered that the safety rods be dropped into place. The reactor had performed as expected and produced atomic power. Eugene Wigner passed around a bottle of Chianti, and everyone drank a bit from paper cups. Compton, who had won a cigar from Lawrence, phoned Conant in Washington, and neither man concealed his excitement. But, as people left the cold squash court, Leo Szilard approached Fermi, shook his hand, and told him gloomily that this was 'a black day in the history of mankind'.[18]

Not every top American physicist moved to Chicago in 1942. Coming out of the September 1941 meeting with Compton and Conant and especially the 6 December meeting in Washington, wherein Bush charged him with producing U-235 for the bomb, Ernest Lawrence, while staying in close touch with the Met Lab, was more determined than ever to maintain Berkeley as a center for nuclear research. Since the late 1920s, Lawrence had been interested in smashing atoms, exploring their intricacies and unleashing their energy, and he had built larger and larger machines to help him do this. These were his cyclotrons, circular structures that allowed him to fire atomic particles around magnetized racetracks at tremendous speed; his latest, the frame of which he had showed Marcus Oliphant the previous summer, might (he hoped) accelerate particles to an energy of 100 million volts, if it did not first spring a leak, blow a tube, or cause a blackout on campus and in nearby neighborhoods of Berkeley. The atom-smashing all but accidentally produced radiation, unknown to Lawrence and unmeasured because of his impatience to increase the energy of his cyclotron while neglecting to activate Geiger counters near the machine. When Joliot and Curie reported, in *Nature*, inducing radioactivity in their Paris lab, Lawrence and his 'boys' quickly mimicked the French team's findings. As Gregg Herken writes, it was 'suddenly obvious to the cyclotroneers that they had been creating radioactivity artificially, and unknowingly, for more than a year'. By late 1937 Lawrence's cyclotron was engaged full time in making radioactive isotopes. Lawrence's work won him the 1939 Nobel Prize in physics, though, because he felt the war made it too dangerous for him to cross the Atlantic, he got the award on the Berkeley campus, with the Swedish consul general presiding.[19]

The imperative to produce U-235 moved Lawrence to rethink his cyclotrons. Into his machine he now fitted a mass spectrograph. The cyclotron's magnet would divide ionized uranium beams into two streams, the U-235 atoms pulled into a tight arc, the heavier U-238 atoms curving further out, by about three-tenths of an inch, than their lighter cousins. The U-235 could be gathered as a kind of metallic smudge where it came to rest. This method of electromagnetic separation of uranium ions differed from gaseous diffusion, favored by Harold Urey and others; separation by centrifuge, undertaken by Jesse Beams at the

University of Virginia and plausibly predicated on the principle that heavier atoms, if spun, would fly further out than lighter ones; and thermal diffusion, whereby lighter atoms ran more quickly than heavy ones from a hot to a cold plate. Some skepticism surrounded Lawrence's electromagnetic separation method: 'there were many technical difficulties to be overcome,' was Arthur Compton's terse assessment. But by mid-1942 Lawrence's great machine, chauvinistically dubbed the Calutron for its university home, was steadily producing U-235 enriched to a promising 35 percent.[20]

5. Oppie

Lawrence was a confident man, but he knew himself to be far stronger as an experimentalist than a theoretician. Having suffered, in 1932, the embarrassment of being scoffed at professionally by the likes of James Chadwick and Werner Heisenberg, Lawrence had retrenched intellectually, and had brought into his circle his Berkeley colleague J. Robert Oppenheimer. The initial stood for Julius, his father's name, but no one called him that. His family called him Robert; fellow graduate students in Europe dubbed him 'Oppie'. Oppenheimer grew up in privileged circumstances in Manhattan and on Long Island. His father, a German Jewish immigrant, found success in the New York City clothing trade. His mother, the daughter of immigrants, was a painter with a well-tuned aesthetic sense: Robert and his younger brother Frank lived in apartments and houses wherein hung paintings by Van Gogh and Renoir. Emotionally protected by his mother, and physically cosseted—he held up the start of his second-floor classes in school because he refused to climb stairs and would only take a balky elevator—Robert blossomed intellectually, showing an early interest in language, poetry, chemistry, and physics. Young for his class, he took a year off between high school and college, spending the summer of 1922 with friends in New Mexico, where he learned to ride a horse and where he first climbed the Jemez Mountains and saw the Los Alamos Ranch School, which was in the business of teaching and toughening overprivileged boys. Robert started at Harvard the following year. His appetite for work, or at least exposure to a variety of subjects, was prodigious, and he indulged himself by taking five courses and auditing five more each semester. 'He retreated', write his two most recent biographers, 'into the security his powerful intellect assured.' He chose, eventually, to focus on physics, training with the theoreticians Edwin C. Kemble and Percy Bridgman, the latter the realist who believed that science should be kept separate from politics. Robert had decided on a career path, he said, of the 'purely useless'.[21]

He went off to Cambridge, the English one, hoping to work with Ernest Rutherford. Bridgman's letter supporting him was qualified: Robert was a highly promising theorist, but weak 'on the experimental side'. 'It appears to me', Bridgman concluded, 'that it is a bit of a gamble as to whether Oppenheimer will ever make any real contributions of an important character, but if he does make good at all, I believe that he will be a very unusual success, and if you are in a position to take a small gamble without too much trouble, I think you will seldom find a more interesting betting proposition.' Like Einstein and God, Rutherford did not throw dice. Robert ended up in the lab of J. J. Thomson, and only with the stipulation that he enroll in a course in laboratory technique; Robert admitted to an 'inability to solder two copper wires together'. He was lonely in Cambridge, thought the lectures 'vile', and, while hiking along the cliffs of Brittany, he considered suicide. Things improved as he met other, younger physicists, and Cambridge also entertained Niels Bohr (who had appeared at Harvard when Oppenheimer was there) and Max Born. The latter thought Oppenheimer showed promise in quantum physics and invited him to Göttingen for the next academic year. Oppenheimer accepted. There, despite annoying Born by interrupting him during seminars and irritating some of his fellow students with what appeared to them as cultural and intellectual snobbery, Oppie found himself as a theoretical physicist. In 1927 he published with Born a paper on the quantum mechanics of molecules, and he finished his doctorate. He returned to the United States that fall with a postdoctoral fellowship from the National Research Council, teaching at Harvard for one semester then the California Institute of Technology in the spring. Ultimately he settled on a dual appointment at Caltech and Berkeley—then a 'desert' in physics and attractive to Oppenheimer as a place 'to try to start something'.[22]

Lawrence had got to Cal first, and had begun to start something with his cyclotrons. He and Oppenheimer had personal lives 'more complementary than similar', as Herken puts it. Lawrence was a Lutheran from South Dakota who avoided profanity. Oppenheimer, an assimilated, or ambivalent, New York Jew, was a touchy, chainsmoking polymath who quoted (and wrote) poetry, took Sanskrit in his spare time, hosted at his hillside residences spirited parties lubricated by strong martinis, and cooked for his friends, with a zest Lawrence thought perverse, a Malay noodle dish called nasi goring (which Lawrence called 'nasty gory'). They did not always get along. 'Robert could make people feel they were fools,' said Hans Bethe, the Cornell physicist who would play a key role at Los Alamos. 'He made me, but I didn't mind.' (A dubious claim.) 'Lawrence did . . . I think Robert would give Lawrence a feeling that he didn't know physics, and since that is what cyclotrons are for, Lawrence didn't like it.' Lawrence resented the intrusion of Oppenheimer's increasingly left-wing politics into the physics lab, as when Oppenheimer scribbled on the lab's blackboard word of a benefit for the Loyalists during the Spanish Civil War. In general, though, the two men recognized their complementary strengths and worked together harmoniously. Lawrence would run his experiments, commanding apparatus with an expertise that Oppenheimer could not hope to match. Oppenheimer would interpret the results of these tests with recourse to a theoretical way of thinking that was alien to Lawrence. Oppenheimer wrote to his brother that he considered Lawrence 'a marvelous physicist'; when Lawrence recommended Oppenheimer for promotion to full professor, he called him a 'valued partner' in the lab. The two men drove together to Death Valley during winter breaks. Lawrence sent roses to Oppenheimer's dying mother in 1931, while the Lawrence children called Oppenheimer 'Uncle Robert' and looked forward to his visits.[23]

No one questioned Oppenheimer's brilliance. There was less conviction about the soundness of his physics. While many of his scientific colleagues, evidently less gifted, won Nobels or are remembered for insights of special profundity, few in the field recall today any professional paper written by Oppenheimer. (Perhaps his most notable contribution, David Cassidy concludes, was his prediction of collapsing stars that would be identified over three decades later as black holes.) His friend and colleague I. I. Rabi conjectured that Oppenheimer's physics suffered from his knowledge of subjects outside his field, Hinduism in particular, which 'surrounded him like a fog' and so mystified his physics as to rob him of the confidence he needed to follow his scientific instincts and publish. He was better when he stood at a bigger canvas, synthesizing and interpreting the solid experimental work of others, seeing connections and organizing meetings of scientists whose work Oppenheimer, often alone, understood as intersecting. The broadly educated theoretician was also something of a scientific impresario, whose insight and good manners might override his arrogance.[24]

As John Adams and Peter Sellars have recognized, there is an operatic quality to Oppenheimer's life: its trajectory rose as the pampered boy genius got established in the international community of physicists, and then became the mastermind of the world's first atomic bomb—after which it plummeted, as Oppenheimer's own agonized doubts about his achievement, coupled with Cold War–inspired suspicions of his past political involvements, gave his enemies the chance to humiliate him, strip him of his fame, and leave him, like Sophocles' Oedipus, to 'live with every bitter thing' until his death in 1967. This version of Oppenheimer's life is, of course, too pat. Yet it is hard to miss the tragic quality of Oppenheimer's story. Oppenheimer looked like a man who had known tragedy, inspiring comparisons to tormented religious figures; with his arrestingly blue eyes, his 'halo' of dark hair, and his thin, in times of stress nearly emaciated body, he looked, thought a friend, like one of the apostles in a Renaissance painting. Given at times to philosophical musing and self-doubt, Oppenheimer clearly felt guilty about his role in building the bomb, telling President Harry S. Truman, on 25 October 1945, that he (or, in some accounts, 'we') had blood on his (or 'their') hands. 'Never mind,' Truman later claimed he replied sarcastically. 'It'll all come out in the wash'; or the President may have given Oppenheimer a handkerchief to wipe the blood off. He had passed security clearances during the war and again in 1947. Using the same evidence unearthed then, but with the Cold War in full swing, the Atomic Energy Commission, in 1954, cast doubt on Oppenheimer's loyalty and revoked his security clearance. Thereafter he lived in a sort of professional limbo, an uncomfortable symbol, for Americans and perhaps others, of scientific and technological success and moral ambivalence about the bomb.[25]

Much has been written about Oppenheimer's politics and their role in the atomic and then the hydrogen bomb projects, and the subject is of limited relevance here. But there is perhaps one point to be made before moving on. Like many Americans, Robert Oppenheimer was associated during the 1930s with the Communist Party, and with individual Communists and causes that would later be stigmatized as Communist or Communist-affiliated. Robert's brother Frank and Frank's wife joined the Communist Party in 1937, and Robert's serious girlfriend, Jean Tatlock, whom he met in 1936 and continued to see during the war, was in and out of the Party. Robert became, as noted, a supporter of the Spanish Loyalist cause, and he contributed money to several organizations that were said to have Communist sympathies, including the Consumers Union. Robert's wife, Kitty, had been married to Joe Dallet, a Communist who died fighting in Spain, and Kitty herself had once been a Party member. And Robert was friendly with Haakon Chevalier, a member of Berkeley's English department and a Party member, and acquainted with Steve Nelson, Dallet's commander in Spain who turned up in 1941 as boss of the local branch of the Party. When questioned later about these associations, Oppenheimer was inconsistent and had difficulty remembering potentially incriminating meetings and conversations.[26]

Having digested much of the abundant recent biographical literature on Oppenheimer, Thomas Powers concludes that 'Oppenheimer's politics were ... —like his physics—mainly theoretical'. Oppenheimer had a streak of righteousness and a willingness to support groups that seemed to him to promote good causes, even while he naively blocked out other, less savory features of these groups. Communists supported social justice and the right side in Spain; that the ones running the Soviet Union murdered millions of their fellow citizens and signed on with Hitler in 1939 either did not register or did not signify. David Cassidy argues that Oppenheimer probably added 'the cachet of communism to his portfolio as an intellectual bohemian', and, though the metaphors mix awkwardly, the sentiment seems right. The Party's ethos established a sense of community attractive to Americans left rootless by the experience of discrimination or religious assimilation, and this may have been its appeal for Oppenheimer. Many of his friends were Communists, and Oppenheimer's 'associations with Communists were a natural and socially seamless outgrowth of his sympathies and his station in life', write Kai Bird and Martin Sherwin. Cassidy doubts that Oppenheimer actually joined the Communist Party. It was the folly and the tragedy of the Cold War to divide the world into strict categories of guilt (card-carrying Communists and fellow travelers) and innocence (patriotic Americans) and finally to sort Oppenheimer into the first. It is tempting to compare Oppenheimer's politics to his sexuality: in his youth, he wrote wistfully erotic-sounding letters to his friend Francis Fergusson, and in Pasadena he evidently developed a crush on the chemist Linus Pauling. Yet he had girlfriends, married, and fathered children. As he defied simple sexual categorization, so he was intimate with Communists and liked some of what they were about. He did not, however, so far as one can tell, betray to the Soviets any secrets, or any information at all, concerning the bomb.[27]

6. Groves

The man who gave Oppenheimer leadership of the bomb program, who brushed aside fears that Oppie was a security risk despite what he termed the scientist's 'very extreme liberal background', was Leslie Groves, who was chosen, in September 1942, to take charge of what was now guardedly called the Manhattan Project. The atomic program had not been Groves's choice. He was 46 years old in 1942 and still a colonel. He hankered for a combat assignment and a promotion to general, especially after overseeing construction of the Pentagon, a job that had pedestrian satisfactions. It was time, he thought, for some excitement.[28]

It was, but not through combat. Groves was picked to guarantee careful military oversight of the bomb project. Vannevar Bush wanted an army man to place a firm hand on it. Fermi had not run his pile yet, and in the fall of 1942 the bomb program generally remained a small part of the massive mobilization effort the United States had undertaken to that point. But there was promise, and, if someone tough and competent could be found to lead the enterprise, its promise might be fulfilled. Groves's military superiors had Groves in mind from the start. When he first met Groves on the afternoon of his appointment, Bush was not sure the generals had made the right choice. Groves, who weighed nearly 300 pounds (he had a taste for chocolate creams, a supply of which he kept in his office safe), came on strong, even to the patrician Bush. He was prudish (having been raised by a father who was a Presbyterian army chaplain of abstemious habits), brusque to the point of rudeness, overbearing, and contemptuous of sentiment. 'I'm afraid he may have trouble with the scientists,' Bush anxiously told an officer after the meeting. To Harvey Bundy, the special assistant to Secretary of War Henry L. Stimson, Bush said: 'I fear we are in the soup.' When Groves got home that evening, he told his wife and daughter, and wrote to his son, then at West Point, that he had a new, secret job that no one was to talk about.[29]

If Groves got off on the wrong foot with Bush, he nevertheless quickly established himself as a demanding and effective advocate for his new cause. On his first full day on the job, Groves sent his assistant, Lieutenant Colonel Kenneth Nichols—'uninspired but punctilious', according to Peter Wyden—to New York to strike a bargain with Edgar Sengier, the Belgian head of Union Minière du Haut Katanga, who was, it may be recalled, sitting on more than 1,200 tons of uranium and prepared to do business. Nichols made the deal, sanctified on a sheet of yellow scratch paper. The following day, a Saturday, Groves authorized purchase of a substantial plot of land in Tennessee, for the purpose of building an enormous plant for the creation of uranium isotopes, and he met Donald Nelson, head of the War Production Board, whom he bullied into assigning the Manhattan Project the government's highest priority rating, loosening bottlenecks and cutting red tape that had previously frustrated the bomb effort. On 23 September, minutes after he had been promoted from colonel to brigadier general, Groves met Stimson, Bush, Conant, and a few others. Stimson suggested a committee of seven to manage the project. Groves countered with a request for just four—Bush, Conant, a navy representative, and himself—and Stimson acceded. At this point, Groves rose and said he had to leave: he was on his way to Tennessee and did not want to miss his train. Bush began to think that Groves had been a good choice after all.[30]

Groves seems to have braced himself to deal with the Manhattan Project scientists. He was an engineer, and proud of his grasp of mathematics, but he knew nothing about quantum physics, a disability in his own mind that he sought to cover with bluster. He came to Chicago on 5 October to inspect Arthur Holly Compton's Met Lab. Groves and Compton, both sons of Presbyterian ministers, found they nevertheless had differences: Groves referred privately to Compton, for some reason, as 'Arthur Hollywood', while the gentler Compton thought Groves guilty of an 'unfamiliarity with scientists'. The two men were ultimately reconciled. Not so Groves and Leo Szilard, whose animosity toward each other was legendary, and in high relief emblematic of the mistrust that existed between scientists and the military men assigned to keep them on task. (The Groves–Szilard feud began at the Met Lab, when Groves, out of his depth, insisted on discussing with Szilard cooling systems for nuclear reactors.) The Chicago scientists ran some equations for their visitor. At one point Groves caught a small transcribing error, which the offending scientist remedied with a finger stroke, leaving Groves smug about his own expertise yet worried at the feckless imprecision of the men and women in his charge.

'Dr Compton, your scientists don't have any discipline,' Groves insisted later. Compton remonstrated that 'responsible' scientists had a kind of discipline, but that it was 'not possible for anyone to tell a scientist what he must do'. However calmly put, that was exactly what Groves feared.[31]

The general went next to Berkeley, and Ernest Lawrence's Radiation Lab. Still on his mettle because of his experience in Chicago, Groves thought Lawrence was trying to patronize him with breezy talk about his cyclotron—engineer's talk, perhaps, but not what Groves wanted to hear. He wanted to know how much U-235 Lawrence was making, and how quickly. When Lawrence confessed that the separation process remained in its infancy, Groves steamed. 'Professor Lawrence,' he said, in front of the Rad Lab staff, 'you'd better do a good job. Your reputation depends on it!' Lawrence was stunned, but only temporarily; he got his own back at lunch: 'General Groves, you know...my reputation is already made. It's *your* reputation that depends on this project.' Thereafter the relationship improved; it worked best to stand up to Groves. But Lawrence still could not say much about U-235 production, and in particular about its necessary level of purity. For that, Lawrence suggested, the general should ask Robert Oppenheimer.[32]

Groves and Oppenheimer looked so unlike each other that it was funny: 'Godzilla meets Hamlet,' someone later said. Their backgrounds, politics, and areas of expertise were dramatically different. Yet both men, insecure in their positions, wanted to make a mark, do something extraordinary, and they seem to have recognized in each other a means of doing that. Or maybe something just clicked. Groves admired Oppenheimer's high intelligence and knew of his reputation in physics. While he, like others, had serious concerns about Oppenheimer's administrative abilities—'he couldn't run a hamburger stand', exclaimed a colleague—Groves believed that he himself could manage the administration of the program, leaving Oppenheimer to keep the scientists focused on building a bomb. As for Oppie's 'left-wandering' politics, Groves preferred to have the physicist close at hand, where he could keep an eye on him. A week after first meeting him in Berkeley, Groves summoned Oppenheimer to Chicago. They met, with Nichols and a second colonel, in a cramped compartment aboard a train bound for Detroit, and they talked for hours about the needs of the Manhattan Project. In the end, cognizant of the unorthodoxy of the appointment but unable to imagine or select a better candidate, Groves chose Oppenheimer to coordinate the construction of the world's atomic bomb.[33]

7. Centralizing the project

Both men agreed that the project demanded further coordination. The scientists actually building the bomb needed to work in one place so as to preserve security (always Groves's chief concern), avoid duplication of effort, cooperate across labs and disciplines (always Groves's worst nightmare, but to Oppenheimer essential), and finally test the bomb. Groves also insisted that the site be isolated yet accessible to transportation, be susceptible to enclosure and have some buildings, and be far enough from the West Coast as to avoid what Groves called 'the ever-present threat of Japanese interference'. Army Major John H. Dudley had scouted sites in Utah and New Mexico; to the latter state Groves, Oppenheimer, and fellow Berkeley physicist Edward McMillan came, on 16 November, to have a look. Dudley had proposed a canyon some 40 miles northwest of Santa Fe, but Oppenheimer and McMillan found the site dark and thus depressing. But the canyon was shadowed by the Jemez Mountains, not far from where Oppenheimer had first ridden twenty years earlier when he had come upon the Los Alamos Ranch School. Dudley had seen the mesa and now drove the party there, over rutted trails. Groves approved Los Alamos instantly. The place looked 'beautiful and savage' to physicist Emilio Segrè when he first saw it; Laura Fermi found the mesa 'covered by the dust that the wind whirls up from the desert below'. 'Nobody could think straight in a place like that,' fumed Leo Szilard. Oppenheimer was thrilled. The government took possession of the school, Groves picked Oppie's home university to serve as contractor, and almost immediately the building began.[34]

Groves found Oppenheimer at least superficially willing to accept a military-style organization of the scientific effort at Los Alamos and of the scientists themselves. The general wanted the men in uniform, to which Oppenheimer agreed, but at which many of his charges balked. Groves backed down. The general hoped to impose on the Los Alamos scientists the discipline he had found lacking at the Met and Rad Labs. He thought the scientists should learn to salute officers—in this he was denied as well. But, Groves insisted, there would be no backing down on the matter of security. German and Japanese spies were always a possibility, and Russian agents were doubtless everywhere; vigilance was necessary, particularly given Oppenheimer's political reputation. The scientists, Groves informed a gathering of them, were 'the greatest collection of crackpots ever seen', and, if they were not to wear uniforms or salute, they must at least follow the rules of 'compartmentalization' he set for them. This meant that the scientists must 'stick to their knitting', concentrating on their individual tasks without regard for the whole. Information about the bomb itself was to be shared solely on a 'need to know' basis. Groves would always pretend that the Los Alamos scientists had adhered to his compartmentalization rule, and he claimed after the war that the policy had prevented any serious breaches of security. In fact, the scientists routinely defied the system— openly, as in seminars led by Oppenheimer and briefings about the project by physicist Robert Serber (who discomfited even Oppie by referring at first to 'the bomb', only later agreeing to call his subject 'the gadget'); and quietly, as Szilard and others would testify, in order to make the process work better.[35]

8. Fissions: uranium and plutonium

The decision to assemble Manhattan Project scientists at Los Alamos, followed less than three weeks later by the chain reaction under Stagg Field, gave impetus and clarity to the project. There were many technical problems to be solved and strategic decisions to be made, but what Groves and Oppenheimer knew they needed, as soon as possible, was a fissionable core for the bomb. It could be made of U-235 or plutonium (Pu-239), with the precise amount of these materials needed remaining a matter of speculation, though not wild speculation. To produce both substances the project would need as much U-238 ore as Groves could put his hands on. Here was a task Groves readily understood, and he undertook it with his usual relentless determination. He believed, at first, that monopolizing the world's uranium supply was possible. The Germans had Joachimsthal, but the United States had Sengier, who not only sold his Staten Island supply to Kenneth Nichols but who promised another 3,000 tons from the Congo. (In the end, the United States would amass some 6,000 tons of uranium during the war. The Congo was the source for 3,700 tons, Canada's Great Bear Lake 1,100, and the rest came from the United States itself.)

Groves also hoped to control the world's supply of thorium, a radioactive element often contained in monazite sands, which were abundant in the Netherlands East Indies, Brazil, and especially the Travancore Coast of southern India. In all these gathering efforts he gained the cooperation of the British.[36]

Having secured his uranium, Groves now faced the need to refine it on a mass scale. Compton and others had planned to erect a pilot plant for making plutonium in the Argonne Forest, 20 miles outside Chicago. It emerged, however, that the uncertainties of plutonium production made risky the presence of a plant, even the so-called semi-works, so near a big city, and it seemed more sensible to place it closer to the full-scale facility where the production work would actually occur. Groves, it will be remembered, had already purchased a large plot of land in the Tennessee Valley, as close to modest Knoxville as Argonne was to Chicago. But the immediate area was sparsely populated and its residents poor. Through the winter of 1942–3 contractors descended on the place, building a railroad extension, laying down new roads, and putting up homes for workers and plant facilities staggering in their size and facelessness: the enormous dark box of the K-25 uranium separation plant covered some 42 acres. The town thus created was called Oak Ridge (its inhabitants dubbed it 'Dogpatch' after the rundown spot in the *L'il Abner* comic strip); the place altogether was known as the Clinton Engineering works. To the site came thousands of workers. Many were not sure what they were supposed to be making. Those who thought they knew were compartmentalized and sworn to secrecy. Mail was censored, phone calls monitored, and when boredom set in there was little for entertainment except movies and games of checkers.[37]

They were trying at Oak Ridge to make quantities of U-235. By the summer of 1943 scientists at Los Alamos were calculating that they would need some 88 pounds (40 kilograms) of U-235 to build the kind of bomb they had in mind. Part of the Oak Ridge enterprise was given over to Ernest Lawrence's electromagnetic separation technique, of which both he and Conant were enamored. They wanted Groves to build 2,000 Calutrons there. Groves, less convinced but nevertheless willing to place at least some of his chips on the magnets, built 500. In theory, these Calutrons should have produced enough U-235 for a bomb within two years, but design and construction problems resulted in the great machines' shorting out with dismaying frequency. Mice and birds found their way into the Calutrons and shut them down until the animals' remains were discovered and removed. By late 1943 the Calutrons had yielded virtually nothing. Much of the rest of the Clinton Works was devoted to separation by gaseous diffusion, in which Harold Urey played a key role. Yet here, too, manifold problems existed, especially with the manufacture of the delicate metallic barriers that were to filter the uranium hexafluoride gas through a series of cascades, producing the U-235 isotope. Debate over the composition of the barriers raged into early 1944, theory foundering more than once as it encountered the realities of engineering.[38]

Groves and the scientists had also originally intended to make plutonium at Oak Ridge. But the Tennessee Plant could not do everything, and if something went wrong with the plutonium-making process, and 'the wind was blowing through Knoxville', as Groves worried it might, there could be substantial loss of life, a shutdown of the Calutrons and gas diffusers, and, worst of all, a breach of security. Groves wanted yet another site on which to build a plant to conjure plutonium. His criteria were water power, a favorable climate, and, above all, isolation—'at least twenty miles between the piles and separation area and the nearest existing community of one thousand or more inhabitants'. John Dudley had helped Groves find Los Alamos; in December 1942 the general asked Lieutenant Colonel Franklin T. Matthias to locate a place to make plutonium. With two engineers from the Du Pont Company, Matthias settled on a high desert cut by the Columbia River in southern Washington State, near the small town of Hanford, population 100. Groves reviewed the site and approved.[39]

Another massive building project ensued. Construction crews were recruited to live in barracks, segregated by sex and race, paid somewhat higher than wartime scale, and treated to an abundance of good food—a treat in 1943. They were building a city, one with the single purpose of producing an elusive element for a mysterious project based elsewhere. The Hanford site proved wilder than Oak Ridge. At one point there were over 50,000 people working in the remote desert, putting in nine hours daily and extra time nights and Sundays. They entertained themselves as best they could, in an enormous beer hall, a gambling hall with slot machines, movie theaters, and a bowling alley. There were fights—'occasionally bodies were found in garbage cans the next morning', wrote the physicist John Marshall—suicides, and prostitution.[40]

Du Pont was responsible for design and construction at Hanford; the Manhattan Project thus involved not only Big Science but Big Business. Some scientists were as suspicious of the men in suits as they were of those in khaki uniforms. Groves's position, shared by Bush, Compton, and Lawrence, was that no one but a large firm could do a job on this scale. Needed at Hanford were three reactors, exalted versions of Fermi's pile, and four plants at which plutonium would be chemically separated from slugs of uranium that had undergone a chain reaction within the piles. Eugene Wigner designed the reactors: enormous cylinders of pure graphite shot throughout with aluminum tubes, into which went 200 tons of uranium metal slugs, themselves 'canned' in aluminum. Water from the Columbia River coursed through the tubes and around the cans, cooling the uranium as it reacted. Cooked in the reactor for at least 100 days, the canned slugs were pushed out of the back of the pile into pools to contain their radioactivity, and months later—two months were the minimum necessary for safety, with four more desirable—they were taken off to the separation plants to have their bits of plutonium teased out. From the start there was a serious glitch. The Hanford B reactor, run at full power as no test reactor had been previously, produced quantities of the element xenon, which absorbed neutrons and 'poisoned' the chain reaction. The engineers and scientists determined to overmatch the poisoning by stuffing more uranium slugs into extra tubes Du Pont had drilled into the graphite. The B reactor was restarted.[41]

In the summer of 1944 Oppenheimer recommended to Groves the pre-enrichment, by thermal (hot to cold plate) diffusion, of feed uranium for the Oak Ridge Calutrons. That made production of U-235 creep toward the level needed for a bomb—64 kilograms in the event. At Hanford, progress was steady once the xenon poisoning problem was solved, but still too slow for Groves's taste. He ordered Du Pont officials to move things along: he needed roughly 6 kilograms for a test shot and another 6 for the first plutonium bomb. Du Pont obliged, with Groves's permission, by taking shortcuts, among them reducing the amount of time workers left the radioactive slugs in their post-reactor baths. That greatly increased the danger to those who then transported the slugs to the separation plants, and especially to those who then removed the slugs from the aluminum cans, which meant dissolving the aluminum in acid. Groves decided he could live with the risk, and that his workers could too, especially if they were not informed of its possible magnitude. Los Alamos got its first delivery of Hanford plutonium in February 1945. Taken by convoy, escorted by men wielding shotguns and submachine guns, the stuff came in stainless steel flasks, each holding, writes Robert Norris, 'eighty grams of the bluish green slurry'.[42]

9. Life and work on 'The Hill'

The uranium and plutonium came into the eager hands of the men who were to build the bombs on the New Mexico mesa. 'Oppenheimer's Army', they were called. Oppenheimer recruited his people in late 1942 and early 1943, and by spring they had started to turn up in Santa Fe. Lansing Lamont describes the arrival:

> They filtered in by twos and threes: bewildered, sleepless, irritated men who had sold their homes, deceived their friends and families, and deserted laboratories and students to sally forth to an unmentionable spot that might as well have been in the land of the yeti. They arrived in the old Spanish capital after hours and days of fighting crowded trains, missed planes and flat tires.

They were instructed to go to 109 East Palace, an old Spanish house fronted by a courtyard. In a small room at the back of the yard they would be greeted by Dorothy McKibben, who would try to calm the physicists and answer their questions and place them at a local home until the next bus could take them to 'Site Y' or 'The Hill' as it came to be known, 35 miles to the northwest. Their address was now simply PO Box 1663, and they were never to address each other in town as 'Doctor' or 'Professor'; the most famous of them were given pseudonyms. The bus ride up to the mesa, at 7,200 feet, was a sobering exercise in withdrawal from anything familiar, anything seemingly civilized. They entered the site through a security checkpoint at the eastern gate, which pierced the barbed-wire fence enclosing the newly sprung town.[43]

Oppenheimer proved an effective recruiter. He signed up Hans Bethe and Edward Teller. Fermi promised to come when he could get away from his work at the Met Lab, and soon he and his wife, Laura, had moved to Los Alamos for the duration, taking over nondescript Apartment D in building T-186, rather than accepting a fancier cottage offered them: the Fermis wanted to avoid distancing themselves from junior scientists and their families. Princeton's Robert R. Wilson was seduced by Oppenheimer's vision of life on a starkly beautiful New Mexico mountain, where brilliant and dedicated scientists would work on a top-secret project that would win the war. Wilson's wife asked about the salary; Oppie assured her they would be rich. Wilson, who had grown up riding horses in Wyoming and had recently finished reading Thomas Mann's *Magic Mountain*, was sold. Stanislaw and Françoise Ulam came, as did George Kistiakowsky, Emilio Segré, Oppenheimer's former students Robert Serber and Seth Neddermeyer, the witty Richard Feynman, and the navy captain and ordnance specialist William 'Deke' Parsons. John von Neumann was a visitor and consultant. As they arrived they were greeted by Oppenheimer, wearing a pork pie hat, chewing on his pipe, as relaxed and happy as his colleagues had ever seen him. On 7 December 1944 Kitty Oppenheimer (who was far less happy) gave birth to a daughter, Katherine.[44]

Throughout these developments, the Americans had played an uneasy game with their British scientific allies. Originally having been jolted out of their lethargy by British scientists, the Americans were at first eager to learn as much and as quickly as possible from the British. Having served as executor of the jolt in the summer of 1941, the British had then been standoffish toward the Americans. On 11 October 1941, two days after his pivotal meeting with Bush and Henry Wallace, Roosevelt had written to Winston Churchill: 'It appears desirable that we should soon correspond or converse concerning the subject which is under study by your MAUD Committee, and by Dr Bush's organization in this country, in order that any extended efforts may be coordinated or even jointly conducted.' At this point, the British were ahead of the Americans in imagining and building a bomb, and possibly for that reason Churchill delayed replying to Roosevelt for two months; when Churchill did respond, he did so vaguely. Having thus delayed their pursuit of a joint effort, the British found that, by the time they decided to undertake it in mid-1942, the Americans had raced ahead and lost much of their enthusiasm for collaboration. Meeting Churchill at Hyde Park in June 1942, Roosevelt did agree that the nations should continue 'fully sharing the results' of their nuclear work 'as equal partners'. As American behavior thereafter suggested that perhaps not everyone involved with the Manhattan Project had got the message, Churchill met FDR again, this time at Quebec in August 1943. The leaders there signed the Quebec Agreement, which acknowledged that the development of an atomic weapon 'may be more speedily achieved if all available British and American brains and resources are pooled', and looked ahead to the time postwar, when US primacy in 'industrial and commercial aspects' of nuclear power would be manifest. Since Groves was responsible for carrying out the terms of the agreement, and since Groves was suspicious of attempts by outsiders to breach the walls of his allegedly compartmentalized operation, the general tried to give the British only a limited view of the project in its totality.[45]

A British team nevertheless came to Los Alamos by invitation in late 1943 and early 1944. Nineteen British scientists observed and assisted with the work there. (James Chadwick and Bohr, who had escaped Copenhagen for Sweden, then Britain, in the fall of 1943, served as 'consultants' to the team.) On the team were Otto Frisch, just weeks earlier made a British citizen, Rudolf Peierls, William Penney (a specialist in blast effects), and Penny-in-the-Slot Klaus Fuchs. The British scientists and their families blended smoothly into the current of life and work on the mesa. One afternoon, Genia Peierls organized a picnic in Frijoles Canyon, nearly 20 rough miles from the town. Laura Fermi agreed to come but was afraid to drive her car, so an 'attractive young man ... with a small, round face and dark hair with a quiet look' took the wheel He seemed nice but said little during the drive. Fermi later learned it was Fuchs. The British team contributed wholeheartedly to the bomb effort; even the grudging Groves admitted as much. (Several would remain at Los Alamos after the war, and Penney would coordinate the American test blasts at Bikini Island in 1946.) Margaret Gowing concludes that the British had 'given everything they could to the project and to Anglo-American collaboration. In narrow terms, however, they undoubtedly received far more than they gave.' And, of course, as Groves pointed out, if the British had not come to Los Alamos, Klaus Fuchs would have done a good deal less damage to the American pursuit of atomic bomb secrecy after the war.[46]

The men and women of Los Alamos were trying to build a bomb of unprecedented power, using materials never used before as an explosive. They knew that U-235 or Pu-239 would make for a devastating weapon, but beyond that were puzzles. By calculating and experimenting, they gradually determined how much fissionable material to place at the bombs' core. They concluded that using a tamper, an envelope of graphite or some other substance, would allow them to reduce the size of the bomb's critical mass and would keep the bomb from exploding prematurely: as the official report on the development of the bomb put it dourly, 'the bomb tends to fly to bits as the [chain] reaction proceeds and this tends to stop the reaction'. Detonation of the bomb required the perfectly timed coming-together of two pieces of subcritical material. The best way to bring together the uranium, the experts decided (and Frisch and Peierls had already determined), was to fire one piece, like a bullet, into a target sphere of the other piece. This would mean placing a gun assembly inside the bomb to shoot the bullet. In 1944 and 1945 ordnance specialists on the Hill fired projectiles into a large sandbox, hoping to learn how big a gun was needed, how fast the uranium bullet would be, and what shape both uranium forms should take in the guts of the bomb. Concluding that the gun assembly would not work with plutonium, the Los Alamos scientists pioneered the touchy physics of implosion, whereby the fissionable spherical core would be encompassed by a jacket of explosive that would squeeze inward with equal, simultaneous pressure. A theoretically more efficient means of starting a chain reaction, and one therefore requiring less precious Pu-239 than had been feared, implosion proved in practice very difficult to perfect. Eventually, with the application of remarkable ingenuity by American, British, and Hungarian scientists, it was made to work. The different triggering mechanisms gave their bombs different shapes: the slimmer, uranium gun-assembly bomb was christened 'Thin Man', then 'Little Boy'; the bulky implosion 'gadget' was 'Fat Man'. They were, some claimed, named for Franklin Roosevelt and Winston Churchill respectively—though Robert Serber imagined them as movie stars William Powell (*The Thin Man*) and Sidney Greenstreet.[47]

As work proceeded on the mesa, rumors abounded as to what was going on up there. It was, some said, a mysterious New Deal project, or a site for building a new kind of submarine, never mind the distance from the ocean, or a shelter for pregnant servicewomen. The military commander at Los Alamos, Colonel Gerald Tyler, was the audience for a man on a train who assured him that the compound was guarded by wild African dogs, who had already torn to shreds a number of foolish trespassers. Neither Groves nor Oppenheimer minded the stories, as the reality was often stranger. The isolation and unfamiliarity of the setting, combined with the intensity of the work and the idiosyncracies of many of the scientists, bred behavior that ranged from eccentric to twisted. Edward Teller banged away on his piano in the middle of the night—it helped him think, but drove the neighbors in his apartment block mad. George Kistiakowsky won a good deal of money teaching the Hungarians how to play poker, though by the summer of 1945 they had learned the game and proved a match for him. Others played baseball, skied (Kisty made a slope by removing trees with explosive charges), hiked, and fished. Richard Feynman deduced the combinations of high-security safes, opened them, and left notes that read, 'Guess Who?' The lower-status non-scientists found what leisure they could. The food was abundant, including steak most days, and the construction workers, machinists, and enlisted men and women had plenty of beer. There were antelope hunting, tarantula and rattlesnake eradication, square dances, and poker, for lesser stakes than the scientists played for. An army private from New York City reminded himself of home by suspending a bagel from his ceiling.[48]

10. A different sort of weapon

Hard work as it was, it was also thrilling. To be among the greatest floating seminar of physicists ever assembled, confronting some of the most fundamental problems of the universe and wedding the solutions to these problems to a device that might end the war, created a magisterial, almost holy feeling. 'It was the most exciting part of my career,' recalled Hans Bethe some years later. 'It was our whole life to make this test work.' The scientists imagined themselves as Prometheus, stealing fire, or the openers of Pandora's box, or, in Oppenheimer's case, the Hindu god Brahma in the epic *Mahabharata*: 'I am become Death | The shatterer of worlds.' They worked, wrote Robert Wilson, with 'missionary zeal'. As they raced to build a weapon that would bring victory over Fascism, their language reflected their feelings of rectitude about the enterprise and their role in it: they were serving freedom by unlocking the atom's secrets, 'liberating' the energy of the nucleus, or 'releasing the forces of nature'—there could hardly be anything more natural or noble than that. And it was, after all, 'superb physics', as Enrico Fermi liked to say to silence doubters, with an aesthetic beauty, or a 'technical sweetness', in Oppie's phrase. The enchantment with science and technique may also have allowed the physicists to distance themselves from the obvious implications of their work. 'I don't believe', wrote the perceptive Laura Fermi, 'they had visualized a destruction whose equivalent in tons of TNT they had calculated with utmost accuracy.'[49]

In fact, before they tested the bomb, the men who built it were not entirely sure how powerful it would be. At one point during the summer of 1942 Edward Teller estimated that a bomb might ignite the atmosphere's nitrogen and thus destroy the world. Oppenheimer, briefly rattled, had rushed off to consult Compton, and the men agreed that, if Teller's calculus held, the project must end. Hans Bethe ran the numbers again and found the chances of apocalypse to be a mere three in a million. The experiments had resumed. Prior to the test explosion at Alamogordo on 16 July 1945, the scientists famously organized a betting pool, in which each participant was to guess how much blast the shot would generate. The most powerful high-explosive bomb then in use was the British 'Blockbuster', which packed the equivalent of 4.6 metric tons of TNT, with a metric ton being about 10 percent heavier than a conventional ton. The pessimist in the pool was Oppenheimer, who guessed 300 tons, while Teller, who had earlier predicted the destruction of the atmosphere, picked highest at 45,000. I. I. Rabi entered the game late, and with few options left took 18,000. Rabi won the pool bet when the Trinity test gadget produced 18.6 kilotons of blast.[50]

The test atomic bomb would thus deliver an explosion orders of magnitude larger than any weapon previously used. Still, the blast effect of the bomb was measurable on the same scale that was used for what would soon be called, misleadingly, conventional (that is, non-nuclear) weapons. Those who dropped the first two atomic bombs anticipated that the bombs' explosive effects would be profound yet recognizable. Those whose cities were struck by the bombs, to some extent anyway, would also recognize the explosive effects of the bomb blasts and the fires that followed them: while Hiroshima and Nagasaki were largely undamaged by bombs before August 1945, they were not entirely so, and information about other bombed Japanese cities was sufficient to bring the residents of the two fated places to a fearful understanding of what might be coming. There is no suggestion here that humans can prepare themselves psychologically for the shock of being bombed. There is also no comfort to be sought in the vague familiarity that one has with bombing on a second or subsequent— or second-hand—encounter with it. But there was, in Japan in 1945, a vague familiarity with bombing: we, or someone like ourselves, have been through this before. Indeed, millions had suffered blast and fire from bombing raids across the globe—in Shanghai and Pearl Harbor, in Warsaw and Rotterdam, London and Coventry, Hamburg and Dresden, and in Tokyo in March 1945, when in one night American bombs took some 90,000 lives. But no one had been through an atomic bombing before Hiroshima in August. No one had suffered such an intense blast and searing fire resulting from a single bomb. And, above all, no one had experienced the effects of indiscriminate radioactivity, which spewed from the core of the Little Boy uranium bomb and fell to earth that day. Hiroshimans would call the hidden killer 'poison', and the word was appropriate, given how excess radiation acted upon the human body. Radioactivity was insidious in the way that gas had been during the First World War. It was mute and invisible. It seemed even less discriminate than fire. It killed from the inside out, violating the body more outrageously than any other hideous result of bombing.

To what extent did the scientists who conceived and built the bomb and the civilian and military officials who authorized its use know that radiation from the weapon would kill human beings? They knew some things. The Frisch–Peierls Memorandum of 1940 had warned that a significant portion of 'the energy liberated in the explosion' would be in radioactive form, and that radiation might cling to the debris created by the blast and thus 'be fatal to living beings even a long time after the explosion'. The MAUD Committee thereafter discussed radioactivity in some detail. Anyone exposed directly to the bomb's fissions would die of blood damage. 'The effects of radioactive products would be considerable,' Margaret Gowing summarizes the Committee's finding, and 'they might or might not be of secondary importance'. The committee urged that the possible impact of the bomb's radioactivity be thoroughly studied before the weapon was used. The committee's interest seems to have been technical, not moral. And the MAUD report itself, which would transform the American weapon project, made scarce mention of the radioactivity issue. 'Perhaps... we should have considered whether radioactivity was a poison outlawed in spirit by the Geneva Convention,' one of the MAUD scientists later reflected. 'But we didn't.' Neither did the Americans, at least to any great extent. Compton was concerned enough to implement safety measures at the Met Lab by the middle of 1942, calling in medical experts to check employees' levels of radiation exposure and issuing radiation-sensitive badges to those who worked in the most vulnerable areas. One of Groves's nightmares was runaway radioactivity after the Trinity test in July 1945; he prepared evacuation plans for the surrounding ranches and communities just in case.[51]

But, like the MAUD Committee members, scientists working on the Manhattan Project never dwelled on the bomb's radioactivity, and tended to avoid conjecture that they were producing a dirty weapon. This was partly because they did not believe, or would not let themselves believe, that radioactivity would cause damage beyond the enormous blast area of the bomb. Briefing the Los Alamos scientists, Robert Serber estimated that radiation would kill everyone within 1,000 yards of the blast center—but that it wouldn't matter because the blast itself would kill everyone within 2,000 yards. Norman Ramsey, the Columbia physicist who served as science adviser to the Air Force on Tinian Island, whence the atomic bombers took off for both their missions, affirmed that 'the people who made the decision to drop the bomb made it on the assumption that all casualties would be standard explosions casualties... Any person with radiation damage would have been killed with a brick first.' Oppenheimer himself told the membership of the Interim Committee, formed to advise President Truman on how (not whether) to use the atomic bomb, that the 'neutron effect of the explosion would be dangerous to life for a radius of at least two-thirds of a mile'—an assertion more open-ended than those made earlier by Serber and later by Ramsey, but one that nevertheless implied that radiation damage would be circumscribed by the scope of the blast. Groves claimed, in his postwar memoir, that he 'had always insisted that casualties resulting from direct radiation and fallout be held to a minimum', and that he had decided on an airburst, above the target cities, for that reason; the radioactivity from the bomb would disperse in the air, rather than spreading over the ground or pushing into the earth, like H. G. Wells's Carolinum, and thus contaminating much of the surrounding area.[52]

Groves, then, was well aware of the potential impact of radioactivity, and the Interim Committee, whose members included not only Secretary of War Stimson but Bush, Conant, near-future Secretary of State James F. Byrnes, and Army Chief of Staff George C. Marshall, heard

Oppenheimer's judgment about the 'neutron effect'. Stimson briefed
Truman on committee deliberations. But it is not clear how much Truman,
or for that matter his predecessor, knew about the potential for human
damage by radioactivity from the bomb. In his 1961 memoir, Clement
Attlee, who became British Prime Minister in late July 1945, claimed that
neither he nor Churchill nor Truman knew anything about 'the genetic
effects of an atomic explosion' or about 'fall-out and the rest of what
emerged after Hiroshima'. Attlee's view is not authoritative, since he hardly
knew about the bomb until he became Prime Minister, and it is telling
that he conflates radioactivity's 'genetic effects' with 'fall-out and the rest'.
These are not the same thing. There were, in fact, several ways in which
bomb-borne radioactivity could injure or kill human beings. First, radiation
could affect those who were not killed by blast or fire; Serber and the
others were wrong to think that the blast would cover more ground than
the radioactivity. This was 'direct radiation'. It was possible, second, that
radioactivity could remain in the bombed area, potent enough to sicken
those who came into it hoping to help or in search of loved ones in the
days after the bomb had been dropped; this was 'indirect radiation'. Finally,
either those immediately exposed or those affected later might, while
remaining alive, carry cellular radiation damage to children as yet unborn or
conceived.

Gowing finds little evidence that scientists anticipated the genetic effects
of radiation on a bombed population. She notes that experiments had
shown, in 1928, that radiation distorted the genes of plants and insects,
but the studies apparently stopped there. With one exception: during
the war a British doctor raised the possibility that human mutations
would occur should the Germans attack Britain with 'radioactive fission
products' in some form. It would not have been a great intellectual
leap to the conclusion that an atomic bomb might produce the same
effects. Evidently, no one made the leap. The first volume of the official account of the atomic bomb, written on behalf of the US Atomic
Energy Commission and 655 pages long, contains but a single paragraph on
radioactivity, and it concerns Compton's worries about exposing Met Lab
workers.[53]

Were the scientists and statesmen ignorant about radioactivity? Probably
so. To what extent was their ignorance willful, predicated, that is, on a
desire not to know about the harm that radioactivity could do? That is a
harder question to answer. To read about the men who built the bomb

is to feel some sympathy for them. They thought carefully about their place in the world and were not slaves to an arbitrary authority. They read the Bible (Compton), Shakespeare (Edward Condon), and the Bhagavad Gita (Oppenheimer, in Sanskrit). They hiked, fished, played music, drank, punned, and played jokes on each other. They loved their wives and children.

They were enraptured by their technically sweet and Promethean mission to build the bomb. And they hated Nazi Germany. The moral implications of what they were doing, especially with regard to the insidious killing power of radioactivity, paled unto disappearance when they contemplated the evil of Naziism. (Japan, as we will see, was for some of them another story.) They willed away their scruples because they came to believe that anything that would destroy Hitler's Germany was morally admissible. The world had rushed to condemn the use of poison gas after the First World War, and in the early 1940s most continued to regard it as abhorrent, a touchstone of the inconceivable even in a world gone mad with otherwise-total war. In December 1941, just as the United States entered the war, the Princeton physicists Henry DeWolf Smyth and Eugene Wigner issued a report in which they compared radiation to 'a particularly vicious form of poison gas'. The comparison proved an inspiration to Edward Teller, who, in the spring of 1943, contemplating the worrisome prospect that an atomic bomb might not be possible, suggested instead spraying fission products from Hanford over 100 square miles of German territory, killing its inhabitants and leaving the area a no man's land. Enrico Fermi also raised with Oppenheimer the possibility of using radioactivity as a weapon against Germany; Oppie replied, casually, that plans existed to poison 'food sufficient to kill a half million men', though how he planned to prevent women and children from dying instead he did not say. Ernest Lawrence embraced radiological warfare after 1945 as a way to make war more humane. Bands of radioactivity, he declared, would create a 'cordon insanitaire' around the people and territory one wished to protect.[54]

Convinced of their rectitude, absorbed by the project and hope of saving lives by quickly ending the war, willing to work on behalf of the US military and the government if not always on the military's terms, their minds at least temporarily closed against moral doubt, the scientists and engineers at Los Alamos, supported by thousands of men and women in Chicago, Berkeley, Oak Ridge, and Hanford, built the bomb between 1943 and 1945. It was America's bomb, of course, authorized by the President and paid for, albeit unwittingly, by American citizens. It was also the world's bomb. Its fabricators and components, the ideas that enabled it, came from everywhere. Its victims would be mainly Japanese, but also Koreans, Chinese, and even some Americans, luckless enough to be caught in Hiroshima in early August 1945. Like the republic of science that produced it, and like the radiation that issued from it, the bomb's impact would respect no boundaries.

FIVE

The United States II: Using the Bomb

In the months and years after the atomic bombs were dropped on Japan in August 1945, those in some way involved in the decision offered a variety of reasons for their actions. Let us begin this pivotal chapter with statements from four such people. We can start with Robert R. Wilson, the young Princeton physicist who came to Los Alamos in 1943 imagining himself as Hans Castorp arriving at Thomas Mann's Magic Mountain. Why test, then drop the bomb? Wilson's reminiscence here came nearly a quarter century after the Pacific War had ended:

> Perhaps events were moving just too incredibly fast. We were all at the climax of the project—just on the verge of exploding the test bomb in the desert. Every faculty, every thought, every effort was directed toward making that a success. I think that to have asked us to pull back at that moment would have been as unrealistic and unfair as it would be to ask a pugilist to sense intellectually the exact moment his opponent has weakened to the point where eventually he will lose, and then to have the responsibility of stopping the fight just at that point.

There was momentum behind the scientists' decision to build the bomb. The momentum carried through construction of the test gadget, the test itself, *and* the decision to use the bomb against an opponent—or such is the implication of Wilson's analogy. Once under way, the Manhattan Project became a means that required an end, a force of logic that could be satisfied only by resolution in the cause of battle—that is, against people.[1]

The second statement comes from a more familiar source: Harry S. Truman, who became President of the United States following Franklin Roosevelt's death on 12 April 1945 and was in office when the bombs were dropped and the war against Japan ended. More than anyone, Truman made the decision to use atomic bombs, though a search for a particular document or statement by Truman actually authorizing the bombings is curiously unfulfilling. In any case, it was to his president that Samuel McCrea Cavert, the general secretary of the Federal Council of Churches of Christ in America, wrote on 9 August, just after the second atomic bomb had been dropped on Nagasaki. Many Christians, Cavert wrote, were 'deeply disturbed over [the] use of atomic bombs against Japanese cities'; the weapons were 'indiscriminate' and set an 'extremely dangerous precedent'. Truman replied tersely on the 11th. 'My dear Mr Cavert,' he began:

> Nobody is more disturbed over the use of Atomic bombs than I am but I was frankly disturbed over the unwarranted attack by the Japanese on Pearl Harbor and their murder of our prisoners of war. The only language they seem to understand is the one we have been using to bombard them.
> When you have to deal with a beast you have to treat him as a beast. It is most regrettable but nevertheless true.

Vengeance, then, was part of Truman's motive: the Japanese had attacked first, and treacherously, and had mistreated American prisoners. Evidently, too, the Japanese were impervious to reason, understanding only force, war's lingua franca. And, most memorably, there is Truman's description of the Japanese as 'a beast', vicious, violent, less than human. Atomic bombs were necessary, according to this logic, and they were legitimate, because no one cared that or how a beast was exterminated, least of all the beast.[2]

Statement three comes from Truman's successor as President, Dwight D. Eisenhower. It is actually two comments, combined as many other historians have combined them, but in fact recorded in two different places. In 1945 Eisenhower was commander of Allied Forces in Europe, and in this role he attended the conference at Potsdam, where the Big Three—Truman, Joseph Stalin, and (temporarily, as it turned out) Winston Churchill—discussed the fate of Central and Eastern Europe and the endgame of the war against Japan. In the first volume of his memoirs, published eighteen years later—that is, after his presidency—Eisenhower recounted that Secretary of War Henry Stimson had told him at Potsdam that the atomic bomb would be dropped on Japan. The general recalled his reaction:

> I voiced to him my grave misgivings, first on the basis of my belief that Japan was already defeated and that dropping the bomb was completely unnecessary,

and secondly because I thought that our country should avoid shocking world opinion by the use of a weapon whose employment was, I thought, no longer mandatory as a measure to save American lives. It was my belief that Japan was, at that very moment, seeking some way to surrender with a minimum loss of 'face'.

Then, the quotable coda, which appeared not in the memoirs but in *Newsweek* in November 1963: 'It wasn't necessary to hit them with that awful thing.'[3]

The passages suggest, in the first place, the possibility that a leading American general distinguished between the use of a nuclear weapon and other forms of warfare, judging the first 'unnecessary' and 'awful', more awful at least than other weapons already being used. More significantly, it suggests that there may have been reasons other than the quest for swift and sure victory why Truman decided to use bomb(s) anyway. Surely Stimson would have taken seriously the military judgment of his general (Japan was looking to surrender); surely he would have accepted Eisenhower's logic that the atomic bomb was not necessary to win the war. That he apparently did neither of these things—that he did not refrain from recommending use of the bomb—must therefore mean that Stimson had other reasons to want his president to use it. Revisionist historians, indeed, have found in the Eisenhower quotations evidence that, for Stimson, Secretary of State James Byrnes, and Truman, the real target of the atomic bomb—Japan being, as Eisenhower said, all but defeated without it—was the Soviet Union. If atomic bombs were dropped on Japan, the war would end more quickly, depriving the Soviets of much involvement in the war's endgame and thus of a prominent place in the postwar occupation authority in Japan. And if the United States dropped atomic bombs, the Soviet leadership might be intimidated by American power and become more agreeable in negotiations on the political future of Germany and Eastern Europe, already a matter of friction between the Allies.[4]

One more statement, this from Stimson himself. Henry Stimson, who was 77 years old in 1945, was a dedicated public servant who played a critical role in the drama of the atomic bomb. It was he who told Truman, hours after Truman became President, of the existence of 'a new explosive of almost unbelievable destructive power' then under development, who chaired the secret Interim Committee that advised the President about how to use the bomb, and who removed the city of Kyoto from the bombs' target list, overriding the objections of Leslie Groves. By early 1947, as the Cold War intensified, there were rumblings in US policy circles and in the American press that the bombs had been aimed primarily at the Soviets, not the Japanese, and had thus been militarily unnecessary. Stimson responded, in the February issue of *Harper's* magazine, with 'The Decision to Use the Atomic Weapon', a piece meant to disarm critics by revealing the inside version of official deliberation in the months leading up to the bombing of Hiroshima. Why, then, did the United States drop the bomb?

> My chief purpose [Stimson wrote] was to end the war in victory with the least cost in the lives of the men in the armies which I had helped to raise. In the light of the alternatives which, on a fair estimate, were open to us I believe that no man, in our position and subject to our responsibilities, holding in his hands a weapon of such possibilities for accomplishing this purpose and saving those lives, could have failed to use it and afterwards looked his countrymen in the face.

The bomb, according to Stimson, was not used for some nefarious or secret reason, but because it promised to end the war sooner and thus save lives. It was American lives that Stimson cherished and mentioned in the passage, but in his following paragraph he noted that, by ending the war, the atomic bombs ended the firebombing of Japanese cities and the blockade of Japan by US ships and thus saved Japanese lives too. The atomic bomb was justified as the most humane way to prosecute, then terminate, the atrocious war.[5]

It will be noted that all four of these statements were made after the bombs had been dropped: Truman's within a couple of days, Stimson's over a year later, Eisenhower's nearly two decades and Wilson's a quarter of a century afterwards. Perhaps Truman had not had much time to think before sending a response to Samuel Cavert, but the others had had plenty of time, and were surely conscious that they were setting down their positions for posterity on a subject fraught with controversy. During the war itself, in the heat of battle, most scientists, generals, and statesmen had neither the time nor the inclination to ask themselves whether the atomic bombs should be used. The modifier 'most' is essential here, since, as we will see, there were those (not Eisenhower) who urged at the time that the bombs not be dropped, that an alternative be found to end the war that did not involve using nuclear weapons against undefended cities. These arguments were either ignored or considered and rejected. The context in which they were made was that of total war against an enemy widely regarded as ruthless and disinclined to surrender unless utterly defeated. Franklin Roosevelt had insisted early in 1943 that Germany, Italy, and Japan surrender without condition; not only the capacity of the Axis nations to make war but their ideological tendency to do so must be expunged. Harry Truman accepted the demand for unconditional surrender as part of his predecessor's legacy. Defeat alone was insufficient; the enemy must be destroyed. Atomic bombs would facilitate his destruction.

1. The progress of the war against Germany

The Manhattan Project began because of fears that Nazi Germany would move rapidly to build an atomic bomb, and that a bomb in Nazi keeping would mean catastrophe for the civilized world. When President Roosevelt had agreed, on 9 October 1941, to move ahead with developing an atomic bomb, Germany and its allies had established control over much of Europe, had substantial forces in North Africa that appeared to threaten also the Middle East, had waged war from the air against Great Britain (with serious psychological though without decisive strategic results), and, the preceding June, had broken the Molotov–Ribbentrop Pact of 1939 and invaded the Soviet Union, with frightening success to that point. The United States and Germany were not yet at war, but their relations were icy and their ships were firing at each other in the North Atlantic, as American vessels carried supplies and munitions to Britain and the Soviet Union and provided cover against German submarines for their own ships and others. War came, by German declaration, two months later. Through 1942, as the Americans improved the coordination and tightened the secrecy of their bomb effort, as Ernest Lawrence began producing minute amounts of uranium 235 in his Berkeley Calutrons and Enrico Fermi built his atomic pile in a University of Chicago squash court under the aegis of Arthur Compton's energized Met Lab, and as Leslie Groves went from colonel to general as he took vociferous command of what was now the Manhattan Project, the German grip on power started gradually to loosen. The Battle of Britain went the way of the Royal Air Force; the invasion of the Soviet Union sputtered, then stalled. The German atomic bomb project was frustrated by decentralization, scientific missteps, and lack of sympathy at the political top, though the Allies did not know this. In the summer of

1942 the first American bombs struck targets in occupied Europe. The
Battle of the Atlantic turned in the Allies' favor. In November, while
workers in Chicago skidded on residue from Fermi's graphite and Groves
and Robert Oppenheimer sealed their functional courtship by agreeing to
build the bomb at Los Alamos, American and British troops were landing
in North Africa (Operation Torch) to begin the destruction of the Nazi
empire from the outside in. Winston Churchill called the strategy 'closing
the ring'.

As the scientists moved to Los Alamos in the spring of 1943 and
construction progressed at the massive plants at Oak Ridge and Hanford,
German military reverses multiplied. The invasion of North Africa bore
fruit that May, when Allied forces defeated the German Afrika Corps and
took a quarter of a million prisoners. The tide turned in the Atlantic
that spring too, as the Americans and Canadians built supply ships more
quickly than German U-boats could sink them and improvements in
Allied sub detection and defense took hold. In April the Germans lost
fifteen subs to Allied attack; in May the figure was forty, and their commander, Karl Dönitz, was forced to pull them back. The Allies, who
had lost over 1,800 ships to the Germans in 1942, would sacrifice barely
800 in 1943. The Germans surrendered at Stalingrad on 2 February,
prompting propaganda minister Joseph Goebbels to admit publicly the
growing seriousness of the German military position and to exhort his
audience to greater efforts. The Soviets marshaled a counteroffensive. That
summer the British and the Americans attacked Sicily, and Allied troops
set foot in Italy in early September, prompting a near-immediate Italian
surrender.

The Germans fought on, in Italy and Eastern and Western Europe.
As the Manhattan Project scientists, along with Groves, confronted
problems—not enough atomic fuel, puzzles concerning bomb size and
implosion and how best to trigger the weapon—Allied troops continued
to tighten the circle. Rome was finally captured on 5 June 1944. The
Russians liberated Romania, Bulgaria, Yugoslavia, Poland, and Hungary
through the year and into 1945. Stalin had chafed while awaiting a British–
American assault across the English Channel; D-Day came finally on 6
June, and France was restored in August. Everywhere, German armies were
falling back and ordinary Germans were dying. And yet there might still be
surprises, as in the German counterattack at the Battle of the Bulge in
December 1944. That the Germans were not close to having an atomic

bomb was established with certainty by Alsos only in the spring of 1945—
indeed, the Germans had started building a new atomic pile in Haigerloch
that February. Until they were sure that Hitler was dead and Germany
defeated, those working on the American bomb felt they could not afford
to let up, and they did not.

2. The allies and the strategic bombing of Germany

There was one important facet of the European war of particular interest
to those at the highest level of the Manhattan Project, and that was the
strategic bombing campaign against Germany. Chickens hatched during
the First World War, then coaxed to maturity by bombing theorists such
as Hugh Trenchard, Arthur Harris, Giulio Douhet, and Billy Mitchell,
were roosting thickly by the 1930s. Far from being represented as mass
murderers, warplane pilots were portrayed as gallant individualists, knights
of the air whose noble mission was to end wars quickly. As British Prime
Mnister Stanley Baldwin had put it in 1932, 'the bomber will always get
through', holding civilians hostage and therefore requiring their governments to sue for an early peace. Thus, presumably in the name of reducing
casualties overall, Italian planes bombed and strafed Ethiopian villages (and
hospitals) in 1935. Thus the Japanese bombed Chinese cities in 1937 and
after without regard for civilian casualties. The Germans, after practicing
bombing technique at Guernica in 1937, attacked Warsaw, Rotterdam,
London, and other cities, aiming ostensibly at military or industrial targets but in reality exercising little care over where the bombs dropped.
Attacks on Britain alone had killed 40,000 by May 1941. In the early
fall of 1940 the British began the 'area bombing' of German cities by
night; with Prime Minister Churchill's permission, air crews made only
perfunctory efforts to drop their bombs on factories, and then only on
fully moonlit nights. Their true target was the morale of the German
populace.[6]

The American position on bombing was at that point unsettled. Air doctrine, established by the American Air Corps during the 1920s, endorsed
bombing 'attacks to intimidate civil populations', without saying precisely
that such populations would themselves be bombed. When other nations

had targeted civilians, however, the US government had condemned the practice. Roosevelt's secretary of state, Cordell Hull, called the Japanese air attacks in China 'barbarous', and his decision to embargo the sale of airplane parts to the Japanese was pointedly linked to this bombing. The military commentator Fielding Eliot foresaw in 1938 the need for US air attacks against Japanese cities should it come to war, but suspected that the American public would reject such a course, and that American fliers would also resist targeting civilians 'unless driven to do so as a measure of reprisal for like enemy conduct'. As war threatened in Europe in 1939, Roosevelt declared his government and people opposed to 'the unprovoked bombing and machine-gunning of civilian populations from the air'. When elements of the US Army Air Forces (AAF) first came to England in the spring of 1942, their commanders refused to join the RAF in its newfound commitment, under Butch Harris, to 'de-house' German workers. Instead, the AAF would rely on precision, daylight bombing of German military and industrial targets, in this way destroying Germany's warmaking capacity without, the commanders told themselves, slaughtering civilians like the profligate and debased Europeans. Besides, the AAF thought that attacks on civilians might increase their will to resist.[7]

Notice, however, the qualifications in these statements: the American people would forbear from air attacks, wrote Eliot, 'unless driven...as a measure of reprisal for like enemy conduct'; the United States would refrain from 'unprovoked' attacks on civilians, Roosevelt declared; the AAF at first shunned British air doctrine in good part because of doubts concerning not its morality but its effectiveness. The American knights of the air who flew daylight missions against German targets, mainly in the Low Countries and France, beginning in 1943, could believe, if they wished, that they were fighting more ethically than their British counterparts, bombing, as Air Force General Henry Arnold put it, 'in accordance with American principles using methods for which our planes were designed'. What they were doing in fact was subjecting the enemy to constant bombing—the Americans by day, the British by night—and to the bombing of targets of every description. Arnold and others also believed that the Americans were better suited than the British, by training and equipment ('methods for which our planes were designed'), to launch precision raids by day. While they did, according to Ronald Schaffer, keep an eye on American public opinion, the air generals nevertheless acted largely out of utilitarian conviction rather than an abiding sense of moral scruple. General Carl (Tooey) Spaatz, the first commander of the Eighth Air Force, said after the war that 'it wasn't for religious or moral reasons that I didn't go along with urban area bombing', but rather because of his belief that going after 'strategic targets' was more likely to end the war sooner. Ira Eaker, who succeeded Spaatz, 'never felt there was any moral sentiment among leaders of the AAF'. The Americans also scoffed at British warnings about the dangers and ineffectiveness of daylight precision bombing. What the RAF had failed to do, the Americans would manage, without killing Dutch civilians or angering German civilians and thus increasing the latter's resolve to fight on.[8]

The Americans' plans failed to work. Their navigation was imperfect, the daylight bombing allowed the Germans to mount successful counter-measures using interceptor planes and anti-aircraft fire, and the weather over northern Europe provided a challenge the Americans were unused to. Panicky air crews dropped their payloads prematurely ('creep-back'), not only resulting in missed targets but inadvertently killing civilians in occupied countries. Postwar estimates were that the Eighth Air Force placed only 20 percent of its bombs within 1,000 feet of its intended targets. The British, ironically, felt themselves compelled to advise Eaker that the Americans were alienating captive populations with their inaccuracy. Henry Arnold scolded his commanders, reminding them that each American pilot 'is handling a weapon which can be either the scourge or the savior of humanity, according to how well he uses it'.[9]

The problem, the pilots would have replied, was not with their determination and courage but with the AAF's strategy. The discrepancy between the AAF's results and those of the RAF were vividly pointed up in July 1943, when Harris and Eaker sent their bombers over the German port city of Hamburg. The RAF struck first, on the night of the 24–25 July. Their coordinates rigged against creep-back, and protected by a new technology known as 'Window'—aluminum shreds that, dumped from British bomb bays, distracted German radar operators—nearly 800 planes dropped high explosives and incendiaries, killing some 1,500 people, 'de-housing' thousands more, and, as intended, stretching beyond capacity Hamburg's firefighters. The result was not decisive enough for Harris, so three nights later the RAF struck again. This time, conditions were perfect; as Michael Sherry has written, 'the second Hamburg raid ignited the war's first great firestorm'. Thousands burned to death, or simply melted into lumps of flesh in the 1,400° heat. Some who tried to run were caught in the melting asphalt of the streets. Others, seeking shelter underground as those suffering attack by explosives were advised to do, were asphyxiated as the firestorm intensified and sucked the city center dry of oxygen. Firefighters who survived the onslaught were helpless; small 'children lay like fried eels on the pavement'. Perhaps 45,000 people died in Hamburg that night, mostly women, children, and old men. 'Hamburg', Jörg Friedrich has written, 'found itself in a room for three hours not where life dies—that always happens—but rather, where life is not possible, where it cannot exist.' It was a horror 'transcending all human experience and imagination'.[10]

On the mornings after the nighttime raids, the Eighth Air Force attempted to fulfill its part of the mission, which was to attack Hamburg's shipyards (including a submarine base) and an aircraft engine factory. Smoke from the preceding night's attacks on both mornings hid the Americans' targets, and the Eighth did little damage. When the results of the Hamburg attacks were assessed, the Americans began to rethink their strategy. If efficiency was the goal of bombing, and if there was no compelling moral impediment to bombing the centers of cities, Hamburg seemed to prove that the British had been right all along. Eaker's subordinate Frederick Anderson now waxed enthusiastic about the possibility of a daylight attack on Berlin, which would, if successful, have a 'terrific impact' on the German population. In October the Eighth carried out its first daytime attack, on the city of Münster. The use of Window made such raids safer for the attackers, and over time the degradation of German defenses helped too. Similar assaults were made, with satisfyingly bloody results, in Axis Bulgaria and Romania the following year. And Hamburg was instructive on another front: in its aftermath, Roosevelt called it 'an impressive demonstration' of what might be done by American bombers in Japan.[11]

The best known and most notorious of Allied bombing raids on Germany came at Dresden, the capital of Saxony and a cultural center, though not altogether devoid of military and industrial targets. It was a city of refugees, many of them running from the advancing Red Army, and in its suburbs were some 25,000 Allied prisoners of war (including the future American novelist Kurt Vonnegut Jr.). It was early 1945, and, despite the rapid crumbling of German resistance, Churchill wanted to continue bombing undefended German cities. The British struck first, on the fatally clear night of 13 February, unleashing high explosives and incendiaries. The Americans followed up the next morning, Valentine's Day and Ash Wednesday, and, as in Hamburg, unable to see much of the target for the smoke and flame left by the British the previous night, bombed the area without discrimination. Neither attack encountered much opposition; indeed, the Luftwaffe was altogether absent from the sky over Dresden. The death toll came to some 35,000. The bombing was, recalled Arthur Harris's deputy, 'one of those terrible things that sometimes happen in wartime, brought about by an unfortunate combination of circumstances'. And it was, as Frederick Taylor has written, 'a terrible illustration of what apparently civilized human beings are capable of under extreme circumstances, when all the normal brakes on human behavior have been eroded by years of total war'. Dresden would be remembered as an example of wanton destruction, and of killing, without evident military purpose, of a large number of people who wanted no part of war and had contributed nothing notable to its prosecution.[12]

3. The war in the Pacific

So would go the war with Japan. With the decision to attack Pearl Harbor, the Japanese embarked on a military campaign designed to conquer East Asia and consolidate their new empire, called the Greater East Asian Co-Prosperity Sphere, before the Americans could recover from the blow and while the Soviet Union was under siege by the Germans. (The Japanese military command was at least publicly contemptuous of the American will to fight in the wake of a serious setback.) The Japanese followed Pearl Harbor with coordinated assaults on Guam and Wake Island, attacks in Southeast Asia, including Singapore, the Dutch East Indies, and the Philippines, and continued aggression against China. Better planning and technological superiority on the sea and in the air contributed to Japan's early victories. Having underestimated the Japanese even more completely than the Japanese had underestimated them, the Americans were shocked to discover that they were outgunned. 'It was a terrific blow to us, all our pilots particularly, to find that the Japanese Zero was a better airplane than anything we had,' said a rueful US Admiral Arleigh Burke. By spring 1942 the Japanese held virtually all Southeast Asia, had taken the American surrender of the Philippines, were ensconced in South Pacific island redoubts including the Solomons, Guam, and Wake Island, and seemed to threaten British Ceylon and India, New Guinea, and even Australia and New Zealand.[13]

By mid-year, however, fortunes started to turn. American naval units managed a stalemate with the Japanese in the Coral Sea in May. The following month, the Americans defeated the Japanese fleet attempting to capture Midway Island, dispatching four Japanese aircraft carriers and a heavy cruiser and killing scores of Japan's best pilots. While not fully recognized at the time, Midway proved the turning point in the war. Thereafter the Japanese largely assumed a defensive posture, hoping to wear down the Americans in a war of attrition in the Pacific. But, as American war production increased manyfold and Soviet success at Stalingrad set the Germans on their heels, a war of attrition did not favor the Japanese. The US Army General Douglas MacArthur, despite having been forced out of the Philippines, took charge of the Southwest Pacific theater and engaged the Japanese in New Guinea. Navy Admiral Chester Nimitz, who commanded US forces elsewhere in the Pacific, opened a campaign that summer to liberate Pacific islands with an attack on Guadalcanal in the Solomon chain. The Americans seized an airfield there, survived a devastating attack on their ships in nearby Savo Bay (four sunk, three damaged), and undertook a bloody ground campaign against Japanese troops whose ranks were intermittently reinforced. The Americans and Japanese fought each other on Guadalcanal through the summer and fall, past Christmas and into the new year. 'It is almost beyond belief that we are still here, still alive, still waiting and still ready,' wrote an American correspondent. 'The worst experience I've ever been through in my life.' A Japanese NCO named Kashichi Yoshida jotted a poem of despair:

> Covered with mud from our falls
> Blood oozes from our wounds
> No cloth to bind our cuts
> Flies swarm to the scabs
> No strength to brush them away
> Fall down and cannot move
> How many times I've thought of suicide.

It ended in early February when the remaining Japanese withdrew. Thousands had died on both sides.[14]

Like their German allies, the Japanese fought on, with growing desperation as the circle closed around their home islands. In January, as the

Japanese gave up the struggle for Guadalcanal, Roosevelt at Casablanca announced Allied resolve to win 'unconditional surrender' from the Axis belligerents. The Americans, with Australians and New Zealanders, fought their way west through the Japanese-held islands: Tarawa that November, Kwajalein and Truk in early 1944, Bougainville in March, Tinian that summer. The Philippines campaign began in October, while British and Indian troops pushed the Japanese hard in Burma and reopened the Burma Road in January 1945; they would liberate Mandalay in March. US marines assaulted Iwo Jima, less than 700 miles south of Tokyo, beginning in mid-February. The Japanese, dug into caves, tunnels, and pillboxes, fought back fiercely. The Americans blasted them with grenades and artillery and burned them out using tanks equipped with flamethrowers. Iwo was declared secure on 26 March. The Japanese lost nearly 22,000 dead, virtually all the island's defenders. Iwo cost the Americans 7,000 dead and almost 20,000 wounded. 'I hope to God', groaned a wounded marine, 'that we don't have to go on anymore of those screwy islands.'[15]

Nimitz had another in mind. Okinawa was at the center of the Ryukyu chain, about midway between Taiwan and Kyushu. It was 60 miles long and between 2 and 18 miles wide, and a possible base for American ships and planes. The Okinawans had been ruled by the Japanese since 1879. The commander of the Japanese garrison on the island, General Mitsuru Ushijima, had 70,000 troops, but knew he faced an American force far larger than his (180,000), and thus decided to abandon defense of Okinawa's beaches and retreat mostly to the southern end of the island, where limestone ridges, caves, and a network of bunkers offered hope of concealment, protection, and positional advantage. When the Americans disembarked warily on 1 April, they met little resistance. For a week, as they advanced, things remained quiet. Then, on the 8th, the 24th Marine Corps ran up against the outermost picket of Ushijima's defenses, Kakazu Ridge. It was the beginning of a nightmarish period of assault, withering machine gun and artillery fire, retreat, counterattack, and—if all went well—survival to fight another day. Meanwhile, the US fleet that had delivered the troops and shelled Japanese positions came under attack from the air. On 6 April the Japanese mustered 700 planes, half of them *kamikaze* fighters on suicide missions, and struck the US vessels. 'The strain of waiting, the anticipated terror, made vivid from past experience, sent some men into hysteria, insanity, breakdown,' wrote a correspondent. The Americans lost three destroyers, a mammoth cargo carrier, and two ammunition supply ships, and ten other ships suffered damage.

American commanders elsewhere in the theater chafed at the slow progress made by the assault force. But there was precious little the marines could do. The Japanese were well armed, and they fought intelligently and remorselessly. And they were almost impregnably dug in. 'We poured a tremendous amount of metal in on those positions,' recounted a marine commander. 'Not only from artillery but from ships at sea. It seemed nothing could possibly be living in that churning mass where the shells were falling and roaring but when we next advanced, Japs would still be there, even madder than they had been before.' It took two months and three weeks to take Okinawa. Some 110,000 Japanese combatants, including pilots and sailors, were killed—almost without precedent, 7,400 surrendered—and between 45,000 and 80,000 Okinawans died, victims of the shelling, the crossfire, and by suicide, the result of their own fears, stoked by the Japanese, that the Americans had come to rape and torture them. Combined US Army, Navy, and marine deaths in the campaign came to 12,500; total US casualties approached 50,000. Three days before the end on Okinawa—that is, on 18 June—President Truman met the Joint Chiefs of Staff to discuss strategy for defeating Japan. Many at the meeting argued that the United States would have to invade Japan, beginning with the southern island of Kyushu. Truman approved an invasion plan, but added his hope that 'there was a possibility of preventing an Okinawa from one end of Japan to another'.[16]

Truman's strategists hoped so too. They knew that American ships and planes had made it nearly impossible for the Japanese to move soldiers and supplies between Japan and the Asian mainland. The seas surrounding the home islands had been seeded with mines, complicating transport between the islands and thus overtaxing the Japanese rail system, already strained by bottlenecks and maintenance problems. The American blockade could be tightened over time, starving Japan and finally bringing its surrender. Another possibility was the threat or fact of Soviet entry into the war against Japan. At the Big Three conference at Yalta, held the previous February, Stalin had agreed, after securing from Roosevelt a handful of significant territorial concessions in East Asia, that the Russians would enter the war against Japan within three months of the defeat of Germany. That meant the Soviets would move by early August. Given the pace of Soviet force build-ups in the areas just north of Manchuria, Soviet intervention was a

THE UNITED STATES II

formidable threat to the Japanese, one that, combined with the dissolution of the Pacific empire at the hands of the Americans, offered a possible endgame without the need for a US invasion.[17]

4. The bombing of Japan

There was another way to go, not in distinction but in addition to a tightened blockade and possible Soviet entry. Since early in the war—indeed, since before the United States went to war and well before the American Air Force began bombing civilians in Germany—American military planners had envisioned attacking the Japanese from the air, without discriminating between soldiers and noncombatants. In mid-November 1941 Army Chief of Staff George Marshall had proposed (secretly) to the American press that, in the event of war, American planes would 'be dispatched immediately to set the paper cities of Japan on fire ... There won't be any hesitation about bombing civilians,' Marshall asserted. 'It will be all-out.' White American racism, and the contempt it fostered for the Japanese, enabled Marshall and others to contemplate attacks on Japanese cities without reservation or fleeting second thoughts; if incinerating Germans troubled them temporarily and slightly, no similar scruples kept them from imagining Japanese cities put to the torch. 'Perhaps the best way to offset this initial defeat is to burn Tokyo and Osaka,' mused a military official two days after Pearl Harbor. At that point the United States did not have the capability of attacking Japanese cities—a one-off raid on Tokyo led by Lieutenant Colonel James Doolittle in April 1942 raised American morale but did little damage—but, as US forces pushed toward Japan in early 1945, such attacks became possible. For a time, strategists maintained that the targets of bombing, as in Germany, were military and industrial, and the persistence of this claim allowed for considerable self-delusion along the way. In fact, throughout 1943 air-force analysts built careful models of Japanese (and German) cities in the Utah desert, then experimented with various combinations of incendiaries to determine how best to burn them down. The mock Japanese houses were even stocked with tatami mats taken from Japanese–American homes in Hawaii.[18]

The attacks on Japan, aided by the availability of new B-29 Superfortress bombers for China and the Marianas, began in earnest in mid-1944, with

a raid on a Kyushu coke and steel plant. The attack failed, and heralded
a series of failures resulting from Japanese defenses, logistical problems at
Chinese airfields, bad weather, and defects in the B-29s, in ascending order
of importance. The final two problems also plagued the bomber campaign
launched from the Marianas. As American pilots had found in Germany,
it was hard to hit a single target, even one as large as a steel or munitions
plant. Recognizing this, officials in Washington raised the priority of what
they called blandly 'urban industrial areas' to second on the targets list, still
behind 'the aircraft industry' but now ahead of steel plants, oil refineries,
and everything else. When the commander of the Marianas-based XXI
Bomber Group, Haywood ('Possum') Hansell Jr., proved reluctant to implement the new policy, he was replaced in early January by General Curtis
LeMay, who had recently achieved some success against long odds with
China-based B-29s and had never exhibited compunction about unleashing
incendiaries against civilians. LeMay was a man of few words, pugnacious
looking with what seemed a perpetual glower and a cigar clamped in his
teeth. He had been impressed with the results of an 18 December raid on
the Japanese base at Hankow, China, in which his planes had dropped over
500 tons of incendiaries and burned the city lavishly. 'To worry about the
morality of what we were doing—Nuts,' declared LeMay after the war. 'A
soldier has to fight. We fought. If we accomplished the job in any given
battle, without exterminating too many of our own folks, we considered
that we'd had a pretty good day.' LeMay tried, like his predecessor, to hit
industrial targets, but the memory of Hankow burning stayed with him,
and a successful incendiary raid on Tokyo on 25 February—a pretty good
day—persuaded him to change his tactics. He would target not factories but
urban neighborhoods. He would replace many of his planes' high-explosive
payloads with incendiaries. And, given the evident weakness of Japanese
defenses, he would remove all guns and gunners from the B-29s and order
his pilots to fly at lower altitudes over their targets, thereby improving
bombing accuracy, saving fuel (and preserving weight for payloads), and
reducing the chances that his planes might be hit by enemy or fratricidal
gunfire.[19]

The target was to be Tokyo. LeMay selected as a site for the incendiaries
an area of roughly 12 square miles in eastern Tokyo encompassing the
Asakusa ward. It had a population density of 103,000 per square mile.
(Deliberately excluded from the target zone was the Imperial Palace; the
sight and smell of nearby burning would be enough to send a message to

its leading resident, the Emperor Hirohito.) On the evening of 9 March, B-29s took off from Guam, Saipan, and Tinian, rendezvoused, and headed west, 334 in all. Each bomber carried up to 6 tons of napalm, phosphorous, and oil-based incendiaries. Japanese radar detected the force and sounded an early warning at 10.30, but inaccurately reported that the attackers had headed off over the sea. The first of the incendiaries—napalm, so as to illuminate the target for the second wave of bombers—came down just after midnight, followed by M-69 magnesium cluster bombs that burst just above the ground. Japanese air defense broadcast an attack warning belatedly at 12.15. The fires spread rapidly, enveloping the target area and an additional 4 square miles besides. Back on Guam, LeMay was uncharacteristically nervous. 'I'm sweating this one out myself,' he told his public information officer. 'A lot could go wrong. I can't sleep. I usually can, but not tonight.' He was worried about his crews. There were flak and some interceptors over the city, but the biggest danger the Americans faced was from turbulence, the result of the powerful updrafts caused by the fires below them. Crew members donned oxygen masks to block the stench of napalm and burned flesh. Nearly all the B-29s returned safely to their bases. (One B-29 crew claimed they had monitored Radio Tokyo during the attack, and insisted they had heard the American songs 'Smoke Gets in Your Eyes' and 'My Old Flame'.)[20]

The 25 February attack and others ostensibly on industrial targets meant that the people of Tokyo were no strangers to the B-29s—indeed, one of the nicknames given them was 'regular mail'. But they were unprepared for the waves of bombers that set fire to the city after midnight on 10 March. What anti-aircraft batteries they had were deployed near major factories and were aimed not by radar but by searchlights. Tokyo had trenches and some tunnels, but citizens who managed to reach these found them no protection from the oxygen-sucking heat of the incendiary fires. Houses were made of wood and paper and tightly packed together; efforts to cut fire lanes between them had foundered on labor shortages that had left in place the wooden remnants of structures that had been demolished. Police, firefighters, and hospital workers were unable to cope with the scope of the disaster they faced. 'To fight ultramodern incendiary bombs', wrote Robert Guillain, a French journalist who was in Tokyo during the attack, 'the populace's basic weapons were straw mats soaked in water, little paper sacks of sand and, in quantity, water buckets that had to be filled from the cisterns at each house'. Families had been told that, in case of an attack, they were to protect their homes and avoid panic.[21]

Mostly, people ran. They wrapped themselves in hooded air-raid cloaks, thickly padded with cotton, gathered together what family they could, and ran, hoping to find a way out of the flames, certain that they would not survive if they stood still. Whipped by a strong wind, the *akakaze* or 'red wind' off the Tokyo plain, the flames ignited the cloaks and trapped their wearers. Water was their hope. Firefighters tried to douse running people with water, hoping it would protect them from the blaze, or people threw themselves into barrels of water that the parsimonious had placed by their houses to fight fires. People ran to fetid canals and immersed themselves, with only their mouths and noses above the water line. But many of them died anyway, gulping at the deoxygenated air, trampled by others frantically seeking relief from the fires, or boiled by the superheated shallow water in which they stood. Others made it to the Sumida River, only to be swept away by the swift current or drowned as the tide rose: fire or water, they chose their fate. Some ran up rises toward bridges, only to find that the bridge they sought had collapsed, and only then to be crushed or pushed into the water by the crowd that had followed them up the fruitless approach. Or they made it onto an undamaged steel bridge, placed their hands in relief on its railing—and twisted off in agony as they were burned by the scorching metal. The Buddhist temple to Kwan-yin, survivor of the great earthquake and fire of 1923, burned with its monks and refugees and its famous tall gingko trees. In the red light district of Yoshiwara men died with their prostitutes; residents of Nihombashi, funneled by police to the imposing Meiji Theater, tried to protect themselves from the flames by lowering the great steel stage curtain, only to suffocate when toxic fumes penetrated the curtain, which had stuck in place.

As the dawn came in Tokyo, survivors of the bombing were caught in a paralysis of wonder, shock, and nausea. The city stank with the 'sickeningly sweet odor' of melted, rotting flesh. A reporter found 'long lines of ragged, ash-covered people struggl[ing] along, dazed and silent, like columns of ants'. Nearly everyone remarked on the astonishing quiet of the eastern part of the city, the silence broken only by the sound of people coughing or calling out to loved ones. Dedicated as they were, policemen, doctors, and civic officials quailed at the task of collecting the dead. 'In the black Sumida River countless bodies were floating, clothed bodies, naked bodies, all as black as charcoal. It was unreal,' recounted Dr Kuboto Shigenori. 'These were all dead people, but you couldn't tell whether they were men or women. You couldn't even tell if the objects floating by were arms and legs or pieces of burnt wood.' A police official explained that he was told to report on the situation in the city. 'Most of us', he said, 'were unable to do this because of horrifying conditions beyond imagination...I was supposed to investigate, but I didn't go because I did not like to see the terrible sights.' (His interviewer noted that at this he laughed, uncomfortably.) Many of those who survived the attack felt guilty and apologetic, no matter how badly wounded they were or how much they had lost. Michael Sherry has noted that Tokyoites did not give any indication of hating Americans after the raids, though he adds, shrewdly, that hatred may have been 'cancelled out by other emotions'. Not entirely. Robert Guillain, though French, felt unprecedented hostility from people in Tokyo in the days after the bombing. And after another firebomb attack on 23–24 May burned to the ground Tokyo's military prison, investigators found that, while every one of the 400 Japanese inmates had survived, all 62 American aviators imprisoned there had died. (Occupation authorities would convict the prison's commandant of war crimes.)[22]

'Hell could be no hotter,' concluded Guillain. No one knew, or knows, how many died that March night. Some bodies were no doubt uncounted because they were consumed by fire; others were quickly buried in mass graves so as to eliminate stench and prevent an epidemic; still others who might have been registered as dead may have left the city prior to the bombing, unbeknownst to relatives or (more likely) the only survivors in their families. Gordon Daniels quotes estimates made by officials in Tokyo of between 76,000 and 83,000 killed, though his own guess is closer to 90,000. That roughly 40,000 were injured by the bombing—that is, about half the number killed—suggests something of the fire's intensity.[23]

5. The firebombings and the atomic bombs

Many commentators have compared the Tokyo firebomb raid of 9–10 March to the atomic bombings of Hiroshima and Nagasaki that followed five months later. One ought to be cautious when making this comparison, as there are significant differences between the attacks. Sherry points out, for example, that Tokyo, unlike Hiroshima, underwent 'a process of destruction', one that unfolded over time as the American bombers dropped their incendiaries. 'The observer', Sherry writes, 'could see the destruction take place and watch the thing come alive, becoming some living, grotesque organism, ever changing in its shape, dimensions, colors, and directions.' (This was Guillain's experience: not being in the area that was bombed, he and his neighbors stood on their terraces and watched, 'uttering cries of admiration . . . at this grandiose, almost theatrical spectacle'.) There was no such unfolding or 'process' at Hiroshima, only what the bomb's Japanese witnesses called *pika-don*—'flash-boom'— an enormous blast, a searing heat and light, with no dramatic narrative, just a climax. Of course, the very singularity of the atomic bomb made it different from other weapons. The psychological effect of being attacked by well over 300 bombers is surely different from that of seeing one's city devastated by a single bomb dropped from a single plane. Radioactivity, the unseen evil that penetrates the body and keeps on killing and maiming a later generation, was the offspring only of the atomic bomb.[24]

And, yet, there were also many compelling similarities between these two events, and they make comparison irresistible. Lacking the dramatic explosion and the lingering radiation of the atomic bombings, the firebomb attack nevertheless produced enormous shock of its own, leaving its victims—the accounts say it repeatedly—dazed, vacant-eyed, as if in a bad waking dream. The incendiaries produced no radioactivity, but the heat and flame they generated left survivors with grotesque burns, and the eerily smooth scars called keloids that would become better known as shame-inducing features of atomic-bomb victims. People who experienced either of these events compared them to natural disasters, including volcanoes, typhoons, and most commonly earthquakes, as a way both of normalizing the attacks by naturalizing them and of assigning their causes to other-than-human hands—which may help explain the overall lack of hostility encountered by Americans in Japan after August 1945. Above all, the firebombings and atomic bombings were alike in their unabashed targeting of non-combatants for destruction. Before the March raid on Tokyo, Curtis LeMay might have convinced himself that he was going after military targets; in retrospect he claimed that all one had to do was 'visit one of these targets after we'd roasted it, and see the ruins of a multitude of tiny houses, with a drill press sticking up through the wreckage', in order to understand what little distinction existed between industrial and residential areas. As Little Boy and Fat Man were prepared for use that summer, Harry Truman reassured himself that the bombs would be dropped only on military targets. Both LeMay's and Truman's claims were delusional. But they represented the decay that had for some years rotted away the barricade separating soldiers and civilians as targets placed in the cross hairs by combatants.[25]

Two years after the war had ended, David Lilienthal, the chair of the US Atomic Energy Commission, reflected on the end of the distinction between soldiers and civilians:

> Then we burned Tokyo, not just military targets, but set out to wipe out the place, indiscriminately. The atomic bomb is the last word in this direction. All ethical limitations of warfare are gone, not because the *means* of destruction are more cruel or painful or otherwise hideous in their effect upon combatants, but because there are no individual combatants. The fences are gone.

The atomic bombs provided an exclamation point at the end of a continuous narrative of atrocity.[26]

And yet—again; the very subject of the atomic bomb inspires topic sentences that reverse the story's course. The men and women who imagined then built the bomb thought they were doing something different from what other makers of weapons did, thought they were engaged in something special. No one recalls the names of those who developed napalm and other incendiaries. No other single weapon project received $2 billion in government funds. (Radar cost more, but it was not a weapon as such.) Knowing what they knew about the power of a nuclear chain reaction, and whatever they may have guessed about the impact of radioactivity beyond the perimeter of the blast, some scientists and some government policymakers felt a need to think especially hard about how, and against whom, the atomic bomb was used. Curtis LeMay was permitted by Air Force strategic doctrine to firebomb Tokyo with many tons of incendiaries, but he made the decision to launch the attack himself. There were no high-level meetings to discuss the use of napalm. The opposite, of course, was true for the atomic bomb.

6. Doubters

There was, as Robert Wilson suggested, an assumption in the air that, if a bomb became feasible while the enemy—any enemy—was still in the field, it should be used; it would have been, as Wilson put it, 'unrealistic and unfair' to have asked the scientists to stop their work and the United States to stop its fight. Roosevelt seems to have assumed this, and when, in late 1943, Leslie Groves began retrofitting a B-29, largely designated for use in the Pacific theater, to carry the bomb, it was clear that he, too, planned to use his weapon against any and all enemies. Roosevelt's and Groves's decisions were the ones that mattered most, and most of the scientists working on the bomb, like Robert Wilson, accepted this. But even before Germany had surrendered, several of those involved with the Manhattan Project, convinced that the great evil of Naziism had been subdued and the danger of a German atomic bomb had passed, argued that the bomb ought not to be used against Japan. In other words, the target of the bomb should be understood as having been defeated, and the bomb's aiming point not merely shifted to another nation. It must be said that there was not much sympathy for the Japanese themselves—while the Jewish refugee scientists especially regarded them as less malignant than the Nazis, most also remembered Pearl Harbor, read the news of the ferocious island-hopping campaign, and shared the view, held by most white Americans, that the Japanese were not quite human. Instead, the scientists' major concern was that combat use of the bomb against Japan would set a bad precedent for the rest of the world and would in particular antagonize the Soviet Union, which would feel threatened by the US attack and would consider it necessary to race ahead with a bomb-building project of its own.[27]

Niels Bohr was an early advocate of informing the Soviet Union about the bomb project, thereby hastening a return to the republic of science and an 'open world' of information exchange. Bohr had traveled to Los Alamos in 1944 and had there advocated, in his elliptical way of speaking, the use of the bomb as a symbol of international hope and an opportunity for international cooperation. He did not, apparently, recommend specifically against using the bomb in Japan, but he stressed the singular evil of Hitler and told Oppenheimer confidently that 'nothing like' Naziism 'would ever happen again'. Leo Szilard went further. Szilard had energetically promoted the bomb, and to him belongs a good deal of credit for harassing US authorities into taking the project seriously early in the European war. Gradually, however, Szilard's gifts as a scientist became less relevant to the task of crafting the bomb itself. In early 1945, as Germany's defeat loomed, Szilard decided to talk to Roosevelt about the urgent need for postwar control of nuclear weapons. He solicited a letter of introduction from Albert Einstein, gained permission to take his cause to the President from Arthur Compton, and secured, through Eleanor Roosevelt, an appointment at the White House—for 8 May 1945. When FDR died on 12 April, Szilard managed to reschedule with Truman. He got as far as the office of Truman's appointment secretary Matthew Connelly, who assured Szilard that his boss took him seriously, then shunted him off to South Carolina for a meeting with James Byrnes, the man who was soon to be secretary of state, though Szilard did not know this.[28]

Szilard took Harold Urey and University of Chicago dean Walter Bartky along for support; the men arrived by train in Spartanburg on 28 May. Szilard presented Byrnes with Einstein's letter and read a memo, which suggested that dropping a bomb on Japan would probably move the Soviets more quickly toward making a bomb of their own. Byrnes remonstrated. Groves, he said, had told him that there was no uranium in the Soviet Union. Having spent $2 billion on the bomb, not to use it against Japan would ultimately dismay Congress and make it difficult to get funding for nuclear research in the future. And, Byrnes implied, the Soviets, who seemed to him up to no good in the East European nations they had liberated from Germany, might be easier to deal with if the United States dropped an atomic bomb. At this point, Szilard remembered, 'I began to doubt that there was any way for me to communicate with Byrnes in this matter.' Szilard and his colleagues took their leave in a fog of depression.[29]

Szilard returned to the Met Lab and discovered he had, as he often had, generated controversy. The Army was angry that Szilard had been permitted to get to Connelly and especially Byrnes. Bartky was reprimanded by Groves and scolded for giving Szilard's memo to Byrnes; Groves considered Szilard 'an opportunist' with 'no moral standards of any kind'. Compton loyally backed his scientists, and, as the high-level Interim Committee began its deliberations, he deputed James Franck, the head of Met Lab's chemistry section, to write a report examining the probable consequences of the bomb's use. Franck had serious reservations about using the bomb, and had in fact exacted a promise from Compton, in 1942, that, if an

American bomb was ready before Germany or another nation had one, Franck could object to its use at the highest level of government. Franck, who was fondly called 'Pa' by his co-workers and had a reputation for rectitude, rushed to his conclusions, and sent his thirteen-page report to Secretary of War Stimson on 11 June—though, as things turned out, it did not reach Stimson's desk.[30]

Franck knew the reasons why many were promoting the use of the bomb, or he anticipated them with remarkable acuity. Some said that using bombs would end the war quickly and thus save American lives. Franck doubted that the first generation of nuclear weapons would be powerful enough to discourage the Japanese from continuing the fight. Moreover, even if the bombs did shorten the war and thus keep American soldiers alive, that benefit 'may be outweighed by the ensuing loss of confidence and wave of horror and repulsion' the world would feel if the bombs were dropped. The huge expense for the Manhattan Project, mentioned to Szilard by Byrnes, did not require the bombs' use; the American public would understand 'that a weapon can sometimes be made ready only for use in an extreme emergency', and that nuclear weapons were in this category. The 'compelling reason' to build the weapon had been the scientists' fear that Germany might be building one too, but that was no longer an issue. Above all, using the bomb against a Japanese city would so shock the world as to make future control of nuclear weapons unlikely. The bomb was 'something entirely new in the order of magnitude of destructive power'. Given that, the way forward was to arrange a demonstration of the weapon in 'the desert or [on] a barren island', to which representatives from all nations, including of course Japan and the Soviet Union, would be invited. If the Japanese saw the awful power of the bomb, they might surrender. If the Russians and others saw that the Americans had the bomb but were too merciful to use it, they might be persuaded to place nuclear weapons work under international control.[31]

Military and government officials either remained unaware of the Franck Report or ignored it. Still, dissent continued. A gas diffusion engineer named O. C. Brewster got a letter through to Stimson on 24 May in which he insisted that, if the United States dropped the bomb, 'we would be the most hated and feared nation on earth'. George Harrison, Stimson's special assistant, wrote to his boss on 26 June of scientists' concerns about the bombs' use leading to a nuclear arms race. In July, Szilard tried again, circulating at the Met Lab a petition calling on the government to refrain,

THE UNITED STATES II

'on moral grounds', from using the bomb against Japanese cities. He got fifty-three signatures at first, then toned down his language slightly and gained seventeen more. But he could not win over the Lab's chemists, nor could he persuade Oppenheimer or Edward Teller, both at Los Alamos, to sign. (Oppie refused even to circulate the document.) The petition went through channels to Groves, who sat on it until 1 August, when he sent it to Stimson. President Truman, who had been in Potsdam and was then returning home aboard ship, never saw it.[32]

There were also several high-ranking doubters, men involved in atomic-bomb decisionmaking, who shared, perhaps independently, the scientists' concerns about dropping the bomb on Japanese cities, or who had different concerns that nevertheless brought them to some of the same, troubled conclusions. With Barton J. Bernstein, we can probably dismiss the postwar statement of wartime opposition to using the bomb made by Dwight Eisenhower. Bernstein casts similar doubt on *post facto* remarks criticizing the attacks by three of the four members of the 1945 Joint Chiefs of Staff: Admiral Ernest King, Army Air Force General Henry Arnold, and Admiral William Leahy, the chairman of the chiefs whose 1950 memoir, incongruously endorsed by Truman, described the use of the bomb as barbaric. The fourth member of the JCS, George Marshall, did privately urge Stimson, on 29 June, to confine use of the bomb to a genuinely military target. When the administration instead agreed to target Hiroshima and other cities, Marshall kept his counsel. Joseph Grew, the Undersecretary of State and former Ambassador to Japan, urged Truman in late May to signal the Japanese that even in surrender they could retain control of their political system, meaning that the office and the person of the Emperor would be preserved. Grew's proposal came in the aftermath of the latest firebombing attack on Tokyo; the atomic bomb lurked only in shadow form behind his argument to the President. Truman sent Grew off to see Stimson and several military leaders, who objected that such a concession would signal weakness to the Japanese even as the battle continued for Okinawa. Most forceful among the dissenters was Ralph Bard, undersecretary of the navy and a member of the Interim Committee. Bard was convinced, as he wrote to George Harrison on 27 June, that the Japanese were looking for a way to capitulate. If perhaps Japan was warned about the bomb, even a few days before it was to be used, and if perhaps the President could make 'assurances' to Tokyo regarding the Emperor, the Japanese would surrender unconditionally. Bard saw nothing to lose by trying.[33]

7. The dismissal of doubt

All these dissents, doubts, and inklings of doubt were overridden by the determination, among bomb-builders and policymakers, to use the new weapon as long as the enemy refused to surrender unconditionally, as the US government defined the adverb. The strenuous concerns of Szilard and Franck, along with the more qualified ones of Marshall, Grew, and Bard, could not match the combination of assumption and conviction on the part of those who saw no reason *not* to use the bomb and various and substantial benefits to using it. Franklin Roosevelt, typically cautious and non-committal about nearly anything not requiring an immediate decision, did apparently wonder to Vannevar Bush, in September 1944, whether the bomb 'should actually be used against the Japanese or whether it should be used only as a threat with full-scale experimentation in this country'. He was thinking aloud, advocating for the devil, trying something new on for Bush—for otherwise there is nothing in the record to suggest that Roosevelt would have hesitated to use the weapon he himself had authorized and had discussed without reservation many times with Bush, Stimson, Churchill, and others. The assumption that the bomb would be used also governed the deliberations of Truman's Interim Committee. Established in late April at the behest of the President, the committee was broadly charged by Stimson to 'study and report on the whole problem of temporary war controls and later publicity, and to survey and make recommendations on post-war research, development and controls, as well as legislation necessary to effectuate them'. Its members were Stimson, in the chair (George Harrison served as chair when Stimson could not be present), Bard, Bush, Conant, Karl Compton, and Undersecretary of State William Clayton. Attached to the committee was a Scientific Panel, including Oppenheimer, Ernest Lawrence, Arthur Compton, and Enrico Fermi. James Byrnes was added as the personal representative of the President.[34]

To some small extent, as Michael Sherry has pointed out, the Interim Committee's discussion of how to use the atomic bomb 'sometimes slipped over into pondering whether to use it all'. Bard, after all, concluded that the Japanese should be warned in advance about the bomb and offered a guarantee that the emperor would be retained, conditions that bore at least as much on the question of 'whether' as the matter of 'how'. Even more striking is the speed with which the first formal discussion of the committee, on 31 May 1945, went in the direction of the future of nuclear power and prospects for its international control. The membership talked for over three hours that morning hardly mentioning Japan, though just before lunch there was a conversation about how to handle the Russians. When at last the subject of Japan came up, number eight on an agenda with eleven substantive items, it was encapsulated in the title 'Effect of the Bombing on the Japanese and their Will to Fight'. The subsequent discussion concerned similarities and differences between the atomic bombing and ongoing non-nuclear strikes, possible targets, and whether to drop just one bomb at a time or several at once. (Groves, who was present, and was ultimately invited to every Interim Committee meeting, urged use of a single bomb, in part because the effect of a multiple strike 'would not be sufficiently distinct from our regular bombing program'.) No one at this point voiced reservations about using the bomb. In summarizing the deliberations, R. Gordon Arneson, who took notes at the meeting, recorded 'general agreement' with the conclusion that 'we could not give the Japanese any warning' that the bomb was coming.[35]

Some members of the committee had talked at lunch, for around ten minutes, about the possibility of using a non-combat demonstration of the bomb to convince the Japanese to give up. Arthur Compton later said he raised the issue with Stimson, who put it to the others seated at the table. (Another account has Byrnes taking the initiative with Lawrence.) In either case, everyone hearing the argument objected to it. The Japanese could attack the demonstration site or the plane delivering the bomb. The bomb might be a dud. Even if it exploded, Japan's 'determined and fanatical military men', in Compton's words, might be unimpressed. America's war prisoners might, somehow, be placed in the demonstration area. The element of surprise, crucial to shock the Japanese, would be lost. And, finally, someone added, would the threat of the bomb or its non-combat display move a people whose cities had already been firebombed? The Interim Committee had been treating the atomic bomb as something special, but its membership still was not sure that in every respect it was, or that its victims would see it so.[36]

The committee met several more times in June and July. On 1 June it was joined by four leading industrialists, whose firms had been involved in plant construction and other projects concerning the bomb, and whose postwar involvement in the nuclear industry was deemed to be vital. That afternoon, after the industrialists had left, the committee agreed that 'the bomb should be used against Japan as soon as possible; that it be used on a war plant surrounded by workers' homes; and that it be used without prior warning'. That decision was reaffirmed at the next meeting on 21 June in response to Arthur Compton's report of Szilard's protest movement at the Met Lab. At this session the members also discussed at some length how to treat publicly news of the dropping of the bomb, and unanimously agreed to the revocation of Clause Two of the Quebec Agreement with the British, which required the 'mutual consent' of the signatories before the bomb could be used against a third party; no one at this stage wished to ask the British for permission to drop an atomic bomb on Japan. The committee also agreed that, when Truman met Josef Stalin at Potsdam later that summer, the President should tell Stalin that the United States was 'working on this weapon' with optimism for its success 'and that we expected to use it against Japan', but that Truman should rebuff any further Soviet enquiries concerning the weapon's 'details'. More discussion of this forthcoming exchange followed when the committee convened again on 6 July, and the members revisited the language of statements to be issued following the bombing, particularly in the light of suggestions made in the meantime by British scientists. The committee met a final time on 19 July, three days after the bomb had been successfully tested in New Mexico, with Truman, Stimson, and Byrnes in Potsdam, and without its scientific advisers. Once more the focus was on the future, with discussions concerning continuing nuclear research, a memo by Bush and Conant recommending that the new United Nations establish some 'mechanism' for international control of atomic energy, and a lengthy consideration of Congressional legislation regarding both these matters and others. In the light of the recent bomb test, the committee agreed to send a letter of congratulation to Oppenheimer. No date was set for the next meeting, and as it happened no other meeting was held.[37]

James F. (he was called 'Jimmy') Byrnes had been Franklin Roosevelt's Director of War Mobilization. It was an important position for a powerful man known as 'the assistant president'; indeed, Byrnes was passed over for the vice-presidential nomination in 1944, which would have made him Roosevelt's heir apparent, in favor of Truman only because Roosevelt thought Byrnes was too conservative to win the northern votes that he judged were essential for victory that year. Byrnes briefed Truman on the atomic bomb just a day after Stimson did so—that is, on 13 April—telling the new president that 'we were perfecting an explosive great enough to destroy the whole world', then adding that 'the bomb might well put us in a position to dictate our own terms at the end of the war'. Truman, who feared Byrnes slightly and thought him 'conniving', nevertheless found his political experience useful and was unduly impressed with Byrnes's international expertise. He asked Byrnes to be his secretary of state, effective that summer, and Byrnes accepted.[38]

Byrnes harbored no apparent doubts about using the bomb. As head of War Mobilization he had known of the project early on, and had told Roosevelt of his worries that the gadget was costing too much with no certainty of return. (Stimson would tell the President, during their last meeting in mid-March 1945 that he considered Byrnes's anxieties 'jittery, nervous, and rather silly'.) As we have seen, when Szilard approached Byrnes with his objections to using the bomb at the end of May, Byrnes put him off, echoing the arguments he had previously rehearsed with Truman: the bomb was too expensive not to use, and dropping the bomb could make the Soviets better behaved in Eastern Europe. During meetings of the Interim Committee, Byrnes voiced no concern about dropping the bomb, only returning with emphasis to his belief that the Soviets should not receive information about the bomb lest Stalin insist on a 'partnership' the Americans must never offer. More consistently than any other US official, Byrnes came to see the atomic bomb as a vital instrument of wartime and postwar diplomacy toward the Soviet Union. With Truman at Potsdam in July, and having just heard that the bomb had been successfully tested, Byrnes confided to Special Ambassador Joseph Davies that he thought the Russians would ultimately see things the Americans' way with reference to the thorny issue of German reparations, and that September, with the war won, Byrnes went off to a Foreign Ministers' Conference in London, according to the troubled Stimson, with 'the presence of the bomb in his pocket' to 'get [him] through'.[39]

Byrnes thought of the bomb as an unalloyed benefit to the United States. Not so Henry Stimson. The Secretary of War, clearly aging and often incapacitated by fatigue and migraine headaches, nevertheless commanded enormous respect in Washington and beyond in 1945. His experience of government was far greater than that of Truman, and virtually everyone else. It was Stimson who had deflected the enquiries of then-Senator Truman in 1944 when Truman, chair of the Committee to Investigate the National Defense Program, had tried to probe a very expensive but secret construction project called Manhattan. Stimson was not as convinced as Byrnes that the Soviets were untrustworthy, and he regarded the atom bomb, as he told the President in late April, as 'the most terrible weapon ever known in human history', one that carried with it 'a certain moral responsibility'. When a scientists' Target Committee placed the city of Kyoto at the top of its list of objectives for an atomic-bomb crew, Stimson, who had twice visited it, demanded its removal: Kyoto was a cultural and religious center that would become, if destroyed, an example of American cruelty, and, if spared, a symbol of American decency and restraint. No amount of entreaty from Groves would persuade the secretary to put Kyoto in the cross hairs. Stimson also took it on faith that civilians should be spared, 'as far as possible', from the weapons of war.[40]

'As far as possible'—there was a loophole that admitted morally dubious acts backlit by self-delusion. In gravitas, in the regard with which others held him, in his willingness to allow his decisions about the bomb at least occasionally to trouble him, he was the government's counterpart to Robert Oppenheimer (who found Stimson impressive). The bomb, Stimson jotted in notes to himself before his first meeting with the Interim Committee, 'may *destroy or perfect* International *Civilization*' and 'may [be] *Frankenstein or* means for World Peace'. But, if there was distress in these perceptions, so alien to the likes of Groves and Byrnes, there was also an unwillingness to allow them to prevent the bombs from being used. Stimson needed to discuss how and where the bomb(s) would be dropped, and he was genuinely concerned about the consequences of dropping the bombs on Japanese cities. He did not, however, question the need to drop them, never recognizing any 'profound qualitative difference' between them and non-nuclear weapons, as Martin Sherwin puts it. Stimson guided the Interim Committee to its decision that the bomb should be used as soon as it was ready, and it was he, along with Marshall, who formally authorized the 20th Air Force to 'deliver' the bombs to Japan. Perhaps he extinguished his doubts with his strenuous effort to keep Kyoto off the target list; having secured the safety of the Buddhist temples and shrines and the lives of the citizens of Kyoto, Stimson could tell himself that he had acted decently, even morally, or had gone as far as circumstances would allow. Perhaps instead, as Sherry argues, he deluded 'himself that "precision" bombing remained American practice' in 1945. In any event, to gain the surrender of Japan, Stimson wrote in 1947, it seemed necessary to administer a 'tremendous shock which would carry convincing proof of our power to destroy' Japan. That meant the bomb.[41]

Harry Truman relied on Stimson for guidance about the bomb, so it is no surprise that the President came to share his secretary's self-delusion about its target. Overwhelmed by the job—on the first afternoon following Roosevelt's death he told reporters that he 'felt like the moon, the stars, and the planets had fallen' on him—Truman exhibited on the atomic-bomb issue a combination of feigned indifference and zealous over-involvement characteristic of the insecure. There is little evidence that he saw the bomb as a moral matter, at least before the second bomb was dropped on Nagasaki on 9 August. He nevertheless felt compelled to tell himself, like Stimson, that the atomic bombs whose use he authorized, or to whose use he acceded, were to be aimed at military targets. It was in a mid-May 1945 meeting with the President that Stimson declared that Air Force firebombings had targeted the Japanese military, and that 'the same rule of sparing the civilian population should be applied as far as possible to the use of any new weapons', like the atomic bomb. Two weeks later came the Interim Committee meeting that resolved, according to Stimson, that the 'most desirable target' of the bomb 'would be a vital war plant employing a large number of workers and closely surrounded by workers' houses'. Truman accepted this recommendation. After conferring with Stimson about the bomb again at Potsdam, on 25 July, Truman wrote in his diary:

> I have told the Sec[retary] of War, Mr Stimson, to use it so that military objectives and soldiers and sailors are the target and not women and children. Even if the Japs are savages, ruthless, merciless and fanatic, we as the leader of the world for the common welfare cannot drop this terrible bomb on the old capital [Kyoto] or the new [Tokyo]. He and I are in accord. The target will be a purely military one.

Anyone who knew, as Stimson and Truman did, what the firebombs had done to Hamburg, Dresden, and Tokyo, and what the test of the plutonium bomb in New Mexico had revealed nine days earlier, also knew that these weapons unleashed upon cities did not magically kill only their military inhabitants, or destroy factories and 'workers' houses' while sparing tea shops, hospitals, and the homes of teachers. Here, again, was self-deception—undertaken at the highest level and on the most critical of issues. Probably, like Stimson, Truman told himself that sparing Kyoto (and, belatedly, Tokyo) absolved him of charges that he was targeting innocents. Having thus persuaded himself that he was merely engaged in the accepted strategic practice of war, Truman slept soundly on those midsummer nights.[42]

8. To Alamogordo, July 1945

That decisions needed making, that self-delusion seemed necessary, were results of the Manhattan Project's success in producing a functional atomic bomb. While Truman struggled to find his footing as president, while Byrnes, Groves, and especially Stimson tutored him about the bomb, while the Interim Committee discussed how to use the bomb, and scientists, generals, and government officials debated targets, Oppenheimer's army in New Mexico labored to solve the bomb's technical problems and thus fulfill its destiny. Szilard, Franck, and several others thought the bomb should not be used automatically against Japan. Oppenheimer was having none of it. He turned aside Szilard's provocative petition, and threw himself so fully into the work of finishing the plutonium test bomb that Groves wondered if he would have time for policy meetings in Washington and friends worried about his health. There remained difficulties with the implosion mechanism, the series of detonators that needed to fire simultaneously, 'within a fraction of a millionth of a second', if the bomb's plutonium was to chain react properly. Equally troublesome was the bomb's gumball-sized initiator (codenamed 'urchin'), which lay within the plutonium core and would start the release of neutrons. A brave Canadian named Louis Slotin spent his days at a gunmetal desk, pushing toward each other, then quickly separating, two hemispheres of plutonium. He was trying to figure out exactly how much of the volatile element would be needed for the shot. No one had a more dangerous job; 'tickling the dragon's tail,' it was called. (Nearly a year later, Slotin was still tickling. His screwdriver slipped, the hemispheres joined for a split second of criticality, and Slotin, who threw his body over the hemispheres even as he wrenched them apart, died an agonizing, and secret, death nine days later.[43])

It was serious and sophisticated work. Preparing the test bomb gave the male scientists a sense of masculine power: they named their bombs Little Boy and Fat Man and planned to label any unsuccessful test device 'a girl'. The work allowed them to presume to control nature. Nuclear energy was the fundamental force in the universe; to command it 'in a pint pot', wrote the physicist Freeman Dyson, was to 'produce an illusion of illimitable power'. Oppenheimer called the test site (and ultimately the shot itself) Trinity, inspired by the 'three-person'd God' of a John Donne sonnet. Preparation for the test was, at times, almost shockingly quotidian. Once the Trinity bomb was under assembly, scientists found several holes in its volatile core, which they plugged with shreds of facial tissue. Some of the bomb's detonator charges required snugging by means of Scotch tape. The bomb was taken by car and truck to the test site at Alamogordo, 200 miles south of Los Alamos; the core, separated of course from the rest of the assembly, traveled in two suitcases with thermometers attached. As the test gadget was hoisted into a tower, wherein it was to be detonated, technicians threw dozens of army-issue mattresses beneath it, hoping to cushion it if it tore loose from its fittings and plunged to earth. As the bomb lay in place throughout the day and night of 14 July, thunderstorms sparked throughout the area, making the scientists jittery and more than once inspiring them to gallows humor.[44]

Through the next day and night they figuratively held their breath. Groves fretted about the unstable weather and unhappily contemplated postponing the test. Oppenheimer, agitated, worried that postponement would mean that 'I'll never get my people up to pitch again', as he put it. Vannevar Bush, onsite for the shot, was awakened prematurely when the wind blew down his tent; he gave up on sleep and walked to the makeshift mess hall for breakfast at 3.45 in the morning of 16 July. Men chainsmoked and drank coffee. Enrico Fermi, oddly, tore a piece of paper into scraps. (After the blast, he would use these as primitive but effective indicators of the test bomb's power.) At 4.45 project meteorologists reported a short break in the storms. Groves and Oppie decided to test Trinity at 5.30. Those witnessing the test got pieces of smoked welder's glass through which to watch. Richard Feynman, the brilliant trickster, refused to use his, reasoning that at a distance of 20 miles his eyes would be protected sufficiently by the windshield of the truck in which he sat. Edward Teller, on the other hand, put on gloves, a pair of sunglasses under the welder's glass, and a generous portion of anti-sunburn cream. Samuel Allison, from Chicago's Met Lab, read the countdown on a radio station that crossed frequencies with another playing a Tchaikovsky serenade, which provided surreal background music for Allison's steady voice. At 5.29 Allison reached zero. A split second later, ground and heaven burst open.[45]

Oppenheimer thought of a regnant Brahma from the epic *Mahabharata*.
'A foul and awesome display,' was Kenneth Bainbridge's verdict. Fermi,
seemingly oblivious to the light and heat and shock, dropped his paper
scraps and watched as the blast wave carried them. Cocky Richard Feynman
turned away, temporarily blinded. Others cheered and danced. The Trinity
shot produced a light brighter than any seen previously in the world,
bright enough to have been seen from space. Its core temperature was four
times greater than that at the center of the sun. The pressure from the
blast was unprecedented; the radioactivity it threw off, as Lansing Lamont
calculated, was a million times more than that emitted by all the radium
on earth. The light, then blast wave, reached Groves, Bush, and Conant,
lying side by side and facing away from the tower at a distance of about
16,000 yards. The men shook hands, then Groves said, 'we must keep this
whole thing quiet'. An army major standing nearby tapped Groves on the
shoulder: 'Sir,' he said, 'I think they heard the noise in five states.' If not
quite that, Trinity nevertheless drew a good deal of attention. An 18-year-
old blind woman named Georgia Green, in a car with her brother-in-law
on the road to Albuquerque, registered the bomb's light. Windows broke
in Texas, terrified people called police or newspaper offices to report an
earthquake or plane crash; a New Mexico man named Hugh McSmith
found himself shivering in bed, the sheets and blankets having been blown
off him. Groves put it out that an ammunition dump had exploded. In his
memorandum to Stimson on the test, Groves included an account written
by Brigadier General Thomas F. Farrell, who had witnessed the blast from
the Alamogordo control room 10,000 yards south of the blast site. 'The
effects', wrote Farrell, 'could well be called unprecedented, magnificent,
beautiful, stupendous, and terrifying.'

> The whole country was lighted by a searing light with the intensity many
> times that of the midday sun. It was golden, purple, violet, gray, and
> blue . . . Thirty seconds after the explosion came first, the air blast pressing
> hard against people and things, to be followed almost immediately by the
> strong, sustained, awesome roar which warned of doomsday and made us
> feel that we puny things were blasphemous to dare tamper with the forces
> heretofore reserved to The Almighty. Words are inadequate tools for the job
> of acquainting those not present with the physical, mental, and psychological
> effects. It had to be witnessed to be realized.[46]

As Groves struggled to contain information about the test—a harbinger
of American efforts to prevent specific knowledge of the bomb's works

from reaching the international community once the war had ended—he faced a dangerous, related problem. Soon after the shot was fired, Robert Wilson led an observation team north out of Trinity. Needles on the Geiger counters carried by the team members suddenly jumped. Radioactivity, in a reddish-brown cloud, was drifting north, threatening small communities and cattle ranches and raising the distressing possibility that these might have to be evacuated. Updrafts from the narrow canyons intensified the winds and caused them to blow promiscuously across the area. The small town of Carrizozo was endangered, as were larger communities such as Coyote, Ancho, and Vaughn, 112 miles north of Trinity. A radiation monitor named Joe Hirschfelder drove through the worrisome landscape and returned to Base Camp with radioactive tires and a skin exposure reading so disturbing that he found it impossible to hitch a ride to Albuquerque with nervous colleagues, even after a shower. Several cattle ranches on a mesa west of Carrizozo were contaminated with radioactive ash, a circumstance the government labored to keep secret. Groves's report to Stimson on the test did not alert the secretary to any potential problem with radioactivity from a bomb blast, though Groves admitted that assessments were not yet final.[47]

At the site itself, among the scientists especially, reflection and sobriety soon set in. Initial jubilation gave way to a silent breakfast, for those with an appetite. Project director Kenneth Bainbridge shook hands with Oppenheimer and said to him quietly: 'Now we're all sons-of-bitches.' Oppie discovered on the desert floor a turtle struggling on its back, having been overturned by the bomb's blast wave. Oppie flipped him over and watched him scuttle away; 'that's the least I can do,' he thought. 'I am sure', said George Kistiakowsky after the test, 'that at the end of the world—in the last millisecond of the earth's existence—the last men will see what we saw.' And yet they were at least as sure of something else: that the atomic bomb would prove to be the winning weapon against the Japanese. When Thomas Ferrell saw Groves after the test, the first thing he said was: 'The war is over.' 'Yes,' replied Groves, 'after we drop two bombs on Japan.'[48]

9. Truman at Potsdam

Jubilation trumped reflection in Potsdam, where Truman had arrived on 15 July. Truman had agreed to the summit with reluctance, nervous as he was during his first summer as president that Stalin and, to a lesser extent, Churchill, would outmaneuver or bully him. ('I'm on my way to the high executioner,' Truman wrote glumly to his wife, Bess.) He knew that the Trinity test was imminent, and he held out hope for its decisiveness. But he nevertheless came to Potsdam expecting to need the Russians' help to finish off Japan. And, though it is often forgotten now, and particularly by authors of books about the atomic bomb, Truman not only played the endgame of the Pacific War at Potsdam but confronted a host of issues on which he anticipated Soviet troublemaking: the amount and direction of German reparations, the vexed and ongoing question of the new German–Polish border, and whether the United States and Great Britain would extend diplomatic recognition to the Soviet-liberated states of Finland, Bulgaria, Romania, and Hungary, all of which seemed to be falling under Moscow's control. Japan was much on Truman's mind as he and his delegation— Byrnes, aide William Leahy, and Soviet expert Charles Bohlen—took up residence in a three-storey yellow stucco building at No. 2 Kaiserstrasse. But the Soviets were in his face.[49]

Byrnes had excluded Stimson from the entourage, seeking to assert his own control over the President and suspecting that the old man had grown soft. The Secretary of State for all of two weeks, Byrnes had from the start clung fast to the doctrine of unconditional surrender and hoped very much to avoid sharing information with the Soviets about the atomic bomb. Other advisers, including Stimson, who had invited himself to Germany despite his exclusion from the formal delegation, wanted to warn the Japanese explicitly about their imminent destruction, sweetening the threat with a promise that Japan could retain the emperor in a constitutional monarchy if it surrendered. This need not be construed as a shift away from unconditional surrender but a redefinition of it. It was Stimson who brought news of the Trinity test to Kaiserstrasse on the evening of 16 July, delighting Truman and Byrnes. When the Secretary of War returned the next day with further details of the shot, he also proposed an early warning to the Japanese. Byrnes brushed the suggestion aside and instead described a 'timetable' for using the bomb, and, when Truman failed to intercede, Stimson concluded that the President had already adopted Byrnes's posi- tion. Byrnes subsequently informed his department that neither the early warning nor a guarantee of the emperor would be forthcoming.

Truman had his first meeting with Stalin that same day. After apologizing for arriving in Potsdam a day later than expected—he had been ill, and had been negotiating with the Chinese—Stalin raised a number of issues, and declared that his armies would be ready to go to war with Japan by mid-August, providing an agreement on territorial concessions could be reached with the Chinese. The meeting lasted two hours. Afterwards, Truman seemed satisfied, recording in his diary that Stalin was 'honest—but smart as hell', and a man he could 'deal with'. Still not altogether sure of the magnitude of the Trinity test, the President appeared pleased to have Stalin's pledge of help: 'Fini Japs when that comes about,' he wrote, though it may have been that his expectation of Japan's demise had to do not only with the anticipated Soviet intervention (assuming successful negotiations with China) but with the use of atomic bombs even sooner.[50]

As reports from Alamogordo continued to arrive in Potsdam, carried dutifully by Stimson to Truman, Byrnes, and Churchill, the President's confidence rose, and so did his doubts about the need for Soviet involvement in the war. By the 18th, Truman seemed to Stimson 'greatly reenforced' in his determination to make the Soviets see reason. The next day, as he boasted to Bess, he managed a 'tough meeting' with the Russians when he 'reared up . . . and told 'em where to get off and they got off'. Having received a final, detailed report on Trinity on the 21st, Truman turned even more bumptious, quarreling vigorously with Stalin on Germany and the political future of Eastern Europe. Churchill was surprised at Truman's performance—until Stimson gave him a copy of the latest Trinity report the following day. 'Now I know what happened to Truman yesterday,' the Prime Minister said. 'When he got to the meeting after having read this report he was a changed man. He told the Russians just where they got on and off and generally bossed the whole meeting.' It was not just the President's attitude that had changed. Prodded by Byrnes, he now made it clear that he was disinclined to bend to Soviet demands, 'apparently', Stimson wrote privately, because he was 'relying greatly upon the information as to S1'. The bomb meant, perhaps, that the Soviets would get less than they wanted from China—control of Outer Mongolia and the railways in Manchuria and leaseholds on the cities of Dairen and Port Arthur—that they would prove yielding in their occupied zones of Eastern Europe and Germany, and that, assuming the bomb ended the war quickly, they would not, in Byrnes's words, 'get so much in on the kill' and thereby have only a small role to play in the post-surrender occupation of Japan.[51]

While the British, then, were promptly and fully informed about the Trinity test, the Russians were not, and the question remained: what, if

anything, should they be told? Stimson and others thought Stalin should
hear something about the bomb from official sources. Jimmy Byrnes
wanted to stonewall, to let the Russians find out when others did, after
the bomb had been dropped. Truman decided on a sort of compromise,
though one tipped toward Byrnes's position. At 7.30 in the evening of
24 July, the eighth plenary session of the Potsdam conference took a recess.
Instructing Bohlen, his Russian interpreter, to stay put, Truman walked
across the room to Stalin, turned him away from the group, and told him,
with a casualness that was clearly strained, that the United States had 'a new
weapon of unusual destructive force'. According to Truman, Stalin replied
that 'he was glad to hear it and hoped we would make "good use" of it
against the Japanese'. Truman and other US officials thought Stalin's reply
indicated that he did not know what weapon the President was talking
about—no more, that is, 'than the man in the moon', as Truman said later.
They were wrong. Stalin had in June received information, gleaned from
Klaus Fuchs at Los Alamos, that a bomb test was scheduled for later in
the summer, and the intelligence was later refined. Following the plenary,
Stalin called Lavrenti Beria, head of the secret police, to ask what Soviet
intelligence knew about the shot. Beria said there had been no information
that a test had taken place, whereupon Stalin flew into a rage and told Beria
he had been misinformed. Back at his villa Stalin, cursing 'in ripe language'
about American machinations, declared that he would not be manipulated
and vowed to speed production of a bomb.[52]

Out of the Potsdam conference came the eponymous declaration that
spelled out surrender terms to the Japanese. Stimson, along with Joseph
Grew and Secretary of the Navy James Forrestal, had in June drafted a
statement of terms that offered a slight but significant modification of
unconditional surrender: that the Japanese might retain 'a constitutional
monarchy under the present dynasty'. The 'Committee of Three', as the
men called themselves, hoped that such a promise might tip the balance
in the Japanese Cabinet, allowing its 'peace faction' to lead an exit from
the war because the emperor, who might now be enlisted in the quest
for peace, would escape punishment, removal from office, or humiliation.
On 18 July, just after the conference had begun, the Joint Chiefs of Staff
offered their support for retaining the Emperor as the only figure on the
scene who could persuade the soldiers loyal to him to lay down arms. But
Byrnes disliked the new draft of terms. He may have feared that seeming to
soften US conditions, however subtly, might encourage Japanese hardliners

to continue the fight in the hopes of gaining further concessions. Equally likely, Byrnes's focus, as ever, rested on domestic politics, and he worried that the loophole made by the modification would enrage an American public bent on bringing to its knees the nation that had perpetrated Pearl Harbor, the Bataan 'Death March', and scores of reported atrocities against American (and other) prisoners.

This was Truman's concern too. It was his view that Franklin Roosevelt had committed the United States to the policy of unconditional surrender, just as FDR had assumed, in authorizing a program to build an atomic bomb, that the bomb should be dropped when it was ready. The new president was willing to offer the Japanese a hint of leniency in the Potsdam Declaration, or what he believed was a hint: the Japanese could establish a government 'in accordance with the[ir] freely expressed will', though only in the presence of US occupation forces and only after other conditions had been met—among them the elimination of 'the authority and influence of those who have deceived and misled the people of Japan into embarking on world conquest', and the administration of 'stern justice' to all 'war criminals', perhaps including the Emperor. When Byrnes removed the imperial retention clause from the draft declaration, Truman tacitly agreed with his secretary of state by accepting the change. The Potsdam Declaration, issued on 26 July by the United States, Great Britain, and China (the Soviets were not asked to sign), thus offered Tokyo no meaningful modification of terms, only the peace of the vanquished, and in harsh language. Japan's choice was 'unconditional surrender' or 'prompt and utter destruction'.[53]

So the die was cast. When the Japanese government did not immediately accept the Potsdam Declaration—Prime Minister Kantarō Suzuki reportedly said, on 28 July, that Japan would 'ignore' it (mokusatsu)—the Americans moved ahead with their plans to drop an atomic bomb on the first target city, Hiroshima. The uranium core of the bomb, encased in a cylinder of lead and weighing 300 pounds, had left San Francisco on the day of the Trinity shot and arrived at Tinian Island in the Marianas, seized from Japan the previous summer, on the 26th, the day the Potsdam Declaration was issued. Tinian was the home of the Air Force's 509th Composite Group, members of which had been designated and trained to deliver the bomb. Colonel Paul Tibbets would command the B-29 that would carry Little Boy to its target. Delivery was set for 6 August, as long as the weather cooperated.

10. Why the bombs were dropped

How had it come to this? In the months and years after Hiroshima, historians and other commentators offered a variety of explanations for the US decision to use the atomic bomb against Japan. One of them, heard increasingly in recent years, is that white American racism caused, or at minimum enabled, the United States to use a devastating weapon on the Japanese, brown people whom they considered inferior to themselves, barbaric in their conduct of war, and finally subhuman—'a beast', as Truman put it. It is certainly true, as John Dower, Ronald Takaki, and others have demonstrated, that the Pacific War was fought with a savagery unfamiliar to those who had engaged each other in Europe, where enmities were bitter but vitiated by the fact that the adversaries were white. On the west coast of the United States, beginning in 1942, Japanese-Americans were rounded up and placed in internment camps. There was no means test given for loyalty: 'a Jap is a Jap', insisted General John L. DeWitt, head of the US Western Defense Command, and all 'Japs' were potentially treacherous. Or, as the Los Angeles *Times* had it: 'A viper is nonetheless a viper wherever the egg is hatched—so a Japanese-American, born of Japanese parents, grows up to be a Japanese not an American.' Home front officials and publications depicted Japanese and Japanese-Americans as insects, vermin, rodents, and apes, and in this way inspired exterminationist fantasies, for who could object to the eradication of lice, spiders, or rats? Marshall Fields department stores in Chicago bought a two-page newspaper ad depicting a simian-like Japanese soldier cringing beneath the shadow of a bomber; the caption asked, 'Little men, what now?' The Elks Lodge in Harrisburg, Illinois, promised 'to knock out Hirohito but it won't be easy... Rats are dangerous to the last corner.' Even more sophisticated publications erased the distinction between soldiers and civilians in Japan. According to the *New Republic*: 'The natural enemy of every American man, woman and child is the Japanese man, woman and child.' It was race that mattered, blood that told; no Japanese, anywhere, could or should be spared.[54]

The Americans who fought Japanese in the Pacific theater were, if anything, even more scathing in their characterizations of them. Admiral William F. ('Bull') Halsey, commander of the US South Pacific Force, told reporters that 'the only good Jap is a Jap who's been dead six months'. Not to be outdone, Halsey's Atlantic counterpart, Admiral Jonas H. Ingram, explained that, 'if it is necessary to win the war, we shall leave no man, woman, or child alive in Japan and shall erase that country from the map'. 'When you see the little stinking rats with buck teeth and bowlegs dead alongside an American, you wonder why we have to fight them and who started this war,' said Lieutenant General Holland M. ('Howlin' Mad') Smith. 'The Japanese smell,' he added. 'They don't even bleed when they die.' Soldiers took their cues from their officers, whose views in any case reinforced their own about the kind of enemy they were fighting. Robert Scott Jr., author of the bestseller *God Is My Co-Pilot*, relished combat in Southeast Asia. 'Personally,' he wrote, 'every time I cut Japanese columns to pieces . . . strafed Japs swimming from boats we were sinking, or blew a Jap pilot to hell out of the sky, I just laughed in my heart and knew that I had stepped on another black-widow spider or scorpion.' E. B. Sledge, island hopping with the marines in the South Pacific, marveled at the refusal of Japanese soldiers to surrender and noted many examples of 'trophy-taking' by his fellow marines—the result, he thought, of a 'particular savagery that characterized the struggle between the Marines and the Japanese'. Marines prized enemy ears, fingers, hands, and, most often, gold teeth:

> The Japanese's mouth glowed with huge gold-crowned teeth, and his [American] captor wanted them. He put the point of his kabar on the base of a tooth and hit the handle with the palm of his hand. Because the Japanese was kicking his feet and thrashing about, the knife point glanced off the tooth and sank deeply into the victim's mouth. The Marine cursed him and with a slash cut his cheeks open to each ear. He put his foot on the sufferer's lower jaw and tried again. Blood poured out of the soldier's mouth. He made a gurgling noise and thrashed wildly.

Compassion for Japanese was rare, Sledge noted, and scorned by most American soldiers as 'going Asiatic'.[55]

The men who made the decision to drop atomic bombs and decided where to drop them shared the sharply racialized sentiments of their officers and fighting men. 'Killing Japanese didn't bother me very much at that time,' recalled Curtis LeMay. 'So I wasn't worried particularly about how many people we killed in getting the job done.' The South Carolinian Byrnes routinely referred to 'niggers' and 'Japs'. Discussing the Hiroshima bombing with Leslie Groves on the day after it had happened, Chief of Staff George Marshall cautioned against 'too much gratification' because the attack 'undoubtedly involved a large number of Japanese casualties'.

Groves replied that he was not thinking about the Japanese but about those Americans who had suffered on the Bataan 'Death March'. Truman himself was a casual user of racial epithets for African Americans, Jews, and Asians. The Japanese, in his lexicon, were 'beasts', 'savages, ruthless, merciless, and fanatic'.[56]

While there is no question that white Americans, at least, exhibited anti-Japanese racism, it is unlikely that racism explains why the United States dropped atomic bombs on Hiroshima and Nagasaki, though perhaps it helped policymakers justify the decision to themselves after it had been made. The coarsening of ethical standards concerning who got bombed and how was virtually universal by 1945. Americans hated Japanese more than they hated Germans, but that did not prevent them from attacking Hamburg and Dresden with firebombs, targeting the citizens of these cities just as surely and coldly as those in Hiroshima and Nagasaki were targeted— or, for that matter, the citizens of London and Shanghai. There is no evidence to suggest that the Americans would have foregone use of the atomic bomb on Germany had the weapon been ready before V-E Day. If Berlin or Bonn or Stuttgart had been the a-bomb's target, Groves could not have satisfied himself afterwards that Bataan had been avenged, but he might instead have mentioned Rotterdam, the Battle of the Bulge, or even Auschwitz, as he put aside all possible remorse. Or he and the others could have said that the atomic bomb had ended the European war more quickly and thus saved lives, American and enemy, as they would say about the atomic bombings of Japan. The war on both fronts had by 1945 reached a level of savagery that matched even the poison of anti-Asian racism.

A rather stronger case can be made for the American use of atomic bombs as a way of compelling the Soviets to behave more cooperatively in negotiations concerning especially Eastern and Central Europe, and as a way of ending the war quickly and thus foreclosing a major role for the Soviets in the occupation of Japan. The argument for 'atomic diplomacy', as this is called, has been made most forcefully down the years by Gar Alperovitz, though others have put forward their own versions of it. The case made by these 'revisionists' relies on establishing that Japan was militarily defeated by the summer of 1945, that the 'peace faction' of the Japanese government was assertively pursuing terms of surrender by then—chiefly a guarantee of the emperor—and that US policymakers *knew* that Japan was beaten *and* that the peace faction's exploration of terms had imperial backing, were specific and sincere, and thus worthy of taking seriously.

(This explains the revisionists' use of the 1963 Eisenhower quotation: 'It wasn't necessary to hit them with that awful thing.') The Americans also *knew* that a Soviet invasion of Manchuria and north China, promised by Stalin for August, would destroy what remained of Japan's will to fight on and in this way allow the Soviets to help shape the postwar Japanese political economy. Rather than permit this, and in the hopes of making the Russians more agreeable in negotiations elsewhere, the Americans dropped the atomic bombs, needlessly and perforce cruelly, on a prostrate nation.[57]

There is plenty of evidence that key US decisionmakers linked the bomb to their effort to intimidate the Soviet Union. Stimson, like Truman and Byrnes, thought of diplomacy as a poker game, in which the atomic bomb would prove part of 'a royal straight flush' or the 'master card', and in mid-May Stimson told Truman, regarding the proposed (and delayed) summit at Potsdam, that, when it finally convened, 'we shall probably hold more cards in our hands ... than now', meaning a successfully tested bomb. Byrnes was troubled at the thought of the Russians 'get[ting] in so much on the kill', as he put it. He told Navy Secretary James Forrestal that he 'was most anxious to get the Japanese affair over with before the Russians got in, with particular reference to Dairen and Port Arthur. Once in there, he felt, it would not be easy to get them out.' Byrnes later recalled wanting 'to get through with the Japanese phase of the war before the Russians came in'. He also assured Special Ambassador Joseph Davies at Potsdam 'that the atomic bomb assured ultimate success in negotiations' with the Russians, over German reparations and presumably other things. And Truman's sense of heightened confidence on learning of the Alamogordo test, his new assertiveness with Stalin, and his desire to rethink the matter of Soviet involvement in the war against Japan, all indicate the extent to which the bomb made an impression on the President and planted it firmly in the diplomatic realm.[58]

When they thought about the bomb, then, Truman and his advisers thought about what it might suggest for relations with the Soviets. But that does not mean that policymakers used the bombs primarily because they wished to manipulate the Russians. They did not know for certain that the Japanese were close to surrender before 6 August, that the addition to the battle of Soviet divisions, the withering American firebombings coupled with the strangling naval blockade, or even the threat of American invasion of the Japanese home islands, would bring speedy capitulation. They did want to end the Pacific War at the soonest possible moment, and one of the reasons they wished to do so was to keep Russian soldiers out of China and Soviet officials out of Japan once the war was over. All this was, however, best described, as Barton Bernstein has put it, as a 'bonus' added to the central reason why the Americans dropped the bombs. 'It seems likely', writes Michael Sherry, 'that even had Russian entry been greeted with open arms, rather than accepted as a painful aid and inevitability, the bomb would have been used on the same timetable.' As much as it mattered to US decisionmakers that the Russians be impressed and even cowed by the use of atomic bombs against cities, that the Russians become more tractable in negotiations, something else mattered more.[59]

What mattered more was the assumption, inherited by Truman from Roosevelt and never fundamentally questioned after 1942, that the atomic bomb was a weapon of war, built, at considerable expense, to be used against a fanatical Axis enemy. This was 'a foregone conclusion', as Leon Sigal has put it, 'unanimous' among those most intimately involved in wartime decisionmaking. 'As far as I was concerned,' wrote Groves, Truman's 'decision was one of non-interference—basically, a decision not to upset the existing plans.' Groves would subsequently liken Truman's role to that of 'a surgeon who comes in after the patient has been all opened up and the appendix is exposed and half cut off and he says, "yes I think he ought to have out the appendix—that's my decision".' A kind of bureaucratic momentum impelled the bomb forward, from imagining to designing to building and then to using. It would have taken a president far more confident, far less in awe of his office and his predecessor, to reflect on the matter of whether the atomic bomb should be used. Even then, it is difficult to picture how the momentum toward dropping the bomb would have been stopped. Truman and his advisers saw no reason not to drop the bomb.[60]

That they did not had to do with their self-deception—the bomb would be used only on a military target, Stimson and Truman assured themselves—and much to do with the belief, by now hardened into assumption, that non-combatants were unfortunate but nevertheless legitimate targets of bombs. From the first decision by an Italian pilot to aim recklessly at a Turkish camp in Africa, through the clumsy zeppelin bombings and British retaliation for them in the First World War, the 'air policing' of British colonies during the 1920s, and the ever more deadly and indiscriminate attacks by the Germans, Japanese, British, and Americans, ethical erosion had long collapsed the once-narrow ledge that had prevented men from plunging into the abyss of heinous conduct during war. Civilians could and would be killed by bombs. To shift the analogy slightly, and, as Richard Frank has written: 'The men who unanimously concurred with the description of the [atomic bombs'] target experienced no sensation that their choice vaulted over a great divide.' Indeed, their 'choice' was only which Japanese cities should be struck, not whether any of them should be. Once heralded as 'knights of the air', American pilots and their crews were now more often regarded as 'hooligans', or worse. Still, they were doing their nation's bidding: three days after Pearl Harbor, two-thirds of Americans polled said they supported the indiscriminate bombing of cities in Japan, a sentiment sustained throughout the war. There was equally little compunction about civilians in Germany, where estimates showed that by 1945 Allied bombers had killed between 300,000 and nearly twice that many. Psychologically, yes, there was something horribly different about the atomic bomb, a single bomb, with what Oppenheimer called its 'brilliant luminescence' and its capacity to create such destruction by itself. Functionally, it was merely another step on a continuum of increasingly awful weapons delivered by airplanes.[61]

US policymakers believed that killing Japanese as quickly and efficiently as possible would save American lives. They were never sure how many, of course. An invasion of Kyushu was scheduled for 1 November 1945. Policymakers estimated how many Americans might be wounded or die in the invasion by extrapolating from losses sustained during recent campaigns in the Philippines, Iwo Jima, and Okinawa. They concluded that US losses 'should not exceed the price we have paid for Luzon'—31,000 killed, wounded, and missing—during the first thirty days of the invasion of Kyushu. The figures were mentioned at the meeting between the Joint Chiefs, Stimson, Truman, and several others on 18 June 1945.

An acrimonious debate rages among historians over the extent to which policymakers made more precise estimates of possible American invasion casualties during the summer of 1945. In the end, it is unlikely that estimates, whatever they said and whoever made them, made much difference to Truman; he surely would be scornful of the debate over them were he alive now. For, if the President could save even a handful of American lives, he would not have hesitated to allow atomic bombs to be dropped on Japan. Intelligence indicated that Japanese plans for *Ketsu-Go*, the defence of the homeland, were well advanced by that summer. They included the use of as many suicide *kamikazes* in the first three hours of the invasion as had been deployed in Okinawa over three months. Two Japanese divisions and a smattering of other units had bled the Americans at Okinawa. Fourteen or more divisions, well dug into caves and bunkers, were expected to oppose the invaders on mountainous Kyushu. Near the end of the 18 June meeting, Truman told the Joint Chiefs to 'proceed with the Kyushu operation'—after saying, recall, that he 'hoped there was a possibility of preventing an Okinawa from one end of Japan to another'. Victory without an invasion at all remained a wish to be cherished.[62]

11. Alternatives to the atomic bombs, and moral objections to attacking civilians

None of this is to say that there were not, in some metahistorical sense, possible alternatives to using the atomic bombs. Barton Bernstein has laid them out and assessed their likely efficacy. There was the 'noncombat demonstration' of the bomb, endorsed in the Franck Report of June 1945 (unlikely, in Bernstein's view, to have achieved Japan's surrender). Alternative II was to modify or redefine the demand for unconditional surrender, as Grew and Stimson wanted to do, by guaranteeing the position of the emperor ('*quite unlikely*—but not impossible ... [to] have produced a Japanese surrender before 1 November on terms acceptable to the United States'). Another possibility was to follow up the Japanese 'peace feelers', extended by some Japanese officials through intermediaries in Switzerland that summer, and apparently indicating that peace might come about if (again) the United States offered to preserve the imperial system (only a 'slim hope' of success, in Bernstein's view). Alternative IV was to rely on Soviet intervention to push Tokyo to its breaking point—but no American decisionmaker believed Soviet entry alone would quickly finish the job, and none in any case desired it. A final option was to continue the bombing of Japan's cities and the naval blockade of the home islands. Bernstein thinks this alternative the most likely to have produced surrender by 1 November, the chances of success being 'maybe 25–30 percent'. Bernstein does say that some combination of these alternatives might 'very likely' have done the job. And yet, as Bernstein recognizes, his analysis is doubly counterfactual: one cannot know what the divided Japanese war cabinet would have done had the Americans pursued one or several of these courses instead of dropping the bombs, and, more significantly, it is difficult to imagine the Truman administration deciding to depart from the course established by Franklin Roosevelt's creation of the Manhattan Project in the first place. Why *not* drop the atomic bombs?[63]

There were a few men and women, at the time, who remonstrated against what was, after the Nazi genocide, the crucial moral enormity of the war: bombing civilians. The French philosopher Jacques Maritain made the utilitarian argument that attacking cities from the air increased popular anger and resistance and thus, immorally, prolonged the conflict. In March 1944 an obscure American religious magazine called *Fellowship* ran an article by the English pacifist Vera Brittain condemning urban bombing. Pacifists A. J. Muste and Mohandas Gandhi criticized the atomic bomb as the worst excess of a war they had opposed more generally. But the vast majority, of officials and citizens, military men and civilians, in the United States and everywhere else, had by 1945 undergone a profound eclipse of conscience. They knew that the atomic bombing was by itself unprecedentedly powerful, yet even after the Trinity test they could not imagine destruction and horror beyond what they had already witnessed, and perpetrated. Most did not accept Maritain's argument that mass bombing would prolong the war; instead they felt, as the air theorists had felt during the 1920s, that by increasing the horror they were shortening the war and therefore finally saving lives. Harry Truman was interested in saving American lives, and believed that by using the bomb he had done so. 'It was a terrible decision,' he wrote to his sister Mary. 'But I made it. And I made it to save 250,000 boys from the United States and I'd make it again under similar circumstances. It stopped the Jap war.' Six years after the bombing, Truman recalled for an interviewer that he had been told that the population of Hiroshima in 1945 was 60,000—an underestimate of some 200,000—and that he thought it 'far better to kill 60,000 Japanese than to have 250,000 Americans killed'. 'No one at the time regarded the bomb's use as an open question,' according to Michael Sherry. The atomic bomb may have been 'a transcendent form of power', but it would be 'conceived and used in the familiar ways'. Nor were the Americans alone in imagining without compunction the use of the weapon. 'Indeed,' writes Bernstein, 'it is difficult to believe that any major World War II nation that had the bomb would have chosen not to use it in 1945 against the enemy.' This is surely true. Had the British, Germans, Russians, or Japanese developed the bomb first—and that they did not had nothing to do with any ethical impediment to doing so—they would have dropped it on civilians with no more hesitation than the Americans showed.[64]

Like his boss, Truman aide George Elsey was interviewed years after the bombs had fallen and the war ended. Elsey understood that Truman had inherited the bomb from Roosevelt, and that the bomb had developed a logic and momentum of its own. 'Truman made no decision because there was no decision to be made,' Elsey said. 'He could no more have stopped it than a train moving down a track. It's all well and good to come along later and say the bomb was a horrible thing. The whole goddamn war was a horrible thing.'[65]

12. The threshold of horror: Poison gas

There remains one (at least) theoretical and historical problem to confront with respect to Elsey's argument that use of the bomb was foreordained, that it formed not a break but a continuum with the recent past practice of killing civilians from the air. In his June 1945 plea to arrange a non-combat demonstration of the bomb on a deserted island, James Franck pointed out that the American public, apparently, believed there *was* a threshold of horror beyond which certain weapons ought to be prohibited for use, even against an enemy widely regarded as subhuman. The American people, Franck insisted, drew the line at using poison gas in East Asia. This was true, 'even though gas warfare is in no way more "inhuman" than the war of bombs and bullets.' A few military officials and those in charge of the government's Chemical Warfare Services in fact urged that gas or other chemical or biological agents be used to rout the Japanese from their Pacific island strongholds or against the home islands. Following Iwo Jima, the CWS proposed to the Joint Chiefs the use of chemical weapons on Okinawa, but the matter ended there. The subsequent struggle made several of the generals reconsider. General Joseph W. Stilwell, who had fought the Japanese in China, wanted George Marshall to permit the use of chemicals should it come to an invasion of Japan, and General Douglas MacArthur and Brigadier General William A. Borden both offered qualified support for deploying poison gas. Marshall himself, a decent man who, it may be recalled, had private doubts about dropping atomic bombs, raised the subject on 29 May 1945, with Stimson and Assistant Secretary of War John J. McCloy. Shaken by the tenacity of Japanese units on Okinawa, the Chief of Staff suggested developing 'new weapons and tactics' to overcome the 'last ditch defense tactics of the Japanese'. Marshall proposed the use of mustard gas, the specter of Ypres in 1917. McCloy was willing to study the proposal, with an eye toward a public growing daily more alarmed at rising American casualties. Stimson could not stomach it. Neither could William Leahy, chairman of the Joint Chiefs and Truman adviser, who pointed out that Roosevelt had made public statements against the use of chemicals that were 'beyond the probability of change'. There is no evidence that Truman sympathized with one side or the other in this debate; in the event, the United States used no chemical or biological weapons against the Japanese.[66]

Why not? Why atomic bombs but no mustard gas? There are several reasons. First, the military branches regarded the use of chemical agents as unprofessional, even unsporting, in a way that dropping bombs or firing explosive shells was not. The Navy and Army Air Force especially also believed they might find themselves starved of their preferred weapons and resources should chemicals be authorized for use in island warfare. Institutional rivalry thus to some extent trumped a willingness to fight with absolutely no restraint. Second, and unlike atomic weapons, gas had a history of use in combat, and fairly or not a particularly ugly reputation among both military and civilian constituencies. The world had recoiled in revulsion when gas was used in the First World War; not only was American public opinion unreconciled to its use in 1945 but so was the international community, several of its European members having experienced the release of chemical agents first hand. If not absolute, prohibitions nevertheless existed on the use of gas, while no treaty or arrangements yet governed nuclear weapons. Finally, and most important, the resistance to using gas had much to do with the way in which gas killed. As noted earlier, death from explosion and fragment and fire—from outside in, as it were—was more readily countenanced than death by an insidious agent that might enter the body undetected and then kill from the inside out. Death by gas was a violation of the body, unfair in a way that bombing (bizarrely) was not. The difference was even partly aesthetic, with trauma by explosion held more bearable than an end brought on by slow suffocation. Small comfort, perhaps, but the general abdication of conscience undergone by the world's citizenry had not altogether eradicated its scruples concerning chemical and biological weapons.[67]

An odd coda: just after Harry Truman's final speech to the nation as president in mid-January 1953, Atomic Energy Commissioner Thomas Murray wrote seeking reassurance that Truman did not regard the use of atomic weapons as 'immoral'. Truman responded: 'I rather think you have put a wrong construction on my approach to the use of the Atomic bomb. It is far worse than gas and biological warfare because it affects the civilian population and murders them by the wholesale.'[68]

Carried by an aging and ill-fated cruiser called the *Indianapolis*, the carefully cosseted core of the world's first combat atomic bomb had arrived on Tinian on 26 July, the day of the Potsdam Declaration. It was joined to the rest of the bomb assembly on 1 August in an air-conditioned hut. When finished, Little Boy looked like . . . a bomb. It was 14 feet long, 5 feet in diameter, and it weighed approximately 10,000 pounds. Its proximity fuse, set for an altitude of about 1,800 feet, was designed to touch off a small explosion at the rear of the bomb, which would send a uranium bullet hurtling toward the bomb's nose. There it would collide with a 'cap' of fraternal U-235. If all went as planned, that would ignite an atomic explosion that would destroy the center of Hiroshima and transform the world.[69]

SIX

Japan: The Atomic Bombs
and War's End

There was a loud boom—of course there was. A 30,000-pound bomb had exploded less than a mile above the city. But what people in Hiroshima remembered most about the morning of 6 August was silence. A fisherman tending his nets on the Inland Sea, 20 miles from Hiroshima, heard a great explosion, but few in Hiroshima claimed later to have heard any noise at all. The silence that followed the bombing, with its blast and light and burning heat, was profound. 'The hurt ones were quiet,' wrote John Hersey, albeit in retrospect. 'No one wept, much less screamed in pain; no one complained; none of the many who died did so noisily; not even the children cried; very few people even spoke.' Dr Michihiko Hachiya, who was among the bombed that morning and worked heroically to treat the wounded, observed that 'one thing was common to everyone I saw—complete silence'. Kenzaburō Ōe was a boy on the quiet island of Shikoku in August 1945. He became a writer, and discovered the victims of Hiroshima in 1963. Ōe, too, found and recorded silences from that day: the silence of those with terrible injuries, of those who had suffered unimaginable loss, of those who 'raising both hands skyward and making soundless groans', jumped into the Ōta River 'as though competing with one another'—even the silence, jealously insisted upon, of those survivors who steadfastly refused to talk about their experiences that day, demanding silence as their right as victims.[1]

1. Japan in retreat

By August 1945 Japan's military position was parlous. Since the reversal at Midway Island in June 1942, victories had been few and short-lived, stalemates generally the best that could be hoped for, and defeats had come with greater frequency and often catastrophic results. The American and Allied conquests in the Pacific from late 1942 on—at Guadalcanal and New Guinea, Tinian and Saipan, the Philippines, Iwo Jima, and Okinawa—were, of course, devastating Japanese defeats. An old poem, set to music in 1937, began with the words 'Umi yukaba' (in English 'Across the sea'); Japanese soldiers said or sang it to their families before they left for the front. By 1943 it had become a melancholy phrase of parting, and it introduced radio descriptions 'of battles in which Japanese soldiers "met honorable death rather than the dishonor of surrender" '. In mid-1943 the American General Douglas MacArthur launched Operation Cartwheel against Japanese forces in New Guinea. Beaten by Australian units at the coast town of Finschhafen, the Japanese retreated (a 'fighting withdrawal', they called it) toward the interior of the island. The Japanese main force crossed a steep gorge and blew up the suspension bridge over it, stranding thousands of their straggling comrades. Masatsugu Ogawa was one of those left behind. He recalled men dying in droves, their corpses stinking in the hot sun, stripped of their useful gear by the living and covered by so many worms they looked silver from a distance. Ogawa prayed that his artillery, much reduced, would not fire at the enemy, for one Japanese shell inevitably attracted hundreds in return. Men lost their minds; Ogawa and his fellow soldiers shot them to put them out of their misery. Of the 7,000 soldiers assigned to Ogawa's 79th Regiment over the course of the campaign, 67 survived.[2]

Recognizing that Saipan would provide the Americans with airfields within a bomber's distance of Japan, Prime Minister Hideki Tōjō declared it 'an impregnable fortress' in the spring of 1944 and sent thousands of troops to reinforce it. Among them was Takeo Yamauchi, a Russian-language student and closet socialist who reluctantly accepted conscription and arrived at Saipan on 19 May. The Americans launched an air attack on 11 June and sent in the marines four days later. A squad leader, Yamauchi nevertheless had no appetite for battle, and when the armies clashed at close range he, along with several others, headed for the relative protection of the mountains to their rear. They encountered a fellow soldier from their squad, who started to tell them 'glorified stories of bravery'. Yamauchi told the man to shut up. He wandered the island for days, doing his best to avoid having to fight as men died around him. Overwhelmed, discouraged, and hungry, he surrendered to US forces on 14 July. He was unusual. The Japanese government later estimated that, of the 43,682 men sent to defend Saipan, 41,244 died, along with some 14,000 civilians. The fall of the 'impregnable fortress' brought down Tōjō's cabinet.[3]

Emperor Hirohito now ordered his armies to raise the cost of America's island campaigns, if nothing else buying time to prepare for the defense of the home islands. That is what General Tademichi Kurabayashi did on Iwo Jima in February and March 1945, sacrificing his entire force of 20,000 while inflicting heavy casualties (7,000 dead, up to 19,000 wounded) on the Americans. Okinawa came next. Kikako Miyagi was a 16-year-old schoolgirl when the land assault began on 1 April. Mobilized into the Himeyuri Student Corps (boys the same age entered the Blood and Iron Student Corps), Miyagi was pressed into service as a nurse in a cave at the south end of the island. The wounded started coming, 'thousands of them', she remembered, men a little older than herself with toes, arms, even faces missing. The older girls had the task of restraining men whose limbs were being amputated. The relative respite at night gave the girls a chance to carry corpses outside, where they threw them into shell craters. At the end of May they withdrew; the wounded were given cyanide, told to die gloriously, and left where they lay. Miyagi walked, staggered, crawled, trying to stay alive and avoid capture by the advancing American 'demons', whom she was sure would defile and kill her. Finally, on the first day of summer, she was captured, still gripping a grenade but too exhausted and frightened to pull the pin. She was well treated and later reunited with her parents.[4]

Those few who survived these terrible battles, including Ogawa, Yamauchi, and Miyagi, could not have been optimistic that Japan would hold out, and had seen enough of war to turn away from it in revulsion. Had they known the state of the Japanese atomic-bomb projects, NI and F, they would have been even more certain that the game was up. As noted in Chapter Three, the Japanese program had never flourished, despite the ingenuity of its leading scientist Yoshio Nishina, the respected 'Old Man' of Japanese physics. Short of money, short of uranium ore and the equipment needed to separate from it fissionable U-235, short of electricity and basic lab equipment, and short especially of confidence that a bomb was worth pursuing, scientists had let the two parallel projects languish. By the time the Americans had laid siege to Okinawa, Nishina's Riken Institute, in the Koishiwa District of Tokyo, had produced but a fleck of U-235. Then, on the night of 13 April, Curtis LeMay's bombers attacked. Nishina, along

with over 600,000 others, were burned out of their homes. Much of the
Riken was destroyed. At the end of the month, Nishina summoned to his
office Masashi Takeuchi, who had been in charge of uranium separation
despite being out of his depth. Takeuchi, said Nishina, had failed. He must
now resign. He did so the next day, and transferred to the Navy, where
he worked to improve radio communications. Nishina moved his family
to a Riken building the fires had spared and resumed desultory work on
fission. (When the Los Alamos theoretician Robert Serber visited Nishina
at the Riken several weeks after war had ended, he found that the remaining
scientists were growing vegetables on the grounds. 'They were just trying
to live,' Serber explained.)[5]

But the suffering of Japanese soldiers and civilians and the absence of an
atomic bomb were not enough, in the spring of 1945, to shake the cabinet's
resolve to fight on, if the alternative was unconditional surrender. That is
not to say that the Japanese leadership remained altogether insensitive to the
nation's declining military fortunes, nor that there was unanimity among
policymakers concerning the response to the decline. On 5 April, just days
after the Americans had landed on Okinawa, the cabinet of Prime Minister
Kuniaki Koiso fell, in part because of its inability to devise a plan to take the
country out of war. Koiso was replaced by Kantarō Suzuki, an aging admiral
whose wife had been the boy Hirohito's most influential nurse, and with
a reputation for loyalty to the emperor and battlefield bravery. Suzuki was
not himself committed to an early peace—indeed, he told associates that
he thought the war should continue for two or three more years—though
he was willing, or in any case found it necessary, to place in his cabinet
two men known to favor a settlement: as navy minister, Mitsumasa Yonai,
and as foreign minister, Shigenori Togo, who insisted that, as a condition of
their signing on, Suzuki authorize an honest investigation of Japan's military
and diplomatic situation. Suzuki also appointed, as army minister, General
Korechika Anami, who was known to be a hardliner on the war and who
extracted from Suzuki a promise to fight on until the war was won. Anami's
place in the cabinet guaranteed that the high-level struggle over the fate of
the fast-eroding empire was certain to continue.[6]

At least equally crucial in determining Tokyo's position toward Allied
surrender terms was the attitude of Emperor Hirohito. In the years following the end of the Pacific War, Americans and Japanese together promoted
the useful fiction that Hirohito had never been more than a figurehead,
a symbol of transcendent greatness to which the Japanese people might

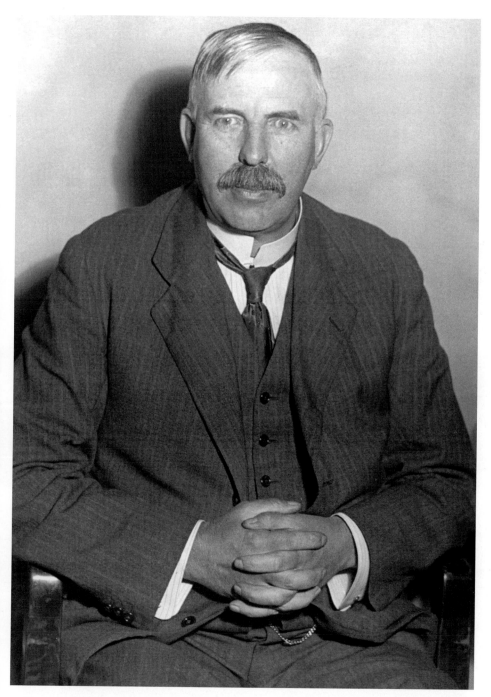

1. Ernest Rutherford: A New Zealander who came to the United Kingdom in 1895, Rutherford was one of the pioneers of modern nuclear physics. He found, contrary to his own expectations, that atoms were not stable but changeable, and that they packed enormous energy. If he and his colleagues weren't careful, he said, "some fool in a laboratory might blow up the universe unawares."

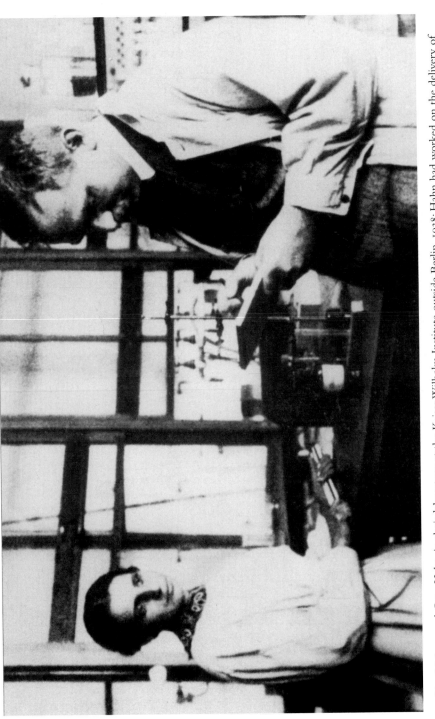

2. Lise Meitner and Otto Hahn, in their laboratory at the Kaiser Wilhelm Institute outside Berlin, 1938: Hahn had worked on the delivery of poison gas during World War I, though he later concluded that using a nuclear weapon would be "contrary to God's will." He and Meitner nevertheless are credited with the discovery of fission—the splitting of a nucleus that results in the release of a great deal of energy, among other things.

3. Ernest Lawrence, Enrico Fermi, and Isidor Rabi: Three physicists who played important roles in the development of the first nuclear weapons. Lawrence built, first at the University of California, great machines that produced enriched uranium; the Italian Fermi, having fled Europe following the rise of Adolf Hitler, assembled the world's first nuclear reactor, which went critical in Chicago in late 1942; Rabi, who had serious misgivings about the atomic bomb, nevertheless served as a "senior consultant" at Los Alamos, New Mexico, the bomb's birthplace.

4. A US government propaganda poster, "Lookout Monks!": Throughout the war, the British and American governments encouraged citizens to imagine the destruction of Germany and Japan by bombers. This poster offered simian depictions of Hitler himself and a generic Japanese, suggesting that, while both enemies were less than human, it remained possible to distinguish between good Germans and bad ones, while all Japanese were similarly loathsome. Such distinctions did not, however, prevent the bombing of both German and Japanese cities.

5. Johann Strasse, central Dresden, 1945: American and British air forces bombed the German city of Dresden on the night of 14–15 February, 1945. While not without military targets, Dresden was also an undefended city of gracious old buildings and a large number of refugees. The attack brought criticism at the time and has done so since. Bombing non-combatants was a well established practice by the time the atomic bombs were dropped later that year.

6. Yoshio Nishina: Trained by Ernest Rutherford, Nishina was Japan's leading physicist during the Second World War. Pictured here is the cyclotron he built at Tokyo's Riken Laboratory. Japan did not come close to developing an atomic bomb—Nishina doubted it could be done, Japan lacked uranium, and resources for the project were scarce— but after the war the Americans destroyed the cyclotron anyway. Having visited Hiroshima and Nagasaki soon after they were bombed, Nishina died of cancer in 1951.

7. Leslie Groves and J. Robert Oppenheimer: Groves was made a general and put in charge of the top-secret Manhattan Project in September 1942. He was brusque, secretive, and, as it turned out, very good at getting scientists, engineers, laborers, and military officials to work together to build nuclear bombs. Oppenheimer was a sensitive soul and a brilliant theoretician who coordinated the scientific effort for Groves. "Bambi meets Godzilla," someone described the pair. But theirs was an effective partnership.

8. The Americans destroy a German "uranium burner": The Germans had sophisticated nuclear physicists during World War II, and the Allies feared the Germans would beat them to the bomb. Hitler's mistrust of physics as "Jewish science" and several miscalculations by leading physicists, including especially Werner Heisenberg, in fact prevented substantial progress, as the Allies discovered to their relief in early 1945.

9. The Japanese emperor, Hirohito, walks through Tokyo neighborhoods wrecked by American bombs: During the spring of 1945, and most famously or notoriously on the night of March 9–10, American bombers struck the Japanese capital with incendiaries, burning several parts of the city nearly beyond recognition and killing many thousands. Hirohito, whose palace was spared, toured the ruins, eliciting, according to observers, the quiet anger of shell-shocked residents.

10. Unloading the plutonium core of the Trinity test gadget, July 1945: It was about two hundred miles from Los Alamos, where the bomb and its core were developed, to the test site near Alamogordo. The core was boxed and driven carefully to the Trinity site on July 12, "in the backseat of an Army sedan," Richard Rhodes has written, "like a distinguished visitor." The successful test shot took place at dawn on July 16.

11. The "Big Three" at Potsdam, July 1945: The Soviet Union's Josef Stalin, US President Harry S. Truman, and British Prime Minister Winston Churchill came together at Potsdam, in defeated Germany, to discuss the end of the war with Japan and the shape of the postwar world. Truman learned soon after arriving that the Trinity shot had succeeded. He told Churchill as much; to Stalin, he reported that the United States had a powerful new weapon. Espionage and logical deduction assured that Stalin knew what Truman meant.

12. Ruined Hiroshima: The atomic bomb codenamed "Little Boy" struck near the heart of Hiroshima on 6 August 1945. A man stands amid the wreckage, staring at one of the few structures remaining near the hypocenter: the Hiroshima Prefectural Industrial Promotion Hall, built three decades earlier. The building looks today much as it did following the bombing, and is meant to be a symbol of peace.

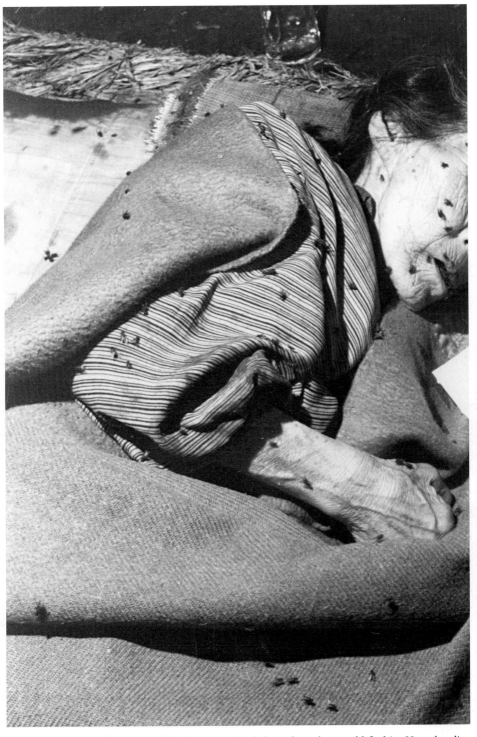

13. The bombed, 1: The living in Hiroshima sought shelter where they could find it. Here they lie in the city's main train station.

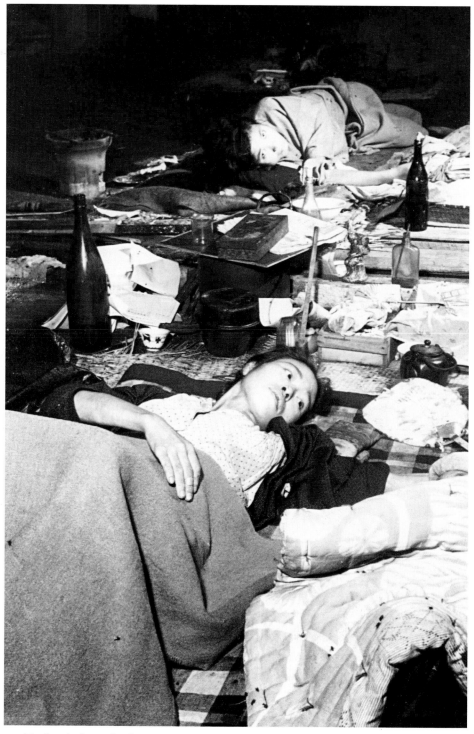

14. The bombed, 2: A family at a makeshift hospital ward. The city had forty-seven hospitals; only three were sufficiently undamaged after the bombing to be able to accept patients.

15. Standing at attention: The American Marine Corps photographer Joe O'Donnell took this picture in September 1945 in Nagasaki, struck by an atomic bomb on 9 August. A boy stands erect, having done his duty by bringing his dead brother to a cremation ground. "I wanted to go to him to comfort him," O'Donnell later wrote, "but I was afraid that if I did so, his strength would crumble."

16. No handshake for a hated enemy: The Americans ordered the Japanese to send a surrender delegation to Manila. Fifteen men, led by General Torashiro Kawabe, arrived at Nichols Field from Tokyo on 19 August. Kawabe extended his hand to Colonel Sidney F. Mashbir, who refused to take it, merely gesturing with his thumb toward a line of cars that would take the envoys to US headquarters. There waited General Douglas MacArthur with surrender terms.

17. Yuli Khariton and Igor Kurchatov: The two physicists most responsible for the creation of the Soviet atomic bomb program in the 1940s. Both were well treated by a grateful Josef Stalin, as the table setting here suggests.

18. The Indian reactor at Trombay: The CIRUS reactor, built with Canadian help and supplied with moderating heavy water by the United States, came online in 1960. The Indians had assured their benefactors that they sought nuclear power only for peaceful purposes, but they would soon derive weapons-grade plutonium from the reactor's fuel rods.

rally, but someone detached from the messy and controversial details of day-to-day decisionmaking. The fiction of imperial detachment was useful to Hirohito himself and to his advisers, who naturally wished to keep the Emperor free of stain from the failed war and preserve his reputation and influence once the conflict had ended. It was useful as well to General Douglas MacArthur and other architects of the American occupation of Japan, because the Emperor offered a stable (and conservative) touchstone for Japanese society, and not incidentally a powerful, anti-communist presence in Japanese politics after 1945. The historian Herbert Bix has in recent years forcefully corrected the impression of Hirohito as a passive monarch. In fact, argues Bix, the Emperor was energetically engaged in wartime policymaking. Hirohito 'gradually became a real war leader,' writes Bix, 'influencing the planning, strategy, and conduct of operations in China and participating in the appointment and promotion of the highest generals and admirals.' He was aware of the situation on the battlefield and, guided by his leading adviser, Lord Keeper of the Privy Seal Marquis Koichi Kido, made vital interventions in policy decisions at the top level, including those involving the termination of the war. Hirohito was neither prime minister nor commander-in-chief. But he did make the decision to go to war with the United States by attacking Pearl Harbor in later 1941, and on the day itself Hirohito dressed in his naval uniform and, according to Bix, 'seemed to be in a splendid mood'.[7]

Even after touring his ravaged capital following the American incendiary attack of 9–10 March 1945, Hirohito seems to have believed that his people's morale was holding up and that a final battle for the homeland was a reasonable prospect. His falling-out with Prime Minster Koiso and his choice of Suzuki to replace him reflected a desire to fight on; as he took office, Suzuki told an interviewer that he remained confident of victory. But by June the tide had shifted. Defeat on Okinawa, no matter how costly to the Americans, was a devastating blow to the leadership. Even before its magnitude became clear, the unconditional surrender of Japan's German ally had dampened spirits considerably. Along with leaving Japan to face the United States alone, it also raised the distressing possibility that the Soviet Union would abrogate its April 1941 Neutrality Pact with Japan, even though it had another year to run. Several Japanese leaders suspected that the Soviets had agreed, at Yalta in February, to enter the war against Japan in exchange for Asian territorial concessions made by Roosevelt and Churchill. (They were right.) On 5 April the Soviet foreign minister, Vyacheslav Molotov, called in the Japanese ambassador to Moscow, Naotake Sato, and informed him that the Soviet Union was renouncing the Neutrality Pact. The situation had changed since 1941, Molotov declared: Russia was now allied with the United States and Britain, against whom the Japanese were fighting. Sato remonstrated, to the extent of getting Molotov to agree, with great reluctance, that the Pact would remain in force through the end of its term in 1946. This concession would require what Stalin called 'strategic deception', since the Soviets were already mobilizing to attack Japanese forces in China.[8]

The Soviet decision to abandon the Neutrality Pact, in a year's time or immediately, came as a blow to the Japanese leadership's wishful thinkers, who had previously imagined that their nation could, by concentrating solely on defending the home islands against the Americans, wear the enemy down and win improved surrender terms. Soviet involvement against them meant disaster. The new situation encouraged the quickening of 'peace feelers' undertaken by an assortment of Japanese officials in a variety of European capitals. (Since the Americans had cracked Japanese codes and the Japanese knew it, 'secret' discussions with European diplomats were intended for American ears.) Foreign Minister Togo directed Ambassador Sato to try to persuade the Russians to stay out of the war, then went behind Sato's back to instigate private discussions between the Soviet ambassador in Tokyo Iakov Malik and former prime minister Koki Hirota, with an eye toward possible Soviet mediation. Japanese representatives in Stockholm, Bern, and at the Vatican attempted to pursue with diplomatic counterparts the definition of unconditional surrender. None of these efforts bore fruit. Stalin was by now bent on war with Japan as soon as his armies were ready and satisfactory arrangements made with the Chinese. The multisplendored peace feelers spread throughout Western Europe were never authorized by the cabinet or the Emperor and were renounced when discovered.[9]

The 'peace faction' did assert itself more and more as summer arrived. Talks with the Russians grew frantic; even as Stalin, through Molotov, put Sato off, the Emperor himself decided that Soviet mediation was essential and dispatched to Moscow Fumimaro Konoe, the respected former prime minister whose advisers and friends had been drafting position papers calling for significant Japanese concessions. By late June, Tsuyoshi Hasegawa has written, Japan had reached 'the crucial moment when Hirohito became actively involved in the effort to terminate the war'. The Emperor was deeply worried about the preservation of the 'national polity', or *kokutai*, meaning largely his own position in postwar Japan. The nation experienced a flurry of acts of *lèse majesté*, ongoing since the beginning of the war but increasingly troubling to the authorities by 1945. A Home Ministry report noted then that 'antiwar thoughts and feelings finally have come to the point where they even curse and bear resentment against His Majesty'. Hirohito was derided, in letters, comments, and graffiti, as a 'fool' (*baka*), 'stupid fool' (*bakayarō*), and 'big stupid fool' (*daibakayarō*), or even 'Little Emperor'. When Hirohito toured Tokyo following the first great B-29 raid in March, he claimed to find no diminution of popular morale. But an aide had noticed that the vacant expressions of those picking through the rubble 'became reproachful as the imperial motorcade went by . . . Were they resentful of the emperor because they had lost their relatives, their houses and their belongings?' That he felt compelled to ask the question was itself significant.[10]

And yet, despite a certain degree of realism about Japan's situation, a growing understanding that the Soviets were no friends and the Americans unyielding in their demand for unconditional surrender, the cabinet, as a group, would not let go its insistence on negotiating terms for the nation's capitulation. While Hirohito (in mid-June), his advisers, and key members of the cabinet sought Soviet help to bring the war to an end, they were not prepared during June and July to accept the American conditions for doing so. From Moscow, Sato, ever the realist, implored his superiors 'to make the great decision' to surrender unconditionally. 'If the Japanese Empire is really faced with the necessity of terminating the war,' he wrote to Togo on 12 July, 'we must first of all make up our own minds to terminate the war.' 'I send this telegram,' Sato finished, 'in the belief that [it] is my first responsibility to prevent the harboring of illusions which are at variance with reality.' Togo replied five days later. After reminding Sato that the Emperor himself sought Soviet mediation, he added: 'Please bear particularly in mind, however, that we are not seeking the Russians' mediation for anything like an unconditional surrender,' which remained unacceptable. Indeed, not even the 'peace faction' could agree on what concessions to make. Sato wrote back on the 19th, charging that officials in Tokyo were 'out of touch with the atmosphere prevailing here'. Nevertheless, Togo responded on the 21st: 'With regard to unconditional surrender we are unable to consent to it under any circumstances whatever. Even if the war drags on and it becomes clear that it will take much more than bloodshed, the whole country as one man will pit itself against the enemy in accordance with the Imperial Will.' The Americans read these exchanges. President Truman, meanwhile, was now at Potsdam, and he had learned on 16 July that the atomic bomb had been successfully tested.[11]

Postwar critics of the US decision to drop the atomic bombs charged, among other things, that Japanese peace feelers were genuine in the summer of 1945, that Hirohito urgently sought to end the war as long as his position was guaranteed, and that he could and would have pulled the cabinet with him to surrender if the Americans had offered him assurances much like those belatedly provided after the a-bombs had fallen and the Russians had entered the war. That is possible—it is difficult, after all, to predict the emotional and psychological impact such a concession would have had on the Emperor and those advising him—but the evidence suggests it is unlikely. For one thing, while the peace faction was riven with disagreement over what conditions should be attached to Japan's concession, the influential hardliners, including General Anami, Yoshijiro Umezu, and Soemu Toyoda, were united in their determination to prevent capitulation and to fight to the end. (Premier Suzuki waffled between the groups.) The final condition—the guarantee of the emperor—emerged as an option by itself only after the bombs had been dropped; previously it was accompanied by others, including an American promise not to occupy Japan, which was clearly unacceptable to Washington. There remained in Tokyo, despite Sato's forceful missives from Moscow, fond hope that the Russians might take a hand in negotiations, and might at least refrain from attacking Japan. The Americans listening to the decoded intercepts of Japanese correspondence concerning terms thus heard not a clear, single message but a cacophony of voices, clashing and confusing, insusceptible to careful reading of a sort the Americans were disinclined to do anyway.

2. Preparing to fight the invaders

Above all, and as the Americans also knew, while various Japanese experimented with peace feelers through third countries, the Japanese military moved forward resolutely with plans for a final, all-out battle to defend the home islands. The defence plan was called 'Ketsu-go', or 'Decisive Operation'. Adopted by Imperial General Headquarters in March 1945,

Ketsu-go correctly anticipated that the Americans planned to invade the southern island of Kyushu and the Kanto Plain surrounding Tokyo. Military coordinators of the plan decided, first, to allow the Americans a beachhead on Kyushu—there seemed little choice, given US firepower as exhibited elsewhere in the Pacific—then to concentrate forces and lacerate the enemy before they could regroup and move inland. Second, the Japanese would use *tokkō*, suicide attacks by planes, human torpedoes, and other devices manned by those willing to give up their lives to protect the homeland. Finally, planners envisioned full-scale mobilization of the population to attack the Americans with homemade weapons—pitchforks, shovels, improvised explosives, and whatever else came to hand. Over two dozen divisions of Japanese troops would deploy to southern Kyushu, there to await the invader. *Kamikaze* would take to the sky. Local civilians would help build roads, unload trucks, and torment the invaders with guerrilla tactics. Assistance would come also in the form of Kyushu's topography, jagged and forbidding; the beaches gave way to high bluffs that would be difficult for the Americans to negotiate. Japanese commanders reminded their troops that twice in the thirteenth century invading Mongol armies had been wrecked at Kyushu—the second time by a providential typhoon the Japanese had christened 'Divine Wind', or *Kamikaze*.[12]

The American plan for invading Japan was drawn up in later May 1945. Called 'Downfall', it envisioned an attack on Kyushu beginning on 1 November ('Olympic'), then an assault on the Kanto Plain ('Coronet') starting on 1 March 1946. The American planners, principally the Joint Chiefs of Staff and theater commander MacArthur, underestimated the number of divisions the Japanese intended to shift to southern Kyushu. But they knew the attack would be sharply contested. US intelligence that summer detected strenuous efforts by the Japanese to build artillery emplacements and to mine the land just beyond the beaches. In a move that was reminiscent of Okinawa, the Japanese were preparing cave defenses on the bluffs. The Americans worried that the limited number and poor quality of roads in the area would slow the invasion's progress. And they took seriously statements duly recorded from Japanese government and media sources: the morale of the people was high, and—as on Okinawa—they would gladly fight to the death rather than surrender. The Japanese suspected that killing a large number of Americans in Kyushu's interior would so alarm American public opinion that the US government would

be forced to come to terms well short of its tiresome demand for unconditional surrender.[13]

What worried US planners most was their perception that the Japanese
would do anything to defend their homeland, that the fighting during
'Downfall' would be more brutal on a massive scale than anything American troops had encountered thus far. They knew about Iwo and Okinawa,
of course, and judged the merciless defense of those islands a logical extension of Japanese atrocities proved or rumored to have occurred previously
elsewhere. The 'Rape of Nanking' in December 1937 was reported to
have produced between 10,000 and 20,000 Chinese dead within its first
few days—figures later revealed to have been too small by a factor of
ten. Japanese soldiers raped Chinese and Korean women and forced them
into prostitution on a scale as incomprehensible as it was appalling. Even
before the Westerners had engaged in indiscriminate bombing of cities,
the Japanese had rehearsed such a strategy against the Chinese war capital
of Chungking, killing an estimated 5,000 civilians. Less well known, but
even more heinous, was the use of poison gas, produced on the island of
Okunoshima near Hiroshima, against the Chinese fighting in the mountains of Shanxi, and bacteriological agents, employed in Manchuria by the
notorious Unit 731. The Japanese also launched over 9,000 'balloon bombs'
from Honshu into the Pacific jet stream in late 1944 and early 1945. Bearing
antipersonnel and twin incendiary bombs, a handful of these odd weapons
reached the northwestern United States and caused several casualties, and
served further to remind Americans, if further reminder was needed, of
Japanese ingenuity and nefariousness.[14]

Most of all, the Americans feared Japanese suicide attacks. In the fullness
of time, it is clear that these tactics were far more costly to the Japanese than
to the Americans they targeted. Saburō Ienaga has estimated that 'no more
than 1 to 3 percent of the suicide pilots actually hit Allied warships', and
various other macabre devices—the ōka (Cherry Blossom) 'flying bomb',
the shinyō plywood motorboats with high explosives strapped to their bows,
and the submarine kaiten human torpedo—proved even more unreliable,
except as death traps for those driving them. Yet these statistics were not
clear at the time. The tokkō weapons terrified the Americans, and the threat
of their lavish use in Ketsu-go deeply concerned them. Certainly there was
commitment to these weapons on the part of their operators. Yokota Yutaka
was a kaiten pilot whose missions were scrubbed because of malfunction
or an absence of enemy targets. Ashamed of what he considered his own

failure to fulfill his destiny, he was miserable (and disbelieving) when he heard the war had ended. His comrades had died, not him. 'Tears sprang to my eyes,' he remembered. 'I cried bitterly. "I'll never launch! The war is over..."' During Ketsu-go Japanese command planned to target troop transports, slow, unarmed, and thus more vulnerable than warships. *Shinyō* would strike the anchored ships at night; *kaiten* would be deployed at close range; 'Crouching Dragons' *(fukuryō),* frogmen, submerged and holding mines at the ends of wooden poles, would ram US landing craft in the shallows off Kyushu. Five thousand *kamikaze* would strike during the first ten days of 'Olympic.'[15]

Such carnage as 'Downfall' would bring—10,000? 50,000? No one knew, and the guess hardly mattered—*might* be avoided altogether if atomic bombs were dropped on Japan, accompanied or not by Soviet entry into the war. 'Think of the kids who won't get killed,' Truman wrote to his wife, Bess, on 18 July, having heard about the Trinity test and having got Stalin's agreement to enter the war. On the same day, he wrote in his diary: 'Believe Japs will fold up before Russia comes in. I am sure they will when Manhattan appears over their homeland.' The uranium core of the Little Boy bomb was by then en route to Tinian. It arrived on the 26th. (Norman Ramsey, the chief scientist on the island, estimated the value of the uranium and accordingly signed a receipt for it, later wondering, with chagrin and amusement, how the government might dock his pay half a billion dollars if anything went wrong.)[16]

3. Preparing to drop Little Boy

The nuclear element of the bomb came into the hands of the 393rd Bombardment Squadron, the business end of the 509th Composite Group, which included support personnel for the 393rd's pilots. The 509th had been constituted the previous October at Wendover Field, Utah, on the edge of the great salt flats that had long discouraged travelers to the American west but now provided a practice range for the unit's fliers. The group was commanded by Paul W. Tibbets, a 29-year-old lieutenant colonel who had extensive experience as a bomber pilot in Europe. When given his command, Tibbets had been told about the Manhattan Project, the offspring of which might win the war. He would be given the best pilots and crews, the new, state-of-the-art B-29 bomber (which would arrive in

Utah that December), and access to whatever resources he needed to make
his group work, though he was not to tell his men what kind of weapon
they would be carrying. Tibbets would build the 509th to a strength of
1,800, 117 of whom were formed into thirteen B-29 crews and trained,
unwittingly, to drop atomic bombs. They practiced over Utah, Nevada,
and California through the winter of 1944–5. In clear daylight, they flew
to 30,000 feet, took aim at circular targets inscribed for them on the desert
floor or at a white raft in California's Salton Sea, and released monstrously
heavy bombs made of concrete and with high explosives lodged in their
noses. These were painted orange and thus christened 'pumpkins'. Tibbets
instructed his men to turn sharply, at 155 degrees, just after they had released
their pumpkins, and to fly away quickly once they had made their drops.
In their off hours men blew off steam over the border in Nevada casinos,
but they were closely monitored by security police. No one was to talk
about what they were doing or the size or shape of the pumpkins. Trans-
gressors were banished to a base in the Aleutian Islands for the rest of the
war.[17]

Through the spring, as firebombs devastated Tokyo and officials chose
other Japanese cities to be spared temporarily for subsequent atomic bombings, Tibbets continued to drill his fliers. He sent a group to Batista Field
in Cuba, whence they practiced carrying heavy loads for distance over
water, dropping 10,000-pound bombs accurately from high altitude, then
returning to base with a limited supply of fuel. Tinian's airbase, already
home to B-29s flying missions over Japan, began receiving elements of the
509th late in the spring; Tibbets and his pilots and crews arrived on 15
June. There they practiced some more, dropping pumpkins on Japanese
targets in the Marianas and Carolines through mid-July, then dropping
the bombs on cities in Japan starting on the 19th. Curtis LeMay himself
approved each mission; Tibbets was withheld from all of them. (The 393rd
ultimately conducted thirteen pumpkin attacks on Japan, with the final
mission numbered 14, reserving lucky 13 for Hiroshima.) Command hoped
not only to prepare its crews for the a-bomb runs, but to lull the Japanese
into thinking that attacks by single B-29s failed to amount to much and
were hardly worth opposing. 'The pumpkins were respectable bombs,'
recalled an engineer for the 509th, though not worth Japan's trouble of
sending up scarce fighter planes or even sounding citywide alarms. Apart
from these raids, 509th crews appeared mostly to sit in their mysteriously
well-guarded compound while men in other units took on duties far

more frequently and at greater risk. The 509th huts were thus on the receiving end of rocks tossed resentfully over the barbed-wire perimeter. The men grinned and bore it and even named their well-used movie theater 'The Pumpkin Playhouse'. They still did not know why they were there.[18]

They finished assembling Little Boy on the last day of July. Brigadier General Thomas Farrell, on Tinian as Groves's deputy, wired his boss that the bomb could be dropped as early as the next day. But the weather looked bad, and there was a bit more to do. On 2 August, Tibbets, with his bombardier Thomas Ferebee, met LeMay at the general's headquarters on Guam. LeMay confirmed what they had long discussed: Little Boy's target was Hiroshima, a southern port city on Japan's Inland Sea. LeMay had a recent reconnaissance map of the city, and he asked Ferebee to choose an aiming point. Ferebee quickly spotted the Aioi Bridge, a distinctive T-shaped structure that spanned the Ōta River close to the center of the city; the others approved. Seven B-29s would take part in the mission: three would fly ahead, over Hiroshima and the alternative targets of Kokura and Nagasaki (the latter a fresh addition to the targets' list), to check on the weather; another would be flown to Iwo Jima, where it would serve as a backup carrier for Little Boy if something went wrong with the bomb-bearing plane in flight; and two more—Charles Sweeney's *Great Artiste* and George Marquardt's prosaically named *No. 91*—would accompany the atomic bomber, carrying blast measurement instruments and cameras respectively. The seventh B-29 would be piloted by Tibbets himself. It had never been named.

Back on Tinian on Saturday 4 August, Tibbets summoned the crews of the mission bombers to the unit's briefing hut. He had two officers pull aside drapes to reveal blackboard-mounted maps of the three target cities. He then stepped aside for William 'Deke' Parsons, head of the Manhattan Project's Ordnance Division, who was instrumental in developing the uranium gun at the heart of Little Boy and who would arm the bomb on mission day and fly with Tibbets. Parsons had brought with him a film clip of the Trinity test and started to screen it for the men, but the projector jammed irretrievably—whereupon Parsons described the blast from mem-ory. He never used the words 'atomic' or 'nuclear', but he warned the pilots against straying too close to the mushroom cloud the anticipated explosion would generate. They could not know for certain what would happen, Parsons concluded, but the consequences of a successful drop were likely to be enormous. Tibbets then finished the session with reminders about routes and timings and reassurances concerning rescue should any of the planes be forced down over water. He told the crewmen not to say anything about the mission, in letters home or on base. He ended with a pep talk—and the declaration that the bomb 'would shorten the war by at least six months'. Thus sobered, and encouraged, the men shuffled off to contemplate their course. Tibbets then took his crew for a final rehearsal over Tinian. He flew straight and level and Ferebee released a pumpkin over the sea. It all checked out.

4. Mission No. 13

On the following day, having scanned the weather forecast, LeMay gave the word: the mission was on for the 6th. Little Boy was taken from the 509's air-conditioned assembly hut and pulled gently, by a tractor, to a pit on the runway. Several of the men had written messages on the bomb with crayons. Some were obscene missives for the Japanese, but Major John E. Moynihan, the public-relations officer for the mission, wrote, 'No white cross for Stevie'—his young son at home. The bomb was loaded into the pit, and the annointed bomber, *No. 82*, was towed over it. The bomb was winched into the plane's forward bomb bay and secured with a central shackle and several braces. The loading went smoothly. Meanwhile, Tibbets had decided his plane needed a name. He summoned from a base softball game a sign painter and instructed that 'Enola Gay', his mother's first and middle names, be painted on the fuselage. The bomber's usual pilot, Robert Lewis, was unhappy to discover the change, but Tibbets was now in charge and anyway the paint had already dried. Lewis would serve as Tibbets's co-pilot on the run to Hiroshima.

The plan called for Deke Parsons to ready the bomb while the plane remained on the ground, inserting into its rear end the explosive and the detonator that, once activated, would fire it off, sending the uranium bullet home. Parsons had wanted to perform this operation once the plane was in flight, but Groves, worried about turbulence and the tiny space in which Parsons would have to work, said no. Parsons had accepted the verdict—until he saw the alarming rate at which B-29s taking off from Tinian's Runway A, the one to be used by the *Enola Gay*, had crashed short of liftoff. A crash with a nuclear bomb on board might obliterate Tinian. Now he confided in Farrell: he would do the final bit of assembly only after the plane was airborne. Farrell cautiously consented, and Parsons folded himself into the tiny space behind Little Boy and practiced inserting the charge until his hands bled. Farrell offered Parsons a pair of gloves, but Parsons refused; 'I've got to feel the touch,' he said. By the time Farrell did his duty and cabled Groves about the important change in procedure, there was nothing Groves could do but ratchet up an already serious case of nerves.

They would take off at 2.30 the next morning, 6 August. Men tried to sleep but mostly failed. The final briefing came at midnight, where Tibbets blandly repeated his description of the bomb they carried as 'very powerful', and the Lutheran chaplain on base prayed with the crew that 'they bring this war to a rapid end'. The men had an early breakfast of eggs, sausage, and pineapple fritters, a favorite of Tibbets. They were driven to their B-29s at 2.00 and arrived to a cacophony of sound and harsh lights worthy of a Hollywood movie set (thought an unhappy Tibbets) or, as someone else put it, 'a drugstore opening'. Photographs were taken of the *Enola Gay*'s crew, after which they climbed into their plane. The men all had pistols, and Tibbets secretly carried a metal box holding twelve cyanide capsules; if the plane went down over Japan, any crewman left alive would choose suicide by self-inflicted bullet or self-administered poison. 'Let's go,' said Tibbets at 2.45, and he throttled his plane forward. It was heavy, some 15,000 pounds over spec with its weighty bomb and extra fuel, and Tibbets badly frightened co-pilot Lewis by using nearly all of Runway A to gain speed. At what seemed the last second Tibbets lifted the plane's nose, and the *Enola Gay* rose over the night sea, flying northwest at low altitude to save fuel and ease the task of Parsons, squatting behind the bomb in the unpressurized bomb bay.

Parsons inserted cordite charges into Little Boy's back end, but he left a key circuit undone so the bomb was not yet armed. Tibbets tried to sleep, failed, and chose instead to disclose at last the full truth about their payload. The sky grew lighter, indicating fair weather ahead. Just before 6.00 (5.00 in Japan) they reached Iwo Jima, where Tibbets climbed to 9,000 feet and rendezvoused with the *Great Artiste* and *No. 91*, the instrument and photo planes. Parsons and his fellow weaponeer Morris Jeppson finished arming the bomb. 'It won't be long now,' said Tibbets over the intercom. The *Straight Flush*, the B-29 that overflew Hiroshima, sent word that the skies over the primary target were largely clear, so Tibbets committed to his course and brought his plane to bombing altitude, 31,000 feet. The crew, though not their pilots, put on flak suits, and all drew on smoked-glass goggles to protect their eyes from they knew not what. Bombardier Ferebee spotted the target and took charge of the *Enola Gay*'s course for the bombing run. The other two planes slowed and let the *Enola Gay* run to the target alone. Ferebee saw the Aioi Bridge. 'I've got it,' he called. Then, just after 8.15 Hiroshima time, the bomb-bay doors opened and the bomb tumbled out. Ferebee later said he could see it turn its nose to the ground, as it was supposed to. Free of its load, the *Enola Gay* leaped up. Tibbets's months of training took over, and he dived and sheared off, speeding frantically away from the blast area. The bomb's proximity fuse was set for roughly 1,850 feet above the ground, which meant that the bomb should explode 43 seconds after it had left the bomb bay. Jeppson was counting it down. He got to 43—nothing. 'It's a dud,' he thought. Then an intense light lit the plane, followed by a powerful jolt. It felt, recalled the navigator, Dutch Van Kirk, as though he had been sitting on a metal garbage can that someone had hit with a baseball bat. Tibbets first thought it was flak. Then came a second blast wave, and the pilot calmed down; he knew what it was, and that there would be no more.

They saw the fireball, then the mushroom cloud that Parsons had told them about during the briefing ages before. 'The city was hidden by that awful cloud,' Tibbets wrote later, 'boiling up, mushrooming, terrible and incredibly tall.' 'A column of smoke is rising fast,' said the tailgunner, Robert Caron, into a voice recorder. 'It has a fiery red core . . . Fires are springing up everywhere . . . there are too many to count.' Tibbets radioed Tinian that the bomb had produced 'good results', which staggered Deke Parsons: ' "Good"? Hell, what did he expect?' On his own, he wired Farrell that the visual effect of the bombing had been 'greater than [at] Alamogordo'. Jake Beser, in charge of preventing Japanese jamming of the mission's communications, likened the sight to sand stirred in shallow water at the beach; Robert Lewis thought the cloud resembled 'a pot of boiling black oil'. Lewis gave silent thanks that his war would soon be over, but the displaced pilot of *No. 82* had other thoughts too: 'My God,' he wrote in his journal, 'what have we done?' 'If I live a hundred years,' he added, 'I'll never quite get these few minutes out of my mind.'[19]

The *Enola Gay* and its escort planes headed for home. They lost sight of the mushroom cloud only after 363 nautical miles. Many of the men on Tibbets's plane now slept, exhausted. Aboard the *Great Artiste*, the physicist Luis Alvarez, who had monitored the blast in part by dropping instrument-bearing parachutes simultaneously with Little Boy, grew pensive, and decided to write his 'first grown-up letter' to his 4-year-old son, Walter. 'What regrets I have about being a party to killing and maiming thousands of Japanese civilians this morning', he wrote, 'are tempered with the hope that this terrible weapon we have created may bring the countries of the world together and prevent further wars.' As the planes approached Tinian, Charles Sweeney slowed his craft so that Tibbets would have the honor of landing first. No one threw stones at the 393rd crews as they clambered down from their planes; the men were greeted instead as arriving heroes.[20]

President Harry S. Truman was then in the North Atlantic, aboard the cruiser USS *Augusta* on his way back to the United States from Potsdam. He had already let slip to the ship's officers and crew that their country had tested a powerful new weapon—like those briefing the crews on Tinian, Truman had not used the word 'atomic'—calling it 'the biggest gamble in history' but one that might by itself end the war. The President got news of the Hiroshima bombing in the form of a twenty-six-word message, soon supplemented by one somewhat longer. He was at lunch with six enlisted men when an aide handed him the bulletins. Grinning broadly, Truman gripped the captain's hand, and declared: 'This is the greatest thing in history!' He announced to the crew that 'an atomic bomb' had been dropped on a Japanese city, then strode off to the officers' mess to repeat the news. 'It was an overwhelming success,' he told the men. 'We won the gamble!' In the meantime Leslie Groves, who had waited anxiously for word of the attack (he eventually received Parsons's message to Farrell, delayed by a communications' glitch), had released an official presidential announcement about the bombing. Unsure yet about the impact of Little Boy on its target city, Groves described instead its power, slightly overestimated, on the basis of the Trinity shot, at 20,000 tons of TNT. 'It is an atomic bomb,' the announcement went on. 'It is a harnessing of the power of the universe.' Groves described Hiroshima as 'an important Japanese Army base'.[21]

5. The bombed city

That was true, as far as it went. Hiroshima was headquarters to the Japanese Second Army and Chugoka Regional Army and had been a transit point for soldiers and supplies bound for war. Hiroshimans had hailed the Fifth

Army as it left their docks to attack Singapore in early 1942. The city's ammunition depot was one of the country's largest, and several thousand nearsighted local men over the age of 40 had recently been recruited into the Eleventh Infantry Regiment by the increasingly desperate military; their families had bid them farewell as the sun rose on 6 August. There were between 24,000 and 40,000 soldiers in Hiroshima that day, and they were going nowhere, for the Americans had mined the Inland Sea so thoroughly that shipping of men and goods had reached a standstill. Their mission was to defend the area against invaders they felt sure were coming. There was some manufacturing in Hiroshima, but most of the factories were newly built and on the outskirts of the city, and thus would survive the atomic bomb.[22]

'Hold out your left hand, palm down, fingers spread, and you have a rough outline of the shape of Hiroshima,' write Fletcher Knebel and Charles Bailey II. 'The sea is beyond the fingertips. The back of the hand is where the Ota River comes down from the hills to the north. The spot where the bomb exploded is about where a wedding ring would be worn, just south of the main military headquarters and in the center of the residential–commercial districts of the city.' There were approximately a quarter of a million people in Hiroshima on 6 August; it is hard to be more precise than that because the city had undergone five large-scale evacuations and a sixth was under way, scattering Hiroshimans throughout the surrounding countryside. Not all residents were Japanese. Indeed, some 20 percent—50,000 people—of Hiroshima's population was Korean, most of them men and women brought involuntarily to the city as conscripted laborers and prostitutes. There were hundreds of Chinese there and 3,200 Japanese-Americans, some of them trapped in Japan by the sudden outbreak of war in 1941, and over a thousand of whom would become casualties of the atomic bomb. There were smaller numbers of workers, students, and missionaries. Some two dozen US prisoners of war were locked away in the city, their existence either unknown, ignored, or denied by American military officials. There were just 150 stores open in Hiroshima, 200 doctors, 1,780 nurses, 2 big Army hospitals, and 45 smaller civilian ones.[23]

What the citizens of Hiroshima were doing early in the morning of 6 August 1945 was disturbingly ordinary. Some were still asleep. Some were cooking breakfast on household charcoal braziers. Others were dressing for work or school, reading newspapers—heavily censored, these exhorted people to valor and maximum effort on the home front—sitting on the toilet, puttering in the garden. Many were on their way to work or school, or had just arrived at these places. Thousands were involved in a program to create firebreaks and widen fire lanes in the city, which involved the dolorous destruction of wood and paper houses, sometimes their own. During the night people had twice been awakened by air-raid sirens, and at 7.10 that morning a third alert was sounded when air defense spotted the atomic mission's weather plane heading for the city. When the plane passed harmlessly overhead, the authorities sounded the all clear. Perhaps wary of further false alarms, perhaps convinced that single or several B29s carried no danger, spotters who detected the trio of planes—the *Enola Gay*, *Great Artiste*, and *No. 91*—just after 8.00 decided not to restart the siren, though a radio station mentioned the planes and suggested they were doing reconnaissance. There seemed no reason to take shelter. Precaution fatigue had set in.[24]

So had a wishful conviction that Hiroshima would continue to be spared the bombing that had wracked Tokyo, Yokohama, and other Japanese cities. There was a rumor that President Truman had a close relative living in Hiroshima, possibly an aunt or even his mother. Others claimed that Hiroshima (and Kyoto, also as yet untouched) was so beautiful a city that the Americans wanted to turn it into a resort when the war was over. Hiroshima, it was said, was dearer to the United States than other Japanese cities because so many Hiroshimans had relatives in America, and because so many Japanese-Americans were living in Hiroshima. A few may have known about American prisoners held in the city—or felt that because there were so many foreigners generally in Hiroshima the Americans were reluctant to bomb it; a German priest who lived there recalled that local officials would tell him that their city was safe 'thanks to you'. Some even went so far as to say, as to hope, 'that perhaps the city of Hiroshima was not on the American maps'. (Deep down, most knew better: 'Will it be tomorrow or the day after tomorrow?' people asked themselves.)[25]

Pika-don, they called it later: 'flash-boom'. 'A blinding...flash cut sharply across the sky,' recalled a history professor who was more than 3 miles away from ground zero, the spot on the ground over which Little Boy exploded. There came 'a blank in time', that 'dead silence' so many experienced, 'then a...huge "boom"...like the rumbling of distant thunder. At the same time a violent rush of air pressed down my entire body...' Lying exhausted on his living-room floor after a night's duty as an air warden at his hospital, Dr Michihiko Hachiya was 'startled' by two powerful flashes of light that starkly illuminated a stone lantern in his garden. If he heard the boom that followed he did not say so in his memoir. Toyofumi Ogura was out walking: 'Just as I looked toward the sea and noticed the way the waves were sparkling, I saw, or rather felt, an enormous bluish white flash of light, as when a photographer lights a dish of magnesium'—a comparison made by more than one survivor. 'Off to my right, the sky split open over the city of Hiroshima'; seconds later came 'a dull but tremendous roar as a crushing blast of air pressure assailed me'. Children testified with unadorned directness. Kikuko Yamashiro, who was 5 years old: 'In the morning, my big brother and I were playing upstairs. There was a blinding flash and our house fell down.' Kimura Yoshihiro, a third grader, saw something fall from the plane: 'Five or six seconds later, everything turned yellow. It was like I'd looked right at the sun. Then there was a big sound a second or two later and everything went dark.' The flash as bright as the sun brought, first, intense heat, which melted human beings virtually to nothing within a kilometer of ground zero (also called the hypocenter) and burned exposed skin up to 2.5 miles away. Seconds later came the blast wave, knocking over hibachi grills and setting fires, flattening wooden buildings for 2 miles around and concrete structures close to the hypocenter, and tearing the clothes and skin off people, smashing their internal organs and driving splintered glass into their bodies. Finally, unseen and at first unfelt, came radiation, gamma rays and neutrons that penetrated the skin of many who counted themselves fortunate to have escaped burn and blast. Condensation occurred atop the rising cloud of smoke and dirt and debris, and an ashy black rain fell for an hour and a half, drenching the miserable city with the radiation it contained.[26]

6. The bombed people

Silence. Then bewilderment: 'I felt as though I had been struck on the back by something like a big hammer,' recalled a young woman, 'and thrown into boiling oil...I felt as though the directions were all changed around.' Science fiction: the blast blew so hard that a group of boys working in a field were lacerated by blades of the grass that surrounded them. Absurdity:

while birds, insects, lizards, and households pets vaporized, several survivors remember seeing carp swimming peacefully in ponds or cisterns hours after the bomb had struck, and rats were seemingly unaffected. And horror, as people looked up, dazed, or began to stumble, walk, or run—where?—anywhere else, to find water for their burns or thirst, medical help, or loved ones. 'We finally came across some living human beings,' remembered a primary-school student named Iwao Nakamura. 'But maybe it would be more correct to say that we met some people from Hell. They were naked and their skin, burned and bloody, was like red rust and their bodies were bloated up like balloons.' A grocer, badly burned, saw, and participated in, a nightmare:

> The appearance of people was...well, they all had their skin blackened by burns...They had no hair because their hair was burned, and at a glance you couldn't tell whether you were looking at them from in front or in back...They held their arms bent [forward] like this...and their skin—not only on their hands, but on their faces and bodies too—hung down...I can still picture them in my mind—like walking ghosts...They didn't look like people of this world...They had a special way of walking—very slowly...I myself was one of them.

'When I came to my senses,' a soldier told Kenzaburō Ōe, 'I found my comrades still standing erect and saluting; when I said, "Hey", and tapped their shoulders, they crumbled down into ashes.'[27]

They walked to the rivers and to the slopes of Hijiyama Hill, which seemed to offer relative protection from whatever might come next. A military policeman, weeping, stroked a young girl's face, and murmured, 'I have a child this age, how is she now?' At an impromptu aid station in the skirts of Hijiyama, Toyofumi Ogura found several women, badly injured, who 'howled and screamed as if possessed for the children they'd lost'. Nearby was the counterpart to this scene, as children, in agony of pain, cried for their mothers. Futuba Kitayama watched them die, one by one. Amid the horror, Ogura found a friend, Professor Watanabe, feasting on pumpkin roasted by the bomb's heat. Invited to taste, Ogura found it 'surprisingly good'. An officer named Matsumura, bloodied at the waist but feeling the tug of duty, made his way to the hillside headquarters of Lieutenant General Yamamoto, his chief of ordnance. Yamamoto glanced at Matsumura, then asked, 'Is your son [musuko] safe?' The younger man was briefly confused: he had only daughters, as the general knew. Then, seeing Yamamoto smiling, he realized that it was an incredible joke; the general had glimpsed Matsumura's bloody trousers and used a word that meant both 'son' and, in slang, 'penis'. Matsumura was able to assure the general that his *musuko* was intact.[28]

Others hurried to hospitals, hoping to find medical care. Most found disappointment. Of the city's forty-five civilian hospitals, only three were sufficiently undamaged to accept and help patients. Both military hospitals were uninhabitable. Over 90 percent of Hiroshima's doctors and nurses were killed or injured by the bomb; a month after the attack, only thirty doctors were healthy enough to resume their duties. Medicines, supplies, and surgical equipment had been destroyed, patients who had already been in hospitals now needed urgent care from wounds caused by broken glass or fallen plaster, and within days whoever could stand up long enough to help was forced to confront the perplexing phenomenon of seemingly healthy survivors suddenly sickening and dying as if by some evil magic—radiation poisoning, though it took weeks for Hiroshimans to understand what it was. (When Ogura's wife, Fumiyo, died from radiation on 19 August, the death certificate he obtained for her listed the cause of death as heart failure.) Makeshift aid stations around the city were overwhelmed. The healthy, or relatively healthy, or walking wounded, administered to the injured, swabbing wounds with iodine but leaving them otherwise uncleaned. Workers established a system of triage, as they tried to save those who seemed to have hope of surviving. To the consternation of family members, the most severely injured were left on the ground to die.[29]

Michihiko Hachiya, the doctor who had been lifted by the blast off his living-room floor, found himself naked and bleeding from wounds in his neck and thigh. He yanked glass splinters out of his flesh, located his wife, Yaeko, who was also hurt (and who tied an apron around her husband's waist), and headed for his hospital, several hundred yards away. Hachiya's wounds were too much; he sank to the road, urging Yaeko on. Soon colleagues appeared and hoisted him onto a stretcher, on which they bore him, to the Communications Building adjacent to the hospital, which was already too crowded to admit more patients. They passed him through a window into a janitor's closet, now an emergency aid station. 'The rooms and corridors were crowded with people, many of whom I recognized as neighbors,' Hachiya wrote. 'To me it seemed that the whole community was there.' A nurse bathed his wounds in iodine, a treatment he endured through clenched teeth. Then fire broke out in the hospital next door and everyone was evacuated. Drenched with water from a fire hose, providentially working, and dragged into an open area to escape the flames, Hachiya passed out. He came to and looked around. 'Hiroshima', he observed, 'was no longer a city, but a burnt-over prairie.' The fire spared the hospital's first floor and Hachiya was now moved there. A colleague closed his forty wounds with sutures and he fell asleep.

When he awoke he saw the apocalypse. Patients were crowded into the ward 'like the rice in sushi', the overflow under the stairway and in the front garden. Most were burned, and many of these, Hachiya could see from his bed, were gravely ill. His wife lay in the next bed, her face and body white with ointment. Food and water were as scarce as medicine. 'Disposing of the dead', Hachiya observed, 'was a minor problem'—corpses were trucked off by an army detail to be cremated—'but to clean the rooms of urine, feces, and vomitus was impossible', raising fears that disease would spread. Hospital employees who made it in to work over the next several days told harrowing stories of death and grief. Patients, who continued to stagger in, touched Hachiya in their gratitude for a straw pallet on the noisome floor, a spoonful of rice gruel, and a kind word from a nurse. Confined to his bed by his wounds, consumed with guilt while he watched his colleagues attempt to cope with the human tragedy that grew worse each day, Hachiya found himself increasingly desensitized to the misery around him. 'Parents, half crazy with grief, searched for their children. Husbands looked for their wives and children for their parents. One poor woman, insane with anxiety, walked aimlessly here and there through the hospital calling her child's name.' Within two days of the bombing, Hachiya reflected: 'People were dying so fast that I had begun to accept death as a matter of course and ceased to respect its awfulness.' (In the Red Cross Hospital, bedridden and half-dead patients identified themselves by writing their names in blood on the walls beside them.)

Hachiya struggled out of bed on the 11th. He was buoyed by rumors that Japan had retaliated for the bombing of Hiroshima, annihilating, with 'the same mysterious weapon', the major cities of California. He joined his medical colleagues on rounds, ministering to the injured as much as their limited resources would allow. He also left the grounds in search of assistance, supplies, and news. Rumors kept flying: Japan had turned the tide, or was on the verge of being invaded. One proved true—the Emperor would address the nation over the radio on the 15th. At the appointed time, Hachiya and others crowded into an office at the Communications Bureau to listen. They heard an unfamiliar and barely audible voice through the crackle and hiss of static; Hachiya caught only the phrase, 'Bear the unbearable'. At the end of the broadcast the Bureau Chief, who had been closest to the radio, announced that the Emperor had told the nation that the war was lost. Hachiya was stunned. He returned to the hospital. 'The one word—surrender—had produced a greater shock than that bombing of our city,' he recorded. 'The more I thought, the more wretched and miserable I became.' The discovery that death by radiation awaited thousands who had appeared to be recovering was still ahead of him.[30]

It was already hot by 8.00 on the morning of 6 August, so Shin Bok Su, a Korean woman who had come to Hiroshima with her husband eight years earlier, helped her family—grandma, and her children, 7, 4, and 13 months—remove the heavy clothes and protective headgear they had worn in their backyard air shelter the previous alarm-filled night. Su's husband had gone to work. 'Suddenly, "PIKA!" a brilliant light and then "DON!" a gigantic noise.' The world turned upside down. Through the darkness she heard grandma calling for help; she found the old woman lying on top of the baby, trapped by two pillars that had held up the house. Using a knife blade supplied by a neighbor, Su managed to get them free. She could not find the other children. Her husband came home, so covered with soot that she failed to recognize him until he spoke. Fire spread to the house as they dug desperately through the rubble, then soldiers arrived and insisted that they leave, finally dragging them away. They returned the next morning to find the house burned to the ground. Su found the corpses of her children when she discovered a line of buttons from her son's shirt. Her daughter's charred form was barely visible, curled next to her brother's.

'You couldn't walk the streets without stepping over the dead.' A week after the bombing, Su and her husband were told they could pick up their children's remains at their school. When they arrived, they were handed two yellow envelopes. Then opened them and discovered the vertebrae of adults. They consecrated the bones to the river. Meanwhile, in late August, Su's husband, who had appeared to suffer no more than a scraped knee, suddenly sickened, and his hair began to fall out. They took the baby and hopped on a freight train, laden with demobilized soldiers, and headed for Osaka and more sophisticated treatment. But the next morning he died: 'His body turned black. Blood seeped from his skin. He smelled awful.' A friend told Su that the government was prepared to pay death benefits to those who had lost family members in the bombing, so Su went to the

Hiroshima city office and filled out the requisite forms. The clerk looked at the family's surname and rejected the application on the grounds that the dead were Koreans. She protested; her husband and children had died because they were Japanese. 'Who had suddenly decided we were aliens?' 'I don't know,' shrugged the clerk. 'The orders came from above.'[31]

Kimura Yoshihiro heard and saw the American plane. He was in the third grade and had just arrived at school, though, because the teacher had not yet shown up, he and his friends were chatting. There was bright yellow light, then 'a big sound', and Yoshihiro was knocked out. He came to when wood falling on his back stunned him with pain. He found his sister and they hurried home. They discovered rubble, then their father pulling at it frantically. Their mother, he told them dully, was dead, killed instantly when a nail had penetrated her skull. They must leave the city. They sheltered that night under a railway bridge, warming themselves when the rain and wind sprang up by the fires of burning houses. 'There were almost no ordinary-looking people there. They had swollen faces and black lips.' Yoshihiro got thirsty and went to the river to drink. There were so many corpses there that he had to keep pushing them aside to find room to dip into the water. The next day they reached a relative's home in the countryside. Yoshihiro kept crying for his mother. On the 15th his sister died—'a hard death', he remembered, 'for her eyes were open . . . staring at me'. Eventually Yoshihiro's father remarried, and the family moved back to Hiroshima. 'I hate war now from the bottom of my heart,' Yoshihiro told interviewers six years later. 'I don't hate anybody because Mother is dead, but I hate war.'[32]

A footnote: given the scope of the calamity for the Japanese and Koreans in Hiroshima, it can be nothing more. There were about two dozen American prisoners of war being held at three locations in central Hiroshima on 6 August 1945. Most of them were killed by the bomb or by furious Japanese after the bomb had been dropped. Two—a Navy pilot named Norman Roland Brisset, and an Air Force sergeant named Ralph Neal—survived briefly, and were united with a B-29 crew that had earlier been pulled from the water by a Japanese fishing boat and brought to Hiroshima on the 17th. Nearly beheaded by their captors and abused by Japanese still homeless at the East Drill Ground, the Americans were saved by their interpreter, Nobuichi Fukui, from the Dartmouth class of 1928. Fukui put the men on a truck and drove them out of harm's way, but when they reached the train station he removed the prisoners' blindfolds and ordered

them to look. 'One bomb!' he kept repeating. Along the way they stopped
to pick up Brisset and Neal. They were in bad shape. They had heard the
blast and felt the fire and survived by jumping into a cesspool. That night,
they worsened and began screaming in agony. The B-29 crewmen gave
them morphine and asked their captors for additional help. 'Do something?'
asked the Japanese doctor in charge. 'You tell me what to do. You caused
this. I don't know what to do.' The two men succumbed at dawn. They
knew no more about the atomic bomb than the thousands of others it
killed.[33]

7. Patterns of response

Each survivor of the atomic bombing remembered it somewhat differently;
there is no 'standard account' of that day in Hiroshima. But the subjects
of the bombing did share certain responses to it, used some of the same
language and images to describe their experience of it. Many, for instance,
were made naked by the bomb: unclothed, and—worse—stripped of skin,
and thus left not only in terrible pain but also in some cases wracked with
shame. Many who survived, including Dr Hachiya, commented on their
own nakedness and their initial shock on seeing so many others naked too.
A male employee of a war factory saw in the rain a woman of about 18
or 19, naked 'except [for] half her panties, which did not cover her'. She
pleaded for help, and when she supplicated with outstretched hands he saw
that her 'skin was burned off as if she was wearing gloves', and 'her breast
was red from burns'. He wanted to help, but her nakedness stopped him.
Robert J. Lifton finds indication here of 'perverse sexual and aggressive
fantasies', and that may be, though he might have contemplated his own
role as a male interviewer possibly perceived to be soliciting such honest and
uncomfortable testimony. A more benign interpretation of the man's recollections is that he, and everyone, was appalled at circumstances that created
widespread public nakedness, not sexually exciting but a demonstration
of mass exposure and therefore vulnerability. Respectable Japanese do not
walk the streets naked. A feeling of shame was the order of the day. The
unclothed felt it; the clothed felt it when they saw the naked and burned.
Dr Hachiya was ashamed to be as well dressed as he was in a patched
shirt and filthy pants when he saw patients including 'an old lady . . . , in
nothing but an undershirt' and 'a horribly burned young man lying naked

on a pallet', and Toyofumi Ogura, witnessing the naked, despised himself for not having resisted the 'militarists' surrounding the Emperor who had brought things to this pass.[34]

Apart from shame, many in Hiroshima underwent a loss of feeling. They were 'stunned', 'numb', unable to grasp and thus unable to respond to the cataclysm they faced. Human feeling, like light in deep ocean water, may be inaccessible in conditions of unprecedented upheaval and horror. And the enormity of what survivors confronted all but required them not to feel. They had, most of all, to cope with the horror, with the gruesome sights and rotting stench, and with the dead. 'After a while they became just like objects or goods that we handled in a very businesslike way,' a soldier reminisced about removing corpses. 'Of course, I didn't regard them simply as pieces of wood—they were dead bodies—but if we had been sentimental we couldn't have done the work . . . We had no emotions.' Toyofumi Ogura: 'There were objects that appeared to be lumps of flesh lying on the ground. Some of these squirmed from time to time, like exhibits in a freak show at a fair ground.' Without feeling or instinct to guide them, many fell back on following routine, going by the book. A soldier on leave in the suburbs rushed back to his Hiroshima-based unit 'almost without thinking'. It was what he had been ordered to do. Nearly everyone was dead, so he hunted up the military code book—rather, a clump of ashes that had once been the book—and took it off to headquarters the next morning. Looking, aghast, at the destruction around him, Ogura nevertheless resolved that he must go the following day to his temporary job as supervisor of a student work squad at the Nippon Steel Manufacturing Company factory to the east, where his charges were making, of all things, hand grenades.[35]

There was a cruel logic to the order in which people died at Hiroshima. Those closest to ground zero were likeliest to perish. People caught outside without any kind of shielding from the blast—a wall between themselves and the explosion, or a berm created by a ditch—had little chance of escaping serious injury if they were less than 2 kilometers from the hypocenter. Those outdoors but partly shielded might well have escaped blast or burn, but if they were under 1.5 kilometers from the center they had a 'moderate' chance of injury by radiation. It was not necessarily better to have been caught inside a wooden house, as within 4 kilometers of the hypocenter, this was likely to have collapsed in the blast wave, and injury or death by fire or radiation threatened those inside such buildings as much as it did those shielded but outdoors. The safest place was inside a concrete structure. Such buildings were rare near the city center, and even in them radiation injury loomed within a half kilometer of ground zero.[36]

At the same time, there was a bizarre randomness as to whether objects were destroyed and people were hurt or killed or escaped harm altogether. After the bombing, Father Wilhelm Kleinsorge returned to his room to salvage what he could. His wooden desk had been smashed to bits, but his papier-mâché suitcase, which had been under the desk, was unscathed and standing right side up on the floor. Missing its target by 800 feet, Little Boy had detonated in the air above Dr Kaoru Shima's eponymous hospital. The building was obliterated and its staff and patients killed instantly, but Dr Shima himself, up early on his bicycle to do house calls on his suburban patients, was unharmed. A bookkeeper named Tsuneo Okimoto, whose house was 500 feet from ground zero, had left early for work that morning, remembering that a flat bike tire had slowed him down the day before and not wanting to be late. At 8.15 he was on a commuter train a mile from home. The bomb deposited him at the bottom of a heap of his fellow passengers; their bodies protected him from flying glass. Two passengers on what may have been the same train were sitting across from each other on the car's south side. One opened the window next to him, the other kept his closed. When the blast came, the passenger beside the closed window was bloodied by projectile glass. The passenger with the open window, apparently unhurt, lifted his seatmate onto his back and headed off for help. Quickly, however, his face and body swelled with excruciating burns, and the men switched places.[37]

Survivors of the bomb thought the whole world was dying. 'Before 1945,' writes Michael Sherry, 'it had been possible to see in air war the potential for global destruction, but survivors of Hamburg or Tokyo rarely connected the extinction of their cities with the fate of the species. For atomic bomb victims, that connection became indissoluble.' A physicist, temporarily blinded, thought, 'the world is ending'; a Protestant minister 'thought this was the end of Hiroshima—of Japan—of humankind . . . This was God's judgment on men.' The writer Yōkō Ōta thought the bomb heralded 'the collapse of the earth which it was said would take place at the end of the world'. Time stopped. When it resumed, Hiroshima's calendar had changed: 'Day One' or 'That day' meant the day the atomic bomb was dropped. It was followed by 'the next day', 'the day after', and so forth. On the night of 24 August—eighteen days after the bomb had been dropped— Dr Hachiya had a nightmare:

It seems I was in Tokyo after the great earthquake and around me were decomposing bodies heaped in piles, all of whom were looking right at me. I saw an eye sitting on the palm of a girl's hand. Suddenly it turned and leaped into the sky and then came flying back towards me, so that, looking up, I could see a great bare eyeball, bigger than life, hovering over my head, staring point blank at me. I was powerless to move.[38]

Finally, the atomic bombing of Hiroshima brought biological anomaly. What struck most observers of Hiroshima after 6 August was, of course, the unfathomable destruction of the city, the wasteland that had replaced the vital metropolis where people had lived and worked. But soon there was something weird: the blasted moonscape of browns and grays was coming alive with *plants and flowers*. Returning in early September to Hiroshima for the first time since she had been wounded by the bomb, Toshiko Sasaki, 'horrified and amazed' by the extent of the devastation, also saw something that 'gave her the creeps': Hiroshima was becoming verdant with new growth. 'Over everything—up through the wreckage of the city, in gutters, along the riverbanks, tangled among tiles and tin roofing, climbing on charred tree trunks—was a blanket of fresh, vivid, lush, optimistic green.' She saw 'bluets and Spanish bayonets, goosefoot, morning glories and day lilies, the hairy-fruited bean, purslane and clotbur and sesame and panic grass and feverfew'. In less than two years, those who had returned to Hiroshima were able to grow grains and vegetables on a scale that dwarfed production in nearby villages. Tomatoes had always been nearly impossible to grow in the city; 1947 yielded a full harvest of them. That the bomb had eradicated predators was one reason for the newfound bounty. Scientists suggested another: the radiation from the bomb had not destroyed but stimulated the roots of existing plants and left the soil, perversely, richer than it had been before.[39]

8. The shock waves from the bomb

Information about what had happened at Hiroshima filtered out slowly. A technician at the Japanese Broadcasting Company in Tokyo noticed at 8.16 that his telephone connection to the radio station in Hiroshima had gone dead. A report reached the Tokyo newspaper *Asahi* that Hiroshima had been bombed and had 'almost completely collapsed', and army headquarters also learned that something was up. At 1.00, someone at the II Army

Corps, based in Hiroshima, signalled headquarters from the waterfront that the city 'has been annihilated by one bomb and fires are spreading'. The army duly reported the news to the cabinet secretary, Hisatsune Sakomizu, who informed Prime Minister Suzuki and the rest of the cabinet, as well as Hirohito. Several suspected the atomic bomb—members of the government were aware of the Japanese a-bomb project, even though unwilling to fund it much—and their suspicions were confirmed by the Truman announcement, about which Sakomizu learned at 3.30 in the morning of the 7th. Meanwhile, military authorities summoned the managing editors of the five leading Tokyo dailies and asked that their papers downplay the news, reporting it off the front page and treating it like an 'ordinary air raid on a city'. The editors complied. The *Asahi* next morning placed a brief report on the Hiroshima bombing at the end of a general story on recent American bombing attacks, ending this way: 'It seems that some damage was caused to the city and its vicinity.' Trains were turned back from the area or routed around it. When the cabinet met that afternoon to discuss the bombing, the army minister, Korechika Anami, disparaged the internal reports and Truman's announcement and told the group that the army would send its investigators to Hiroshima. Among them would be Yoshio Nishina, Japan's leading nuclear physicist.[40]

Despite these efforts at denial, it is certain that Little Boy administered a tremendous shock. The apparent eradication of a city by a single bomb could hardly have done otherwise. Sakomizu would later claim that cabinet members (though perhaps he did not mean all of them) knew that, if Truman's 'announcement were true, no country could carry on a war. Without the atomic bomb it would be impossible for any country to try to defend itself against a nation which had the weapon. The chance had come to end the war.' And, most tellingly: 'It was not necessary to blame the military side, the manufacturing people, or anyone else—just the atomic bomb. It was a good excuse.' When Marquis Kido spoke to the Emperor on the afternoon of 7 August, once the use of the atomic bomb had been confirmed, Kido noted the sovereign's deep concern and later reported that he had said: 'Now that things have come to this impasse, there is no other way. I don't care what happens to me personally, but we should lose no time in ending the war so as not to have another tragedy like this.' The next morning, Hirohito told Foreign Minister Togo: 'Now that such a weapon has appeared, it has become less and less possible to continue the war.

We must not miss a chance to terminate the war by bargaining for more favorable conditions now ... So my wish is to make such arrangements as to end the war as soon as possible.' The Emperor asked Togo to let Suzuki know his wishes, and Togo evidently did so, prompting a meeting of the Supreme War Council, the so-called 'Big Six': Prime Minister Suzuki, Foreign Minister Togo, Army Chief of Staff Yoshijiro Umezu, Navy Chief of Staff Soemu Toyoda, Army Minister Anami, and Navy Minister Yonai.[41]

Despite such evidence, historians have frequently disparaged the claim that the Hiroshima bombing was by itself decisive in bringing about Japan's capitulation. They point out, variously, that the Kido and Togo reports of what the Emperor said during their audiences with him were articulated only several years after the meetings had taken place, and that Kido's contemporary diary does not record Hirohito's statements in such detail; that, whatever Hirohito said on 7 and 8 August, he nevertheless did not accept the Potsdam Declaration, on which the Americans had insisted; and that, despite the high-level meetings that quickly followed, 'not a single senior official ... changed his prior stand on war termination after the atomic bombing', as Leon Sigal has written. One may quibble over this judgment—after all, no single senior official mattered as much as the Emperor, and, however Kido may have elaborated on his and Togo's conversations with him, there can be no doubt that Hirohito's desire to end the war had significantly increased after Hiroshima had been bombed— but only slightly, for it represents the combined wisdom of historians who have studied the Japanese record most recently and carefully. The more interesting question concerns what one does with this conclusion. It is possible to argue that, because the first atomic bomb did not convince the Japanese to surrender, it was necessary to add to the shock by continuing to drop atomic bombs until they agreed to do so. It took ten plagues to compel the Egyptian Pharoah to agree to the exodus of Jews; perhaps it would require all the bombs the United States could muster to break the will of the Emperor. On the other hand, one could as plausibly argue that the bomb, despite the singular destruction and mayhem it caused, was not and would never be the war-winning weapon. To a leadership determined to sacrifice everything to defend the homeland, and to a populace already exhausted beyond shock by the experience or imminence of incendiary bombing, the annihilation of thousands of people at once was not enough to break Japan's resolve to fight on.[42]

9. Soviet entry and the bombing of Nagasaki

It is, in any case, very difficult to disaggregate the effect of the Hiroshima bombing from the impact of two other profound shocks that soon followed in its train. First, and despite his longstanding pessimism that his government's overtures to the Soviets would amount to anything, Ambassador Sato was nevertheless stunned when Foreign Minister Molotov summoned him, at 5.00 p.m. Moscow time on 8 August, to inform him that, 'as of August 9, the Soviet Union will consider itself in a state of war with Japan'. The declaration fulfilled the promise Stalin had made to Roosevelt and Churchill at Yalta six months earlier. That it came despite the Soviets not yet having got from China a satisfactory territorial agreement suggests that its timing, if not its fact, was in part determined by the bombing of Hiroshima. Stalin had apparently spent much of the previous day discussing the bomb with advisers. James Byrnes, the American Secretary of State, had hoped the bombs would end the war with Japan short of the Russians getting 'too much in on the kill', but the bombing may have moved Stalin to act more quickly than he might otherwise have done. And Molotov's statement to Sato that the declaration would take hold on the 9th was mendacious: it turned out Molotov was referring to the time at the front. Thus, just after midnight Trans-Baikal time—it was 6.10 in the evening of 8 August in Moscow—Soviet troops crossed into Manchuria in force and on several fronts at once. They surprised the Japanese Kwantung Army, which was understrength and demoralized, and drove hard toward the cities of Changchun, Mukden, Harbin, and Kirin. Another force attacked Korea. Some Japanese units resisted, while others withdrew or simply melted away.[43]

As he was driven away from the Kremlin after his stark meeting with Molotov, Sato told his embassy secretary, 'The inevitable has now arrived.' Prime Minister Suzuki said much the same thing when he learned of the Soviet declaration at dawn on the 9th. Togo and leading foreign ministry officials were already awake and discussing the new crisis; they quickly resolved that Japan would have to accept the Potsdam Declaration. Togo called on Yonai, another of the Big Six, who agreed that the time had come to bow to the inevitable. Just before 10.00, the Emperor called in Kido. Because of the Soviet attack in Manchuria, the Emperor said, 'it is necessary to study and decide on the termination of the war', and he directed Kido to sound out Suzuki on the matter. Kido told Suzuki, who turned up at the Imperial Palace ten minutes later, that the Emperor wished to end the war 'by immediately taking advantage of the Potsdam Declaration', though whether Kido had actually heard the Emperor put it this way remains unclear. Suzuki summoned the Big Six, and within twenty minutes the group had been collected and the meeting begun in a room in the palace basement.

Maneuver and intrigue followed; the details of these are best chronicled elsewhere. Suzuki began by arguing for the acceptance of the Potsdam Declaration, for the combination of the atomic bomb and the Soviet invasion made it impossible to win. He and Togo understood that accepting the Declaration meant that the *kokutai* must be preserved—that is, the Emperor would not be punished nor deprived of the privileges and symbols of his office. Yonai, whom Togo had thought had agreed with this position that morning, now suggested that three additional conditions might (not should) be attached to Japan's acceptance, and Umezu and Anami elaborated: the Japanese military should have responsibility for disarmament, there must be no occupation, and the Japanese government should decide who should be designated as war criminals. All four conditions, the two army representatives insisted, must be met by the Americans before Japan would agree to surrender. Thereafter, multiple lines were drawn. Togo advocated surrender with just the first condition, Suzuki and Yonai (according to Tsuyoshi Hasegawa) 'were leaning toward Togo's position' but did not speak against demanding the other three conditions, and Toyoda thought two conditions might be met but doubted that four would be.[44]

Then, an hour into the debate, came the second added shock: the Big Six learned that an atomic bomb had struck Nagasaki.

LeMay had resumed the firebombing after Hiroshima, sending 152 B-29s on the 7th and 373 more on the 8th over Japanese cities, including the industrial hub of Yawata. The second atomic bomb, an implosion device with a plutonium core like the one tested at Trinity, was meanwhile under assembly on Tinian. It was designated for Kokura, a medium-sized city (about 195,000) in northern Kyushu with a substantial arsenal. The attack was scheduled for 11 August. Predictions of stormy weather for the 10th and after persuaded Tibbets to move the mission forward to the 9th. The bomb would be carried by Major Charles W. Sweeney in a B-29 dubbed *Bock's Car*. Fat Man weighed 1,000 pounds more than Little Boy;

Sweeney thought it 'resembled a grossly oversized decorative squash'. Like its predecessor, Fat Man bore messages for the Japanese. The engineer Harlow Russ scrawled verse inside the bomb's tail cone:

> Sappy Jappy started scrappy,
> Bombed Pearl Harbor,
> Pretty crappy.
> Jappy have reached end of scrappy,
> Bomb will knock Japan slappy happy.

Sweeney sought an audience with the Catholic priest assigned to Tinian. The two men discussed sin, Christian ethics, and Thomas Aquinas's conditions for a just war.[45]

Things went wrong. Bock's Car's backup fuel pump failed, leaving inaccessible 600 gallons of precious fuel. Two hours into the flight the red warning light on Fat Man's fuse monitor started flashing, which seemed to indicate that some of the bomb's fuses had been activated, threatening detonation. A weaponeer discovered that ground technicians had misaligned two switches and caused the monitor's circuits to malfunction; he solved the problem. The pilot of the photography plane, James Hopkins, missed the rendezvous point over Yakoshima, forcing Sweeney, already burning limited fuel, to go on without him. The weather over Kokura was supposed to have been clear, but by the time Bock's Car reached the city the wind had shifted and the area was obscured by smoke from burning Yawata, victim of LeMay's incendiaries the previous day. Pursued by flak and Japanese fighter planes, Sweeney tried three passes over Kokura, failing each time to discern his aiming point. He made a quick decision: proceed to the secondary target, Nagasaki. The plane had enough fuel for one bombing run, and even then it might not be enough to get them home. Nagasaki was clouded over. Navigating by radar, the plane's bombardier, Kermit Beahan, found a target 2 miles north of the intended one, in the district where many of the city's Catholics lived near the great Urakami Cathedral. Beahan released Fat Man. 'Bombs away!' he called. Then he corrected himself: 'Bomb away!'

Sweeney got his plane back as far as Okinawa with two engines out and running on fumes. He and his crew were bruised and exhausted. They had left far worse in their wake. Fat Man had blasted to rubble the Urakami Cathedral, beheading some of its stone statues, and the Mitsubishi torpedo factory, whose workers had built the weapons used at Pearl Harbor. The merciful cloud cover and a series of ridges had protected the center of Nagasaki and much of its population, but the toll was nevertheless staggering: estimates of the dead ranged from about 40,000 to nearly 140,000 by 1950, with thousands more injured. Some 7,000 of the dead were Catholics, their families having accepted conversion by European missionaries some generations earlier. Only a few hundred of the Nagasaki dead were military men. Between 60 and 80 American POWs died, their presence in Nagasaki known in advance to US officials, who nevertheless judged their sacrifice necessary for the greater good of ending the war more quickly. More than a month after the bombing, a US navy officer visited Nagasaki. He wrote to his wife: 'A smell of death and corruption pervades the place, ranging from the ordinary carrion smell to somewhat subtler stenches with strong overtones of ammonia (decomposing nitrogenous matter, I suppose). The general impression... is one of deadness, the absolute essence of death in the sense of finality without hope of resurrection.' Terai Sumie remembered the bombing with a sequence of haiku:

> my child's sleeping face
> on this blue earth
> radiation everywhere
>
> to the unknown tomorrow
> the bomb victims'
> prayers turn to sobs
>
> guidepost for the soul
> sunflowers that fill
> the blue vase
>
> as if
> the A-Bomb Maiden incarnate
> a dove flies
>
> constant vertigo
> still I dread
> the White Nagasaki[46]

10. The Big Six debates

The Big Six got its news of the bombing very quickly, from the governor of Nagasaki prefecture. The governor played down the impact of the attack, reporting that the number of dead was 'small', probably (he alleged) because the weapon had been less powerful than the Hiroshima bomb. The news apparently had little effect on the impasse the Big Six had reached—though, as Richard Frank has pointed out, Toyoda's argument, or hope, that the United States had few atomic bombs was undercut by the dropping of the second bomb so soon after the first. The debate went on. The meeting adjourned at 1.00 p.m., deadlocked over whether to insist that the United States meet four conditions or merely one.

That afternoon saw lobbying and intrigue by several groups and individuals on behalf of their positions. The veteran politician-diplomat Prince Fumimaro Konoe met Kido at the palace. Distressed to learn that the Big Six were considering four conditions, and that Kido and presumably Hirohito favored this approach, Konoe, joined in the effort by former foreign minister Mamoru Shigemitsu and Hirohito's younger brother Prince Takamatsu, urged Kido to convince the Emperor to issue a 'sacred decision' (*seidan*) to accede to Potsdam with just the one condition, thereby breaking the high-level deadlock. A small group of military officers pursued the same strategy on a parallel track. Meanwhile, Suzuki, at 2.30, convened an emergency cabinet meeting. There, for a larger audience, members of the Big Six rehearsed and embroidered the arguments they had put forward that morning. Yonai, who had first described the additional conditions that had so troubled the debate, now came forcefully into the one condition camp. Still, three hours later, the cabinet was no less divided than the Big Six. And, when the cabinet reconvened at 6.00, it could get no further. Togo contended that the Americans would never accept the military's four conditions. If not, Anami retorted, let the war go on; the army would make the Americans pay dearly if they invaded Japan.

Suzuki put a stop to it at 10.00. He told the group that he would apprise the Emperor of the debate, and once more gather the Supreme War Council (the Big Six). The plan, hatched that afternoon with Kido, was to turn the meeting into an imperial conference, the Emperor himself presiding. Kido had earlier talked to Hirohito for nearly an hour. His own doubts about the four-conditions proposal having been sharpened by his encounters with Konoe, Takamatsu, and Shigemitsu, Kido had evidently brought the Emperor around with a small redefinition of the *kokutai*, broadening it slightly so as to offer the Japanese greater autonomy in determining its ultimate form. Now, after midnight, the principals in the drama met yet again, this time in a room in the palace basement, and in front of the Emperor. Then came a twist: Baron Kiichiro Hiranuma, chair of the

Privy Council, had been asked by the Emperor to join the deliberations. Hiranuma spoke out of his turn, asked many questions, and went on at length. At the end, he proposed yet another broadening of the definition of *kokutai*: it was to be understood that the Potsdam Declaration 'does not comprise any demand that prejudices the prerogatives of his majesty as a sovereign ruler'. 'In effect', Herbert Bix has written, 'this amounted to an affirmation that the emperor's rights of sovereignty, including the all-important right of supreme command, antedated the constitution and had been determined by the gods in antiquity . . . It was certainly not constitutional monarchy' that Hiranuma had proposed. Either because they accepted Hiranuma's redefinition of the *kokutai* or because they were simply exhausted, the three members of the 'Peace Faction' did not object.

Suzuki now asked the Emperor to decide. While no transcript of Hirohito's exact words exists, the historian Robert J. C. Butow has pulled together a 're-creation' of what he said, using the recollections of those who were there. Hirohito said he agreed with Togo—that they should ask for only the single condition. 'Continuing the war can only mean destruction for the nation and prolongation of bloodshed and cruelty in the world,' he said. 'I cannot bear to see my innocent people suffer any longer.' Despite promises made by the military, Tokyo was poorly defended; indeed, the sovereign said pointedly, 'there has always been a discrepancy between plans and performance.' Painful as it was to give way, it was necessary now to 'bear the unbearable'. With that, Hirohito left the room. All six members of the Supreme War Council promptly signed a statement endorsing surrender on the one condition. At 3.00 a.m. the cabinet provided its endorsement. But Anami, angry at the use of the Emperor to break the deadlock in a way he thought dishonorable, now demanded to know whether, if the United States rejected preservation of the *kokutai*, Suzuki was prepared to continue the fight. Suzuki said he was. Just over three hours later, Japan's terms were transmitted to the Allies via the neutrals, Sweden and Switzerland.[47]

Harry Truman received the news around 7.30 in the morning of 10 August. He gathered Byrnes, Stimson, Leahy, and Forrestal and asked them what he should do. Probably no one in the room understood the subtlety of Hiranuma's conditional language, but Byrnes had already been buttonholed by a trio of Japan specialists in the State Department (one of them Joseph Grew), who insisted that the Japanese condition reserved limitless power for the Emperor and would thus frustrate the effort to demilitarize and democratize the defeated nation. Byrnes was worried enough that compromising in any way the unconditional surrender demand would result in Truman being 'crucified' by the American public, weary of war but nevertheless determined to adhere to declared principle—and to avenge itself fully on the Japanese. Leahy, Forrestal, and most emphatically Stimson disagreed, urging the acceptance of Japan's offer as written. (Stimson later groused in his diary about 'uninformed agitation against the Emperor in this country mostly by people who know no more about Japan than has been given them by Gilbert and Sullivan's "Mikado" '.) Here was a chance to end the war and thus save American lives, and to prevent the Soviets pushing deeper into Manchuria and elsewhere and thereby demanding a significant share of the occupation authority. Forrestal found a way out of the impasse: accept Japanese terms, but in the acceptance honor what he called 'the intents and purposes of the Potsdam Declaration'. Truman approved this ploy and assigned Byrnes to put it in writing.

The result was a reply that left much to interpretation. The Byrnes Note, as it came formally to be called, initially stated: 'From the moment of surrender the authority of the emperor and the Japanese Government to rule shall be subject to the Supreme Commander of the Allied Powers.' Notice here that the continued existence of the Emperor was assumed, and that 'Commander' was a singular noun, 'in order', as Stimson put it, 'to exclude any condominium such as we have in Poland'. (Forrestal, more accurately, said 'Germany'.) Further on, the Byrnes Note allowed as 'the ultimate form of government of Japan shall . . . be established by the freely expressed will of the Japanese people'. This was largely a restatement of a provision of the Potsdam Declaration, though that document had omitted the word 'ultimate', the introduction of which now might suggest a phasing in period during which the Emperor might retain his perquisites. Byrnes won approval for his language at a cabinet meeting that afternoon. As the secretary read out the proposal, according to Vice President Henry Wallace, he 'stopped' and 'laid special emphasis on the top dog commander over Hirohito being an American.' Truman noted that Britain's foreign minister, Ernest Bevin, had already approved the draft, and that it would also be circulated to the Chinese and Russians—though the President thought it unlikely that he would hear from Moscow. He also told the group that he had ordered a halt to the atomic bombing: 'the thought of wiping out another 100,000 was too horrible.' He ended by saying that, when peace rumors had been floated the previous day, the White House had received 170 telegrams in response. All but seventeen 'were for hard terms—unconditional surrender'. With a slight subsequent modification by the British, acceptance by the Chinese, and grudging acquiescence by the Soviets, who had wanted at least a say in choosing the Supreme Commander, the Byrnes Note went to Tokyo, where it was received at 2.00 a.m. on 12 August.[48]

Now the wounds that the Emperor's decision had closed with gossamer thread burst open once again. Togo was shaken by the unmistakable lack of explicit concession in the Byrnes Note; several of his subordinates in the foreign ministry hastily and deliberately mistranslated the note, moderating its language and hoping—fruitlessly, as it turned out—that the Japanese military would ask no questions or try a translation of its own. Yonai remained committed to surrender, but Prime Minister Suzuki wavered until Kido summoned him that night to put some backbone into him. Anami, Umezu, and Toyoda were angry at the American response and inclined to stiffen their position: Japan must fight on. A group of junior officers went further, making hasty plans to stage a coup against their disgracefully craven government and to take control of the Imperial Palace. Apprised of the plot, Anami remained silent. Along with Togo, and for reasons of his own, only Hirohito, guided by Kido, stayed steadfastly devoted to ending the war. Byrnes's Note was not all that might have been hoped for, but even if properly translated it could be construed, by those who wished to see it so, as leaving the *kokutai* intact, albeit subservient to an alien supreme commander. The Emperor wished to see it so. Throughout the humid days of 12–13 August, however, the persistent opposition to a settlement by key military leaders, set against the distinctly audible rumblings of a plot to overthrow the government, prevented a decision to end the war.

Thus, for those days and much of the 14th, the war continued. Recognizing that surrender might be near, the Soviets drove hard against the Kwantung Army in an effort to capture as much territory as possible. Many Japanese units fought stubbornly, but they were overmatched and outgunned, and so fell back on nearly every front in Manchuria. The Russians also attacked Sakhalin Island and were preparing an assault on northern Korea. The Americans went on with their air war. Truman had suspended use of the atomic bomb, but there were no more bombs yet ready for use in any case. He also halted strategic bombing while the United States awaited Japan's reply to the Byrnes Note. Still, it was possible to do nearly anything under the guise of tactical bombing, and there were plenty of high explosives and incendiaries available to US commanders in the Pacific. Early on the 13th, carrier-based fighters and bombers struck Japanese factories at Kawasaki, hit airfields and train stations near Tokyo, and even strafed passenger trains. Rumors flew that the capital would be the target of a third atomic bomb; Radio Tokyo warned citizens to 'Take shelter even from a single enemy plane!' and 'Wear white clothing that will protect you better from burns than dark clothes!' That day, with the Japanese response to the Byrnes Note unforthcoming, Truman lifted the ban on strategic bombing. The decision allowed General Henry H. Arnold to carry out his wish to stage 'as big a finale as possible'. Over a fourteen-hour period on the 14th and 15th, 828 B-29s and 186 fighters bombed and blasted Tokyo.

Meanwhile, the agony of indecision over what to do about the Byrnes Note was at last resolved. Anami played a key role. Though deeply unhappy at the prospect of what seemed to him unconditional surrender and more than willing to fight on—he famously said, 'even though we have to eat grass, swallow dirt, and lie in the fields, we shall fight on to the bitter end, ever firm in our faith that we shall find life in death'—he also felt an abiding and powerful sense of duty to his emperor. When Hirohito appealed to him directly, calling him by name and tearfully begging him to accept the surrender decision, Anami resolved against supporting a coup. Indeed: 'those who disobey must go over my dead body', he told a stunned group of younger officers hoping for a green light from their superior. For Hirohito had intervened once again to break the stalemate in the Supreme War Council and the cabinet. At 10.00 a.m. on 14 August, the Emperor convened his second imperial conference in five days, summoning both the council and the cabinet to the same basement room in the palace. After hearing from the irreconcilables, Hirohito spoke, his voice breaking. He had not changed his mind about the need to surrender. Continuing the war, he said, offered 'nothing but additional destruction'. The American reply to the Japanese proposal he deemed 'acceptable', constituting 'a virtually complete acknowledgment' of Japan's terms. The military must accede to this position. For his part, the Emperor would broadcast a message over the radio to the Japanese people, explaining to them why the end had come, why it was necessary to lay down arms. He asked the assembled group to draft the message, which he then planned to record on a phonograph record in his formal Japanese. Thereafter, as one participant recalled, tears 'flowed unceasingly', and the Emperor left the room.

The coup did come off, as insurgents briefly seized the Imperial Palace that night and tried, unsuccessfully, to locate Kido, the Emperor, and the rumored phonograph record of the sovereign's voice. Without high-level support, however, the revolt never had a chance of success: most of the army remained loyal, and within hours the insurgents had been routed and the leaders committed suicide. Anami shared glasses of sake with several associates, then used his sword to open his belly in ritual *seppuku*. Ignorant of these events, the following afternoon Dr Hachiya in Hiroshima, along with millions of other Japanese, strained to hear, through the static of the record, their Emperor entreating them to accept defeat. Hachiya felt confused and betrayed by what the Emperor said. Robert Guillain, a French journalist living in a village outside Tokyo, reported that few understood their sovereign's stilted words and waited for the radio announcer to explain what he had said. 'Then,' wrote Guillain, 'it was over':

> They had understood, and the sobbing broke out. The knots of people dissolved in disorder. Something huge had just cracked: the proud dream of greater Japan. All that was left of it to millions of Japanese was a true sorrow, simple and pitiable—the bleeding wound of their vanquished patriotism. They scattered and hid to weep in the seclusion of their wooden houses.

In the United States, the reaction to the news was a good deal more celebratory.[49]

11. Explaining Japan's surrender

Lurking at the back of this story is that same fraught question: what was it that compelled Japan to surrender on 14 August 1945? Was it the atomic bombing of Hiroshima? Of Nagasaki? The combination of the two, which by their rapid occurrence in succession raised Japanese fears that the United States had more atomic bombs on the way and an ongoing willingness to use them? Were the bombs less important than the Soviet decision to declare war on Japan? Or would Japan have surrendered before the end of 1945, as the US Strategic Bombing Survey would have it, even in the absence of the atomic bombs, Soviet intervention, or the prospect of imminent invasion by US military forces? Needless to say, historians and other analysts have divided sharply over the answers to these questions. Understandably so—there is much at stake here. If the atomic bombs, either or both, caused Japan to capitulate, then they arguably saved lives, especially (but not only) American lives, and thus justified the scientific effort and government expense and soothed any moral qualms Americans might have felt about their use. Of course, on the other hand, if the Japanese surrendered for reasons other than the use of the bombs against them, then the Truman administration could stand accused of visiting stark and needless cruelty on a people, on a world, that was lurching toward peace without them. 'It wasn't necessary to hit them with that awful thing,' as Dwight Eisenhower would put it after the war.

Was it? As with all critical historical questions, the answer is complicated. It is rare to find in the record what detectives and historian-detectives call a 'smoking gun', a clear expression of cause from a figure in a position to provide one. There is no evidence, for example, that Emperor Hirohito turned to Kido at a crucial moment and said, 'It is not about those bombs— we cannot have the Russians capturing our soldiers and occupying our land.' (Even if that statement were discovered in the record, one suspects that historians would question its provenance or subject it to several inter- pretations.) There is consensus that the views of the Emperor were the key to ending the war, especially as the positions of the members of the Supreme War Council hardly changed between 5 and 14 August. It is true that Yonai's position was sometimes mysterious, that Suzuki's wavered briefly after the Byrnes Notes had arrived, and that Anami, while steadfast in opposition to unconditional surrender, significantly refused to support a military coup against his emperor. But it was Hirohito, ghosted by Kido and doubtless influenced by Togo and others, who decided on the 14th that enough was enough. At the first imperial conference on 9–10 August, recall, the Emperor sought to end the war because its continuation could 'only mean destruction for the nation and prolongation of bloodshed and cruelty to the world'.[50] That could mean atomic bombs, a Soviet invasion, or an invasion by the Americans; Hirohito also criticized the military for its lack of preparedness to defend the beaches east of Tokyo. Just before the second imperial conference on the 14th, Hirohito told three senior army officers: 'The military situation has changed suddenly. The Soviet Union entered the war against us. Suicide attacks can't compete with the power of science. Therefore, there is no alternative but to accept the Potsdam terms,' as explicated or confused by the Byrnes Note. Ending the conference itself with his decision to surrender, Hirohito added little to what he had said four days earlier, only that he believed the American proposal would assure the preservation of the *kokutai*. More revealing was the Emperor's speech to the nation the following morning. He observed that 'the enemy has for the first time used cruel bombs to kill and maim extremely large numbers of the innocent, and the heavy casualties are beyond measure. To continue the war further could lead in the end not only to the extermination of our race, but also to the destruction of all human civilization.' Here was an obvious— not 'oblique', as Tsuyoshi Hasegawa has it—reference to the atomic bombs. Ending the war was by Hirohito's account a 'magnanimous act' designed to save not just the Japanese but all humankind from immolation.[51]

Above all, the Emperor was interested in maintaining his position and in protecting his people from further disaster. His second interest was the servant of his first, for by the summer of 1945 popular disillusionment with Hirohito's rule was growing, fed by the extraordinary vulnerability of common citizens to American bombs. It was bad enough when incendiary bombs burned Tokyo in March 1945; the sullen reception that greeted Hirohito as he toured the damage spoke volumes about the public's mood. The police reported on multifarious acts of *lèse majesté*, including someone who said: 'After having let Tokyo get burned down like that, to hell with His Imperial Highness.' Intellectuals were more and more disaffected. No one knew how the dazed survivors of Hiroshima and Nagasaki would feel about the Emperor and the government generally, but their reaction was unlikely to be good. Even more ominous was the attitude of the military, which, as events proved, found it enormously difficult to concede defeat. The army and navy seemed willing to fight to the last civilian before capitulating, at least as long as the losses came by attrition. The result of the military's recklessness could be its own strengthening at the expense of civilian leadership, or rising popular anger over sacrifices demanded without any hope of success. But the shocks administered by the atomic bombs and Soviet entry gave the Emperor good reason to terminate the war; it was harder after 9 August to seek terms. 'So long as one feels there is any chance left, it is very difficult to say that the chance to quit [has come],' said Toyoda after the war. In his view, Soviet intervention put an end to hope. Earlier, Yonai had told an aide, 'the atomic bombs and the Soviet entry into the war are, in a sense, gifts from the gods. This way we don't have to say that we have quit the war because of domestic circumstances.' A joke that circulated through Japanese political circles after the war had it that the atomic bomb was 'the real *kamikaze*', delivering the country from further humiliation and death.[52]

The shocks of August thus gave the Emperor a convenient out, the opening he needed to justify acceptance of the Potsdam Declaration. It may be nothing more than a historian's common sense to suppose that the infliction of death on many thousands—no one yet knew even roughly how many—by a mere two bombs was, along with Soviet intervention, decisive in ending the war. Given the mix of evidence available, and in the absence of any 'smoking gun', common sense may be the best measure possible.

12. Assessing the damage in Hiroshima and Nagasaki

The surrender announcement, the end of the Emperor's public silence, brought no immediate relief to those in Hiroshima and Nagasaki. Yoshio Nishina had arrived in Hiroshima on the 8th, his trip delayed for a day by a faulty transport plane and the government's evident lack of eagerness to learn what had happened. Nishina strongly suspected that the Americans had dropped an atomic bomb, and felt that, if he was right, he and the Riken scientists should take their own lives out of shame for having failed. His investigation, begun the next morning, quickly confirmed his suspicions. He located the hypocenter and picked through the ruins of the city, gathering soil and water sample for analysis back in Tokyo and discovering packets of exposed X-ray film at the former sites of hospitals and photo shops. He met military officials to discuss radiation illness; he could offer no other help. He left for Nagasaki on the 10th, then returned to the Riken just after the Emperor had made his radio announcement. He told his colleagues that, if the Americans could build an atomic bomb, so could they, and they should set to work with his cyclotron. Gone was any talk of suicide. But four months after he had visited Hiroshima and Nagasaki, Nishina's skin broke out in blotches, the result, he thought, of the probing he had done in radioactive areas. He would die of cancer in 1951.[53]

It took the Americans a month to send a team to see Hiroshima for themselves. Leslie Groves was interested in knowing more about what the bomb had wrought, and he was concerned about a swelling chorus of criticism of the bombings at home and abroad. He dispatched to Japan his deputy, General Thomas Farrell, along with nearly thirty officers and enlisted men, including a number of physicians. Separate groups were sent to Hiroshima and Nagasaki. The Hiroshima team included Los Alamos scientists Philip Morrison and Robert Serber, and it looked altogether serious, equipped with Geiger counters and more sensitive electroscopes and moving briskly through the streets of the shattered city. Members of the team took photographs of the destruction. Morrison calculated, on the basis of shadows burned into concrete walls, that the bomb had exploded at its intended height. No one found lingering radioactivity, and a Japanese guide helpfully pointed out that lotuses in the moat surrounding army headquarters were growing once more. The teams rendezvoused in Tokyo, where Farrell called a news conference. The dying in Hiroshima and Nagasaki was largely over, he said. There was no radioactivity left on the ground; the height of the explosion had ensured that death would come only by blast or fire, as the Los Alamos scientists had predicted. When he was challenged by Australian journalist Wilfred Burchett, who had just returned from Hiroshima and had seen people dying quickly as their skin turned blue and blood streamed from their ears, Farrell waved dismissively. The patients were 'victims of blast and burn, normal after any big explosion'. Burchett had succumbed to 'Japanese propaganda'. (Groves himself would admit that some had perished from radiation poisoning, but remarked, scandalously, that this was 'a very pleasant way to die'.)[54]

Emiko Nishii, a 16-year-old girl, came to the Communications Hospital and Dr Hachiya's care on 28 August. She complained of 'general malaise, petechiae [bluish skin blotches], and inability to sleep'. Like many others, she had seemed healthy enough after surviving the bomb, apart from some dizziness and nausea, and after a week or so had returned to work, despite overall weakness and persistent diarrhea. On the 23rd, her hair began to fall out; four days later she developed more petechiae, severe abdominal pain, and 'restlessness'. Her pulse weakened, her temperature rose to 104°, her breath grew labored. She died, 'an agonized appearance on her face', on the 29th.[55]

Wilfully or not, Farrell had been wrong about radioactivity. While it was true that blast and fire caused most of the casualties in Hiroshima and Nagasaki, many who survived these, because they were protected or sufficiently distant from the hypocenter, later sickened and died from exposure to radiation. At the end of June 1946 the US Strategic Bombing Survey, chosen by the president on VJ Day to analyse the impact of bombing on Japan, issued a report titled 'The Effects of Atomic Bombs on Hiroshima and Nagasaki'. Survey members had studied medical records and talked to medical personnel who had struggled to treat the injured in the weeks and months following the bombings. Contrary to Farrell's claim, and contrary to the conclusion of Stafford Warren, one of Farrell's team physicians who had later testified to the Senate Atomic Energy Committee that radiation was the cause of 7–8 percent of deaths in Hiroshima and Nagasaki, the survey estimated that at least twice that many—15–20 percent—had died from radiation poisoning. With a longer perspective, the committee for the Compilation of Materials on Damage Caused by the Atomic Bombs in Hiroshima and Nagasaki, formed at the request of the mayors of both cities, issued in 1979 a lengthy report that included statistically detailed information about the effects of radiation on those in Hiroshima and Nagasaki on the fateful days or immediately thereafter. The committee found that many who survived blast and fire were exposed to high doses of radiation. For example, an unprotected person 1,200 meters from the hypocenter got 95 rads of gamma rays and 59 rads of neutrons. This was a good deal more than enough to cause leukemia (100 rads in total was considered a dangerous dosage)—and, indeed, between 1965 and 1971 the mortality-by-leukemia rate of those so exposed was seven times greater than that for the rest of Japan. The mortality rate by leukemia for those arriving in Hiroshima within three days of the bombing was three times higher than the national average. Survivors also suffered high rates of thyroid, breast, lung, gastric, and colon cancer, blood disorders, and cataracts. Babies *in utero* whose mothers were exposed to radiation were in disproportion spontaneously aborted, stillborn, or born with microencephaly or severe retardation.[56]

The precise number of people who were killed by the atomic bombs will never be known. One is torn between thinking that it is vitally important to estimate as best one can, to try to account for all the people who lost their lives, and an uncomfortable sense that the ongoing dispute over numbers is somehow obscene. Let us, then, be brief. In August 1946, a year after the bombings, the Information Department of the Hiroshima City Office estimated that 118,661 civilians and approximately 20,000 military personnel had died to that point. Among the hurt were 30,524 rated as 'seriously injured' and another 48,606 'slightly injured'. Many of those in the first category presumably died subsequently from their injuries. In Nagasaki the toll seems to have been around 70,000 killed, virtually all of them non-combatants. It is perhaps worth recalling that some 90,000 were killed in the incendiary raids on Tokyo in the spring of 1945.[57]

Hiroshimans had counted themselves blessed that their city had for the most part been left alone. In the hours after the atomic bombing, they worried that the Americans had more terrible things in store for them: poison gas or a 'cold bomb' that would 'freeze everything', even a bomb that would release 'rotten pigs' that would destroy what remained of the ravaged ecosystem. Before surrender the Americans no doubt regarded such rumor-mongering as salutary; in its wake, and especially in the light of growing criticism of their having used the bomb, they sought to limit the spread outward from the bombed cities of both wild gossip and genuine pathology reports alike. The occupation authority, headed by the Supreme Commander for the Allies in the Pacific (SCAP), General Douglas MacArthur, attempted to censor materials that concerned the bomb, though it did so with an inconsistency that will be familiar to students of bureaucracy everywhere. The writer Tamiki Hara, thwarted from publishing his Hiroshima memoir/story 'Summer Flowers' in one Japanese journal, merely chose publication in two others small enough to evade the censor's gaze. When Yōkō Ōta planned, in 1948, to publish her memoir 'City of Corpses,' she received a visit from an occupation intelligence officer who questioned her closely about the politics of her friends and her publisher. At the end of the interview, the officer told Ōta: 'I want you to forget your memories of the atomic bomb. America won't use the atomic bomb again, so I want you to forget the events in Hiroshima.' That, Ōta replied, was desirable but impossible. A censored version of 'City of Corpses' appeared later that year. John Hersey's *Hiroshima*, first published in the *New Yorker* in August 1946, did not appear in Japanese until 1949.[58]

13. 'Nothing, Nothing': Memories of Hiroshima

To be sure, there was more than a little self-censorship surrounding the surviving victims of the bombs, the *hibakusha*. Few wished to be reminded of the terrible day; even those, like Ōta, who felt compelled to write about the experience of Hiroshima, wished they did not. The victims' vulnerability seemed to embarrass them. They also felt ashamed of their appearance and for the burden they placed on friends and family for their medical care. '*Hibakusha* were not welcome compatriots in the new Japan,' John Dower has written. 'Psychologically if not physically, they

were deformed reminders of a miserable past.' Occupation censorship and
Japanese self-censorship concerning the bombs thus worked in tandem to
the probable satisfaction of all parties; there existed, according to Robert
J. Lifton, a guilt-induced ' "conspiracy of silence" between instigators and
victims' of the bombs. In what may have been an act of displaced guilt,
or perhaps just spite, in November 1945 Groves ordered the destruction of
Nishina's cyclotron at the Riken. US soldiers using torches, sledgehammers,
and crowbars dismantled the machine and dumped its pieces in the bay.
Nishina watched and wept.[59]

Some who survived in Hiroshima expressed resentment of or hatred
for the Americans they blamed for their misery. 'I think they must have
been crazy,' said a bar worker of the Americans. '[Toward them I felt]
nothing but hatred.' A businessman who lost his son in the bombing
acknowledged the 'wonderful things America has done for us' during the
occupation, but added that 'until the moment I die I will feel resentment
toward America', while another survivor focused his 'strong hatred' on
President Truman, whom he characterized as 'a cold-blooded animal'. In
general, though, the anger felt by survivors was either directed elsewhere, or
was sublimated, denied, or transformed into some other emotion entirely.
Kenzaburō Ōe blamed Japan's accelerated modernization for leading to
Japanese aggression in Asia, and, inexorably, to the atomic bombings.
Michihiko Hachiya spared both his emperor and the Americans his rage,
settling instead for 'hating the military authorities' who had 'betrayed
the Emperor and the people of Japan', and another writer agreed: 'the
anger we felt at the end of the war', she told Lifton, 'was not toward the
bomb but the Japanese militarists.' Toyofumi Ogura blamed himself and his
fellow citizens for allowing the military to pursue its disastrous course: the
bomb must be accepted as an 'expiation of these sins'. For others, there
was neither anger nor blame, for the bomb was a powerful abstraction,
a 'surreal new dimension of existence' that was beyond the control of
any human being, even those who had ordered it built and dropped.
No one could be blamed for a force beyond human comprehension or
control.[60]

Mostly, the survivors suffered, and grieved, and tried to get on with
their lives, with the articulate or artistic or merely thoughtful among
them occasionally coaxing forth their responses to being bombed. There
were the writers, like Ōe, Tamiki Hara, and Yōko Ōta, the last of
whom in 1955 published the story 'Residues of Squalor' (or 'Pockets of

Ugliness'). Five women and girls are sleeping in a hovel in post-bomb Hiroshima. The narrator, unable to sleep, watches in horror and fascination as 'countless' slugs crawl over the mosquito net under which her family members lie. Awakened, the narrator's mother and sister prepare salt water in a can, then, using discarded chopsticks, pluck the slugs one by one from the netting and drop them into the can. The narrator has no love for the molluscs, but finds herself revolted by this method of killing them:

> I looked in the can. They were half melting, but not completely melted. Thick and muddy, there was no sign of their having put up resistance to this sole primitive measure...I had begun to suffer from an association. It was about human beings heaped up in a mound of death, half burnt but not completely melted, with no energy to show any sign of resistance. They were so alike.

She cannot see the slugs die without remembering 'the pale white radioactive flash [that] burnt H City as though to toast it'. An ordinary act of pest extermination is transmuted into a vivid metaphor for the annihilation of human beings.[61]

Poetry, especially in its Japanese forms, seemed to lend itself to the expression of shock and lamentation. Haiku in particular captured the intensity of the bomb experience. Herewith three haiku by Hiroshima survivors:

> An empty shell I walk flowers hit my eyes (Isami Sasaki)
> To the jeep that quickly came I refused autopsy (Nobuyuki Okada)
> God suddenly averted His eyes at 8:15 (Genshi Fujikawa)[62]

The *hibakusha* poet Eisaku Yoneda caught the pathos of hope deadened by despair, of 'winter sunshine' overmatched by 'cold wind':

> Going along the dirt road,
> I see the winter sunshine brightly;
> The young shoots are through already,
> Steadily pushing between the ashes.
> And yet I look in vain for my young one,
> Hearing only the far sound of a cold wind.
> I stand on the Aioi Bridge, sick at heart.
> In the deep water something flashes!
> Ah! It is but an image,
> An image of his childhood.[63]

And finally, the unalloyed bleakness of Hiroshima, the dead city, in 'Ruins'. The poet is Sadako Kurihara:

> Hiroshima: nothing, nothing—
> old and young burned to death,
> city blown away,
> socket without eyeball.
> White bones scattered over reddish rubble;
> above, sun burning down:
> city of ruins, still as death.[64]

Last, and hardest, are the stories of survivors, related in letters or memoirs or told to journalists, psychologists, or historians (often Americans), not in soaring or bitter literary phrases but in the straightforward, significant prose of ordinary people. One of these was Fumiko Morishita, a waitress at a Hiroshima restaurant who seemed on 6 August unharmed by the bomb. But she had been exposed to radiation and soon sickened. Her fiancé, a soldier who had been away for years, against all odds returned intact and renewed his suit, despite Fumiko's illness. Having watched from her hospital bed as pregnant women gave birth to visibly damaged babies, she turned him away: it was not fair, she said, to subject him to the likely trauma of having retarded offspring. He persisted, holding her erect as they walked in the hospital garden, insisting that he still wanted to marry. But she would not be swayed and at last they parted company. She would never wed.[65]

Masao Baba was 5 years old and living in Hiroshima on 6 August. 'The atom bomb wrecked our big house and killed my father,' he recalled five years later. 'My brother lost an ear and my little sister lost an eye.' Masao's family left for the countryside but had moved back to the city when his mother received permission to build a 'shelter' there. His mother was running a second-hand store and his brother went to work each day. His sister got teased for having just one eye. Masao told her tormentors off, which temporarily put a stop to the teasing. It was harder for him when adults teased her too. 'If our father were alive, he would take her to the hospital and her eye would get better, but we don't have enough money to do that,' he said. 'I always worry about her and it's hard to study because I worry whether she is being teased or whether she is crying by herself.' When grown-ups laughed at her he thought: 'You just wait, you just wait!'[66]

Walking near a crossroads in Hiroshima two days after the bombing, the historian Toyofumi Ogura came upon a makeshift booth, patched together from bits of wood gathered from the wreckage that surrounded it. 'On the shelves', he observed, 'were rows of small packets made from old folded newspaper . . . like the ones in which peddlers wrap seeds. However, each of these packets contained a small quantity of ash and had a name and address written on them. Many didn't even have names—only a description, such as "Male about thirty years old" or "Forty-year-old female" '. Bereaved family members, Ogura noted, had come to claim the minuscule remains, even if it meant guessing wildly about whose ashes they were getting. Ogura's wife, Fumiyo, was doomed to die less than two weeks later. He continued to write letters about his experience, all of them addressed to her.[67]

Some five years later, after the stories of the *hibakusha* and their lost loved ones had begun to come to light, after censorship about the atomic bomb had eased in Japan and permitted publication of some memoirs and poems, Hanson W. Baldwin, the distinguished military affairs writer for the *New York Times*, published an essay in an edited volume called *Great Mistakes of the War*. Baldwin reviewed what was then known of Japanese decision-making during the summer of 1945 and concluded, in agreement with a number of postwar critics, that the atomic bombs had not been necessary to win the war. The Japanese, he wrote, were on the verge of surrender, the Emperor having aligned himself with the peace faction in July. By using the bombs, the Truman administration had exacted from the people of Japan a terrible price and had compromised America's moral standing in the world. Americans had 'inherited the mantle of Genghis Khan and all those of past history who have justified the use of utter ruthlessness in war', and were 'now branded with the mark of the beast'. Equally troubling was the precedent the bombs established of 'Total War'. By unleashing on defenseless citizens the power of the nucleus, the United States had removed the final restriction on the conduct of war, and it was utopian to assume that the United States itself would now be spared the consequences: 'We sowed there a whirlwind of hate which we shall someday reap.' In an age of bitter Cold War rivalry, and with the Soviet Union having detonated its first atomic bomb the previous summer, Baldwin's prediction had about it the ring of ominous and terrifying common sense.[68]

SEVEN

The Soviet Union: The Bomb and the Cold War

The profound shock felt in Hiroshima on the morning of 6 August rippled outward to the rest of the world, less destructive but hardly less psychologically powerful for its distance from its source. Two days after the bombing, an editorial writer for the Australian *Courier-Mail* was dumbstruck: 'What [the bomb] really is no one can begin to describe. Even scientists are lost for words that will describe the full magnitude of its terrifying force.' 'We still feel dazed by the implications of the new discovery,' wrote the editorialist for the *Shanghai Evening Post* on the 10th. The bomb was 'a thing to crush the mind'. More than a week later, Quebec's *L'Autorité* was still staggered; the bomb had 'left the civilized world dumbfounded'. In London, Palestine, and Rhodesia there was 'wonderment' and 'awe', while in Mexico City the bomb was 'a nightmare and [a] horror'. Little Boy 'was doubtless heard by human ears for hundreds of miles around, but morally it was heard around the world'. Even in New York, reported the *Herald Tribune*, 'one senses the foundations of one's own universe trembling'.[1]

When ordinary words and images failed, writers and analysts resorted to myth. J. E. Gendreau, who directed the Institute of Radiology at the University of Montreal, compared the cracking of the nucleus to the theft of fire by Prometheus. A journalist for *Le Populaire*, in Paris, thought of the biblical Tower of Babel, the handiwork of human arrogance aimed at reaching God. Others invoked Faust; as accounts of Hiroshima and Nagasaki gained circulation, it became easy to believe that scientists and statesmen had been granted the secret of the bomb only by their willingness to deal with the devil. (Bombay's *Statesman* offered this judgment: 'Substantial patent control has been established in America, the United Kingdom, and Canada... All who wish to apply should address communications to S. Lucifer, esq., Evil Patents Universal Unlimited, Nether Region.') Most often, commentators referred to the bomb as Frankenstein's monster, the terrible offspring of a science so self-absorbed, so consumed by its own curiosity or hubris, that it had lost sight of the consequences of its work. 'The legend of Frankenstein came back grimly to life when that bomb was dropped on Hiroshima,' declared the *Rhodesia Herald*, while the *Trinidad Guardian* thought the bomb 'a Frankenstein more terrible even than Mrs Shelley's famous creation', and the *Sydney Morning Herald* warned that scientists 'have called into being a Frankenstein monster which, if unfettered, has the power to destroy its creators'—a somewhat optimistic version of the myth in its willingness to make the monster's destructiveness conditional.[2]

No one doubted that something very dramatic had happened, something new and revolutionary had been ushered in. Some thought the apocalypse loomed. Humans had fashioned the tools of their ultimate destruction; another war, cautioned *Montreal-Matin*, would bring 'the complete annihilation of humankind'. An editorialist in Alberta was more matter of fact: the announcement of the bomb 'means simply that men now know how to blast the whole world to smithereens'. Future war was now impossible, for, if war happened, human civilization would end. The *Palestine Post*, echoing a column in the *New York Times*, imagined a world 'equipped with underground cities in which a race of modern troglodytes might seek shelter from atomic blasts'. There was criticism of the United States for using the bomb and of the British for presumably having helped build it; the Japanese-controlled *Hong Kong News* referred bitterly to the Allies' 'diabolic nature', and Bombay's *Free Press Journal* inveighed against the 'savagery' of destroying whole cities. But other commentary was less accusatory and, sometimes, cautiously optimistic. The bomb was traced not to the Americans or a particular set of perpetrators, but to 'mankind', 'science' in the abstract, or (most often) 'humanity'. Because humans had unleashed nuclear energy, the rational and just among them might now find a way to harness it for some good purpose. The French commentator E. Letellier de Saint-Just hoped for 'a new radiant world where mankind would live in brotherhood' if the alternative was annihilation. The bomb was a double-edged sword, thought the *Trinidad Guardian*, embodying 'undreamed of possibilities... for science knows no barriers'. Recalling the science fiction of H. G. Wells, some writers speculated that the peaceful uses of nuclear energy—supplying power, for example, for lighting, heating, and transportation—might prove the bomb's truest legacy, as long as human beings foreswore further use of atomic weapons.[3]

To an extent, international reaction to the bomb followed the accounts of American newspapers and American-based news organizations. American sources presumably knew more about the bomb than did others, and authority attached itself naturally to scientists who built the device, some of whom were quoted in reports during the weeks following Japan's surrender. Phrases drawn from US newspaper stories, especially from the *New York Times*, found their way unedited into English-language papers across the globe. In that way did the discourse surrounding the atomic bomb begin with a common source, and one not inclined to criticism of the decision to use the weapon. Relief that the war was over, and the conviction that the bombs had contributed enormously to its ending, seemed to cascade in all directions from US and Western media capitals. So too, it should be said, did a measure of sobriety and reflectiveness concerning the means used to end the war. President Harry S. Truman had first exulted when he heard of the Hiroshima bombing—'the greatest thing in history', he had called it—but his tone was different three days later, prior to the Japanese surrender, when he wrote to a belligerent senator: 'I certainly regret the necessity of wiping out whole populations because of the "pigheadedness" of the leaders of a nation and, for your information, I am not going to do it unless it is absolutely necessary.' Winston Churchill, a strong advocate for the bomb project, by the early autumn sounded subdued: 'This revelation of the secrets of nature, long mercifully withheld from man, should arouse the most solemn reflections in the mind and conscience of every human being capable of comprehension.' And Charles de Gaulle, leader of the Free French Resistance during the war, while professing not to be surprised at the news of the atomic bombings, nevertheless confessed himself 'no less tempted to despair at the birth of means that made possible the annihilation of the human race'.[4]

Though influenced by American interpretation of the bomb's meaning, representatives of other nations also responded to the event with images and idioms that were very much their own. The most common description of the exploded bomb, offered first by the air crews who observed the bombings and then in the United States but frequently repeated elsewhere, was a great, mushroom-shaped cloud. But descriptions also corresponded to phenomena, both miraculous and disastrous and always powerful, that were local and familiar. *El Nacional*, the organ of the Mexican government, reported on 7 August that 'the first earthquake-bomb' had struck Hiroshima and focused on the bomb's effects on the city's trains. 'It is interesting' writes Regis Cabral, 'that the newspaper associated the A-bomb with two matters of concern to Mexico, one of them quite serious: Earthquakes and railroad performance.' In Japan the bomb was likened also to an earthquake or typhoon. The *Rhodesia Herald* brought the bomb's impact close to home by pointing out that a single bomb produced enough devastation to destroy the center of Johannesburg—or enough power 'to drive the Witwatersrand gold mines for perhaps weeks'. A Trinidad paper compared the bomb to a volcano, much like Mont Pelé, which had erupted recently on nearby Martinique. (The Reuters news agency called on readers to suggest names for the bomb. 'Doomsday Bomb' and 'Earth-Shaker' earned mention in Reuters stories, but 'The Japatomiser' won a headline in the *Pretoria News*.)[5]

The psychologist Robert Jay Lifton, who interviewed survivors of the Hiroshima bombing during the early 1960s, concluded that many of them regarded the attack and its results as 'unnatural' or even 'supernatural' occurrences, in which 'Buddhist hell' or an utter void had replaced an earthly city of human beings. That may have been a first reaction, allowing as it did some distancing between living victims of the atomic bomb and what they had experienced: what had happened was beyond comprehension because it was part of another world, and one could not get one's mind around it, so it was pointless trying to do so. But the subsequent comparison of the bombing to natural phenomena, in Japan and elsewhere, created a memory of the attack that was at once familiar and abstract. If the bomb was like lightning or an earthquake or a volcano, it was something that a nation had suffered before, and from which it had recovered. It was a horror, but it was nevertheless oddly comforting to connect the unknown impact of the bomb to something as natural as a storm. Making this sort of comparison also permitted people to avoid blaming anyone in particular for having unleashed the bomb. No one is responsible for an earthquake; one can shake one's fist at the earth or God, for all the good it will do. Scientists who built the bomb would tell themselves that the weapon's secret was always somewhere out there, waiting to be discovered, and that they had stumbled on it first. Mushrooms need not be planted by humans—they just appear. Even giant ones can, of course, be picked and eaten and thus tamed.[6]

1. The American response

Among leading American statesmen, reactions to the atomic bombings ranged widely. Secretary of State James Byrnes avoided any open remorse, continuing to treat the bomb as a happily found instrument of war and diplomacy. When, at a foreign ministers' conference in London in September 1945, Soviet Foreign Minister Vyacheslav Molotov asked Byrnes whether he had 'an atomic bomb in his side pocket', Byrnes responded: 'You don't know southerners. We carry our artillery in our pocket. If you don't cut out all this stalling and let us get down to work, I'm going to pull an atomic bomb out of my hip pocket and let you have it.' It was a bizarre reply, but one with a point—Byrnes did not see himself as treading on atomic eggshells. Henry Stimson, on the other hand, had long worried that the bomb would complicate, not clarify, the postwar situation. By his efforts the Japanese shrine city of Kyoto had been spared; he had gone forward with the decision to use the bomb willingly but with a sense of gravity and even occasional torment. On the day of the Nagasaki bombing, Stimson told a radio audience that American elation at having built the bomb 'must be overshadowed by a deeper emotion. The result of the bomb is so terrific that the responsibility of its possession and its use must weigh heavier on our minds and on our hearts.' Several weeks later, on the verge of retirement, the Secretary of War handed Truman a remarkable memorandum in which he urged that the bomb's 'secrets of production' be shared with the Soviet Union: 'The chief lesson I have learned in a long life', he wrote, 'is that the only way you can make a man trustworthy is to trust him; and the surest way to make him untrustworthy is to distrust him and show him your distrust.' Truman himself remained publicly steadfast in his statements. The bomb(s) had been necessary to end the war quickly and save American lives, he said. Robert Oppenheimer may have detected blood on his hands, but the President impatiently reproved him and soon after complained about the ' "crybaby" scientist . . . wringing his hands' in Truman's office. Yet others sensed anguish in the President. There was the note to Senator Russell on 9 August, in which Truman said that he hoped he could avoid 'wiping out' the Japanese population. The next day, Truman told his cabinet, according to Vice President Henry Wallace, that he had decided to stop the atomic bombing while surrender negotiations proceeded. 'He said the thought of wiping out another 100,000 people was too horrible,' Wallace wrote in his diary. 'He didn't like the idea of killing, as he said, "all those kids".' The vehemence with which Truman later asserted his lack of doubt about the bombings might well suggest an element of insecurity concerning the decision.[7]

Leading American military men also experienced a range of emotions concerning the use of the bomb. Fleet Admiral William Leahy, Truman's chief of staff, would place the atomic bomb in the same category of opprobrium occupied by chemical and biological weapons, and concluded his 1950 memoir by declaring: 'Employment of the atomic bomb in war will take us back in cruelty toward noncombatants to the days of Genghis Khan.' Others escaped remorse. 'Like taxes, radioactivity has long been with us and in increasing amounts,' wrote Ralph Lapp of the Office of Naval Research. 'It is not to be hated and feared, but... treated with respect, avoided when practicable, and accepted when inevitable.' Curtis LeMay professed himself unbothered by the need to kill Japanese, by whatever means necessary, in order to end the war, and he made pointed comparison between the atomic bombings and the burning of Japanese cities by incendiaries. In early 1946 the Americans presented Japanese officials with a draft of the new constitution, then removed to the garden while the Japanese reviewed the text. When, having finished reading, Jirō Shirasu joined the Americans among the flowers, General Courtney Whitney remarked: 'We have been enjoying your atomic sunshine,' suggesting not just a lack of remorse but an astonishing callousness concerning the fates of many thousands at Hiroshima and Nagasaki.[8]

Robert Oppenheimer wrung his hands in Truman's office after the bombs had been dropped. When he left Los Alamos that fall, honored with a certificate of appreciation from Stimson via Leslie Groves, he warned: 'If atomic bombs are to be added as new weapons to the arsenals of a warring world, or to the arsenals of nations preparing for war, then the time will come when mankind will curse the names of Los Alamos and of Hiroshima.' So, he added, 'the peoples of the world must be united, or they will perish'. Many physicists shared this hope, that their 'traveling seminar' would now be reconstituted, that Niels Bohr's model of sharing scientific information without regard for inconvenient national borders would rekindle trust and ensure peace. Along with Oppenheimer and

Bohr, Enrico Fermi, Leo Szilard, Albert Einstein, and James Franck all agreed with Eleanor Roosevelt, who several days after Hiroshima told a radio audience that the bomb had been made by 'many minds belonging to different races and different religions', a fact that 'sets the pattern for the way in which in the future we may be able to work out our difficulties'. Secrecy in science was artifice, a sham made temporarily necessary by world war but ultimately doomed to failure. There were no atomic secrets; physicists everywhere, properly funded and sufficiently motivated, would quickly learn how to build a bomb. Arthur Compton, predictably, found religious meaning in the bomb's discovery. It was 'God's will' that America had secured atomic power, and the bomb had been used appropriately to win the just war. He cautioned, however, that humankind must undergo 'a rapid growth in moral stature' if it was to avoid destruction.[9]

There was drift in the scientific community, perhaps an inability to grasp the implications of what it had helped to do. Attending a conference of scientists, philosophers, and religion specialists in late August 1945, a reporter for the *New York Times* was astonished to find the experts seeming to avoid all mention of the bomb, 'fiddl[ing],' he said, 'while the world burned'. At loose ends once Oppenheimer had left the desert, Edward Teller and metallurgist Cyril Smith gathered a group of Taos Pueblo Indians and addressed them concerning the mysteries of the atom. There was much talk, among scientists and others, of the peaceful uses of atomic energy, the hope that from devastation would spring innovation, efficiency, clean energy, and solutions to nearly every problem modernity posed. Physicists found themselves having to disabuse the public of at least the wildest of these schemes. (An Arkansas farmer wrote to scientists at Oak Ridge to ask if they had any atom bombs the right size for blowing stumps out of his fields.) Otto Frisch cautioned that atomic-powered automobiles were not in prospect: 'A few minutes' ride in this car would be enough to kill you.' Bemused by the postwar hype, Fermi said, of atomic power, 'it would be nice if it could cure the common cold'. But the bomb's success also conferred status on the physicists, and status translated into lavish federal funding for their atomic projects. I. I. Rabi and Norman Ramsey built a nuclear research laboratory at Brookhaven, Long Island. Leslie Groves provided $170,000 from the Manhattan District for Ernest Lawrence and his brother-in-law Edward McMillan to build at Berkeley a new generation cyclotron, called by McMillan a synchrotron. By the end of the 1940s, notes

Daniel Kevles, the number of university physics majors had doubled since the years before the war, and the field was regarded as the most exciting among the sciences.[10]

'Isn't physics wonderful?' gushed Rabi as the grants rolled in. Samuel Goudsmit was not so sure. Goudsmit had served with Boris Pash's Alsos team that knifed into Germany late in the war searching for evidence of a Nazi nuclear weapons program. They found only reassurance, but his brush with this threat and his own extensive knowledge of how the weapons worked had left Goudsmit shaken. His young physicist colleagues went off to atomic-bomb tests in the Pacific as 'jaunty' as if on a 'holiday'. They returned not sobered by what they had seen but 'full of jolly little reminiscences' about the enormous blasts. This was a kind of hubris Goudsmit found unsettling; it was hardly so wonderful as Rabi proclaimed.[11]

The American people for the most part reacted favorably to the bombings, believing they had ended the war and thus saved their soldiers' lives. A Gallup poll in late August 1945 found 85 percent approval for the use of the bombs; that fall, a Roper poll indicated that 53.5 percent of those questioned thought the attacks on Hiroshima and Nagasaki had been just right, while nearly 23 percent more wished the military had dropped more atomic bombs 'before the Japanese had a chance to surrender'. (Doubt and even disapproval of the bombings rose over the next two years.) American culture did what cultures do when they feel nervous or threatened: it incorporated the bomb into its language and forms, demystifying and co-opting and even making fun of it. There were Atomic Cocktails (Pernod and gin) and an 'Atomic Bomb' dessert, served in Boston. *Life* magazine ran a photo of a model in a two-piece bathing suit—'Miss Anatomic Bomb'. (Reduced versions of such suits would soon be called bikinis, named after the atoll where the first postwar a-bomb tests took place in July 1946.) There were atomic brooches and earrings, 'atomic sales' at department stores, and a child's 'Atomic Bomb Ring' available for 15 cents and a boxtop from Kix cereal, offering a 'sealed atom chamber' in which the owner could 'see genuine atoms SPLIT to smithereens!' There were songs—'When the Atom Bomb Fell', 'Atom Buster', and 'Atom Polka'—dances, and poems:

> The power to blow all things to dust
> Was kept for people God could trust,
> And granted unto them alone,
> That evil might be overthrown.

A disgruntled fan of the Philadelphia Athletics baseball club urged that team members be administered atomic vitamins.[12]

Anxiety about the bomb largely resulted from fears that others, less trusted by God than Americans—the Soviets especially—would soon learn how to build one. Publicly, at least, leading US statesmen declared themselves unworried by this prospect. In this, they took their cues from Groves, who, as in all else, tended to substitute his own appetites and wishes for careful analysis of scientific evidence, or even plain logic. In the spring of 1945 Groves had told the Interim Committee that it would take the Russians up to twenty years to develop the bomb; in this estimate he simply gainsaid the views of many scientists, who thought it might take three to five years. James Byrnes chose to believe Groves, reporting to Szilard in May 1945 that 'there is no uranium in Russia' (not true), and behaving through that summer and fall as though the US nuclear monopoly was a thing assured. 'When will the Russians be able to build the bomb?' President Truman asked Oppenheimer in 1946. 'I don't know,' replied Oppenheimer. 'I know,' Truman said. 'Never.' Truman would later tell a senator that he doubted 'those Asiatics' would ever solve the mysteries of the bomb. This was not the position of experts from the newly created US Central Intelligence Agency in 1947. But agency analysts nevertheless concluded that it was 'doubtful that the Russians can produce a bomb before 1953 and almost certain they cannot produce one before 1951'. 'There existed toward the end of 1947', Gregg Herken has written, 'a remarkable complacency in the military and in the Truman administration concerning the durability of the atomic secret and of the US monopoly of atomic bombs.'[13]

2. The early Soviet nuclear program

Such complacency was sharply at odds with reality, and especially ignorant of the progress made by Soviet nuclear scientists. It will be recalled that the Soviets had had a sophisticated group of physicists and a reasonably progressive (though generally imitative) nuclear program before the German invasion of June 1941. Josef Stalin's regime during the 1930s limited the movements of physicists and other scientists, frequently preventing them from traveling abroad and making it difficult for their foreign colleagues to visit them. Peter Kapitsa was kept from returning to his work in Cambridge in 1934. Some were tossed into prison or executed. Despite the odds, physics research went forward. In Britain, H. G. Wells had inspired and frightened Leo Szilard by imagining an atomic bomb. In 1908 Alexander Bogdanov published the novel *Red Star*, in which Marxist utopian Martians use atomic power to help achieve the good society. Research on the nucleus began in earnest in the Soviet Union following the *annus mirabilis*, 1932, in which James Chadwick at the Cavendish Laboratory discovered the neutron, Cal Tech's Carl Anderson found the positively charged electron (positron), and Ernest Lawrence used his newly built cyclotron to accelerate protons around a magnetic track. Thereafter Abram Ioffe, head of the Physicotechnical Institute in Leningrad, organized an international physics conference, to which many luminaries and top young Russian physicists came. Within a year, there were four nuclear physics labs in operation at Ioffe's institute, headed by Igor Kurchatov. A cyclotron was built at the Leningrad Radium Institute, in the charge of V. I. Vernadskii and to some extent in competition with Ioffe's establishment, but by the late 1930s Kurchatov had effectively commandeered the machine for his own experiments. In other nuclear labs, in the Ukraine and in Moscow, work proceeded fitfully during the mid-1930s, constrained not by a lack of scientific sophistication but by political rivalries, limited funding, and harassment and worse from the regime.[14]

The discovery of fission in late 1938 and its publicity early in 1939 energized the Soviet physics community. Experimentation sped up in all the labs and produced exciting results, concerning the number of neutrons released during fission and circumstances under which a chain reaction might occur, and including the type of moderating agent that would most effectively allow neutrons to strike nuclei and set the chain in motion. Like their counterparts in Europe and the United States, few Soviet physicists thought in 1939 that practical applications of nuclear energy would soon be realized. David Holloway notes that in early 1941 the physicists Yuli Khariton and Yakov Zeldovich wrote a paper suggesting that 10 kilograms of uranium 235 could yield 'a chain reaction . . . with the liberation of tremendous quantities of energy'—an overestimate, but much closer to the correct answer than most previous overestimates—and pointed out that compressing the uranium with an explosive would induce the reaction to take place. Holloway rightly compares this paper (which was neither published nor attended by the authorities) to the Frisch–Peierls memorandum of the same period, though he also notes that the Russians failed to suggest how a quantity of the 235 isotope might be produced, in this way unlike Frisch and

Peierls. Soviet physics ran on tracks parallel to those laid out in the West, or perhaps just behind on the same tracks. Niels Bohr, virtually alone, noticed and admired Soviet progress, and understood that it would not be undone or reversed. But when Germany attacked the Soviet Union on 22 June 1941, work on fission was for the time being shelved in favor of defense research more likely to be productive in the short run. Kurchatov abandoned his fission experiments; Ioffe's institute was moved east and left unsettled.[15]

Like the British and the Americans, before 1941 Soviet scientists gave little thought to the possibility of atomic weapons, believing them impractical. Peter Kapitsa went to work on, among other things, the production of liquid oxygen (for which Russian industry, he wrote Stalin in disgust, was altogether unprepared), and monitored Western physics and physicists as best he could. Good intelligence on the infant state of the German nuclear program gave further disincentive to push forward into the expensive unknown. But in the fall of 1941 the Soviets learned of the recently written MAUD Report, in which British scientists concluded that the production of atomic bombs might be feasible. Slowly the state reacted. In early 1943, Stalin authorized a limited program to build a nuclear weapon. The decision coincided with the initiation of a Soviet counteroffensive out of Stalingrad, codenamed Operation Uran—'Uranus', or more likely 'uranium'. Stalin did not, in Holloway's view, believe a Soviet atomic bomb would ever prove decisive against the Germans. Instead, 'the project he started is best understood as a rather small hedge against future uncertainties'. Igor Kurchatov, who had vowed not to shave his robust beard until 'Fritz' was beaten, was put in charge of the project, and in early March Foreign Minister Molotov sat him down with a stack of papers smuggled out of Britain by Soviet agents. These materials, concerning especially isotope separation techniques and the morphology of a chain reaction, were, according to Kurchatov, of 'huge, inestimable significance for our state and science'.[16]

3. The Soviets' atomic spies

These materials were transmitted by men working secretly for the Soviet Union and without the knowledge or permission of the British government. Later there would be more, and more valuable, information about the state of the British and American atomic-bomb programs, sent to Moscow by spies such as John Cairncross (the probable source of the data Kurchatov saw in early 1943), Klaus Fuchs, Theodore Hall, David Greenglass, and Julius Rosenberg. That these men, and others, provided important atomic intelligence to the Soviets is no longer in doubt: evidence gleaned from a US National Security Agency (NSA) top-secret codebreaking operation that ran for over three decades following the end of the Second World War, called 'Venona', shows that the Soviets had a number of spies in the United States, several of whom conveyed substantial knowledge of the Manhattan Project through handlers attached to the Soviet embassy or consulates. Venona, revealed fully only after the Cold War had ended in the mid-1990s, contained roughly 3,000 messages sent during the war by Soviet operatives to officials in Moscow. These messages were so highly classified that they were inadmissable as evidence in court cases pursued against accused spies during the early Cold War; successful convictions relied instead on less direct evidence from other sources, confessions, or the credibility to judges or juries of those making accusations of espionage.[17]

The discovery of Venona and the implication of Soviet spies more gen-erally in the transmission of 'secrets' from the West to the Soviet Union has contributed to a triumphalist conservative interpretation of the Cold War. Here is proof positive, some historians have seemed to say, that the Russians were up to no good, that their own nuclear program was nothing without a supply of information from more advanced programs, that they stole and cheated their way to nuclear parity with the United States during the Cold War, as if confirming their general duplicitousness, untrustworthiness, and capacity for serious misbehavior. Each new disclosure about atomic spies, fully substantiated or not, was greeted with a kind of knowing sneer; driving spies out of history's woodwork became an occasion for gleeful bashing of 'revisionist' historians who had dared to imagine more nuanced or numerous causes of the Cold War than Soviet perfidy alone. This tendency was abetted, though perhaps unwittingly, by the term used to describe the acquisition of nuclear weapons by more and more nations after 1945: proliferation. That is a biological, even botanical word, which means reproducing 'by multiplying new parts', as in budding. It suggests that the United States was the sole source of nuclear knowledge, of understanding how to develop a bomb, and that therefore anyone else who learned to do it must have discovered the Americans' secret formula. There was a center and a periphery of nuclear knowledge. Since the Manhattan Project was secret, and since after 1945 the United States prohibited dissemination (another biological term—it means, first, 'to scatter seed') of information about the bomb's construction, it must have been espionage that allowed the Russians to penetrate the American nuclear curtain and test a bomb in the late summer of 1949, many years before Groves, at least, thought such an occurrence possible.[18]

As Kurchatov's excitement over the British material in March 1943 indicates, the Soviets did learn by espionage important information about nuclear physics and bomb building in the West. The Russians gave the codename 'Enormoz' to their 'nuclear research' project in the United States, Britain, and Canada. According to Pavel Sudoplatov, a general in the KGB and by his own account a Soviet 'spymaster' during the war, the Russians had twenty-nine agents inside the Manhattan Project. That is probably an exaggeration—and, even if there were that many, most were of negligible influence—but Enormoz plainly bore some attractive fruit. Quiet Klaus Fuchs, a communist driven from Germany by the Brownshirts, had found physics work alongside Rudolf Peierls at Birmingham; the two men began in earnest to work on the bomb in the spring of 1941. 'When I learned the purpose of the work,' Fuchs would say, 'I decided to inform Russia'—a matter of ideological necessity and strategic duty, he thought. The Soviets, as noted, learned of the MAUD Report, engineering work at the great American plant at Oak Ridge, Tennessee (this courtesy of Fuchs), and evidently something of the composition of Enrico Fermi's University of Chicago squash court reactor. Fuchs went to Los Alamos, part of the British scientific team there, in August 1944. Already in place was a precocious Harvard physics student named Theodore Hall. An expert on the properties of uranium, Hall had been assigned Room T-236. 'Oh, that's just next door to U-235,' he quipped, but no one found it funny. Ted Hall thought the only way to ensure world peace over time was to make sure that the Russians knew what the Americans knew about atomic bombs. Also at Los Alamos, having arrived nine days before Fuchs, was David Greenglass. Not a physicist but a machinist, Greenglass was, along with his wife, Ruth, a member of the Young Communist League, though not of the Communist Party itself. He thought the Soviets were fighting a magnificent battle against Fascism and that Stalin and other Soviet leaders were 'geniuses' who used force against their own people only 'with pain in their hearts'. Greenglass's brother-in-law and recruiter was Julius

Rosenberg, an inspection engineer for the Army Signal Corps and a Soviet agent since 1942.[19]

Through couriers and contacts, these men dispatched to Moscow a good deal of information about the atomic bomb. Fuchs and Hall, both well placed at Los Alamos, contributed material on the implosion core of the plutonium bomb. (None of the scientists underwent body searches when they left The Hill for time in town.) Fuchs provided, in early 1945, 'a quite considerable packet of information', according to his courier Harry Gold, which included an account 'summarizing the whole problem of making an atomic bomb as he then saw it'. Hall offered much the same, telling his Soviet contact that 'all the outstanding physicists of the US, England, Italy and Germany (immigrants), and Denmark are working on this thing', and that he did not want to see the Soviet Union 'blackmailed' by some nuclear fraternity at the war's end. David Greenglass gave Julius Rosenberg a list of Los Alamos scientists and several rough sketches of lens molds that would be used to make devices critical to the plutonium bomb's implosion core. Rosenberg himself, excluded from life on The Hill but a true believer, gave his Soviet contact, Alexander Feklisov, a (non-nuclear) proximity fuse for Christmas in 1944. It was Julius's most important gift to the Soviet Union—ironically, given his fate and his later reputation as an atomic-bomb spy.[20]

Some analysts have concluded that the information passed to the Soviets, especially by Fuchs, was critical to their ability to produce a plutonium-based bomb by August 1949. There is something oddly comforting in this belief, in the idea that Soviet knowledge came by proliferation: the American scientists are accorded a monopoly on perceptiveness, American officials a monopoly on problem solving, and only through underhanded means did the Russians (and ultimately others) gain the information they needed to make a bomb. Soviet intelligence officials, who have an interest in proving the importance of espionage, and some Soviet scientists, who do not, have claimed that they succeeded in building a bomb because of secrets stolen from the Manhattan Project. Kurchatov, who had found the British material of 'inestimable significance' in early 1943, two years later rated intelligence from Theodore Hall 'of great interest', then Fuchs's 1945 report as having 'great value'. (Fuchs provided more details of the plutonium bomb's design in reports in June and September 1945.) Kurchatov later said that the first Soviet bomb, tested on 29 August 1949, was a replica of the one the Americans had dropped on Nagasaki, the design of which had been secured from Fuchs and others. The KGB officer Pavel Sudoplatov argued that the Soviets rejected all American attempts to limit atomic energy starting in late 1945 because they 'had already stolen the information they needed from the United States to build their own bomb'. 'The United States would later accuse the USSR of having stolen their atomic secrets,' wrote Feklisov, the case officer for Fuchs and Julius Rosenberg. 'This is true. I was in a position to know that Soviet nuclear weapons were very closely based on American prototypes,' indeed that the first three Soviet test bombs were 'replicas' of American weapons.[21]

But there are several reasons to think that information purloined from the Americans was not, in itself, the critical factor explaining why the Soviets got the bomb when they did. In the first place, intelligence gained by espionage had to be crosschecked for accuracy. Stalin and Lavrenti Beria, the fearsome KGB chief whom Stalin put in charge of the Russian nuclear-bomb program in August 1945 ('dealing with Beria was no joke', recalled Yuli Khariton), worried that their intelligence was incomplete, or subject to disinformation by the Americans, whom they suspected were on to them. (There is a Soviet myth that, at one point, Kurchatov brought Stalin a plutonium sphere, coated with nickel, to reassure the dictator that the physicists knew what they were doing. 'And how do we know that this is plutonium, not a sparkling piece of iron?' Stalin allegedly asked.) Second, while Fuchs provided sound and specific data on the design of a plutonium bomb, he was not asked to describe the workings of a plutonium-producing reactor, including how to 'can' the uranium (as at Hanford) or how to prepare graphite for use as a moderator. Either the Soviets did not know enough to ask Fuchs about these processes, or their scientists already knew what was needed to make them work. And Americans like Groves underestimated the ability of the Soviet Union's centralized economy to gear up quickly for the production of nuclear weapons. What had been for the Americans an extraordinary wartime effort to mobilize production facilities, knowledge, and resources was for the Soviets, after August 1945, a matter of Stalin readjusting his economy's priorities with a virtual stroke of the pen.[22]

Above all, the claim that the Soviet bomb succeeded *primarily* because of information passed by spies ignores substantial evidence that the Russians had deep nuclear knowledge and a sophisticated research program of their own, both before and during the war. Despite the decision taken to depri-oritize nuclear-weapons work during the war and the dislocation suffered by Ioffe and his physicists, Soviet scientists had not suspended their thinking about nuclear power and atomic weapons. Peter Kapitsa, mired in a liquid oxygen project and believing in any case that no bomb was in prospect any time soon, nevertheless suggested to a group of scientists in October 1941 that an atomic bomb, capable of destroying 'a major capital city with several million inhabitants', was theoretically possible. Popular science magazines carried reasonably accurate stories about the Soviet 'discovery' of fission and ongoing nuclear work in well-appointed labs. Russian physicists, who had before the war read and replicated the experiments of their counterparts elsewhere, and who had made discoveries of their own, did not forget what they had learned while the war raged. Stalin's 'hedged' bomb project started in 1943. Khariton, Zeldovich, and others never abandoned work on explosives; engineers dedicated themselves to projects of a scale commensurate with what would be needed to create a bomb. As Holloway points out, the Soviets managed to test, in 1951, a gun-assembly uranium core bomb, for which Fuchs had provided no help. What did help, and despite more Soviet suspicion of American disinformation, was publication, just weeks after the atomic bombings, of an official US report called *Atomic Energy for Military Purposes*, usually called the Smyth Report after its author, Princeton physicist Henry D. Smyth. As they had with their agents' reports from the United States, Soviet authorities read the Smyth Report 'with great interest'.[23]

What most determined the timing of the first Soviet bomb test in 1949 was not information learned from spies but, Holloway concludes, the availability of uranium in the Soviet Union. 'As soon as uranium became available in sufficient quantity,' he writes, 'Kurchatov was able to build and start up the experimental reactor.' Fuchs, who had not visited the Soviet Union, thought that he had accelerated the Soviet bomb project 'by one year at least'; Holloway is willing to make this one to two years' time saved through intelligence information, and notes that the British, who were far better represented at Los Alamos than the Soviets, took five years from deciding to build a bomb to testing it, about a year longer than the Russians. 'One should not overestimate the importance of [the] Soviet intelligence community in setting up the atomic program although its efforts and its contribution were commendable,' wrote Khariton, who was there. Emphasis on the role of espionage in the Soviet project exaggerates the extent to which proliferation explains the extension of nuclear know-how. A better model is polycentric, acknowledging as it does multiple sources of knowledge and multiple sites of imaginative and productive work on the nucleus. Physicists in the Soviet Union can share the credit and must share the blame for their efforts to build an atomic bomb after 1945.[24]

4. Stalin decides to build the bomb

Truman had told Stalin at Potsdam on 24 July that the United States had a powerful new weapon, though he failed to specify what it was. 'We guessed at once what he had in mind,' said Foreign Minister Molotov some years later, and the general G. K. Zhukov claimed that Stalin had said, 'we'll have to have a talk with Kurchatov today about speeding up our work'. According to Tsuyoshi Hasegawa, Stalin now knew that he must try to enter the war against Japan before the Americans dropped the first of their bombs; in the event, of course, he did not quite make it. After Hiroshima, Stalin realized the strategic importance of the bomb. With the United States ambassador Averell Harriman and counselor George Kennan on 8 August, the dictator seemed sanguine, though he let the Americans know the significance of Soviet intervention in the Pacific War and hinted that atomic secrecy was unlikely to be permanent. Privately, Stalin brought together the Kremlin's commissar (and commissariat) of munitions and Igor Kurchatov. 'A single demand of you, comrades!' he told the group. 'Provide us with atomic weapons in the shortest possible time! You know Hiroshima has shaken the whole world. The balance [of power] has been destroyed! Provide the bomb—it will remove a great danger from us.' To Kurchatov alone, Stalin said: 'If a child doesn't cry, the mother doesn't know what he needs. Ask for whatever you like. You won't be refused.'[25]

Under the gimlet eye of Beria, who treated his scientists with a bluntness Leslie Groves had fantasized about, the Soviet atomic-bomb project moved forward. Kurchatov's student Igor Golovin wrote: 'every institute capable of helping solve the atomic problem was called upon to mobilize its scientific resources and contribute under an integrated scientific plan.' Golovin was caught up in the excitement; he came to admire Beria's 'administrative abilities' ('Meetings did not drag on for hours; everything was decided quickly'), and assumed that Beria's use of slave laborers, pulled from four nearby prison camps, was simply necessary to build a bomb before the Americans saw fit to attack Moscow. Less enamored of the work conditions,

Beria's highhandedness, and what he considered a mistaken approach to bomb building, Peter Kapitsa resigned from the project, writing to Stalin, 'there is much that is abnormal in the organization of the work on the atomic bomb'. And, Kapitsa felt, political leaders refused to trust their scientists. There was a good deal to this last criticism in particular, but Khariton and his colleagues, along with engineers and technicians who learned as they went on with the project, maintained morale sufficient to work at a rapid pace. Whatever his suspicions, Stalin made sure the project was fully funded and the scientists provided for. He had built for Kurchatov, on the forested grounds of his laboratory, a beautiful eight-room house with parquet floors and marble fireplaces.[26]

Groves wrote in the *Saturday Evening Post* in 1948 that the Soviets lacked the scientific know-how and 'precision industry' to keep up with the United States technologically. The Russians used 'axle grease where we use fine lubricating oils. It is an oxcart-versus-automobile situation.' Groves underestimated Soviet talent, resources, and resourcefulness. There was uranium in the Soviet Union—in Central Asia, the Ukraine, and eastern Siberia—and the Russians also demanded ore from Czech Jachymov and especially the German side of the Erzgebirge, extracted with prison labor. An experimental reactor, conceived by Khariton in 1943, went critical on Christmas night 1946, just over four years after Fermi's pile had succeeded. (Beria, at the scene a few days later, was disappointed that high-speed clicking and jumping instrument needles offered the only evidence that the pile was working and asked to enter the reactor itself. Kurchatov may have been tempted, but he dissuaded Beria from going in.) A full production reactor came next. Uranium would be refined to plutonium at a site called Chelyabinsk-40, east of the Ural Mountains and about 15 miles from the village of Kyshtym. There the Soviets built a reactor called Annushka ('Little Anna'), using for a reaction moderator graphite refined onsite, much of it a Lend Lease gift from the United States. There were mistakes, accidents, occasional fires, and alarming small explosions. Annushka was nevertheless ready to start in June 1948. Almost immediately, the aluminum cans surrounding the uranium slugs corroded and had to be replaced. Then the slugs themselves swelled so much they could not be discharged from the pile. Khariton had the canned slugs removed, rebored the slug channels in the reactor, then replaced the uranium in the machine. The glitch cost the Russians nearly six months.[27]

Chelyabinsk-40 was like Hanford. The Soviet Los Alamos was near a town called Sarov, roughly 400 kilometers east of Moscow but at the edge of a forest and fairly isolated. The site was named Arzamas-16 after a small city to the north; as Holloway notes, 'it was also—inevitably—referred to as "Los Arzamas"'. There experimenters replicated tasks that their Los Alamos counterparts had undertaken several years earlier. To Georgi Flerov, one of the co-discoverers of spontaneous fission in an experiment set up in a Moscow subway station in February 1940, fell Louis Slotin's dangerous job: establishing the criticality of two plutonium hemispheres as they moved closer together. Scientists disagreed for a time over whether they had allowed for sufficient compression to produce implosion. The problems were solved, and by summer 1949 Kurchatov was ready to test his bomb. The Soviet Alamogordo was near the town of Semipalatinsk, in northeast Kazakhstan. It was steppe country, very hot in summer, and far away from prying eyes. The bomb was assembled at the foot of a 100-foot tower. Yuli Khariton nested the initiator between the plutonium hemispheres, then, at 2.00 in the morning of 29 August, the 'article', as the bomb was nicknamed, was carried up the tower in a freight elevator. At the top the bomb was armed, by Flerov among others. Kurchatov went off to the command post, Beria to an adjacent cabin to sleep. As with Trinity, it rained during the night, causing a brief delay in the test. As with Trinity, the weather improved a bit as dawn arrived. Kurchatov ordered the countdown. At 7.00 it reached zero. The steppe turned white with illumination; the shock wave struck the command center, breaking the glass. 'It worked,' said Kurchatov. Beria hugged and kissed him and Khariton. If the bomb had not worked, a scientist later recalled, 'they would all have been shot'.[28]

The test bomb was the equivalent of 20 kilotons of TNT, roughly the same as the gadget had yielded at Alamogordo four years and one month earlier. Beria confirmed the shot's success with an observer who had witnessed an American test several years earlier, then called Stalin with the news. Grumpy at having been awakened, Stalin told Beria that he already knew the result and hung up, once more inciting Beria to fury. The scientists responsible were secretly awarded high state honors, with the highest—Hero of Socialist Labor—going to those slated to be executed if the test shot had failed. The Soviets had entered the nuclear age.[29]

5. The bomb and the onset of the Cold War

The timing and context of the explosion are impossible to ignore: 1949 was a year of extraordinary tension in the Cold War world. There is, of course, much to say about the Cold War, though most of it is best said somewhere else. Suffice it to say here that, by 1946 anyway, the United States and the Soviet Union had fallen out in a bitter dispute over a host of issues. They disagreed over the disposition of postwar Germany: To what extent should it be punished? Should its size be reduced? Should it be united or divided into spheres of influence controlled by its liberators? They argued over other European states too, with the Americans insisting on free elections in the Soviet-liberated nations of Eastern Europe (especially Poland), while the Russians argued that whoever liberated a country got to shape its political future; as the British and Americans had done in Italy in 1943–4, so the Soviets would do in Bulgaria, Romania, and any other nation where the Red Army had sacrificed soldiers to the elimination of Fascism. There were quarrels over money and goods—the United States had an abundance of both, some of which the Russians wanted for relief and reconstruction—over ideology, principles, and values, over who constituted a danger to whom, over such seeming arcana as the internationalization of waterways, the repatriation of German prisoners, the meaning of language in treaties and agreements, and the definition of such terms as 'imperialism', 'freedom', and 'socialism'. On 9 February 1946 Stalin accused the capitalist West of having started the Second World War in an effort to 're-divide the "spheres of influence" in their own favor', insisting that capitalism 'contains in itself the seeds of a general crisis and of warlike clashes'. Two weeks later, the Moscow embassy's George Kennan warned, in his famous 'Long Telegram', that the Soviet Union represented 'a political force committed fanatically to the belief that with the [United States] there can be no permanent modus vivendi', and on 5 March Winston Churchill claimed, before an American audience and with Truman sitting next to him, that the Soviets had rung down an 'Iron Curtain' between Eastern and Western Europe, and that the proper response, 'strength' and not 'appeasement', must be made by 'a fraternal association of the English-speaking peoples'. Stalin equated the speech with an attack, and there quickly followed in the Soviet Union a campaign of conformity and messianic Marxism-Leninism spearheaded by the ideologue Andrei Zhdanov. Matters declined from there.[30]

The atomic bomb played a role in the onset and intensification of the Cold War. 'Before the atom bomb was used, I would have said, yes, I was sure we could keep the peace with Russia,' said Dwight Eisenhower after visiting Moscow just after the war ended. 'Now I don't know . . . People are frightened and disturbed all over. Everyone feels insecure again.' The bomb, argue Gar Alperovitz and Kai Bird, was 'a primary catalyst of the Cold War', not only initiating a dangerous arms race between the adversaries but enabling the American reconstruction of West Germany along capitalist lines, easing US strategic concerns for Western Europe enough to permit American interventions in Korea and Vietnam, and broadly negating any possibility of accommodation between the two powers because of Soviet suspicions regarding the bomb's use and American efforts to preserve its secrets. Certainly the bomb lurked like a specter at the table during every Cold War colloquy. Certainly, too, the Soviets and Americans, along with their friends, allies, and international subordinates, regarded the bomb as an ominous presence even in their day-to-day affairs. Molotov's weirdly jovial exchange with Byrnes—'I'm going to pull an atomic bomb out of my hip pocket and let you have it', Byrnes 'joked'—in September 1945 indicated the Soviets' acute consciousness of the bomb's influence. 'Atomic bombs', Stalin told a British journalist a year later, 'were meant to frighten those with weak nerves', implying that his nerves were steady but perhaps leaving the opposite impression. In January 1948 he told the Yugoslav diplomat Milovan Djilas that the bomb was 'a powerful thing, pow-er-ful!' Djilas thought Stalin's expression 'full of admiration'. When six months later Stalin ordered a land blockade of Berlin, the United States responded with an airlift of supplies to the beleaguered residents of the West and, more pointedly, by sending sixty B-29s to bases in Britain. While the bombers were not armed with nuclear bombs nor even equipped to carry them, the Truman administration maintained a studied silence about these facts. Perhaps the presence of the bombers in Europe made Stalin more cautious than he otherwise would have been; in any event, he ended the blockade in May 1949. It is plausible that the B-29s reminded him, if a reminder was needed, that the Americans had the bomb and at that point he did not.[31]

The Americans, too, were keenly aware of their monopoly of the bomb from 1945 to 1949. Rationally, it was not always clear that it provided them with a strategic advantage in the Cold War. Some derided the possibility of maintaining the 'secret' of the bomb for any length of time, in spite of Groves's optimistic (and continually sliding) estimate that the Soviets would not have the bomb for decades. Stimson knew the 'secret' would not last and thus proposed, in his memo of 11 September 1945 to the President, that information about the bomb should be shared with the Russians. Henry Wallace, the Secretary of Commerce until Truman fired him in September 1946, noted that research on the nucleus had 'originated in Europe . . . It was impossible to bottle the thing up no matter how much we tried.' Vannevar Bush, director of the Office of Scientific Research and Development and leading scientific adviser on the Manhattan Project, told Truman in September that the atomic 'gun on our hips' had limited diplomatic and strategic utility. 'There is no powder in the gun, for it could not be drawn, and this is certainly known,' he said. So Byrnes evidently discovered at London that same month. (Bush later wrote incredulously of Admiral William Leahy: 'His view was like the postwar attitude of some of the public and many in Congress: There was an atomic bomb "secret", written perhaps on a single sheet of paper, some sort of magic formula. If we guarded this, we alone could have atomic bombs indefinitely.') Truman himself had bleak thoughts that fall. Following Byrnes's failure to sway the Soviets on a range of issues at London, the President glumly told his budget director, Harold Smith, 'there are some people in the world who do not seem to understand anything except the number of divisions you have'. Smith objected: 'Mr President, you have an atomic bomb up your sleeve.' 'Yes,' came the reply, 'but I am not sure it can ever be used.'[32]

Sensing the same thing, and worried over growing Congressional efforts to take control of the atomic-energy issue, Byrnes, in January 1946, called Undersecretary of State Dean Acheson and appointed him chair of a new committee charged to 'draft a plan for the international control of atomic energy'. Acheson objected that he knew nothing about the issue; Byrnes told him not to worry, because the committee would include men who did, among them Bush, James Conant, and Groves. Not satisfied, Acheson added a board of consultants to the committee, including several engineers, Robert Oppenheimer, and, as head, David Lilienthal, former czar of the Tennessee Valley Authority. Part of the point was to outflank or outvote Groves. Acheson had doubts about the way the administration had thus far handled the issue of international control—'Byrnes and Truman didn't understand anything about the bomb,' he told Lilienthal. As Acheson knew, or soon learned, Oppenheimer's and Lilienthal's doubts ran even deeper. '*What* is there that is secret?' Lilienthal wrote in his journal following his appointment to the consultants' group. 'If my hunch that in the real sense there are no secrets (that is, nothing that is not known or knowable) would be supported by the facts, then real progress would be made.' Tutored after hours in nuclear physics by Oppenheimer, Acheson, along with Lilienthal, steered the committee away from Groves's insistence that nothing of significance be shared with the Soviets. In mid-March, the committee produced its findings, dubbed the Acheson–Lilienthal report. It called for the creation of an international Atomic Development Authority, empowered to control radioactive raw materials including uranium, oversee the process of fission worldwide, and manage all research involving atomic explosives. There was deliberate vagueness in the plan, and it established no timetable for the release to the international body of information and resources by the United States. But Acheson and Bush were clear when they described the report on the radio: 'The extremely favored position with regard to atomic devices, which the United States enjoys at present, is *only temporary. It will not last.* We must use that advantage now to promote international security and to carry out our policy of building a lasting peace through international agreement.'[33]

Faced with such a flexible yet resolute commitment to the internation-alization of atomic research—a possible return to a 'republic of science', or at least a global oligarchy—Truman balked. Rather than approve the Acheson–Lilienthal plan and release it to the public, as Acheson urged him to do, the President instead appointed Bernard Baruch head of the US delegation to the United Nations Atomic Energy Commission, and asked that he 'translate' the report 'into a workable plan'. Baruch, who had made a fortune in the stock market, was in 1946 75 years old, nearly deaf, and puffed with pride over his reputation—'without foundation in fact and entirely self-propagated', thought Acheson. 'I am one tough baby,' Baruch proclaimed on accepting the translator's job. He now refused all scientific counsel on the bomb, because, as he told Bush, 'I know all I want[ ] to know. It went boom and it killed millions of people.' Appalled at what he considered Acheson–Lilienthal's generosity toward the non-nuclear world and especially the Soviets, Baruch translated the report by transforming it. He emphasized, in his amendments, the need for inspections, sanctions levied against wrongdoers, and maintenance, during an indeterminate process of divulging atomic 'secrets' to something called the International Atomic Energy Authority (IAEA), of a virtual veto on decisionmaking by the United States. Under his plan (for it soon gained independent status as the 'Baruch Plan'), presented to the United Nations in June 1946, 'the Americans would still retain their arsenal of atomic weapons long after the Russians had surrendered the crucial information about their raw materials sources and the state of their research and development', as Daniel Yergin has written. In the midst of the UN debate on the American plan on 1 July, the United States tested an air-dropped atomic bomb at Bikini atoll in the South Pacific. Missing its target, the worn out battleship *Nevada*, by 2 miles, the bomb nevertheless impressively went boom. The test seemed to punctuate Baruch's intention to retain an atomic monopoly for as long as possible. The Soviets counterproposed with the destruction of existing nuclear weapons, the retention of national control over nuclear weapons' programs, and the endurance of individual vetoes on the IAEA. By September Baruch, who refused to bend on his proposal, admitted to Truman that talks had reached an impasse, and by the year's end, as Gregg Herken has put it, 'the atomic curtain had been firmly rung down'. The Russians applied the *coup de grâce* with a veto in the Security Council.[34]

So the Americans would go it alone, testing weapons openly at Bikini in the summer of 1946 and again, at Eniewetok atoll in the Marshall Islands, in the spring of 1948. The latter series of tests in particular signaled to the Soviets that the United States had enough atomic bombs to afford the luxury of detonating three of them just to see how well they worked—and indeed one of them yielded 49 kilotons, easily the most powerful bomb yet. The Russians, and for that matter the British and others, could glean what clues they wanted from the tests, but there would be no decision to release atomic information. 'It was [Baruch's] ball, and he balled it up,' wrote a disgusted Acheson. The United States hid behind Groves's misplaced faith that the Soviets were years away from developing a bomb, hoping, somehow, that its nuclear monopoly would preserve its security and that of Western Europe, hoping, somehow, that its scientists had caught lightning in a bottle, a feat of genius, technology, and good luck that would be impossible for others to duplicate.[35]

This was wishful folly. But so too, in all likelihood, was the hope of Stimson, Lilienthal, and Acheson that an international agreement that envisioned, even in the short run, an American nuclear monopoly might dissuade Josef Stalin from building his own bomb. In the way that the American decision to drop the bomb on an enemy's city was largely determined by Franklin Roosevelt's decision to develop the bomb in the first place, so also was the Soviets' resolve to make a bomb of their own established with unbreakable momentum by Stalin in August 1945, and perhaps even with Stalin's authorization of a small nuclear project in spring 1943. The bomb was central to the Cold War; the Soviet leadership felt it as acutely as did the American. Stalin was not certain that the atomic bomb would prove, in itself, a militarily decisive weapon in a future war. Officials from the Soviet embassy in Tokyo who visited Hiroshima in September 1945 reported that, although destruction was great and death plentiful from the bomb, the effects of the bomb generally had been exaggerated by the Japanese press. Of course, as long as the Russians lacked the bomb they tried to reassure themselves that they were not in mortal danger from an American bomb. After his bizarre repartee with Byrnes at London in September 1945, Molotov met the secretary again, in Moscow in December. Also present at this meeting was James Conant, determined to get a reading of the Soviet attitude toward the bomb. Incredibly, Molotov repeated his performance of three months before, this time asking Conant (the American recorded) 'if I had an atomic bomb in my pocket', and joking, in a Christmas Eve toast, that Conant should reveal the bomb he had no doubt stashed in his 'waist-coat pocket'. Stalin interrupted Molotov. The bomb, he said sternly, was 'too serious a matter to joke about'. 'We must work together', he added, 'to see that this great invention is used for peaceful ends.' After dinner, Conant walked over to Stalin to say good night. Stalin offered 'heartiest congratulations to the American scientists for their accomplishment' and repeated his hope that the bomb would inspire world peace. And, he admitted, Russia was currently 'behind in science'. The following September, Stalin told the British *Sunday Times* correspondent Alexander Werth that atomic bombs 'cannot decide the outcome of a war, since atomic bombs are quite insufficient for that'.[36]

Stalin was right about this. The American military, which began devising plans for a nuclear strike against the Soviet Union, realized that a bomb dropped on Moscow and other cities would leave the Red Army, intact and angry, in Europe, while bombing the Red Army could have disastrous consequences for the innocent people living nearby. Yet the strategic conundrum the Americans faced, possibly understood by Stalin, was hardly enough to curtail the urgency of his pursuit of his own bomb. If he did not claim, with some American planners (like Baruch), that the bomb would be the 'winning weapon' in the Cold War, he nevertheless felt that the US monopoly had damaged the balance of power between the two sides. As long as the Soviets believed the Americans might use it against them as they had against the Japanese, the bomb was a diplomatic tool of considerable force. Or so Stalin evidently told Kurchatov and Commissar Boris Vannikov in mid-August 1945: 'Hiroshima [he said] has shaken the whole world. The balance has been destroyed.' Stalin found confirmation for his fears as the Cold War unfolded. The Americans he viewed as moderates— Harry Hopkins, Stimson, Wallace—were shunted aside in Washington. Churchill threatened, Byrnes swaggered, and Truman seemed to endorse them both. The Americans refused to provide, on reasonable terms, a loan to the Soviets. They made clear, by the fall of 1946, their intention to keep Germany divided and to restore to prominence the western half of it. They would not discuss making the Dardanelles as accessible to the Russians as the Suez was to the British or Panama to themselves, and when he contrived to see Stalin's hand at the back of a communist insurgency in Greece, Truman responded, in March 1947, by dividing the world into two ideological camps and requesting economic and military assistance for Turkey and Greece, two nations much closer to the Soviet Union than to the United States. Three months later the Americans announced a clever plan of aid for all of Europe and the Soviet Union, one containing a poison pill requiring Soviet economic transparency and that Moscow donate rather than receive funds. And, above all, there was Baruch's grotesque charade, performed to mask the essential truth that the Americans had no intention of sharing the atomic bomb. So thought the Soviets.[37]

And it rankled. More than anything else, the atomic bomb had become a symbol: of American prowess and power, but also of great power status, of scientific status ('we have to learn five times, ten times more than we need to know today,' Khariton told his group at Sarov in 1947), of ideological fitness and bureaucratic efficiency—even of male potency, for, while Soviet scientists called their experimental plutonium reactor 'Annushka', they called the test shot itself 'Stalin's rocket engine'. Archibald Clark Kerr, the British ambassador in Moscow, wrote in late 1945 of Soviet psychology concerning the bomb. The Russians, he said, had felt good about their victory over Germany and their position in the world. 'Then plump came the Atomic Bomb'. The balance of forces was in their judgment 'rudely shaken'. The vast divisions of the Red Army no longer seemed so powerful. The Russians briefly hoped that their American allies would share the bomb's secret, continuing a pattern of cooperation established during the war.

> But as time went on and no more came from the West, disappointment turned to irritation and, when the bomb seemed to them to become an instrument of policy, into spleen. It was clear that the West did not trust them. This seemed to justify and it quickened all their old suspicions. It was a humiliation also and the thought of this stirred up memories of the past.

'We may assume', Kerr concluded, 'that all these emotions were fully shared by the Kremlin.' It was a safe assumption. David Holloway has written: 'As the most powerful symbol of American economic and technological might, the atomic bomb was *ipso facto* something the Soviet Union had to have too.' Thus, even if the United States had made a good-faith effort to share the bomb with the Soviets—and the Acheson–Lilienthal plan, whatever its inadequacies and notwithstanding its hijacking by Baruch, was such an effort—the Soviet project to develop the bomb would have continued apace. 'Stalin', concludes Holloway, 'would still have wanted a bomb of his own.'[38]

The Soviets did not immediately publicize the successful test of 'Stalin's Rocket Engine'. An American B-29 airborne just east of Soviet Kamchatka on 3 September registered a sharp spike in atmospheric radioactivity on its test filter paper. For several days American and British pilots and scientists chased the cloud as it spread in both directions from Kazakhstan. Officials in Washington were informed on the 9th. Louis Johnson, the Secretary of Defense, refused to believe the Russians had detonated an atomic bomb, first dismissing the intelligence that indicated it, then deciding that a Russian reactor must have exploded. Truman also refused to believe it, or rather to accept that it had happened. Like Johnson, he doubted the intelligence; when persuaded of its accuracy, he told Lilienthal that 'German scientists in Russia did it'. When Lilienthal pressed, the President agreed to authorize the appointment of a committee of experts to sift the evidence. Bush was made the chair, but he relied heavily on Oppenheimer's expertise. A year earlier, Oppenheimer had told *Time* magazine that the US 'atomic monopoly is like a cake of ice melting in the sun'. Now, after meeting for five hours on 19 September, the committee concluded that the ice had become water. Lilienthal carried this finding to Truman. Still disbelieving, the President wanted Lilienthal and the other committee members to sign a statement 'to the effect [that] they really believed the Russians had done it'. Four days later, Truman announced that 'an atomic explosion'—he still hoped it might have been a reactor—had 'occurred in the USSR'.[39]

6. Call/response: Developing the 'super'

In December 1945 a group of physical and social scientists at the University of Chicago published the first edition of the *Bulletin of the Atomic Scientists of Chicago*, though the city name was soon dropped from the title. The readership of the *Bulletin* remained small, but the journal gained public attention in June 1947, when editors placed on its cover the Doomsday Clock, whose minute hand indicated the level of crisis then facing the world. Hands at midnight meant nuclear war; in mid-1947 the editors showed the time as seven minutes to midnight. Following Truman's announcement of the Soviet atomic-bomb test, the large hand moved forward four minutes. The changed situation was reflected as well in the reaction in the scientific community. I. I. Rabi thought the Russian shot 'brought the prospect of war much closer'. William Golden, an aide to Lewis Strauss, heard the news in Italy. He stayed up all night writing a letter to Strauss, urging the development of the next generation of nuclear 'superweapons'. Edward Teller called Oppenheimer on the phone. 'What should we do now?' he wailed. 'Keep your shirt on,' came the sharp reply. But for most Americans, it was no time for patience.[40]

The 'superweapons' of which Golden wrote had for years been a gleam in Teller's eye. At Los Alamos, Teller had run afoul of fellow scientists by insisting that work be done on the creation of an awesomely powerful 'Super' bomb, in which a fission bomb would serve as a mere trigger for a far greater explosion. It was Enrico Fermi who imagined such a weapon in the fall of 1941. What if, Fermi asked Teller, a fission bomb was used to set off a larger device that would cause a thermonuclear reaction, similar in nature to the energy produced by the sun? Experiments existed to suggest that the intense heat generated by the fissioning might cause the fusion of two chemically light nucleii—in this case of deuterium, an isotope of hydrogen with a neutron added to its proton nucleus—into a nucleus of helium, which had two protons and one neutron. The offspring of this union would be an incredible burst of energy, its limit determined only by the amount of liquid deuterium fired by the fission bomb. In theory, Fermi calculated, 12 kilograms of deuterium would produce a blast equivalent to a million tons of TNT. A cubic meter of deuterium ought to make an explosion worth ten million tons.[41]

Teller's near-obsessiveness about the Super at Los Alamos had been an annoyance. The focus of the Manhattan Project, thought Oppenheimer, must be a fission weapon, far less complicated than a hydrogen bomb (the Super's less casual name) and thus more likely of attainment before the end of the war. He placated Teller as best he could, meeting him weekly to discuss whatever was on the Hungarian's mind and promising him that the Super would have its day, after the group had succeeded in making a fission bomb. Teller took out his frustrations by banging away on his piano. Perhaps because Hiroshima and Nagasaki had changed him, or perhaps because he had never had much faith that a fusion bomb was practical or desirable, after the war Oppenheimer pulled away from his pledge to build the Super. In September 1945, writing for a Scientific Advisory Panel including Fermi, Arthur Compton, and Ernest Lawrence, Oppenheimer urged that the Super be temporarily shelved. Compton added, in a letter to Henry Wallace, that the Panel advised against going forward 'primarily because we should prefer defeat in war to victory obtained at the expense of the enormous human disaster that would be caused by its determined use'. There was more than a hint here of ethical qualm. As most scientists left the mesa in the fall of 1945, Teller continued to work on the Super there, even writing a top-secret report titled 'The Super Handbook'. But he felt isolated and dispirited. On 1 February 1946 he and his family headed for Chicago, where Edward had accepted a position at the university.[42]

The Soviet atomic-bomb test seemed to change the political and scientific climate overnight. Oppenheimer at first remained sanguine, unconvinced of the Super's practicality. 'I am not sure the miserable thing will work', he wrote Conant, 'nor that it can be gotten to a target except by ox-cart.' He would later point out that, had the Americans had the Super in August 1945, they could not have used it over Hiroshima: the target was 'too small'. Conant reinforced Oppenheimer by insisting that the H-bomb would be built only 'over my dead body'. Hans Bethe agonized but decided against, Compton had enduring moral doubts, and David Lilienthal drew back in horror at the prospect of the Super: 'Is this all we have to offer?' he asked in despair. Berkeley's Luis Alvarez and Ernest Lawrence joined Teller as enthusiasts for the new weapon; Lilienthal found their 'drooling' over the Super unseemly. The military leadership, not fully apprised of the Super, did not speak with one voice on the issue, but air-force chief of staff Hoyt Vandenberg told a Congressional committee in mid-October 'that it was the military point of view that the super-bomb should be pushed to completion as soon as possible, and that the general staff has so recommended'. Brien McMahon, the Democratic senator from Connecticut whose name adorned the Bill that had created the Atomic Energy Commission (AEC) at the end of 1946, and now chair of the Joint Committee on Atomic Energy, was not given to subtlety. Regarding the Soviets, 'what he says adds up to one thing,' wrote an observer. 'Blow them off the face of the earth, quick, before they do the same to us—and we haven't much time.'[43]

The AEC had a General Advisory Committee made up of scientists and appointed by the president. Oppenheimer was its chair. The GAC met over the weekend of 28 October 1949, amidst the rising volume of alarm over the new strategic situation, to discuss what to do about the Super. Gregg Herken has astutely pieced together an account of the committee's discussion. The generals in attendance thought the United States needed an H-bomb. Lewis Strauss agreed, while Bethe simply summarized the state of work on the Super and Oppenheimer merely listened. Conant spoke emotionally against the new bomb on moral grounds, and he apparently pulled other committee members with him, notably Rabi and Fermi. On Sunday afternoon Oppenheimer brought the meeting to a close with a report, written by himself and John Manley, who was associate director at Los Alamos. It strongly reflected Conant's views: 'We believe a super bomb should never be produced. Mankind would be far better off not to have a demonstration of the feasibility of such a weapon, until the present climate of world opinion changes.' A majority of committee members signed the report. Rabi and Fermi produced instead a one-page letter, in which they called the Super 'necessarily an evil thing considered in any light', though their insistence that the United States not go forward with a program was contingent on other nations also exercising forbearance. Oppie signed the more strongly worded majority report and adjourned the meeting.[44]

Teller was profoundly discouraged by the GAC recommendation; he told Manley that he now expected to 'be a Russian prisoner of war in the United States within five years'. Oppie, 'naively', thought the H-bomb was scrapped, at least for now. But Brien McMahon was furious. Reading the GAC report at an AEC meeting the night after it had been finalized—Halloween 1949—McMahon declared that its conclusion 'just makes me sick' and resolved to pressure the President to reject it and move ahead with the hydrogen bomb. Lobbied in one ear by McMahon, Strauss, and other advocates for the Super, and in the other by Lilienthal and a few other members of the AEC, Truman decided, in mid-November, to appoint a special committee (Committee Z of the National Security Council) to resolve the matter. He chose for its membership Louis Johnson, the Secretary of Defense whom he knew to support the Super, Lilienthal, whom he knew to oppose it, and Acheson, now Secretary of State, whose position was unclear to the President, as it was to Acheson himself. The secretary had far more respect for Lilienthal than for Johnson, and a better working relationship with him. He talked to Vannevar Bush and Oppenheimer. 'I saw my duty', he would write in his memoirs, 'as gathering all the wisdom available and communicating it amid considerable competition.' That is slightly self-serving. In fact, Acheson believed in the existence of evil, and thought it naive to compromise with it—or, in this case, to hope that forbearance in building an H-bomb would encourage similar forbearance by the Soviets. He would not have said publicly, as Louis Johnson did, that 'we want a military establishment sufficient to deter [an] aggressor and sufficient to kick the hell out of her if she doesn't stay deterred'. But neither would he have taken issue with such sentiment.[45]

Acheson may also have sensed that Truman wanted the Super. What happened, ultimately, was that the Joint Chiefs grew impatient over the GAC's placidity and the evident divisions on the Z Committee. In mid-January they wrote to Johnson endorsing the Super, calling it 'foolhardy altruism' to suppose that the Soviets would fail to build a hydrogen bomb if the Americans renounced theirs. Johnson forwarded this memo to the President without showing it to the Committee. 'And that', writes Richard Rhodes, 'was that.' Truman read the JCS memo and told Sidney Souers, director of the NSC, that the Chiefs' proposal 'made a lot of sense and that he was inclined to think that was what we should do'. The Z Committee met Truman on the last day of January 1950 and recommended that the

United States try to establish the 'feasibility' of the Super. Lilienthal took the floor to dissent; Truman cut him off after a few minutes: 'What the hell are we waiting for? Let's get on with it.' It was, Lilienthal remarked ruefully, like saying ' "No" to a steamroller'. Later that day Truman announced that the AEC was 'to continue its work on all forms of atomic weapons, including the so-called hydrogen or superbomb'. The President's phrasing elided any differences between fission and thermonuclear weapons—both types coexisted under the rubric 'all forms'—in much the same way that American strategists had allowed themselves to imagine that using atomic bombs on Japanese cities was no different from using firebombs, which practice seemed to have been accepted by all the belligerents. Four days after making his decision, Truman told an aide that 'there was actually no decision to be made on the H-bomb ... We had to do it—make the [H-]bomb—though no one wants to use it. But,' he said, 'we have got to have it if only for bargaining purposes with the Russians.'[46]

Once more, the lights came on at Los Alamos, and another massive effort of physics and engineering began. Teller would have his day, at last. He had difficulty getting other scientists to rejoin him in the desert: many were busy elsewhere, while others had moral reasons to avoid building the Super. Teller faced serious design problems. Another scientist had helpfully suggested using not deuterium but tritium to create a thermonuclear reaction; tritium is radioactive hydrogen 3 (that is, with one proton and two neutrons in its nucleus), and it requires a much lower ignition temperature than deuterium. But tritium was rare, and for the effort needed to make enough for an H-bomb one could manufacture enough plutonium for twenty fission weapons. When analysts drew plans for Teller's Super, the result more closely resembled a house than a bomb: 30 feet long, 162 feet wide, with an imbedded fission core weighing 30,000 pounds and craving much more tritium than Teller had earlier estimated. No existing plane could carry it; it might have to be delivered to its target aboard a warship, presumably unmanned. If a way could be found to use the weapon, especially by dropping it, somehow, from the sky, it was likely to destroy everything within a 1,000-square-mile radius 'by shock', and inflict burns at an astonishing distance of 100 miles from ground zero. The morality of such a bomb remained, for obvious reasons, an issue. So did its utility.[47]

By 1949 the Russians had been working seriously to make a hydrogen bomb for over three years. The Russian decision may have been prompted by material on American thinking about the Super provided by Klaus Fuchs. The German-born spy had in April 1946 attended a conference on the Super at Los Alamos, and Soviet scientists, including Yakov Zeldovich, who had explored chain reactions with Yuli Khariton, read Fuchs's report of this meeting with care. But the Soviets had already begun to speculate on how fusion might be generated. Given the rudimentary state of American thinking about the Super, Fuchs could not have managed more than to signal to his employers that there was American interest in the subject; to have pursued to any length American theorizing at that stage would have left Russian physicists on the wrong foot altogether. Fuchs himself doubted that he gave the Russians much help with the project—a self-exculpatory judgment, but accurate. The Soviets were already managing fine on their own. 'By the summer of 1948', according to Holloway, Zeldovich and others 'had done calculations for a specific design' for a hydrogen bomb.[48]

Kurchatov now asked Igor Tamm, a theoretical physicist at Moscow University's Physics Institute (FIAN), to check Zeldovich's math and oversee the project. Tamm, in turn, tapped several of FIAN's young physicists to help with the work. One of them was Andrei Sakharov, the 27-year-old son of a physics teacher. The joke was that Tamm picked Sakharov because he pitied his young colleague's housing situation, and knew that elevating Sakharov to the thermonuclear team would bring quick improvement. Tamm knew better: Sakharov was already well known and deeply respected by Soviet physicists. 'He distinguished himself', wrote a colleague, 'through the clarity and correctness of his thought, and the conciseness of expression of his ideals.' Sakharov joined the quest to develop an H-bomb. Partly, he felt, there was no choice: if he demurred he might be marginalized, arrested, or worse. He also admitted that he was drawn to the beauty of the physics involved. For Sakharov, as for Fermi and even Oppenheimer, the intellectual excitement of fashioning bombs, coupled with an attraction to the work that was aesthetic and even sensual, was irresistible. And this principled man, like many other men, was strongly affected by his direct experience of total war and Cold War. 'I understood, of course, the terrifying, inhuman nature of the weapons we were building,' wrote Sakharov. 'But the recent war had also been an exercise in barbarity; and although I hadn't fought in that conflict, I regarded myself as a soldier in this new scientific war.' He would later say that the rough balance of terror achieved by the Soviet triumph in both fission and fusion weapons forged a deterrent to all-out war, though he confessed that he may not have imagined such a thing when he accepted Tamm's invitation.[49]

Sakharov devised in his head a new design proposal for a hydrogen bomb. In his memoirs, he calls this the 'First Idea', but it became known to his project colleagues as a *sloika*, roughly 'Layer Cake'. It was so named because it layered fission and fusion, heavy and light elements, and encased them in a high-explosive frosting. The explosive would cause the cake to implode, setting off an explosion of the fission trigger at its center and in this way initiating, in theory, fusion in the light element layers. In early 1949 Sakharov and his promising design were bundled off to Sarov and Yuli Khariton, over Tamm's fruitless objections: 'Things seem to have taken a serious turn,' observed Tamm. Meanwhile, if Stalin, through his representative Beria, was initially disinclined to pursue another expensive and powerful weapon, Truman's announcement on 31 January 1950 that the AEC was to 'continue work' on a hydrogen bomb turned the leadership around. Almost immediately Beria demanded from Kurchatov a progress report on H-bomb research, and within the month Stalin had ordered that such a bomb be built. 'In other words,' writes Gerard DeGroot, 'the Americans decided to build the Super because they thought Soviets were doing so. And the Soviets did so because they were certain the Americans were building one.' Indeed, these mutual perceptions were basically correct.[50]

Sensing himself vindicated by Truman's decision, Teller pressed forward with his work on the Super. He continued to be frustrated, however, by the reluctance of some prominent scientists to embrace the project, and especially by technical problems with his weapon designs. Teller's penchant for losing his temper made him a poor administrator, and he was frequently unwilling to take advice from others. His suggested designs for the Super had flaws, and the project seemed in jeopardy at the end of 1950. The mathematician Stanislaw Ulam bailed Teller out early in 1951. Ulam's wife found him gazing out the window one afternoon 'with a very strange expression on his face'. When she asked what he was thinking, he replied: 'I found a way to make it work.' His idea was to create compression at the enormous heart of the Super, thereby pushing nuclei closer to each other and causing a faster burning of fuel and a greater production of heat. The fission explosion of the initiating device would release X-rays that would in turn cause compression of the thermonuclear material (this was Teller's contribution). Substituting radiation for blast to implode the thermonuclear fuel, now separated from the fission bomb initiator, would provide the speed necessary to ensure that heat was produced rather than lost. 'This is how you make a hydrogen bomb,' said Teller proudly soon after his meeting of minds with Ulam, sketching on the blackboard the new, 'two-stage' implosion sequence. At that moment, recalled physicist Herbert York, 'I realized: That was it.' Even Oppenheimer, so wary of bigger bombs, so skeptical of the feasibility of building the Super, would admit: 'When I saw how to do it, it was clear to me that one had at least to make the thing . . . The program in 1951 was technically so sweet that you could not argue about that.' Development now moved forward. The Americans built a hydrogen bomb called 'Mike' (or 'The Sausage', after its shape) that weighed 60 metric tons. The test shot took place on 1 November 1952 at the south Pacific coral atoll of Eniewetok, liberated from the Japanese in early 1944. The blast produced a fireball 3 miles wide— 'You would swear that the whole world was on fire,' wrote a sailor who witnessed it—a mushroom cloud that blotted the sky, and a sea-water-filled crater 200 feet deep and over a mile across where the island of Elugelab had been. Mike was 1,000 times more powerful than Little Boy had been.[51]

Beria panicked and demanded that Soviet scientists increase their pace; they now worked, according to Kurchatov's secretary, 'as if American bombs would start raining down on them in a month or two'. The Soviets had technical problems of their own to solve; Kurchatov and Beria pushed them, the latter not gently. The Layer Cake design proved sound, and deuterium and tritium were gradually produced in sufficient quantities to yield a thermonuclear reaction. Their goal was to make a horrible but deliverable H-bomb, unlike the unwieldy Mike a weapon that could conceivably be used against an enemy. Stalin's death in early March 1953 and Beria's arrest on 26 June—the scientists at Sarov learned about Beria when one morning the signs denoting 'Beria Street' had been taken down—did not slow the process. There was an eleventh-hour glitch when Kurchatov realized that the Semipalatinsk test site, which was to be used again, was surrounded by inhabitants whose homes might be reached by fallout from the H-bomb's blast. An evacuation plan was hastily put into effect, and thousands of people were sent away, without explanation, some as late as the eve of the test shot. At dawn on 12 August 1953 Kurchatov started the countdown. The blast nearly knocked the scientists off their feet, exceeding their fondest expectations for power and effect. Awesome as they had been, 'the effects of the first atomic bomb had not inspired such flesh-creeping terror', wrote one scientist afterward. Oppenheimer had rescued a turtle after the Trinity test eight years earlier. At Semipalatinsk, birds that had taken flight with the bomb's flash twitched on the ground, 'their wings scorched and their eyes burned out'.[52]

7. The arms race and nuclear diversity

What followed was, if not inevitable, nevertheless entirely predictable. The 'arms race', as it came to be known, meant that every new weapon tested by one side was interpreted by the other as a challenge to be met. Thus, the Soviet test was followed, on 1 March 1954, by an American test of a deliverable hydrogen bomb, on Bikini. Fallout from this shot, codenamed Bravo, was greater than the Americans had expected, and a cloud of radioactivity settled over the Japanese fishing boat *Fukuryu Maru*— in unfortunate translation, 'Lucky Dragon'. All twenty-three members of the crew developed radiation sickness, and one, Aikichi Kuboyama, later died. Lewis Strauss, now chair of the AEC, issued a series of denials, implausibilities, and prevarications concerning the conduct of the test, but there was no denying that the ever-more powerful weapons being tested were bound to produce radioactivity that did not respect international boundaries or innocent bystanders. Back to Semipalatinsk went Soviet physicists and engineers, goaded now by the new supreme leader, Nikita Khrushchev, and inspired, as before, by Sakharov. This time they would drop an H-bomb from a plane, the way it would be delivered in the event of war. When the drop came, on 22 November 1955, with flash and flame and unearthly roar, Yakov Zeldovich threw his arms around Sakharov and yelled, 'It worked! It worked! Everything worked!' Except that a baby was killed in a nearby bomb shelter, a soldier died when his trench collapsed, half a dozen people were badly injured when a hospital roof fell in, and, at a meat-packing plant in Semipalatinsk, shards of broken window glass were blown into the ground beef. The tit-for-tatting continued. The radioactive clouds, tainted soil, and toxic ground water all grew worse.[53]

Bigger bombs were one way to go, especially so long as they could be delivered by aircraft. The history of nuclear weapons is closely connected to the development of air power and theories of strategic bombing. By the mid-1950s, though, much thought was given instead to other means of delivering nuclear weapons. It was never true, as Stanley Baldwin had predicted, that 'the bomber will always get through'. Military science had increasingly caught up with air power; bomber delivery of explosives was relatively slow and vulnerable to anti-aircraft fire or attack from faster fighter planes. Some of the writers who had first imagined the atomic bomb—Harold Nicolson, for example—had speculated that the weapon would be carried by rockets, far more likely to get through than airplanes. The Germans experimented in the 1930s with rockets that they thought might carry poison gas. They developed instead a liquid fuel rocket called the V-2 equipped with a ton-weight explosive, which they launched at big cities (London, Antwerp) and which killed many thousands during the war. These were Hitler's alternative to nuclear weapons. After the war, nations with nuclear bombs of course envisioned attaching them to rocket bodies and firing them at enemies, at great distance and speed. The induction of German scientists into the American and Soviet scientific communities moved such plans ahead. In August 1957 the Soviets fired a missile that, they boasted, had flown across Siberia. It was the first test of an intercontinental ballistic missile (ICBM). Less than two months later came the launch of *Sputnik*, an unmanned satellite that orbited the earth, emitting a pinging or beeping sound as it transited the heavens. *Sputnik* suggested that Soviet rocket science had moved decisively ahead of American, for its boosters were evidently comparable to those needed for the launch of an ICBM.[54]

The American president, Dwight D. Eisenhower, was not especially worried about *Sputnik*, recognizing that it offered no military threat, but the American media bred panic, and Senator Henry Jackson called for a 'National Week of Shame and Danger'. The first US attempt to launch a satellite that December ended abruptly when its rocket carrier blew up on the launch pad. But the Americans soon made up the technological deficit. A year after the Soviet ICBM test, the United States tested its first long-range missile, the Atlas, a much-enhanced version of the German V-2. It carried a megaton payload, flew up to 6,000 miles, and was reasonably accurate as these things went, falling within 5 miles of its intended target. Steady improvement modernized the American arsenal: heavier Titans (I and II) by the early 1960s, a clutch of intermediate-range (1,500 miles) missiles, sent to Britain, Italy, and Turkey in 1960, and an ICBM called the Minuteman, driven by stable solid fuel and the backbone of the country's missile deterrent from its deployment in 1962—the Minuteman was said to be accurate within a tenth of a mile. These weapons were land based and launched from fixed positions.[55]

Meanwhile, in the mid-1950s, the Americans began developing another innovation in delivering nuclear warheads. As bombers could not always get through, and land-based missiles were potentially vulnerable to strikes by their counterparts in the Soviet Union, military planners thought it desirable to put a third set of weapons in motion, and to permit their concealment from an enemy's prying eyes. These were missiles launched from submarines, or SLBMs. (Robert Oppenheimer had named the Trinity test for John Donne's 'three-person'd God'; the Cold War American nuclear posture would be termed the 'triad'.) Polaris missiles, as they were called, were first deployed in 1960 on the *George Washington*, a nuclear-powered submarine. Second and third iterations of the Polaris improved range and accuracy, and version three could be topped with three warheads, which clustered around a target and thus increased the likelihood of its destruction. Late in the decade, the United States produced a missile that carried up to ten warheads, each of which could be programmed to strike a different target—these were multiple independently targetable reentry vehicles, or MIRVs. What would have taken ten bombers to deliver a decade earlier could now be launched at an adversary with greater speed and accuracy than most air strategists had dreamed of.[56]

Despite such innovations, by 1960 there was in the United States ominous talk of a 'missile gap' favoring the Soviet Union. Yet, by every objective measure, the American nuclear arsenal, its weapons and delivery systems, far outstripped that of its rival. Khrushchev bluffed about Soviet capabilities, bragging about his missiles and crowing that Soviet satellites were growing lonely in space while they waited for their American friends to join them. But no boasting could conceal that the Soviet economy was far less productive than the American throughout the 1950s. The index of American striking power was in 1955 some forty times greater than that of the Soviet Union. The United States had B-47 Stratojet bombers and B-52s, all able to refuel in mid air and thus reach the Soviet Union with their nuclear payloads. Soviet bombers were far more limited. Nor were Soviet air defenses much good; Curtis LeMay believed that the US Strategic Air Command (SAC) could destroy the entire Soviet military apparatus 'without losing a man to their defenses'. US bases in Europe and Asia offered proximity to the Soviet homeland that the Soviets could not match.

And, despite their early gains in missile technology, the Russians quickly fell behind there too: by the end of 1962 the Soviets had roughly two dozen ICBMs on station, while the Americans had 284. As yet the Soviets had no SLBMs.[57]

It was Khrushchev who recognized that nuclear superiority was not essential for his nation to be taken seriously as a great power. It was enough to have some nuclear weapons, tested for all to see, or at least bragged about, and to threaten occasionally to use them. When, in October 1956, Israel invaded Egypt and was quickly supported at Suez by Britain and France, Khrushchev (through a subordinate) asked British Prime Minister Anthony Eden, 'What situation would Britain find itself in if she were attacked by stronger states possessing all kinds of modern destructive weapons?' Khrushchev credited this blunt warning for the British decision to back down. It was Khrushchev's revelation, according to his biographer William Taubman, that the menace of Soviet missiles, small in number though they might be, would be enhanced if they were protected against an American first strike by their placement in underground silos. British and American fears that Khrushchev might be crazy or a 'megalomaniac' gave the Russian leader room to maneuver on the issue of East Germany (and Berlin), though when in 1961 the new US president, John F. Kennedy, did some blustering of his own, Khrushchev knew better than to launch his missiles—at whom?—and instead instructed that the old German capital be divided by a wall.[58]

8. The limits of atomic weapons: The Cuban missile crisis

Nor had the Americans been above making nuclear threats, or privately and seriously considering the use of nuclear weapons—in Korea, China, and Vietnam. General Nathan Twining, the air force chief of staff, wished for the use of 'three small tactical A-bombs' against Viet Minh forces surrounding the French garrison at Dien Bien Phu in 1954. His hope was to 'clean those Commies out of there and the band could play the "Marseillaise" and the French would come marching out of Dien Bien Phu in fine shape'. But the gravest Cold War confrontation would come in Cuba. The revolutionary Fidel Castro had taken power on the island, just 90 miles from Florida, on New Year's Day 1959. Historians disagree about whether Castro came into office committed to communism or whether opposition to his rule by the Eisenhower administration gave the Cuban leader no choice but to shift to the left ideologically and seek Soviet help. In either case, by 1961, when Kennedy took office, Cuba was under boycott by the United States and was receiving extensive economic and military aid from Moscow. The Americans tried to get rid of Castro, first by sponsoring an invasion of Cuba by disgruntled exiles that they hoped would inspire a general uprising (this ended badly at the Bay of Pigs in April 1961), then by orchestrating a series of comic but still nasty attempts to assassinate Castro. Reasonably fearing that his regime and his life might be in jeopardy, Castro asked Khrushchev for help.

Khrushchev had reasons of his own for placing Cuba under the Soviet nuclear umbrella. The Americans had recently made operational their medium-range Jupiter missiles in Turkey, and, while it was true that these weapons were less a military threat to the Soviet Union than were ICBMs based in the United States, their presence was nevertheless unsettling. Khrushchev wanted to even the score psychologically: 'What if we throw a hedgehog down Uncle Sam's pants?' he asked a colleague. He wanted to protect Cuba and to be seen as the island's protector, by the Cubans, the Americans, and most of all the Chinese. He sought the instant credibility he thought putting nuclear weapons in Cuba would give him. He may have had Berlin in mind, for a harsh US response to the placement of Russian missiles in Cuba could have justified an equally tough Soviet move in Berlin. Most of all, Khrushchev wanted to rattle the Americans, to give them a dose of their own medicine, to put them in the penumbra of a nuclear shadow like the one that darkened the Soviet Union each day. Khrushchev hoped to slip missiles into Cuba—three dozen medium-range and two dozen intermediate-range rockets, along with warheads and over 40,000 troops to guard and maintain and maybe fire them—and have them fully installed before American overflights spotted them. Faced with a *fait accompli*, young Kennedy would surely acquiesce in their presence. Even if the Americans tried to take the missiles out, Khrushchev wrote later, some would no doubt remain intact. 'If a quarter or even a tenth of our missiles survived—even if only one or two big ones were left—we could still hit New York, and there wouldn't be much of New York left.' Such a threat would, Khrushchev thought, 'restrain the United States from precipitous military action against Castro's government'.

The insertion of missiles did not, as it turned out, restrain the Kennedy administration from acting forcefully. 'Oh shit! Shit! Shit! Those sons of bitches Russians!' exclaimed Robert Kennedy, the Attorney General and the President's brother, when informed, on 16 October 1962, that US intelligence had discovered the missile emplacements. The President did not immediately authorize a bombing raid to take the missiles out or an invasion of Cuba, as several of his advisers urged. Instead, he took his brother's advice and established a naval blockade, or a 'quarantine', as he called it, of Cuba to prevent further introduction of missiles or supplies. He also demanded that Khrushchev 'eliminate' the missiles that were already in place. Khrushchev was unprepared for such a response. He wrote to Kennedy that he was creating a 'serious threat to peace and security' and demanded that he 'renounce' his quarantine decision. The President's response was to raise the level of SAC's alert status to DEFCON 2, just below that of war, and to reply to Khrushchev firmly that US policy would stick. Khrushchev backed down, at least briefly. In a rambling personal letter to Kennedy, written on 26 October, Khrushchev offered a way through: he would remove the missiles from Cuba if the Americans would agree not to invade the island. Even as Kennedy's advisers were discussing the letter, a second arrived from Khrushchev, dated the 27th, adding the condition that the United States remove the Jupiters from Turkey. (Khrushchev agreed not to invade Turkey.) The Americans were vexed by the addition, and, even though the Jupiters were strategically meaningless, Kennedy objected to their equation with the missiles in Cuba. Then, at noon, a US U-2 spy plane was shot down over Cuba by a Russian missile battery, killing the pilot.

'The smell of scorching hung in the air,' as Khrushchev described it later. He had gone too far, he concluded, and the missiles in Cuba must come out. Robert Kennedy, representing the President, met the Soviet ambassador to the United States, Anatoly Dobrynin, that night. Somberly, he told Dobrynin that, if the missiles were not removed from Cuba voluntarily, the United States would take them out. In return for Soviet cooperation, Kennedy would pledge not to invade Cuba. And, while it would not say so publicly, the administration would agree to extract the Turkish Jupiters once the crisis had passed. The next day, Khrushchev sent written acceptance of these terms. He had 'given a new order to dismantle the arms which you described as offensive', he wrote to Kennedy. The most serious nuclear crisis of the Cold War had passed.[59]

At the time, of course, the principals involved did not know that their crisis would remain the worst. Still, a certain sobriety set in on both sides. The Kennedy administration did not abandon its efforts to get rid of Castro's government, or Castro himself, and it continued to build nuclear weapons. Nor did Khrushchev and the Soviets stop blustering—Khrushchev boasted to the Supreme Soviet in December that the 'forces of peace and socialism' had 'imposed peace' on the world—or persisting in their arms build-up. But observers of both Kennedy and Khrushchev noted a new reflectiveness in both men, who as adversaries had together come to the edge of a nuclear catastrophe. On 10 June 1963, in his commencement address at the American University in Washington, Kennedy expressed willingness to 'make the world safe for diversity' and announced that the United States would stop testing nuclear weapons in the atmosphere, as long as the Russians would refrain too. The speech was greeted with enthusiasm by Khrushchev, who would label it 'the best speech by any president since Roosevelt', presumably Franklin. The two nations subsequently agreed on a 'Treaty Banning Nuclear Weapons Tests in the Atmosphere, in Outer Space, and Under Water', more commonly called the Limited Test Ban Treaty. Kennedy's assassination on 22 November 1963 and Khrushchev's ouster the following October did not stop their nations creeping away from the brink. In 1953, with the test of thermonuclear bombs by both sides in the Cold War, the Doomsday Clock of the *Bulletin of the Atomic Scientists* showed, ominously, that there were but two minutes to midnight. At the end of 1963, it was twelve minutes to midnight, and the Test Ban gave hope that time would continue to run backward. The hope, alas, was premature. As ever, the United States and the Soviet Union were just two of the nations in which nuclear weapons were being developed; more than ever, the reverberations of Hiroshima were still being felt around the world.[60]

EIGHT

The World's Bomb

From mutual suspicion between the United States and the Soviet Union came tension, rivalry, and finally Cold War. An arms race, conventional and nuclear, precipitated out of that. Both of the powers demanded loyalty of the nations on their side of the Cold War barrier, and these nations in turn, having chosen a side or having been compelled, by force or persuasion, to join one, required from their citizens dedication to the Cold War cause. The alliance system that had emerged by the mid-1950s—the North Atlantic Treaty for the United States and its allies, the Warsaw Pact for the Soviet-dominated world—triggered a psychological turning inward by people seeking to maintain their autonomy in an international system that threatened to dissolve the bonds of nationhood. (Renewed affection for one's country was in any case widespread following the liberation of nations from German and Japanese occupation and the growing antipathy for colonialism.) And, in the shadow of the powers' arms race, men and women around the world feared for their safety, now apparently in the hands of officials residing in Washington and Moscow. There was, thus, a natural temptation on the part of smaller or less powerful nations to explore the possibility of building nuclear weapons. Scientific curiosity promoted the pursuit; national pride predicted it; the desire for control of one's own security gave it logic and urgency. As neither the Americans, as the Baruch Plan indicated, nor the Soviets, despite a bit of rhetorical generosity toward fellow Communist states, seemed interested in sharing control of nuclear-weapons development, governments elsewhere began to consider nuclear programs of their own.

Scientists were recruited for this purpose, or in some cases recruited themselves and pressured their governments to act. In the United States, many came to see the Cold War as a continuation of the Second World War, with the Soviets replacing the Nazis. There remained dissenters, as we will see, physicists and chemists who clung to the hope of international control of atomic energy or even the creation of a world government. Still, what Robert Gilpin has called the 'containment school' of scientists assumed greater prominence in the nuclear field. The Americans plucked from defeated Germany scientists they felt might stimulate their nuclear progress, and whose capture by the Russians might dangerously tip the nuclear balance east. This recruitment effort, codenamed by its military sponsors 'Operation Paperclip', made it clear to the Germans, many of whom had worked on 'reprisal weapons' before May 1945, that bygones were bygones and no hard questions would be asked about their previous political affiliations—though the US government did hope it would not be necessary to recruit 'ardent Nazis'. The Soviets, for their part, snatched whatever German scientists they could. Elsewhere, scientists who had before and during the war been involved in studying the nucleus resumed their work, often determined to do for their countries what American scientists had done and Soviet scientists would do for theirs. Beginning in 1946, scientists in the employ of their governments once more immersed themselves in the growing literature of the bomb. The British, the French, the Israelis, South Africans, Chinese, and Indians all moved thereafter, with various degrees of speed, to hunt nearby sources of uranium, to buy or manufacture moderators for nuclear reactors or the reactors themselves, to solve problems of initiators and implosion lenses and the derivation of plutonium, and finally to imagine themselves in possession of a nuclear weapon, with all the strategic and moral dilemmas such a condition would present.[1]

Along with this nationalist involution, there was at the same time a countertendency among the world's scientists to restore the borderless 'scientific republic' of the interwar era. Decrying the security regime their government tried to impose on them, some American scientists sought a return to the days when international conferences and uncensored physics journals allowed the fullest exchange of views among colleagues. The 'fraternity' of physicists, as *Fortune* magazine called it, was in its natural state disinclined to admit secrecy to its ranks. 'Progress belongs to us all', insisted Laura Fermi, 'and secrecy cannot for long restrict it within limited boundaries'—loftily said, and close to the mark for many scientists. Physicists joined philosophers and political figures in pleas to create 'One World', a world government, and the gadfly Leo Szilard suggested the full-scale international exchange of scientists (and their families) to serve as monitors of nuclear control agreements and dispensers of information, or even the 'mining' of American and Russian cities with nuclear bombs, as deterrents to either nation contemplating a pre-emptive strike against the other. In some cases, scientists returned from exile—perhaps from productive nuclear work in the United States, Canada, or Britain—to their home countries and their prewar colleagues. The Dane Niels Bohr remained the conscience of the international community of physicists. In his diffident way, he emphasized the unity of humankind bound by the common threat of annihilation, and urged a return to scientific community and openness.[2]

Curiously, the counterthrusts of secrecy and openness found a common result. Those who sought security through secrecy argued that the national interest would be served best by building or buying nuclear apparatus and implying, as least, that a nuclear weapons program might be under way. An open proclamation of nuclear intentions might aggravate the great powers, invite imitation and espionage by jealous neighbors, provoke domestic opposition, or embarrass scientists and technicians should their efforts fail; secrecy seemed to many nuclear-weapons advocates a logical policy. Secrecy, or 'ambiguity', or 'opacity', about one's nuclear plans might also serve strategic purposes, as Israel and South Africa concluded. Those who urged openness in nuclear matters generally did so because, they claimed, only international trust inspired by sharing information would prevent an arms race by nation states, who in the absence of donated wisdom about the bomb would be more likely to pursue, and jealously guard, an arms program. International control of the nuclear industry would allow nations to relax, secure in the knowledge that advances in nuclear physics would be accomplished and witnessed by everyone. If the sharing of nuclear knowledge meant that any interested and well-equipped state could build a bomb, so be it—though most of those who championed the return of 'fraternity' to world physics hoped instead that sharing would obviate the need felt by nations to make weapons of their own. This was, it turned out, too fond a hope.

The world's first nuclear power harbored its own ambivalence about sharing nuclear information. President Harry Truman believed there was a single, magical nuclear secret; as long as the magician refused to show his audience how his best trick worked, no one would figure it out. He thus supported Bernard Baruch's quest to avoid any equitable international control of atomic energy, endorsing instead a naive reliance on perpetuating the US nuclear monopoly, with secrecy to be assured with the passage of the McMahon Bill in July 1946. The shock of the Soviet atomic test in August 1949 brought only an escalation of the arms race and renewed determination to expose the spies who were said to have divulged to the Russians the magician's secret. Yet the administration's futile commitment to secrecy did not prevent Leslie Groves, one of secrecy's staunchest exponents, from authorizing the 1945 publication of the Smyth Report (after its principal author, the physicist Henry Smyth), a surprisingly frank survey of the science and engineering of the atomic bomb, and an account that Russian and other scientists found valuable for keeping their physicists on the right track. Physicists to some extent resumed their travels after the war, and while their governments' sensitivities made them watch their words, they could not and did not totally abjure old habits of candor and collaboration. Truman's successor, Dwight Eisenhower, shared some of Truman's secretiveness about nuclear matters—he would not, for instance, endorse a ban on testing more powerful and innovative hydrogen bombs in 1952 because, he said of the Soviets, 'they could make tremendous advances where we would be standing still'. But Eisenhower also conceived the 'Atoms for Peace' initiative that resulted in the creation, in 1957, of the United Nations' International Atomic Energy Agency, and thereafter the distribution of US nuclear equipment to nations seeking the benefits of peaceful nuclear power. Eisenhower seemed to recognize, as had an editorialist for the *New York Times* just two days after the bombing of Nagasaki, that 'the very nature of science makes secrecy impossible' and that eventually 'all military powers will recruit enough scientists to develop their own atomic bombs'.[3]

That, of course, is precisely what happened during the half century following the end of the Second World War. Nations fashioned nuclear programs for different reasons: fear of annihilation was prominent among them, but also present were scientific curiosity and ego, bureaucratic momentum (like the kind that took the Americans seamlessly from research to testing to use of the bomb against the Japanese), a desire to prove masculine toughness, an interest in creating substantial diplomatic bargaining chips, and, perhaps above all if difficult to substantiate, a growing sense across the globe that atomic weapons conferred status. The British and French empires were shrinking. Smaller states, including Israel and South Africa, were more and more criticized for their treatment of nonwhite majorities or minorities, and risked becoming pariahs. China felt threatened

by the United States and, increasingly, the Soviet Union, and its supreme
leader, Mao Zedong, concluded that his revolutionary regime would not
gain international stature until it developed a bomb of its own. India felt
threatened by China and Pakistan, and Indian scientists and political leaders
thought they were not being taken seriously by their counterparts in the
West; they decided that possession of a nuclear device might win them
respect.

1. Great Britain

Let us begin with Britain. In 1933 Harold Nicolson had imagined that
Britain was first to fashion an atomic bomb, monopolizing its fuel, Deposit
A, and testing the weapon in the North Atlantic, inadvertently wiping out
much of South Carolina into the bargain. The British were among the
world's leaders in nuclear physics before the war, and with the Frisch–
Peierls memorandum and the formation of the MAUD Committee in
1941 they became the first to contemplate seriously building an atomic
weapon. Marcus Oliphant carried to the United States his message of
urgency late that summer. Following a period of coolness in late 1941
and early 1942, resulting from a British belief that they were ahead of
the Americans in caring about a bomb and planning for it, the British
government had resumed attempts to collaborate with the Americans and
hoped for a full sharing of information concerning nuclear matters. Prime
Minister Churchill thought he had achieved a partnership with agreements
with President Roosevelt at Hyde Park in June 1942 and Quebec in August
1943. The admission of a British scientific team at Los Alamos late that year
was useful and promising.

Yet uncertainty remained—or Churchill's doubts did, and Roosevelt's
vagueness, and his advisers' (especially Groves's) skepticism concerning
the desirability of collaboration. Churchill went to Hyde Park again in
September 1944 seeking greater clarity. There he and FDR produced a
brief aide-mémoire. It contained three points. First, it rejected the pleas
of Niels Bohr that the 'secret' of the bomb be shared with the Russians
after the war. Second, it reassured Churchill, stating: 'Full collaboration
between the United States and the British Government in developing tube
alloys [the British codename for the a-bomb] for military and commercial purposes should continue after the defeat of Japan unless and until

terminated by joint agreement.' Third, the note, with seeming casualness, suggested that 'when a bomb [not "tube alloys"] is finally available, it might perhaps, after mature consideration, be used against the Japanese, who should be warned that this bombardment will be repeated until they surrender.' 'Well done indeed,' a Churchill adviser in London cabled his boss, when word of the Hyde Park Agreement was received. There was no similar reaction from Roosevelt's advisers because the President neglected to inform anyone else about the agreement. (Two months after Roosevelt's death, a British member of the tripartite nuclear Combined Policy Committee, created at Quebec and including the Canadians, 'reminded' the Americans about it. The Americans had not heard of the agreement and asked the British for a copy. Some years later, Roosevelt's copy turned up in a file folder kept by the President's naval aide, evidently because the title, 'Tube Alloys', sounded like something to do with torpedoes.)

American casualness or inconsistency concerning postwar collaboration rightly told the British that the issue would not be easily managed after Roosevelt's death. Like his predecessor, Harry Truman dangled before the British the prospect of nuclear cooperation, in November 1945. He acknowledged the substantial British contribution to the Manhattan Project, in its earliest days and especially at Los Alamos. But in early 1945 Marcus Oliphant, again visiting Berkeley, concluded that British entreaties concerning collaboration gave 'only the impression that we are trying to muscle in on a racket we have been too dumb to develop ourselves'. Oliphant recommended that Britain start work on its own racket when the war was over. 'I am quite sure help from the US is not necessary to enable us to carry out this project in England,' said Sir James Chadwick. 'We can stand on our own feet.' The experience in America and with the Canadians and French at a parallel nuclear project in Montreal during the war—on which more later—had already helped. British engineers understood gaseous diffusion and had worked with irradiated fuel rods from Oak Ridge. William Penney, who was to lead the British nuclear project, rode in the B-29 that served as the observer plane for the Nagasaki mission and gathered from that torn city samples of bent poles and crushed fuel cans just ten days after the bombing. Like other nations, Britain learned from the Smyth Report. And the British had uranium, or access to it, from Canada and Africa, by way of the Belgians and the Portuguese.

US policy was moving, by early 1946, toward greater restriction on the sharing of nuclear knowledge. Truman became fixated on the felt need for greater security, interpreted earlier agreements on collaboration with the British very narrowly, and moved away from the Acheson–Lilienthal plan for international oversight to the Baruch version that sought protection for the American monopoly. The McMahon Bill, which passed the Senate on 1 June and the House on 20 July and was signed by Truman on 1 August, would, as Gregg Herken has written, 'so restrict the interpretation of scientific interchange as to make it meaningless, and would outlaw sharing US technology on atomic energy's "industrial uses" with foreign nations by 1947'. Anyone helping another nation gain nuclear information would thereafter be subject to a large fine, up to twenty years in prison, or both. During debate on the Bill, lawmakers revealed ignorance of previous agreements on American–British–Canadian cooperation and showed no inclination to want to know more. Such behavior indicated to British observers, and everyone else, that the United States was no longer interested in participating in a republic of nuclear science and engineering.

In the end, and as was true for the Russians, the American restrictions may not have been decisive, for the British had already determined to move ahead with a nuclear weapons program. Less than two weeks after Japan had agreed to surrender on American terms, British Prime Minister Clement Attlee, who had taken office the previous month following Churchill's shocking repudiation at the polls, declared, in a memorandum to his advisers, that a decision regarding the atomic bomb was 'imperative'. Already on the drawing board were plans for a plant to enrich uranium. That October, the Chiefs of Staff concluded that a weapons-building project ought to be undertaken at once; 'to delay production' while waiting for the Americans to make up their minds about information distribution and international control 'might well prove fatal to the security of the British Commonwealth'. Churchill, having experienced the frustrations of negotiating Britain's junior partner status with the Americans, chimed in from the Commons in November that 'we should make atomic bombs'— indeed, he regarded the decision to do so as 'already agreed'. Attlee and his Cabinet duly approved the construction of a plutonium pile in December 1945. The Foreign Secretary, Ernest Bevin, was particularly avid. Once the Americans had publicized, in spring 1946, their Baruch Plan, Bevin said: 'Let's forget about the Baroosh [Plan] and get on with making the fissle.' There was a flurry of appointments in January 1946. Charles Portal, now a viscount, who had overseen Butch Harris's strategic bombing of Germany, was named controller of production of atomic energy. Christopher Hinton, an engineer with experience building weapons' plants, took charge of constructing a pile in Lancashire. John Cockcroft, late of successful stewardship of joint nuclear work in Canada, became the director of the Atomic Energy Research Establishment, headquartered at an old airfield called Harwell. Advising the project was Chadwick, who had worked closely with the Americans, including at Los Alamos. And William Penney, who had also been at Los Alamos and over Nagasaki, was appointed on New Year's Day as Chief Superintendent of Armament Research, ultimately the most powerful post of all, its importance much enhanced by the quality of the scientist who filled it. The government, on 1 May, presented the Commons with an Atomic Energy Bill, preceding by three months Truman's signature on the McMahon Bill. The secret decision, in January 1947, to move ahead with bomb building thus ratified rather than established the direction in which the British were plainly heading.

'That autumn', wrote C. P. Snow in *The New Men*, his 1954 novel about the British atomic scientists, 'it was strange to hear the scientists alone, trying to examine their consciences, and then round a committee table.' ' "I don't think we've got any options," says one of them. "Luke's [Penney's?] right, the Barford [Harwell?] boys are right, we've got to make the infernal thing." ' Attlee would explain the British decision as 'essential'. 'We couldn't allow ourselves to be wholly in their hands,' he said of the Americans. Britain 'could not agree that only America should have atomic energy'. Bevin concurred: 'We could not afford to acquiesce in an American monopoly of this new development.' Neither man was explicit about building a bomb, but that is what they meant to do. The decision to go for a weapon, as Margaret Gowing has summarized it, was not 'a response to an immediate military threat but rather something fundamentalist and almost instinctive—a feeling that Britain must possess so climacteric a weapon in order to deter an atomically armed enemy, a feeling that Britain as a great power must acquire all major new weapons, a feeling that atomic weapons were a manifestation of the scientific and technological superiority on which Britain's strength, so deficient if measured in sheer numbers of men, must depend'. Whether any of these desires, 'instinctive' as they were, could have been satisfied by American willingness to collaborate fully on nuclear research and production is a matter of more than a little doubt.

Penney was the project's leader, a brilliant mathematical thinker, resolute and wise in the management of people who worked for him and those who controlled his budget. He decided to build an implosion device, with Fat Man as his model. In June 1947 Penney gathered about three dozen scientists and engineers in the library of the battered Woolwich Arsenal in London and told them, behind drawn shades, that they would build an atomic bomb. He described how they would do this. Construction had already started on a complex of plants where the work would be undertaken: uranium refining at Springfields, Lancashire; at a place dubbed Windscale, in Cumbria, the reactor itself and a facility nearby to extract plutonium; then a gaseous diffusion plant at Capenhurst, Cheshire. The bomb itself was to be assembled at Aldermaston, Berkshire, where, according to the site newsletter, the hasty construction left 'swamps reminiscent of Passchendaele'. Penney's participation in the American project helped a great deal as he oversaw the making of a British bomb, but it did not solve every problem. He had not, for example, worked much on plutonium, and did not know what metal or metals to use to fashion the vessel in which to melt the element. His original design for the bomb's core proved volatile. Penney sought solutions to these and other dilemmas when he and his wife, Adele, invited visiting American nuclear scientists to dinner at their south London home. He had limited success.

There was an unlikely source of help for the first three years of the project: Cockcroft had hired Klaus Fuchs to work at Harwell. Like Penney, Fuchs had benefited enormously from his time at Los Alamos, but unlike Penney he had smuggled out of New Mexico notebooks filled with equations and design sketches, many of which had gone through couriers to Moscow. Now, Fuchs's expertise in physics and espionage helped the British: 'The same notes he had used in drafting summaries for his secret Soviet contacts in the United States', writes Brian Cathcart, 'provided early assistance to the British atomic bomb programme.' Fuchs lectured the scientists about the morphology of the weapon, and he wrote a paper evaluating several versions of the arrangement of plutonium at the bomb's core. The design Fuchs preferred, one in which bomb designers left a bit of space between the plutonium center and the uranium tamper surrounding it, was ultimately chosen by Penney for his test device. (Penney made the decision in 1950, after Fuchs had been imprisoned early that spring.)

By early 1952 Penney had a device nearly ready for testing. A pretrial explosives test blew a 30-foot crater in the Thames Estuary, making a mockery of any lingering efforts to preserve the secrecy of the project. Penney considered detonating his bomb at an American test range, either at Eniwetok in the South Pacific or in Nevada, but when negotiations stalled the British turned instead to the Monte Bello islands, a barren cluster of land forms 50 miles off the northwest coast of Australia. The islands had served as platforms for pearl divers in the past, but without fresh water or much plant life they had been abandoned to birds and sea snakes. The Australian government did not object to an atomic bomb being tested on them. On 8 June 1952 the frigate HMS *Plym* left the Thames with the bomb casing in its hold, headed for Oceania. The core, assembled at Aldermaston, followed in September, flown in stages to Singapore, wherein it was placed on a fast boat for the Monte Bellos. There it was united with the rest of the bomb in the weapons room of the *Plym*. The ship was to be the bomb's container for the test. The operation was called 'Hurricane'.

They counted down and triggered the bomb just after breakfast on 3 October. Photos revealed a towering fireball and a great spout of seawater borne upward by the blast. Men at the base camp some 8 miles away from where the *Plym* was anchored felt the earth shake and caught the bomb's blast wave a half minute after the shot. The blast had yielded at 25,000 tons of TNT. The Monte Bellos were pelted with 'a torrent of toxic rain', according to Cathcart. The scientists and engineers congratulated each other with 'riotous parties' in which 'much liquor was drunk and unprintable songs were sung' (Gowing). Just three weeks later, the Americans tested their first hydrogen bomb at Eniwetok. It was a hundred times more powerful than Hurricane.

The British appear to have been more relieved than elated with their success. Some in government told themselves that their possession of a testable atomic weapon would provide them with a deterrent against a nuclear attack, presumably by the Soviet Union. The bomb had also come to symbolize great-power status by the early 1950s; it was something that anyone with international standing was expected to have. But Hurricane failed to win American or Soviet respect for British physics or military science, in the light of the bigger bombs those nations were developing even as Penney and the others toasted in the Monte Bellos. The Russians evidently ignored the British test. The Americans at first dismissed it as inconsequential, and when asked if he now thought about increasing nuclear collaboration with Britain, a member of Congress said derisively, 'we would be trading a horse for a rabbit'. The British built more atomic bombs, deliverable ones, in a project called, incongruously, 'Blue Danube'. And they went to work on a thermonuclear device, making enough progress by late 1957 for even the Americans to be surprised and impressed. In mid-1958 Congress relaxed restrictions placed twelve years earlier on Anglo-American nuclear collaboration.[4]

2. The French atomic bomb

Like their British counterparts, French scientists had been at the forefront of nuclear research before the war: Marie and Pierre Curie had experimented with radioactive radium as far back as 1898, their daughter, Irène, and her husband, Frédéric Joliot, continued and advanced the Curies' efforts during the 1930s and did pioneering work on fission. (Frédéric would help to remove 185 kilograms of heavy water from Paris to Britain just in advance of the conquering Germans in 1940.) Joliot and other French nuclear scientists developed far-sighted laboratory practices in France before the war. Joliot's chief collaborators on fission research in the 1930s were Hans von Halban, an Austrian, and Lew Kowarski, who was Russian. Both were attracted to Paris by Joliot's reputation and his ready store of radium, first at the Radium Institute, then at Joliot's new labs at the Collège de France. (Also to Joliot's side came Bruno Pontecorvo, an engaging young Italian physicist.) The physical chemist Bertrand Goldschmidt started, in 1933, as the lab assistant of Joliot's mother-in-law at the Radium Institute. Also in Paris at the same time were young physicists Francis Perrin, son of a Nobel Prize winner, and Pierre Auger, who would become Perrin's brother-in-law. Goldschmidt, Halban, and Kowarski were Jews; the latter two were naturalized Frenchmen in 1939. That March, Joliot, Halban, and Kowarski split the uranium nucleus with a neutron, publishing their results, despite a plea for silence from Leo Szilard, in the British journal *Nature* the following month.

The German occupation scattered the nuclear community of Paris and France. While Joliot and Irène Curie stuck it out and did their best to confuse the Nazis about their work, most of the others fled. Halban and Kowarski accompanied the French heavy-water shipment aboard the British coal ship *Broompark* out of Bordeaux to England in June 1940. Both scientists were dispatched to the Cavendish Laboratory at Cambridge, where they drew together a handful of others and resumed their research, hoping to produce more fissions, more neutrons, and ultimately to construct reactors. The following summer, the MAUD Committee reached its conclusion that atomic bombs might be possible to build. But it seemed clear by late that summer that the apparatus necessary to build a bomb was unaffordable in the circumstance of world war and thus impractical on British soil. With collaboration with the Americans a diminishing possibility, the British decided, in the summer of 1942, to send a group to Montreal, Canada, to build a reactor. The scientists and engineers would be safe there, closer to sources of uranium, and closer to the Manhattan Project scientists, from whom they would continue to seek help. And Montreal would be a joint project, including scientists from Canada and France. Halban, the naturalized Frenchman, was eager to go, and was put in charge of the team. Kowarski, increasingly unhappy with what he saw as Halban's highhanded treatment of him, stayed in Cambridge.

Halban had some British and Canadian researchers at his disposal. He also sought to reconstitute the group of French and European scientists with whom he had worked in Paris, or whose work in France he had known there. Frances Perrin was in New York, but Halban passed him over, fearing that he might insist on having patent rights to equipment or procedures Halban's group would have to use without obstacle. He did recruit Perrin's brother-in-law Pierre Auger to head his division of experimental physics. Jules Guéron, a North African Jew who had taught in Strasbourg, joined the Free French, escaped to London, then moved in with Halban and Kowarski's group at the Cavendish. Halban brought him to Montreal to take charge of physical chemistry. Also on the scene was Bruno Pontecorvo, whom Bertrand Goldschmidt would remember as his 'charming Italian colleague from the Curie laboratory' in Paris. Cleared by British security services, Pontecorvo arrived in Montreal in early 1943 prepared to do physics. (Designated by the codename 'Mlad', Pontecorvo passed information about the project to the Russians. He would later join the British nuclear project at Harwell, then, in the summer of 1950, defect with his family to the Soviet Union.)

Bertrand Goldschmidt escaped from France in early 1941. He managed to find passage on a crowded ship to Martinique. There, he ensconced himself at an upcountry hotel run by a black woman with a Jewish father, and inhabited also by a pair of German-Jewish filmmakers and the anthropologist Claude Lévi-Strauss. Weeks later, Goldschmidt found a seat on a tiny seaplane to Puerto Rico (when he arrived there he found Lévi-Strauss in American custody; agents suspected his transcriptions of Amazonian language were an Axis code), then got to New York by mail boat in late May. After months of idleness, Goldschmidt took a volunteer job administering oral radioisotopes to hospitalized cancer patients. He also went to Canada to conduct experiments at a radium processing plant. Halban wrote in March 1942 and asked Goldschmidt to join him. Goldschmidt was interested, but the British were slow to give permission. When at last his hiring to Montreal was authorized, in the summer of 1942, Goldschmidt was astonished to learn that he was to be attached, with American consent, to Chicago's Metallurgical Laboratory, to work in the chemistry lab under Glenn Seaborg. There, as the first and only Frenchman to participate in the Manhattan Project, Goldschmidt worked on uranium and plutonium extraction. He met Fermi, Oppenheimer, Groves ('pleasant, slightly on the plump side, with an engaging manner'), was sworn many times to secrecy, and later called the experience 'the most fascinating of my career'. Halban had finally got to Montreal himself and summoned Goldschmidt, in late October 1942, to induce plutonium while working in the project's chemistry division.

The growing presence of Frenchmen in the Montreal lab was one of the reasons the Americans remained cool to the British scientists who had hired them. The Americans were worried mainly about security, since they viewed the French as unreliable. Groves, supported by Vannevar Bush and James Conant, refused to allow the shipment of heavy water or graphite to Canada, and insisted that nothing specific or technical about nuclear research, only basic science, be discussed with the Montreal team. Halban and the others pushed ahead anyway. In early 1943, Goldschmidt and Auger, who had previously taught at the University of Chicago, and both still in possession of university identification cards, returned to Chicago and were happily received by their former colleagues. Auger returned to Montreal with good information about Fermi's squash court pile, which had gone critical two months earlier, while Goldschmidt pocketed a test tube, courtesy of Seaborg, containing a tiny amount of plutonium that Goldschmidt had helped to distill the previous summer. There were several further openings over the next nine months. The signing, by Roosevelt

and Churchill, of the Quebec Agreement on 19 August 1943, briefly raised
hopes of renewed collaboration, and it was followed by the arrival of
the British team at Los Alamos. In March 1944 Chadwick managed to
persuade Groves to let the Montreal group build a heavy-water reactor
as a pilot plant. Perhaps to placate Groves, the British sacked Halban
as project director and replaced him with John Cockcroft, who had
welcomed Halban and Kowarski to Cambridge nearly four years before
but who was otherwise untainted, in Groves's mind, by association with
France.

Under Cockcroft's measured leadership, and with renewed cooperation
from the Met Lab, the Montreal project went forward. In July 1944
Goldschmidt and Guéron received a shipment of metal slugs, which
had been irradiated in a reactor at Oak Ridge. Experimenting with a
new process to extract uranium from the slugs (the French called them
'hot dogs') by use of a chemical solvent, Goldschmidt went to work.
Meanwhile, Charles de Gaulle, leader of the Free French and destined
to play the leading role in French politics after the war, stopped briefly
in Ottawa during a tour of North America. Auger, Goldschmidt, and
Guéron decided that de Gaulle must learn about the bomb. De Gaulle's
representatives gave them three minutes; it was Guéron who got the
honor of telling the general, and of urging de Gaulle to retain the colony
of Madagascar, which held uranium. Afterwards, in a reception line, de
Gaulle said to Goldschmidt: 'I thank you. I understood you very well.'
With Halban sidelined, the pile expert Kowarski appeared in Montreal.
Reactor work speeded up then, and plans progressed for a large nuclear
complex, run jointly by Britain, Canada, and France, and located 200
kilometers west of Ottawa at a lonely but beautiful place Champlain
had called 'the hollow river' during his seventeenth-century explorations.
(It was now called the Chalk River.) The bombings of Hiroshima and
Nagasaki startled the Montreal team but did not stop it. On 5 September
1945 the Montreal reactor went critical. Kowarski called it Zeep, for
Zero Energy Experimental Pile. Chalk River opened that fall. It was a
rough and ready place, appropriately christened, in November, by Canada's
Minister of Munitions and Supply Clarence Howe, who ceremonially
urinated on an outside wall. Early the next year, the Americans insisted that
Goldschmidt, by then the last French scientist remaining with the Canadian
project, be removed to France, as he was (they claimed) jeopardizing any
possibility of future Anglo-American nuclear collaboration. Goldschmidt

duly left, carrying in his head a good deal of valuable information to France.

The American desire to strip the North American nuclear programs of French participants helped to reunite them in Paris. Like Josef Stalin, de Gaulle had been struck by the power of the bomb that had destroyed Hiroshima, and, though he professed 'despair' at the appearance of atomic weapons in the world, he wasted little time in creating a government agency to oversee nuclear issues: the Commissariat à l'Énergie Atomique (CEA). It was headed by Frédéric Joliot-Curie—who, with his wife, had hyphenated his surname during the war—and Raoul Dautry, an engineer and former minister of armaments who was an astute administrator and, unlike Joliot-Curie, not a communist. Theirs was a fruitful relationship, and it moved the French nuclear project briskly forward. Guéron, Auger, Perrin, Kowarski, and Goldschmidt were all involved. They set up shop at an old fort at Châtillon, on the edge of Paris. The French had contracted with Norsk Hydro for heavy water in March 1940; the shipment, 5 tons, was now delivered, six years later. Joliot-Curie also requisitioned 8 tons of uranium oxide that had been hidden from the Germans in Morocco since June 1940, and 9 tons of sodium uranate, the basis for the product called yellowcake, turned up in a boxcar in Le Havre. Laboratory glassware he purchased from a pharmacy that was going out of business. In the summer of 1947 construction began on a small reactor, the sort with which Goldschmidt and Kowarski had extensive experience. Kowarski, who liked naming machines, called the pile Zoe. Goldschmidt, using the Moroccan uranium oxide, prepared its fuel.

Zoe went critical on 15 December 1948. Kowarski had the honor of pressing the button that sent heavy water into the machine. 'Of course,' Goldschmidt wrote later, 'no one could see anything, because everything took place behind the shielding provided by a thick concrete cube, several meters on each side, located at the center of a kind of shed.' Joliot-Curie kept track of the measurements. Zoe would be put to use producing radioisotopes for research. The French program quickly expanded thereafter, with more funding and other reactors. It turned out that there was naturally occurring uranium in France, which supplemented supplies from Africa. Goldschmidt teased out the first milligram of plutonium late in 1949. Joliot-Curie had renounced the creation and use of nuclear weapons, but his open embrace of communism made him an increasing liability in France's relations with the West, and, in the aftermath of Klaus Fuchs's arrest in Britain in early 1950, Joliot-Curie was dismissed as head of the CEA.

Building a nuclear weapon was a related but different matter. Leslie Groves had long doubted that the French could build bombs: when he asked an American engineer about French prospects ('How about the Frogs?'), he was told that 'you can never get two Frenchmen to agree', so it would be 'damn near eternity' before the French would have the necessary reactors up and running. Perrin, who succeeded Joliot-Curie as head of the CEA, was no more enthusiastic about nuclear weapons than his predecessor. Such high-level doubt left weapons' work 'only a drawing board project' in the early 1950s, according to the CIA. Still, a 1946 poll had revealed that a majority of French citizens wanted their scientists to make nuclear weapons. De Gaulle believed, as Spencer Weart has noted, 'that a country without nuclear weapons would not be taken seriously', and in 1954 Prime Minister Pierre Mendès-France, smarting over the imminent loss of Indochina, declared: 'A country is nothing without nuclear armaments.' He thereupon authorized a program to build a weapon, a decision accelerated by the French, British, and Israeli rebuke at Suez in 1956 and affirmed by de Gaulle when he became premier in 1958. De Gaulle wanted France to have an independent military force, called *force de frappe*, that would include nuclear weapons. The CIA now reported that 'most French political parties have taken the position that atomic armament is a necessary condition of independence'. Bombs conferred status, and the French craved status. By 1960 creation of nuclear weapons came second in the French military budget, trailing only funding for the suppression of the Algerian revolt. 'Admission to the "nuclear club" is a symbol in French eyes of immediate parity with the other nuclear powers,' concluded US intelligence. France tested its first bomb, a 70-kiloton plutonium weapon, at the Reganne Oasis in Algeria in February 1960.[5]

3. Israel: Security and status

The French were willing to share their nuclear knowledge with others, and once Joliot-Curie had been sacked it became easier to accept French help without fear of seeming to embrace some side project of the Comintern. Perhaps the chief beneficiary of French openhandedness was Israel. Born into conflict, Israel had security concerns from the start of its existence in 1948. Its first Prime Minister, David Ben-Gurion, was haunted by the Holocaust, and he feared the genocide against Jews would be continued by Arabs in the Middle East. If Israel had a nuclear weapon, or if other nations thought it did, enemies would refrain from attacking the Jewish state out of concern for their preservation. Ben-Gurion was also aware that Jews had played a key role in nuclear physics and chemistry before and during the war, and he hoped to collect a world-class scientific community in Israeli universities and institutes. Avner Cohen, who has written the definitive history of Israel's nuclear project, says that Ben-Gurion began thinking seriously about a nuclear reactor (at least) during the 1948 War of Independence, as the Israelis called it. (Israelis fought Arab armies in part with a wildly inaccurate mortar nicknamed the Davidka, the shell from which created a small, mushroom-shaped cloud when it landed in the desert; the Arabs insisted the Israelis were using nuclear weapons against them.) The Israeli government sent six young physicists abroad in 1949, expecting them to learn some sophisticated nuclear science, and combed the Negev Desert in a futile search for uranium. Reasoning that expertise might eventually be traded for resources, Israeli scientists explored innovations in the production of heavy water and the refinement of uranium.

Ben-Gurion's interest in the pursuit of nuclear power, and ultimately a nuclear weapon, was joined in the mid-1950s to the willingness of other nations to assist him in at least the first quest. The Americans' Atoms for Peace program, announced by President Eisenhower in December 1953, soon brought an offer to the Israelis of a small research reactor. Better still, in mid-1956 the French, seeking Israeli help with their plans to seize the Suez Canal from Egypt, dangled as payment a reactor complete with uranium fuel. This was not exactly a purchase of Israel's cooperation but an 'implicit incentive', according to Cohen, sweetening the deal for an Israeli govern-ment inclined to join the Suez expedition anyway. Forced by US pressure to back off from its aggression (with Israel and Britain), France resolved, as noted, in late 1956 to speed its nuclear-weapons program, and also grew more sympathetic to Israeli security concerns. (Britain, too, evidently got in on this act, funneling heavy water and small amounts of plutonium and enriched uranium to Israel from the late 1950s to the mid-1960s.) France and Israel negotiated an agreement providing French help with building a nuclear compound in Dimona, in the Negev. Signed a year after the Suez fiasco, the deal provided Israel with a reactor capable of yielding up to 15 kilograms of plutonium a year, and evidently (the agreement is still classified) added a reprocessing facility wherein plutonium could be extracted. What the French gained from the arrangement, aside from Israeli gratitude, was not obvious. And, when de Gaulle became premier in the spring of 1958, he tried to put a stop to French–Israeli collaboration, holding hostage further shipments of uranium until Israel agreed to limit itself to peaceful uses of nuclear power and to permit inspection of its plant by the International Atomic Energy Commission. But by then Dimona was fully under construction, and other benefactors had been found: the British, through the Norwegians, sold Israel heavy water, and Jews in the United States, almost certainly knowing what they were doing, sent Israel money directly for the project. The French also permitted an Israeli scientist to watch an early nuclear-weapon test in the Sahara.

The American government only slowly acknowledged to itself that Israel intended to develop nuclear weapons at Dimona. In part this was because Ben-Gurion misled the United States about the purposes of Israeli research, denying publicly and privately that Israel sought to make a bomb. US diplomats were inclined to accept at face value Ben-Gurion's denials: it was easier to hope that Ben-Gurion was telling the truth, and it may have been that the Americans were not altogether unhappy to have doubts about Israeli military capabilities creep into the minds of the Arabs and the Russians. Nevertheless, when incoming President John F. Kennedy asked Eisenhower's Secretary of State Christian Herter about nuclear 'prolifer-ation' in January 1961, Herter replied: 'Israel and India.' Thus informed, Kennedy insisted that Israel allow US inspectors into Dimona, and he noted his nation's 'deep commitment to the security of Israel' as an alternative to Israeli development of a nuclear-weapons capability. Ben-Gurion's response was to allow American 'visitors' (not inspectors) to come briefly to Dimona over several years and otherwise to continue delay and prevarication with regard to the weapons issue. The 'visits' started in early 1964. The Americans' hosts at Dimona were friendly and seemed coopera-tive, but never once allowed the visitors to see the plutonium-reprocessing operation, which would have revealed clearly Israel's intentions. The CIA nonetheless concluded, by 1963, that such activity was probably going on. (The CIA was later accused of having supplied Israel with enriched uranium during this period.) Lyndon Johnson, who succeeded Kennedy following the latter's assassination in November 1963, was less inclined than his predecessor to pressure the Israelis on the nuclear weapons' issue. He

compromised: in exchange for an Israeli pledge not to 'introduce' the
weapons into the region, the United States would supply Israel with conventional arms sufficient in number and sophistication for the Jewish state
not to need atomic bombs. By 'introduce' the Americans may have meant
'create'. The Israelis meant 'use'. It suited both sides to avoid clarifying the
matter.

This calculated ambiguity about its nuclear program—Cohen calls it
'opacity'—allowed the Israelis to proceed with weapons development
under the assumption that Arab states would worry about what might
happen to them unless they avoided direct confrontation. Egypt's leader,
Gamal Abdul Nasser, threatened to attack Israel should it become apparent
that the Israelis were building atomic weapons, but he also denigrated
nuclear weapons as unlikely to be useful or decisive in war and suggested
that Israel might just be trying to intimidate his people by pretending to
develop a bomb. For the most part, Nasser and other Arab leaders thought it
best to keep quiet about the issue, perhaps hoping that the Israelis would be
less likely to build nuclear weapons if their adversaries seemed unconcerned
about them. If so, the strategy failed to work. The Israelis feared an Egyptian
air strike on Dimona. In May 1967, as armies mobilized and tensions rose in
the Middle East, Egyptian MIGs twice flew reconnaissance missions over
the nuclear facility. After the first overflight, on the 17th, Israeli Prime
Minister Levi Eshkol called up thousands of reserves and told aides: 'It
is war, I am telling you, it is war.' Following the second overflight, Ezer
Weizman, the military's chief of operations, concluded that an Egyptian
attack on the nuclear base was imminent, and urged Eshkol (writes Cohen)
'to preempt immediately or at the latest the next morning'. Both sides
stayed their hands, but only temporarily; on 5 June the Israeli air force
struck Egyptian planes on the ground, initiating the Six Day War. Israel
won decisively. But, whatever the outcome, the Israelis' perception of the
threat that preceded—in their view, induced—the war convinced them that
a nuclear weapon belonged in their arsenal. Indeed: at the time war broke
out, it was already there, though it had not been tested and, short of a
catastrophic event that put the existence of the Jewish state in doubt, it
could not be used. Maintaining an air of mystery about its capabilities and
intentions allowed Israel to keep its enemies in a salutary state of uncertainty
about what it might do.

Israel's 'opacity' concerning the bomb persisted. On 1 July 1968 sixty-
five nations signed the Nuclear Non-Proliferation Treaty. Israel was not

among them. Article Two prohibited signatory nations from working toward the acquisition or manufacture of 'nuclear devices', and the Israelis were unready to make this pledge. The Johnson administration pressed Eshkol to sign; the Prime Minister demurred. Meanwhile, the Americans sought clarification of Israel's enigmatic promise not to 'introduce' nuclear weapons to the Middle East. The Israelis, through their ambassador in Washington Yitzhak Rabin, played coy, but, when pushed by the American negotiator, Paul Warnke, Rabin declared that (as Warnke put it) 'an unadvertised, untested nuclear device is not a nuclear weapon'. Because Israel had not admitted having a nuclear weapon and had not tested one, it had no nuclear weapon. The public disclosure of the bomb in Israel's basement, made by Hedrick Smith in the *New York Times* in July 1970, seemed neither to shock anyone nor to change the Israeli position. Virtually everyone continued to abjure talking about the Israeli nuclear weapon. Perhaps they felt there was nothing to be done about it. Perhaps they hoped it would go away.[6]

4. South Africa: To the nuclear brink and back

Like Israel, the Republic of South Africa began thinking seriously about nuclear weapons in the late 1940s, and for some of the same reasons. Both nations had hostile neighbors who regarded them as pariahs: Israel had displaced the Palestinians, while South Africa was governed by a tiny white minority that had disempowered and oppressed the black majority, particularly after the victory of the racist, Afrikaner-led Nationalist Party in 1948. Both nations found sympathy in the United States, which provided both with nuclear technical help under the Atoms for Peace Initiative. Both boasted advanced scientific communities; brains were the leading asset of both nations' nuclear projects. South Africa, like Israel, refused to sign the Non-Proliferation Treaty in 1968 (though the South Africans, unlike the Israelis, eventually did so). And South Africa, like Israel, would find it useful to practice ambiguity with regard to its nuclear-weapons capabilities. It was diplomatically less abrasive to keep other nations guessing than to tell the whole truth about developments, and it ultimately enhanced security, or so both nations argued. Enhanced credibility and prestige were, these governments hoped, natural consequences of a nuclear program about which other nations knew just enough to be concerned.

One major difference between Israel and South Africa was the abundance of uranium available in the latter country. Uranium was a by-product of gold mining, long South Africa's most fabled enterprise, and the nation had abundant reserves of both elements. British and especially American attempts to monopolize the world's uranium led both to muffle any objections they might have had to white South Africans' racist policies and to cooperate with Pretoria's efforts to extract its uranium and prepare it for export: in the early years of atomic energy, the United States and Great Britain bought a good deal of uranium from South Africa, with the Americans alone purchasing some 40,000 tons during the 1950s and 1960s. The South Africans put the sales of their uranium to relevant purpose. They established an Atomic Energy Board (AEB) in 1949, which accepted help from its British and American counterparts, willing to provide know-how and technical assistance in return for continued South African uranium sales. A. J. A. Roux, longtime president of the South African AEB, would laud the help 'so willingly provided by the United States of America during the early years of our nuclear programme when several of the Western world's nuclear nations cooperated in initiating our scientists and engineers into nuclear science'. The British trained South Africa's scientists and permitted the recruitment by South Africa of scores of their own. The Americans provided the South Africans with their first reactor, Safari-1, which went critical in 1965. In the meantime, the AEB had instituted, in 1961, a site for nuclear research and development. Located in the desert west of Pretoria, the site was named Pelindaba, Zulu for 'we do not talk about this at all'. Of its 900 employees, not a single one was black. (A sister site, opened nearby in 1970, was called Valindaba, which means 'we do not talk about this any more'.) Prime Minister John Vorster announced, in July 1970, that South Africa was enriching uranium, but insisted that it had only benign intentions. Among these, it happened, was the creation of peaceful nuclear explosives (PNEs), pioneered by the United States through a program called 'Plowshare'. The South Africans thought they might use PNEs for mining or construction. They nevertheless kept the project secret—an acknowledgment, no doubt, that peaceful and military nuclear explosions were difficult to tell apart.

Also top secret were South African plans to build an atomic weapon. Following Vorster's 1970 announcement, the AEB decided to focus on the gun-style bomb design used by the Americans in Little Boy. The Y-Plant at Valindaba began enriching weapons-grade uranium, though the process was plagued by inefficiencies, and the refined Ur emerged only slowly. The Americans had continued to help, supplying Safari-1 with weapons-grade fuel for a decade after its delivery, but by the mid-1970s the political climate had shifted. Growing popular anger with the segregationist apartheid policy led to American sanctions on trade and investment in South Africa, and the regime's mounting supply of refined uranium made an obvious target for Pretoria's American critics. US shipments were suspended in 1975. At that point, South Africa turned to France, West Germany, and especially Israel for help; growing nuclear polycentrism offered multiple opportunities for exploitation. David Albright estimates that most of the assistance given South Africa through these sources was relatively unsophisticated, though it was supplied 'in violation of international sanctions' against the regime. There were also allegations that the Germans provided advanced jet nozzles for the uranium refinement process and the Israelis offered help with weapon design. Whatever aid they got, the South Africans had their device ready for testing by August 1977, though they lacked sufficient uranium for it. They bored two test shafts deep into the Kalahari Desert and prepared to join the nuclear club, or nearly to do so: the test would be 'cold' in the absence of fissile fuel. Then a Soviet satellite photographed the Kalahari test site, and Soviet Premier Leonid Brezhnev immediately informed the Americans and West Europeans. The powers issued warnings—even the French, thus embarrassed, threatened to end their nuclear cooperation with Pretoria—and South Africa cancelled the test. Weapons development nevertheless continued at Pelindaba and Valindaba. By the late 1970s South Africa had six, gun-type nuclear weapons in its arsenal and enough enriched uranium to fuel them, and was developing a missile system for their delivery.

The government also had a strategic plan in place for their use. Rather like Israel's, it was predicated on ambiguity, the hope that South Africa's neighbors would forbear from attacking the apartheid state out of uncertainty as to the extremity of its response. Should that fail, and should armies mass against it, Pretoria would quietly tell the United States and other western governments that it had nuclear weapons, and thus that it behooved them to act to prevent a war that could have catastrophic consequences for southern Africa. If the West did not respond constructively and the threat of invasion remained, South Africa reserved the right to test a device under or above ground. The government's hope, concludes Albright, was to 'force' western nations 'to place South Africa under their nuclear umbrella in the event of a crisis'.

It never came to this, and in fact the story of South Africa's nuclear program ended as satisfactorily as stories concerning nuclear weapons can possibly do. South African security fears had much to do with the unsettled state of Namibia—unsettled, it should be said, in good part because of South African meddling there—and the presence, during the late 1970s and through the 1980s, of Cuban combat forces in Angola, there by invitation of one of the parties fighting for control of the former Portuguese colony, and over the objection of another one, which was bolstered by the South African military. By 1989 there was a calming of tensions in both places: Namibia was on its way to independence, and the Cubans had left Angola following an agreement between South Africa, Angola, and Cuba. The Cold War was ending, easing South African concerns that the Soviets might sponsor the invasion or subversion of the apartheid state. And it was clear that having nuclear weapons had not enhanced South Africa's prestige as much as it had secured its status as an international pariah. When F. W. De Klerk was elected president in September 1989, he decided, most significantly, to dismantle apartheid and install democracy. He also decided to undo the nuclear-weapons program and sign the Non-Proliferation Treaty. Within months, the six nuclear bombs were taken apart, their enriched uranium cores were rendered benign, the nuclear plants were decontaminated, and even the harmless metal bomb jackets were destroyed. Inspectors from the International Atomic Energy Agency verified all this in 1991. Two years later the South African Parliament, transformed by the crumbling of apartheid, made it illegal for South Africans to develop or help develop nuclear weapons. For the first time in history, a nation had reversed its nuclear development program and eliminated all its weapons.[7]

5. China: The people's bomb

In 1958 the People's Republic of China embarked on Mao Zedong's 'Great Leap Forward', in which China's agriculture, already collectivized, was further consolidated into gigantic 'people's communes', and in which communities and even individuals obligingly built 'backyard smelters' to fabricate steel. Out in Hunan province, in China's west and through which ran the notorious 'malaria belt' wherein the disease was rampant, many thousands of peasants joined geology teams to prospect for uranium. Scrambling over rough terrain, wielding Geiger counters and pickaxes, the peasants managed to unearth a good deal of the stuff, which they fashioned, on the teams' instructions, into yellowcake ready for enrichment. The Great Leap generally registered somewhere between a disappointment and a disaster: in the first category, the backyard smelters produced little in the way of useful steel, while the agricultural collectivization program, combined with rash exhortations by the government to overeat and the export of 'surplus' grain, caused starvation on a massive scale; as many as thirty million people died. For China's nuclear program, the Great Leap's legacy was mixed. As John W. Lewis and Xue Litai note, the reckless quest to find and process uranium on a mass scale left the land gouged and polluted and wasted uranium that was inexpertly dug out and clumsily handled. On the other hand, the peculiar, land-rush approach to uranium prospecting yielded 150 tons of Ur concentrate, China's first batch, and, according to Chinese authorities, sped the development of a nuclear weapon by a year. 'In this limited sense,' write Lewis and Xue, 'the first Chinese bomb was a "people's bomb".'

Mao had once scorned the American atomic bomb as 'a paper tiger', used by the 'reactionaries...to scare people'. But, following the Korean War, during which US troops had encroached on China's eastern border, and especially after the crisis in the Taiwan Straits in 1954–5, featuring explicit threats by President Eisenhower and Secretary of State John Foster Dulles of nuclear strikes against Chinese 'military targets', Mao decided that China needed a nuclear-weapons program too. Like several other nations, China had the main elements for such a project already in place. In the late 1930s the physicist Peng Huanwu worked with Max Born at Edinburgh. An expert in quantum field theory, Peng would become chief of the Chinese project's theoretical division. Qian Sanqiang studied in Paris during the war with Irène Curie; he worked on uranium fissions. Peng and Qian returned to China after the revolution there had taken off and began training students in nuclear physics. (Qian's Paris connection paid off: in the late 1940s and early 1950s, Frédéric and Irène Joliot-Curie helped Qian buy equipment for nuclear-physics laboratories and gave him 10 grams of radium salt to nudge the work along.) The Soviets helped too, though grudgingly. In early 1955 they promised Mao a reactor, a cyclotron, and fissionable uranium sufficient for research. Mao was happy to have the offer but he mistrusted it, as he mistrusted the Soviet Union and it him, and his conviction that China would eventually have to do without much Soviet help guided his decision to send peasants into the hills with pickaxes three years later.

Indeed, by that time the Chinese watchword in nuclear matters was self-reliance. 'We don't have to learn from the Soviet Union,' claimed Mao following icy talks with Soviet Premier Nikita Khrushchev; Mao had wanted, he told his physician, to 'stick a needle up [Khrushchev's] ass', to which Khrushchev responded by rescinding an earlier offer to China of a prototype A-bomb. Alarmed at what they considered Mao's 'adventurism' in the form of twisting the tail of the American paper tiger, the Russians backpedaled from their other nuclear commitments, withdrawing their scientists and technicians from China's labs and reneging on agreements to supply China generously with more equipment and uranium. Of course, the years of exposure to Soviet expertise had helped Chinese scientists, and so too did the American Smyth Report, Robert Jungk's book on the atomic scientists, and the memoir of Leslie Groves, of all people. Still, by 1960 the Chinese considered themselves to be going it alone. The political tumults unleashed periodically by Mao—not just the Great Leap Forward, but several campaigns against 'rightist' intellectuals—brushed the nuclear program but never untracked it, for it was well defended by Premier Zhou Enlai and Nie Rongzhen, head of China's strategic weapons program after 1958. It helped that the project was located in the west, near sources of uranium and away from cities where the various political campaigns and intrigues were most acute. China's gaseous diffusion plant was in Lanzhou, Gansu Province, a place so remote, it was said, that 'even the rabbits won't defecate' there.

Chinese scientists chose uranium for their fuel, gaseous diffusion for its refinement, and implosion as the means of detonating a test nuclear device. A detachment from the People's Liberation Army found a test site in desolate marshland just north of a lake called Lop Nur. The army, using a good deal of prison labor, carved out a compound there in the early 1960s, fighting hunger by eating leaves and using the same scarce water for cooking and washing. The test device came west in 1964, the bomb itself by rail, its core by air. The parts were assembled onsite. Last minute reconnaissance photos revealed a small human settlement within the blast area; expert trackers caught 200 people who turned out to be impoverished holdouts from Chiang Kaishek's Kuomintang. A technician named Yang apparently dreamed the date and time of the test: in the fifteenth anniversary year of the founding of the PRC, fifteen days hence (it was then 1 October), and at 1500 hours. The test duly occurred then. The bomb was hauled up a tower, as at Trinity, and rigged for detonation. At 3.00 on 16 October 1964, the device exploded. It worked perfectly. Several of the scientists present wept for joy. Zhou Enlai, getting word of the success while hosting a large number of actors at the Great Hall of the People in Beijing, announced the shot, then admonished the cheering thespians not to damage the floor.

The Chinese thereafter moved quickly to test a thermonuclear device (June 1967) and to build deliverable warheads. Moved to act by security concerns and status-driven desire to prove Chinese scientific prowess, and in spite of political upheaval and economic uncertainty, the PRC had joined the world's nuclear club within nine years of deciding to do so. The nation had had critical help before 1960. But Lewis and Xue emphasize China's determination to succeed on its own. 'The scientific wonder of fission and its potential', they write, 'enraptured and drew to it men and women of China just as much as it did all attached to that [scientific] fraternity. That this must be said derives more from American parochialism than from anything special about China.' By the end of the twentieth century, China had some 450 nuclear warheads, most of them based on land, though only twenty or so of the long-range (ICBM) variety. And, in the wake of the nuclear test by India, in 1974, China helped Pakistan go nuclear with advice, blueprints, and a supply of weapons-grade uranium.[8]

6. India: Status, religion, and masculinity

India's decision to build an atomic weapon was inspired, in part, by China's success, and in part by fears that rival Pakistan would seek a device of its own and threaten India with it. Like Israel, India tried to mask its strategic intentions and nuclear capabilities, using ambiguity or opacity to leave its adversaries uncertain whether India could, if it wished, strike with atomic weapons. Nor was security India's only cause. Like South Africa and others, India knew that there were strategic limitations on the use of nuclear weapons—what, for example, does one do with atomic bombs when the Pakistanis infiltrate the mountains on India's northwest border? India also sought nuclear capability as a sign of status, especially in the light of a recent colonial past that lingered in the form of Western denigration of Indian science and the anxiety of Indian scientists that the scornful Westerners might be right. The Western sponsors of 'nonproliferation', according to George Perkovich, seemed to replicate the pattern of colonial domination in their insistence that only those who had already tested nuclear devices ought to possess such things. Third World latecomers, like India, were unwelcome in the nuclear club. Yet the Indians' determination to prove themselves scientifically and technologically was complicated by the nation's rhetorical claims to a moral high ground internationally, where conflict was to be shunned or forestalled by reason, discussion, mediation, and finally compromise. In the light of Mohandas Gandhi's insistence on the pacific resolution of disputes, India's avid pursuit of atomic weapons looked unseemly.

The men who made decisions about India's nuclear program for roughly the first two decades of the nation's independent existence were Jawaharlal Nehru, the Prime Minister and Foreign Minister, and Homi Bhabha, who was named by Nehru in 1948 to head India's newly established Atomic Energy Commission. Nehru had worked closely to achieve independence with both Gandhi and other, more coldly pragmatic leaders affiliated with the Congress Party, and, while he had in him some of the Mahatma's moral distaste for war and its weapons—he called for 'neutralism' in the budding Cold War and came across, thought Eleanor Roosevelt, as 'sensitive and gentle'—he could equally be toughminded, especially when he thought the security of his people might be at risk. Nehru also believed in the need for scientific progress, and in the sponsorship of science by the state, though he warned that science was Janus-faced, with a 'destructive side and a constructive, creative side'. Homi Bhabha was a brilliant and enterprising man who came to Cambridge in 1927 to study engineering but switched to physics, working with Ernest Rutherford, James Chadwick, and P. M. S. Blackett and gaining his Ph.D. in 1935. He spent time in labs across Europe, including those of Enrico Fermi and Niels Bohr, returning to India in 1939, whence the war found and stranded him. He persuaded the well-endowed Sir Dorabji Tata trust to fund a school for nuclear research, with himself as its head. The Tata Institute of Fundamental Research was established in Bombay in 1945. It would become, Bhabha wrote, 'the cradle of the Indian atomic energy programme', its dynamism reflecting that of its cultured and worldly director.

During the parliamentary debate over the creation of India's AEC in 1948, Nehru was candid about India's purposes. While he emphasized the benefits of nuclear energy, he pointedly told critics that it was impossible to 'distinguish between' peaceful and military uses of the atom where basic research was concerned. He expressed 'hope that our outlook in regard to this atomic energy is going to be a peaceful one', but he did not categorically rule out weapons work. Nehru's and Bhabha's reputations were nevertheless such that other countries trusted them to stay away from bomb development, or at least from proclaiming that they were building bombs. During the 1950s India got help constructing and fueling reactors from Britain (the Apsara research reactor, Asia's first, which went critical in 1956), and from Canada and the United States, which, respectively, built and supplied with heavy water the CIRUS reactor, online as of 1960. The Indians assured Ottawa and Washington that CIRUS products 'would be used only for peaceful purposes'. In the meantime, however, Bhabha planned a complex nearby—all this activity took place in and around Bombay—that would extract weapons-grade plutonium from CIRUS's fuel rods. Like the South Africans, Nehru and Bhabha spoke of producing Peaceful Nuclear Explosives, and in this they were never discouraged by the United States.

American fantasies about PNEs—using nuclear devices to 'change the earth's surface to suit us', as Edward Teller proclaimed in 1957—help explain the willingness with which the United States provided both South Africa and India with nuclear equipment and information, and the apparent calm with which the Americans regarded India's nuclear opacity. The Americans also, in the late 1940s and early 1950s, hoped to monopolize India's monazite sands, a possible source of nuclear fuel. And the Americans understood, despite any number of policy differences with Nehru, India's delicate strategic situation in South Asia. In September 1961 George McGhee, Undersecretary of State for Political Affairs, suggested to his boss, Dean Rusk, that the United States might assist India to develop an atomic bomb and thereby 'beat Communist China to the punch'. Rusk rejected the idea, but less than five years later he advised President Lyndon Johnson to take 'no dramatic steps to discourage the Indians from starting a nuclear weapons program', and Johnson did not. Nor did other nations place obstacles in

India's way. Meanwhile, China attacked India following a border dispute in 1962 and detonated its device at Lop Nur in 1964, and India and Pakistan fought two limited but sharp wars, in 1965 and 1971. Yet India did not test a bomb until 1974.

The reason for the delay, as Perkovich has it, is that residual moral doubts about producing a nuclear weapon, combined with a lack of official conviction that a bomb would enhance India's security and (perhaps as a result of these two factors) a haphazard decisionmaking process concerning nuclear affairs, slowed momentum toward a decision to test. But official indecision never affected the determination of the nuclear scientific community to push forward. Like their counterparts elsewhere, Indian scientists wanted to test themselves, solve problems, and advance their status, nationally and in the world. Homi Bhabha had reminded delegates at the Geneva Conference on Peaceful Uses of Atomic Energy in 1955 that scientists were a global community that 'stood above history and politics' and that they must never be 'restrained by national boundaries' and jealousies. (Bhabha died in a plane crash in early 1966.) Indian physicists, helped by the British, Canadians, and Americans, and increasingly sophisticated in their own techniques, were mostly ready by the early 1970s to test a PNE, and awaited only government permission to do so. This came, according to Perkovich, in September 1972, in the aftermath of American bullying during the previous year's conflict with Pakistan (and the subsequent formation of Bangladesh), and with Prime Minister Indira Gandhi, Nehru's daughter, under siege politically. If the nation would gain status from testing an atomic device, so, presumably, would its leader. Having worked through some problems concerning the test device's initiator, the team was ready to go by the spring of 1974. Just after 8.00 a.m. on 18 May the Indians detonated a PNE at Pokhran, beneath the Rajasthan desert. Scientists estimated the blast at 12 kilotons, though much later revised the figure downwards; the Americans guessed the shot had produced between 4 and 6 kilotons.

It was 'a peaceful nuclear explosion', and Mrs Gandhi insisted that there was 'nothing to get excited about'. Gandhi's poll numbers spiked. A man delivering newspapers told a reporter for the *Washington Post*: 'Now we're the same as America and Russia and China. We have the atomic bomb.' 'I couldn't escape the current of glee that streaked through me at the thought of what other nations would say,' wrote the politician Raj Thapar, no friend of Mrs Gandhi. 'They wouldn't be able to kick us around as before.' That was not quite the world's reaction. Pakistan's Prime Minister, Zulfikar Ali Bhutto, professed himself 'determined not to be intimidated,' and authorized a quickened pace for nuclear development by his country. China showed public restraint, while Canada made clear its anger over India's evident militarization of its peaceful nuclear assistance. The American ambassador, Daniel Patrick Moynihan, scolded Mrs Gandhi: 'India has made a huge mistake. Here you were the No. 1 hegemonic power in South Asia. Nobody was No. 2 and call Pakistan No. 3. Now in a decade's time, some Pakistani general will call you up and say I have four nuclear weapons and I want Kashmir. If not, we will drop them on you and we will all meet in heaven. And then what will you do?'

The answer was to slip back, for the time being, into a period of nuclear quiescence, under governments less convinced than Indira Gandhi's of the utility of nuclear testing or bomb building, or sufficiently convinced that India's status had been at least temporarily assured by the 1974 blast. Moral doubt about nuclear weapons persisted in some quarters, including those of Moraji Desai, Prime Minister from 1977 to 1979, and Indira's son Rajiv, who served in the office in 1984–9. Still, nuclear science and technology moved ahead. The Indians bought more heavy water (from China!), tested warhead-bearing Agni and Prithvi missiles, and refused, along with Pakistan, to sign on to a significant extension of the Nuclear Non-Proliferation Treaty in 1995. And, with the rise of the Hindu nationalist Bharatiya Janata Party (BJP) in the 1990s, nuclear weapons became even more fully associated with nationalism, however crabbed and threatening to non-Hindus, and associated as well with continuing resentment of the West and a masculine swagger characteristic of BJP leaders. When the BJP won elections in early 1998 and Atul Behari Vajpayee became Prime Minister, the stage was set for a resumption of testing. As one commentator wrote, Indians bitterly recognized the West's 'unstated cultural assumptions: that the subcontinent is full of unstable people with deep historical resentments, incapable of acting rationally or managing a technologically sophisticated arsenal'. The BJP would prove them wrong. Three times on 11 May 1998 and twice more on the 13th, India detonated nuclear devices—weapons, not PNEs. 'We have a big bomb now,' crowed Vajpayee, though the government soon withdrew that comment. *India Today* announced that the 'tests and their aftermath have radically redefined India's image of being a yogi in today's world of realpolitik'—no one feared a gentle yogi—and a BJP official revealed a plan for party functionaries to collect 'sacred soil' from Pokhran and transport it in holy vessels across the country, thereby 'spread[ing] the feeling of national self-confidence' and radioactivity. The American columnist Mary McGrory scolded Vajpayee, 'who wished to establish his machismo' with the blasts; not Vajpayee but the virulent Hindu nationalist Bal Thackeray declared: 'We have to prove we are not eunuchs.' The Pakistanis, of course, felt the same way, firing off five tests on 28 May and two more on the 30th. 'Today,' said Prime Minister Nawaz Sharif, 'we have settled a score.' The Indian Defence Minister dismissed the Pakistani explosions as 'Ping Pong balls', leaving Pakistanis, and others, to draw their own sexual conclusions.[9]

7. The critics of nuclear weapons

Just as nuclear weapons were developed in a number of nations over time, so were the weapons, and nuclear power generally, criticized from a variety of vantage points and for a number of reasons. In the United States, some scientists who had initiated, designed, or built the bomb had profound second thoughts, or articulated emphatically after the war doubts that had crept in earlier. 'If I had known that the Germans would not succeed in constructing the atom bomb,' said Albert Einstein, 'I would never have lifted a finger.' Robert Oppenheimer's deputy at Los Alamos, Samuel Allison, confessed: 'I don't have a comfortable feeling for having helped cremate a hundred thousand Japanese civilians.' Oppenheimer himself later wished that the Japanese had been warned explicitly about the bomb. Cyril Smith, co-director of the Experimental Physics at Los Alamos, told an interviewer: 'Sometimes I wake up at night feeling the plutonium metal in my hands—metal that I personally helped fabricate for the bomb—and realize that it killed hundreds of thousands of people. It's not a pleasant feeling.' Several leading nuclear physicists walked away from weapons' work forever; others, including Arthur Holly Compton and Hans Bethe, would campaign, quietly but openly, against developing a thermonuclear bomb. So too did radical intellectuals, including the pacifist A. J. Muste and the social critic Dwight Macdonald, excoriate the use of the bomb. Muste, and others, compared Hiroshima to Dachau. 'Like all great advances in technology of the past century,' wrote Macdonald in 1945, 'Atomic Fission is something in which Good and Evil are so closely intertwined that it is hard to see how the Good can be extracted and the Evil thrown away.'[10]

In Britain and the Commonwealth, voices were raised against the bomb, though they were at first scattered and most prominent among pacifists (who objected, obviously, not only to nuclear weapons but to war in general) and communists, who could be stigmatized by their countries' governments and whose moral footing became slippery once the Soviets had tested a bomb in 1949. Vera Brittain, one of a few British writers who had protested during the war against the policy of bombing German cities, was bolstered by the surprising extent to which many of her country-men and -women now criticized the attacks on Hiroshima and Nagasaki, appalled if not by the bombing of civilians then at least by the use of nuclear weapons against them. The physicist P. M. S. Blackett was among the first to argue that the bombs had been used as tools of diplomacy against the Russians rather than to end the war against Japan, the implication being that the bombings' purpose had been ignoble and, worse, that they represented, wrote Blackett, 'not so much the last military act of the second world war, as the first act of the cold diplomatic war with Russia now in progress'. Drawing from Aristotle ('one must not do evil that good might come') and Catholic doctrine, the philosopher Gertrude Anscombe attacked the Allied policy of unconditional surrender as 'visibly wicked', rejected arguments based on military necessity for bombing enemy cities, and in 1957 protested when her university, Oxford, gave the atomic bomber Harry Truman an honorary degree. In Canada the government largely preempted opposition by declaring that it would not pursue a bomb, but organizations of scientists and technicians issued statements deploring nuclear weapons anyway. Aus-tralian journalist Wilfred Burchett went to Hiroshima in early September 1945 and found abundant evidence that thousands had died, and continued to die, from exposure to radiation. When American representatives in Japan insisted that radioactivity had not been a problem, Burchett contradicted them. In his home country, a relatively favorable popular response to the atomic bombings in their immediate aftermath had been reversed by late 1948, when by a margin of 10 percent Australians said they had a negative view of atomic energy in general. Speaking as the first anniversary of the bombings neared, Mohandas Gandhi allowed, as Anscombe would not, that 'good does come out of evil'. But the bomb had 'deadened the finest feelings that have sustained mankind for ages', bringing only 'an empty victory to the Allied armies'. The bomb had destroyed two cities in Japan, and over time was likely to corrode the souls of those who had perpetrated the destruction.[11]

Elsewhere in the world, there were glimmerings of anti-nuclear activity as well. In France, Albert Camus wrote immediately after the bombing of Hiroshima of the 'most awful destructive rage' the attack manifested; 'civilization has just reached its final degree of savagery.' An American bomber pilot named Garry Davis renounced his citizenship, set up a tent on the UN office lawn in Paris, and demanded the creation of a world government. Praised by Camus, Jean-Paul Sartre, and André Gide, among others, 'Davis created an enormous sensation' in France, as Lawrence Wittner has noted. The German Social Democratic Party condemned war, though without specifically targeting the bomb; in Italy, the atomic attacks faced sharp criticism from the Vatican, the philosopher Benedetto Croce, and Enrico Fermi's sister, Maria; and peace movements galvanized by opposition to the bomb rose from postwar ashes in Scandinavia and the Low Countries. There were murmurings of anti-nuclear feeling and support for world government in such places as Hungary, the Philippines, and Venezuela.[12]

What precisely the critics wanted was never fully clear. Expressions of worry and dismay became sharper from the 1950s through the 1980s, and movements formed around the world—the Campaign for Nuclear Disarmament in Great Britain, the National Committee for a Sane Nuclear Policy (SANE), especially in the United States, the Campaign for a Nuclear Freeze, and numerous national groups that opposed atomic power and atomic weapons. Influenced in part by such groups, governments moved to curb weapons' testing, prevent new nuclear development in nations that had not yet made bombs, build confidence so as to prevent the accidental launch of missiles or bombers, and, eventually, trim their own nuclear arsenals. The United States and the Soviet Union, far and away the largest possessors of nuclear hardware, signed the Limited Test Ban Treaty in 1963, the Strategic Arms Limitation Treaty (affecting intercontinental missile launchers and anti-ballistic missiles most prominently) in 1972, the Intermediate-Range Nuclear Force (INF) Treaty of 1987, and the Strategic Arms Reduction Treaty (1991), which limited not just launchers but the nuclear warheads that sat atop them. The Nuclear Non-Proliferation Treaty was signed in 1968 and extended indefinitely in 1995. Anti-nuclear organizations surely had a hand in persuading the world's governments to impose these limitations and restrictions; it would be wrong to pretend otherwise, and cynical to claim that the treaties have not done much good. Yet no one is so naive as to claim that the threat of nuclear war has vanished. The powers retain nuclear stockpiles, smaller nations continue to develop weapons or remain mysterious as to their capacity and willingness to do so, and refined uranium disappears from storage facilities to know-not where with alarming frequency. No world government exists to regulate nuclear energy or nuclear weapons; inspectors for the United Nations are viewed with suspicion or derision. And, in some ways, the battle against nuclear weapons, difficult as it is, remains a good deal easier than the philosophically more complicated fight to prevent attacks, of any description, on civilians. One cannot kill as many civilians at once with a 'conventional' bomb or a car bomb as with a nuclear weapon. But, if humankind has, since Hiroshima and Nagasaki, stepped back across the nuclear threshold, it has stridden grimly forward in its willingness to target the innocent. 'Do not do evil that good might come of it.' That would seem to be easier said than done.[13]

Epilogue
Nightmares and Hopes

More than sixty years after the bombings of Hiroshima and Nagasaki, people still have nuclear nightmares. Some imagine a resumption of the Cold War, in which disagreements over human rights or interference in domestic affairs or competition over scarce resources like oil results in a dusting-off of atomic arsenals in the United States, Russia, and China. Others imagine nuclear weapons in the hands of irrational dictators or rogue nations. What if North Korea develops nuclear weapons, as it has frequently threatened to do? Its leader, Kim Jong-Il, an unpredictable man who has nevertheless made a habit of carrying out his threats, might hold hostage to his demands South Korea and Japan, and much of East Asia. What if Iran goes nuclear? Early 2007 estimates are that, if Tehran continues at its current present pace of refining uranium, it could have a bomb as soon as 2009; the Iranian leadership has denied the Holocaust and speculated openly about wiping Israel off the map. The suspicion that Iraqi president Saddam Hussein had obtained yellowcake from Niger was one (of several) reasons given by the George W. Bush administration for launching war on Iraq in the spring of 2003. That suspicion was unfounded. Still, worried about Iran and the chronic instability of the region, Middle Eastern governments have begun pressing forward with nuclear programs of their own. Saudi Arabia in particular has recently shown a desire to have nuclear power, though the likes of Kuwait, Bahrain, Egypt, and the United Arab Emirates have also acknowledged interest. 'We will develop [nuclear power] openly,' declared the Saudi Foreign Minister. 'We want no bombs. All we want is a whole Middle East that is free from weapons of mass destruction,' including both Israel and Iran. The world has heard such denials before.[1]

There is another nightmare, and it is perhaps more frightening because it is harder to predict. A terrorist is supplied with a small bomb built around a core of uranium. He carries the device, fitted into a backpack or a suitcase, into Charles de Gaulle airport, King's Cross Station, or Times Square, and detonates it. While the blast itself would kill only the handful of people unlucky enough to be nearby, a large area would be contaminated with radioactivity, and the psychological effect of such an attack would probably be shattering. In 1997 General Aleksandr Lebed, a former Russian national security adviser, claimed that the Russians had built suitcase bombs—their targets, allegedly, were NATO command bunkers in Europe—and that several had disappeared since the breakup of the Soviet Union. Just weeks after the 11 September 2001 attacks on the United States, the Israelis said they had arrested a Pakistani man trying to enter Israel via the Palestinian Territories with a backpack-borne nuclear device. The event worried Western terrorism experts and law-enforcement officials. In December 2005 US air marshals shot dead in Miami a plane passenger who evidently claimed to have a bomb in his knapsack, though it turned out that the man had a psychological condition and had neglected to take his medication; no bomb was found. Atrocious and indiscriminate bomb attacks on public transport in Bombay, Madrid, and London have raised fears that a nuclear device might be used in the same awful way.[2]

Those who would deliver such weapons, attached to their bodies, are different from the pilots at Hiroshima and Nagasaki. They are not part of a state that has formally declared war. They are reckless with their own lives. But in a fundamental way things have not changed: terrorists with bombs, conventional or nuclear, do not care who they kill, since everyone in a targeted city, country, or civilization is deemed guilty of pursuing an unjust war against them. Their savage logic is that there are among their enemies no non-combatants. All Americans, Israelis, Britons, Shia or Sunni are guilty of transgression against them. Naturally, the intended targets of such attacks find such thinking barbaric, as indeed it is. But let us remember here twentieth-century attacks on non-combatants in 'Mespot' and India, at Guernica, Shanghai, Nanjing, and Warsaw, in Coventry and London, at Hamburg and Dresden, at Tokyo, Hiroshima, and Nagasaki. These attacks were undertaken in the name of 'air policing' (policing is part of security and less than war), unabashedly to terrorize a population and thus force a quicker end to war (a humane strategy, no?), or to 'de-house' war workers (their houses were to be destroyed, not them). Technological advances allowed, in Vietnam and Iraq, the use of 'smart' bombs, which found only military targets—unless they didn't, in which case the result was 'collateral damage,' a term suggesting that civilian casualties were an unfortunate byproduct of an attack on a legitimate target. Alas: no type of bomb is smart all the time. One might argue that those who use technologically sophisticated weapons are at least *trying* to avoid killing civilians; that is not the case for a suicide bomber who blows himself up in a crowded marketplace. And yet, in both cases the result is the horrible and predictable death of innocent people.

It would be pleasant to think that governments and terrorist organizations acknowledge limits to the kinds of attacks they can make, the kinds of weapons they might use. Not since Nagasaki has anyone dropped an atomic bomb on a city, and the energy with which nations have condemned the use of biological or chemical weapons—by the Iraqi government against the Kurds in Halabja in 1988, by the Japanese religious cult Aum Shinrikyo in the Tokyo subway in 1995—inspires hope that the world regards this sort of attack as unacceptable. That such weapons continue to exist, however, and are used at all, suggests a more sobering reality. Where enemies can be totalized and demonized as readily as they are in the contemporary world, restraint is a virtue out of season. What remains is a conviction that non-combatants can be targeted if the danger is great or the cause just, as so often seems to be the case, or that genuine non-combatants cannot exist in a world of polarized ideologies or opposed cultures.

The editors of *The Bulletin of the Atomic Scientists* are not optimistic about the fate of the earth. In January 2007 the minute hand of the 'Doomsday Clock' moved ahead, from seven to five minutes before midnight. 'Not since the first atomic bombs were dropped on Hiroshima and Nagasaki,' warned an editorial, 'has the world faced such perilous choices.' The piece cited as particular dangers a recent North Korean nuclear test, Iran's interest in nuclear power, signs that the Bush administration would consider the use of nuclear strikes on unfriendly nations or terrorist groups holding weapons of mass destruction, and the ongoing insecurity caused by the presence of 26,000 nuclear weapons in the United States and Russia alone. The *Bulletin* acknowledged that climate change also represented a serious threat to the welfare of the earth. But 'nuclear weapons present the most grave challenge to humanity, enabling genocide with the press of a button'. The growing interest in nuclear power, in part as a remedy for global warming, risks spreading nuclear material across the globe; the editorial reminds us that spent fuel from 'peaceful' nuclear reactors can be processed into weapons-grade plutonium, only 1–3 kilograms of which are needed to make a bomb. 'Our way of thinking about the uses and control of technologies must change to prevent unspeakable destruction and future human suffering,' concludes the piece. 'The Clock is ticking.'[3]

Equally important is a change in thinking about human targets in war. It is not easy to find nuclear weapons, but in a happier world warheads can be detected, counted, and even disassembled. The part of the human brain that assists in making moral choices is far more difficult of access. The Japanese butchered Chinese civilians with bayonets; the Americans killed Japanese with non-nuclear weapons and without discrimination, since all Japanese were said to be alike in their inhumaness (the Americans depicted them as rats and roaches). The Nazis exterminated millions of unresisting people during the 1930s and 1940s. The Americans, and especially the British, bombed German cities: in February 1945 Arthur Harris, head of Britain's Bomber Command, said, 'I do not personally regard the whole of the remaining cities of Germany as worth the bones of one British Grenadier.' Much of the world refuses to accept this view. Article 51 of the 1977 protocol to the Geneva Conventions declares that civilians 'shall enjoy general protection against dangers arising from military operations', including 'indiscriminate' attacks such as those 'expected to cause incidental loss of civilian life, injury to civilians, damage to civilian objects, or a combination thereof, which would be excessive in relation to the concrete and direct military advantage anticipated'. Thirty years later, among the nations that have not yet ratified the protocol are the nuclear nations Pakistan, Israel, and the United States, and the nuclear hopeful Iran. Neither, of course, has Al Qaeda announced plans for a signing ceremony.[4]

Who is victimized by weapons ought to be our main concern. And yet, in the end, despite the hundreds of thousands of innocents killed by 'conventional' means during the twentieth century, we always return to Hiroshima, banal in its similarity to other sites of atrocity, appalling in its difference from them. One bomb, which killed not only by blast and flame but insidiously, from the inside of the body out, by radiation. The atomic bomb was new, and its use made Hiroshima special forever. Hiroshima today is a thriving and attractive city of over a million people. It has been massively rebuilt since 1945. An arcaded shopping mall is perpetually crowded with visitors; the best restaurants are jammed; a major league baseball team, the Hiroshima Carp, plays in a downtown

stadium (though is rarely very good). There is an art museum featuring
some French Impressionist painting. In 2004 Hiroshima's central wholesale
market sold 33 billion yen worth of vegetables and about 18 billion yen of
fruit. Shopkeepers and hoteliers are friendly and Hiroshimans are in general
more helpful than Japanese in larger cities. In the summer of 2006 a bus
driver left his bus and ran three blocks in the heat to catch an American
visitor, to whom he was afraid he had given wrong directions. In short,
Hiroshima is a remarkably nice place to spend a few days.

It is also a place that promotes peace. There is a yearly ceremony on
6 August in which the mayor makes a declaration of peace and the victims
of the bomb are remembered. The vortex of peace activity in the city is
the Peace Memorial Museum, on the lush grounds of the Peace Memorial
Park, just where the Ōta River splits in two and within yards of ground
zero. The skeletal dome of the Hiroshima Prefectural Industrial Promotion
hall rises just across the river from the park. In the northwest part of
the park, near a statue of Kannon, the Goddess of Peace, carefully folded
paper cranes hang suspended from wires, gifts from thousands of children
around the world and given in the memory of Sadako, the Hiroshiman girl
who made cranes until the day she died of radiation poisoning. There is
a Peace Clock, a Peace Fountain, a Peace Bell, and a monument to the
Koreans who died in the bombing, built in 1970 and moved into the park,
following some diplomatic wrangling, in 1999. Within the park is the Peace
Memorial Museum, with a main building and an east wing. Its exhibitions
chronicle the history of Hiroshima, including its role as a military center
(information that was added subsequent to criticism of its absence when
the museum first opened). The story of the atomic bomb's development
and the decision for its use is displayed in several panels. The museum
concentrates on the human consequences of the bomb, and the exhibits
that display these are not for the faint of heart: visitors see children's toys
and bottles melted and crushed, a bundle of hair that fell from the head
of a (surviving) radiation victim, scorched *mompei* (cloth work pants) and
harrowing photographs of shadows cast in concrete by *Little Boy's* flash, of
the injuries suffered by the wounded, of the incredulous dead. There are
t-shirts for sale—it is a modern museum—but their messages are tasteful, for
the emphasis throughout the building is on memory, reconciliation, peace.

In the late spring of 2004, as visitors left the formal exhibition space
of the museum's main building and turned right down a window-lined
hall toward the exit, they were stopped by several smiling young women

who asked them to fill out a brief questionnaire. The intent of the form was evident immediately: while everyone understood that visitors came to Hiroshima to visit the museum and park, to encounter the history of the atomic bombing, civic leaders wanted people to know about the city's other attractions. The authors of the questionnaire informed visitors about the shopping centers and the baseball team, about the importance of Hiroshima as a seaport and trading hub, about the zoo, the botanical garden, the trolley cars purchased from cities all over the world, and the nearby island Miyajima, a favorite of Japanese tourists for its graceful temples and its red *torii* shrine, standing sentinel near the island's busy dock. Above all, the questionnaire stressed, Hiroshima, city of the bombed, remembered its past but had also moved on. It was no longer a city of victims but a cosmopolitan place with an international reputation. The first atomic weapon was the world's bomb. Modern Hiroshima, in the aspirations of its leading citizens, is the world's city.

Notes

INTRODUCTION: THE WORLD'S BOMB

1. US Strategic Bombing Survey, *Japan's Struggle to End the War*, excerpted in Barton J. Bernstein, ed., *The Atomic Bomb: The Critical Issues* (Boston: Little, Brown, 1976), 56.
2. Thomas Powers, *Heisenberg's War: The Secret History of the German Bomb* (New York: Knopf, 1993), 437.
3. Richard Rhodes, *The Making of the Atomic Bomb* (New York: Simon and Schuster, 1986), 735–6; Paul Boyer, *By the Bomb's Early Light: American Thought and Culture at the Dawn of the Atomic Age* (New York: Pantheon, 1985), 193; Mahatma Gandhi, 'The Atom Bomb and Ahimsa', in Kai Bird and Lawrence Lifschultz, eds., *Hiroshima's Shadow* (Stony Creek, CT: Pamphleteer's Press, 1998), 258–9.
4. Margaret Gowing, *Britain and Atomic Energy 1939–1945* (New York: St Martin's, 1964), 386.

CHAPTER ONE. THE WORLD'S ATOM

1. J. Bronowski, 'ABC of the Atom', in *Hiroshima Plus 20*, prepared by *New York Times*, intro. John W. Finney (New York: Delacorte Press, 1965), 138; Margaret Gowing, *Britain and Atomic Energy 1939–1945* (New York: St Martin's, 1964), 1.
2. Gowing, *Britain and Atomic Energy*, 5; Daniel J. Kevles, *The Physicists: The History of a Scientific Community in Modern America* (Cambridge, MA: Harvard University Press, 1995 [1971], 75; Richard Rhodes, *The Making of the Atomic Bomb* (New York: Simon and Schuster, 1986), 41–2.
3. Rhodes, *Making of the Atomic Bomb*, 42, 44.
4. Ibid. 50–1; John W. Dower, *Japan in War and Peace: Selected Essays* (New York: New Press, 1993), 64.
5. Laura Fermi, *Atoms for the World: United States Participation in the Conference on the Peaceful Uses of Atomic Energy* (Chicago: University of Chicago Press, 1957), 42; Rhodes, *Making of the Atomic Bomb*, 165.
6. Bronowski, 'ABC of the Atom', 143.
7. Kevles, *The Physicists*, 271; Philip L. Cantelon, Richard G. Hewlett, and Robert C. Williams, eds., *The American Atom: A Documentary History of Nuclear Policies*

from the Discovery of Fission to the Present, 2nd edn. (Philadelphia: University of Pennsylvania Press, 1991), 5; Rhodes, *Making of the Atomic Bomb*, 24.

8. Rhodes, *Making of the Atomic Bomb*, 35.

9. Ibid. 34.

10. Robert Jungk, *Brighter than a Thousand Suns: A Personal History of the Atomic Scientists*, trans. James Cleugh (San Diego: Harcourt, 1958), 5–6, 8–9; Rhodes, *Making of the Atomic Bomb*, 104–33; Dower, *Japan in War and Peace*, 64.

11. Fermi, *Atoms for the World*, 42.

12. R. E. Peierls, *Atomic Histories* (Woodbury, NY: American Institute of Physics, 1997), 45.

13. Victor Lefebure, *The Riddle of the Rhine: Chemical Strategy in Peace and War* (New York: Chemical Foundation, 1923), 31; Amos A. Fries and Clarence J. West, *Chemical Warfare* (New York: McGraw-Hill, 1921), 13.

14. L. F. Haber, *The Poisonous Cloud: Chemical Warfare in the First World War* (Oxford: Oxford University Press, 1986), 24–7, 34.

15. Otto Hahn, *My Life: The Autobiography of a Scientist*, trans. Ernst Kaiser and Eithne Wilkins (New York: Herder and Herder, 1970), 118–19, 128–30; Edward M. Spiers, *Chemical Warfare* (Urbana, IL: University of Illinois Press, 1986), 14.

16. Rhodes, *Making of the Atomic Bomb*, 92–3; Lefebure, *Riddle of the Rhine*, 68; Hahn, *My Life*, 120; Haber, *Poisonous Cloud*, 24, 107, 192–3.

17. Haber, *Poisonous Cloud*, 22–3, 45, 51–3, 290.

18. Fries and West, *Chemical Warfare*, 6, 38, 141; Rhodes, *Making of the Atomic Bomb*, 100–1; Haber, *Poisonous Cloud*, 134; Lefebure, *Riddle of the Rhine*, 176–7.

19. Haber, *Poisonous Cloud*, 239, 292–4, 307–8; Spiers, *Chemical Warfare*, 38.

20. Haber, *Poisonous Cloud*, 235–6; Spiers, *Chemical Warfare*, 22; Fries and West, *Chemical Warfare*, 127; Rhodes, *Making of the Atomic Bomb*, 94.

21. Spiers, *Chemical Warfare*, 39–40; Haber, *Poisonous Cloud*, 248–9, 299; Fries and West, *Chemical Warfare*, 371.

22. Spiers, *Chemical Warfare*, 4, 17; Haber, *Poisonous Cloud*, 292.

23. Hahn, *My Life*, 118; Haber, *Poisonous Cloud*, 2, 126, 138; Lefebure, *Riddle of the Rhine*, 237–41.

24. Kevles, *The Physicists*, 146–7; Hahn, *My Life*, 131–2.

25. Hahn, *My Life*, 131–2; Rhodes, *Making of the Atomic Bomb*, 95.

26. Haber, *Poisonous Cloud*, 26; http://www.energyquest.ugov/scientists/curie/html, accessed 28 Sept. 2005.

27. Etel Solingen, ed., *Scientists and the State: Domestic Structures and the International Context* (Ann Arbor: University of Michigan Press, 1994), 6.

28. David Holloway, *Stalin and the Bomb: The Soviet Union and Atomic Energy, 1939–1956* (New Haven: Yale University Press, 1994), 10.

29. Paul R. Josephson, 'The Political Economy of Soviet Science from Lenin to Gorbachev', in Solingen, *Scientists and the State*, 146–51.

30. Holloway, *Stalin and the Bomb*, 39–40.

31. Ibid. 40–4, 47; Josephson, 'Political Economy', 151–2. See also Thomas B. Cochran, Robert S. Norris, and Oleg Bukharin, *Making the Russian Bomb: From Stalin to Yeltsin* (Boulder, CO: Westview Press, 1995).

32. Kevles, *The Physicists*, pp. ix, 112, 118–31, 138; Robert Gilpin, *American Scientists and Nuclear Weapons Policy* (Princeton: Princeton University Press, 1962), 22.

33. Kevles, *The Physicists*, 132–3, 148.

34. Ibid. 173–5.

35. Ibid. 238–9, 250–1.

36. Marshall Cohen, 'Moral Skepticism and International Relations', in Charles R. Beitz, Marshall Cohen, Thomas Scanlon, and A. John Simmons, eds., *International Ethics* (Princeton: Princeton University Press, 1985), 3–5. See also Robert Westbrook, *Why We Fought: Forging American Obligations in World War II* (Washington: Smithsonian Books, 2004).

37. Michael Walzer, *Just and Unjust Wars: A Moral Argument with Historical Illustrations* (New York: Basic Books, 1977), 21.

38. Gilpin, *American Scientists*, 26.

39. Ibid. 27–8; R. W. Clark, *The Greatest Power on Earth: The International Race for Nuclear Supremacy* (New York: Harper and Row, 1980), 44; Jungk, *Brighter than a Thousand Suns*, 201; Rhodes, *Making of the Atomic Bomb*, 675.

40. Walzer, *Just and Unjust Wars*, 264–5.

CHAPTER TWO. GREAT BRITAIN: REFUGEES, AIR POWER, AND THE POSSIBILITY OF THE BOMB

1. H. G. Wells, *The World Set Free* (Leipzig: Bernhard Tauchnitz, 1914).

2. Mary Wollstonecraft Shelley, *Frankenstein, or, The Modern Prometheus* (London: Oxford University Press, 1969); Edward Bulwer-Lytton, *The Coming Race* (London: G. Routledge and Sons, 1874); Alexandra Aldridge, *The Scientific World View in Dystopia* (Ann Arbor: UMI Research Press, 1984), 10–11.

3. Szilard to Sir Hugo Hirst, 17 Mar. 1934, in Philip L. Cantelon, Richard G. Hewlett, and Robert C. Williams, eds., *The American Atom: A Documentary History of Nuclear Policies from the Discovery of Fission to the Present*, 2nd edn. (Philadelphia, PA: University of Pennsylvania Press, 1991), 7–8; Richard Rhodes, *The Making of the Atomic Bomb* (New York: Simon and Schuster, 1986), 14–17, 21–5; Gerard J. DeGroot, *The Bomb: A History of Hell on Earth* (London: Pimlico, 2005), 5–6.

4. Robert Jungk, *Brighter than a Thousand Suns: A Personal History of the Atomic Scientists*, trans. James Cleugh (San Diego: Harcourt, 1958), 7; Charles Weiner, 'New Site for the Seminar', in Donald Fleming and Bernard Bailyn, eds., *The*

Intellectual Migration: Europe and America, 1930–1960 (Cambridge, MA: Harvard University Press, 1969), 194–5.

5. Jungk, *Brighter than a Thousand Suns*, 53–6; J. W. Boag, P. E. Rubinin, and D. Shoenberg, eds., *Kapitza in Cambridge and Moscow: Life and Letters of a Russian Physicist* (Amsterdam: North-Holland, 1990), 195.

6. Jungk, *Brighter than a Thousand Suns*, 34–6; Jean Medawar and David Pyke, *Hitler's Gift: Scientists who Fled Nazi Germany* (London: Piatkus, 2000), 3, 9, 26–7; Frank R. Pfetsch, 'Germany: Three Models of Interaction–Weimar, Nazi, Federal Republic', in Etel Solingen, ed., *Scientists and the State: Domestic Structures and the International Context* (Ann Arbor: University of Michigan Press, 1994), 198–9.

7. Jungk, *Brighter than a Thousand Suns*, 37; Medawar and Pyke, *Hitler's Gift*, 21; Pfetsch, 'Germany', 199.

8. Medawar and Pyke, *Hitler's Gift*, 26, 33–46, 85–7; Rhodes, *Making of the Atomic Bomb*, 185–6, 192.

9. Medawar and Pyke, *Hitler's Gift*, 87–9; L. F. Haber, *The Poisonous Cloud: Chemical Warfare in the First World War* (Oxford: Oxford University Press, 1986), 306, 312.

10. Medawar and Pyke, *Hitler's Gift*, 80–5, 220–1; Margaret Gowing, *Britain and Atomic Energy 1939–1945* (New York: St Martin's, 1964), 46–8.

11. Leo Szilard, 'Reminiscences', in Fleming and Bailyn, *Intellectual Migration*, 94–141. See also Rhodes, *Making of the Atomic Bomb*, 20–1, 192–3; Medawar and Pyke, *Hitler's Gift*, 213–15.

12. Rhodes, *Making of the Atomic Bomb*, 568; id., *Dark Sun: The Making of the Hydrogen Bomb* (New York: Simon and Schuster, 1995), 56–7; Jungk, *Brighter than a Thousand Suns*, 187.

13. Rhodes, *Dark Sun*, 54–5; Lansing Lamont, *Day of Trinity* (New York: Atheneum, 1965), 29–30.

14. Rhodes, *Dark Sun*, 55–7; Lamont, *Day of Trinity*, 30; Ronald W. Clark, *The Greatest Power on Earth: The International Race for Nuclear Supremacy* (New York: Harper and Row, 1980), 106.

15. Rhodes, *Dark Sun*, 57–8.

16. Medawar and Pyke, *Hitler's Gift*, 85.

17. Edward Said, *Orientalism* (New York: Pantheon, 1978), 259.

18. Jungk, *Brighter than a Thousand Suns*, 48, 71.

19. Baldwin quoted in Horst Boog, 'Harris: A German View', in Sir Arthur T. Harris, *Despatch on War Operations, 23rd February, 1942, to 8th May, 1945* (London: Frank Cass, 1995), p. xli.

20. DeGroot, *The Bomb*, 2; Charles Messenger, *'Bomber' Harris and the Strategic Bombing Offensive, 1939–1945* (New York: St Martin's, 1984), 13; Robin Neillands, *The Bomber War: The Allied Air Offensive against Nazi Germany* (Woodstock and New York: Overlook Press, 2001), 12.

21. Neillands, *Bomber War*, 12–13; Messenger, *'Bomber' Harris*, 13.

22. Andrew Boyle, *Trenchard* (London: Collins, 1962), 221–2.

23. Ibid. 223–4, 229; Dudley Saward, *Bomber Harris: The Story of Sir Arthur Harris* (Garden City, NY: Doubleday and Co., 1985), 17–18.

24. Boyle, *Trenchard*, 56–62, 97, 115–16, 137–41.

25. Ibid. 166, 186–8, 239, 311–12.

26. Ibid. 299; Messenger, 'Bomber' *Harris*, 16–18; Michael S. Sherry, *The Rise of American Air Power: The Creation of Armageddon* (New Haven: Yale University Press, 1987), 19, 24, 34–5; David R. Mets, *The Air Campaign: John Warden and the Classical Airpower Theorists* (Maxwell Air Force Base, AL: Air University Press, 1999), 11–12.

27. Boyle, *Trenchard*, 354, 365–9; Boog, 'Harris: A German View', p. xl.

28. Boyle, *Trenchard*, 369, 388–91; Saward, *Bomber Harris*, 24–31; Sir Arthur Harris, *Bomber Offensive* (New York: Macmillan, 1947), 19–23; Priya Satia, 'The Defense of Inhumanity: Air Control and the British Idea of Arabia', *American Historical Review*, 111/1 (Feb. 2006), 16–51.

29. Messenger, 'Bomber' *Harris*, 8; Saward, *Bomber Harris*, 3, 8–11; Harris, *Bomber Offensive*, 16.

30. Saward, *Bomber Harris*, 16, 21, 24–31; Harris, *Bomber Offensive*, 18–23.

31. Documents accessed at http://en.wikipedia.org/Wiki/Terror_bombing, 11 Nov. 2005.

32. Saward, *Bomber Harris*, 58–61, 67; Harris, *Bomber Offensive*, 23–31.

33. Messenger, 'Bomber' *Harris*, 26; Neillands, *Bomber War*, 31, 35.

34. Sherry, *Rise of American Air Power*, 93; Neillands, *Bomber War*, 44, 52–4.

35. Harris, *Bomber Offensive*, 33; Messenger, 'Bomber' *Harris*, 41–2, 47–8; Harris, *Despatch on War Operations*, 7; Ronald Schaffer, *Wings of Judgment: American Bombing in World War II* (New York: Oxford University Press, 1985), 36.

36. Schaffer, *Wings of Judgment*, 107–9; http://www.ww2guide.com/bombs. shtml#bombs, accessed 15 Nov. 2005.

37. This account of the discovery of fission draws on Laura Fermi, *Atoms in the Family: My Life with Enrico Fermi* (Chicago: University of Chicago Press, 1954), 97–104; Rhodes, *Making of the Atomic Bomb*, 233–75; Jungk, *Brighter than a Thousand Suns*, 59–70; Gowing, *Britain and Atomic Energy*, 21–8.

38. Szilard to Strauss, 25 Jan. 1939, in Cantelon, Hewlett, and Williams, *The American Atom*, 8–9.

39. Harold Nicolson, *Public Faces* (Boston and New York: Houghton Mifflin, 1933).

40. Margaret Gowing, *Independence and Deterrence: Britain and Atomic Energy, 1945– 1952*, i. *Policy Making* (London: Macmillan, 1974), 1.

CHAPTER THREE. JAPAN AND GERMANY: PATHS NOT TAKEN

1. Richard Rhodes, *The Making of the Atomic Bomb* (New York: Simon and Schuster, 1986), 118; Robert D. Nininger, *Minerals for Atomic Energy: A Guide*

to *Exploration for Uranium, Thorium, and Beryllium* (New York: D. Van Nostrand and Co., 1954), 44–6; Martin Lynch, *Mining in World History* (London: Reaktion Books, 2002), 22, 40.

2. Thomas Powers, *Heisenberg's War: The Secret History of the German Bomb* (New York: Knopf, 1993), 10; David Irving, *The German Atomic Bomb: The History of Nuclear Research in Nazi Germany* (New York: Simon and Schuster, 1967), 34–7, 50–5. In the light of what Irving has become—a Nazi apologist and Holocaust denier jailed in Austria in early 2006–it is a bit worrisome to rely, as I have done, on this book. Most scholars of the German bomb nevertheless consider it to be based on sound scholarship.

3. Nininger, *Minerals*, 43–4; Lennard Bickel, *The Deadly Element: The Story of Uranium* (New York: Stein and Day, 1979), 48–51, 53.

4. Lynch, *Mining*, 288–9; Bickel, *Deadly Element*, 56–8.

5. Robert Jungk, *Brighter than a Thousand Suns: A Personal History of the Atomic Scientists*, trans. James Cleugh (San Diego: Harcourt, 1958), 107–8.

6. Ronald W. Clark, *The Greatest Power on Earth: The International Race for Nuclear Supremacy* (New York: Harper and Row, 1980), 58–60.

7. Arthur Holly Compton, *Atomic Quest: A Personal Narrative* (New York: Oxford University Press, 1956), 96–7; Peter Wyden, *Day One: Before Hiroshima and After* (New York: Simon and Schuster, 1984), 57–8.

8. The novelist Robert Wilcox claims, in *Japan's Secret War*, that the Japanese did indeed find uranium in occupied northern Korea, and used it to make an atomic weapon, which they tested successfully on 10 Aug. 1945. The bomb obviously came too late to reverse Japanese fortunes. What evidence of the program they could not destroy fell into Soviet hands. North Korea does have uranium, though its quality is unknown and most sources suggest that it was not discovered until 1964. See, but do not take seriously, Robert K. Wilcox, *Japan's Secret War* (New York: William Morrow, 1985).

9. Wyden, *Day One*, 86; John W. Dower, ' "NI" and "F": Japan's Wartime Atomic Bomb Research', in John W. Dower, *Japan in War and Peace: Selected Essays* (New York: New Press, 1993), 64–5.

10. Walter E. Grunden, *Secret Weapons and World War II: Japan in the Shadow of Big Science* (Lawrence, KS: University Press of Kansas, 2005), 56.

11. Dower, ' "NI" and "F", ', 171; Grunden, *Secret Weapons*, 70, 81.

12. Dower, ' "NI" and "F" ', 84–5; Grunden, *Secret Weapons*, 71; Wyden, *Day One*, 87–8.

13. The foregoing paragraphs are based on Grunden, *Secret Weapons*, 48–82; Dower, ' "NI" and "F" ', 55–100; Wyden, *Day One*, 86–8; Kenji Hall, 'Japan's A-Bomb Goal Still Long Way off in '45', *Japan Times*, 7 Mar. 2003; Rhodes, *Making of the Atomic Bomb*, 580–2.

14. Jeremy Bernstein, *Hitler's Uranium Club: The Secret Recordings at Farm Hall* (Woodbury, NY: American Institute of Physics, 1996), 399–400.

15. Powers, *Heisenberg's War*, p. vii; Rhodes, *Making of the Atomic Bomb*, 115–16; David C. Cassidy, *Uncertainty: The Life and Science of Werner Heisenberg* (New York: W. H. Freeman, 1992), 172–3.

16. Rhodes, *Making of the Atomic Bomb*, 130–3; Cassidy, *Uncertainty*, 228–9, 313, 324.

17. For Heisenberg's visit to the United States, see Powers, *Heisenberg's War*, 3–8; Cassidy, *Uncertainty*, 411–13.

18. Cassidy, *Uncertainty*, 303, 310, 394–6.

19. Ibid. 342–5, 377–93; Powers, *Heisenberg's War*, 40–3.

20. Cassidy, *Uncertainty*, 394–6, 412–13.

21. Irving, *German Atomic Bomb*, 31–7.

22. Ibid. 42–6; David C. Cassidy, 'Introduction', to Bernstein, *Hitler's Uranium Club*, pp. xviii–xix.

23. Irving, *German Atomic Bomb*, 55–6, 62–4, 68, 76–7; Cassidy, 'Introduction', p. xxii; Powers, *Heisenberg's War*, 95–7.

24. See Michael Frayn, *Copenhagen* (London: Methuen, 1998); Mark Walker, *Nazi Science: Myth, Truth, and the German Atomic Bomb* (New York: Plenum Press, 1995), 243–68; Cassidy, *Uncertainty*, 436–42; Powers, *Heisenberg's War*, 120–8; Paul Lawrence Rose, *Heisenberg and the Nazi Atomic Bomb Project: A Study in German Culture* (Berkeley and Los Angeles: University of California Press, 1998), 155–7; Rhodes, *Making of the Atomic Bomb*, 383–6; Jungk, *Brighter than a Thousand Suns*, 98–104.

25. Irving, *German Atomic Bomb*, 56; Powers, *Heisenberg's War*, 98; Cassidy, 'Introduction', pp. xxiii–xxv.

26. Cassidy, *Uncertainty*, 307; Irving, *German Atomic Bomb*, 77, 126–7.

27. Cassidy, *Uncertainty*, 455–7; Albert Speer, *Inside the Third Reich*, trans. Richard and Clara Winston (New York: Macmillan, 1970), 300–3.

28. Irving, *German Atomic Bomb*, 143–70, 187, 193–4, 198, 200–1; Rhodes, *Making of the Atomic Bomb*, 455–7, 513–17; Powers, *Heisenberg's War*, 337–9.

29. Leslie R. Groves, *Now it Can Be Told: The Story of the Manhattan Project* (New York: Harper and Brothers, 1962), 187; Nicholas Dawidoff, *The Catcher Was a Spy: The Mysterious Life of Moe Berg* (New York: Pantheon, 1994); Powers, *Heisenberg's War*, 382–93.

30. Jungk, *Brighter than a Thousand Suns*, 156–64; Wyden, *Day One*, 108–9; Rhodes, *Making of the Atomic Bomb*, 606–7.

31. Jungk, *Brighter than a Thousand Suns*, 168–70; Rhodes, *Making of the Atomic Bomb*, 609–10; Cassidy, *Uncertainty*, 497–500; Cassidy, 'Introduction', p. xiv; Powers, *Heisenberg's War*, 421–4.

32. Bernstein, *Hitler's Uranium Club*, 24, 138–43; Rose, *Heisenberg*, 9.

33. Cassidy, *Uncertainty*, 509; Groves, *Now it Can Be Told*, 140; Wyden, *Day One*, 97–9.

34. Cassidy, *Uncertainty*, 484–5; Jungk, *Brighter than a Thousand Suns*, 81, 170; Bernstein, *Hitler's Uranium Club*, 64.

35. Leo Szilard, 'Reminiscences', in Donald Fleming and Bernard Bailyn, eds., *The Intellectual Migration: Europe and America, 1930–1960* (Cambridge, MA: Harvard University Press, 1969), 106–7.

36. Jungk, *Brighter than a Thousand Suns*, 75–8; Wyden, *Day One*, 30; Martin J. Sherwin, *A World Destroyed: The Atomic Bomb and the Grand Alliance* (New York: Knopf, 1975), 23–4.

37. Wyden, *Day One*, 34–5; Sherwin, *A World Destroyed*, 16–17; Albert Einstein to Franklin D. Roosevelt, 2 Aug. 1939, in Philip L. Cantelon, Richard G. Hewlett, and Robert C. Williams, eds., *The American Atom: A Documentary History of Nuclear Policies from the Discovery of Fission to the Present*, 2nd edn. (Philadelphia, PA: University of Pennsylvania Press, 1991), 9–10.

38. Wyden, *Day One*, 35–8; Rhodes, *Making of the Atomic Bomb*, 314–17.

39. Margaret Gowing, *Britain and Atomic Energy 1939–1949* (New York: St Martin's, 1964), 40–2, 389–93.

40. Ibid. 43; Rhodes, *Making of the Atomic Bomb*, 329–31.

CHAPTER FOUR. THE UNITED STATES I: IMAGINING AND BUILDING THE BOMB

1. Richard Rhodes, *The Making of the Atomic Bomb* (New York: Simon and Schuster, 1986), 340–1; Margaret Gowing, *Britain and Atomic Energy 1939–1945* (New York: St Martin's, 1964), 54, 67; Otto R. Frisch, ' "Somebody Turned on the Sun with a Switch" ', *Bulletin of the Atomic Scientists*, 30/4 (Apr. 1974), 12–18.

2. Rhodes, *Making of the Atomic Bomb*, 359, 362; James G. Hershberg, *James B. Conant: Harvard to Hiroshima and the Making of the Nuclear Age* (Stanford, CA: Stanford University Press, 1993), 146–7; Gowing, *Britain and Atomic Energy*, 66–7; Richard G. Hewlett and Oscar E. Anderson Jr., *The New World, 1939–1946* (University Park, PA: Pennsylvania State University Press, 1962), 37.

3. 'The MAUD Report, 1941', in Philip L. Cantelon, Richard G. Hewlett, and Robert C. Williams, eds., *The American Atom: A Documentary History of Nuclear Policies from the Discovery of Fission to the Present* (Philadelphia, PA: University of Pennsylvania Press, 1991), 16–20; Gowing, *Britain and Atomic Energy*, 76, 104–5; Hewlett and Anderson, *The New World*, 42–3.

4. Peter Wyden, *Day One: Before Hiroshima and After* (New York: Simon and Schuster, 1984), 37; Martin J. Sherwin, *A World Destroyed: The Atomic Bomb and the Grand Alliance* (New York: Knopf, 1975), 28–33; Rhodes, *Making of the Atomic Bomb*, 372.

5. Rhodes, *Making of the Atomic Bomb*, 372–4; Wyden, *Day One*, 43–4; Hewlett and Anderson, *The New World*, 43; Gregg Herken, *Brotherhood of the Bomb: The Tangled Lives and Loyalties of Robert Oppenheimer, Ernest Lawrence, and Edward Teller* (New York: Henry Holt, 2002), 39–40.

6. Arthur Holly Compton, *Atomic Quest: A Personal Narrative* (New York: Oxford University Press, 1956), 6–7.

7. Rhodes, *Making of the Atomic Bomb*, 143–5; Daniel J. Kevles, *The Physicists: The History of a Scientific Community in Modern America* (Cambridge, MA: Harvard University Press, 1995 [1971]), 271–2.

8. Hershberg, *James B. Conant*, 8–9; Compton, *Atomic Quest*, 6–7.

9. Compton, *Atomic Quest*, 6; Rhodes, *Making of the Atomic Bomb*, 363–4; Wyden, *Day One*, 44–5.

10. The foregoing paragraphs are based on Compton, *Atomic Quest*, 7–9; Wyden, *Day One*, 45; Hershberg, *James B. Conant*, 149; Kevles, *The Physicists*, 325; Sherwin, *A World Destroyed*, 30–1, 36–7.

11. On 'big physics', see Kevles, *The Physicists*, 286.

12. Franklin D. Roosevelt, 'Roosevelt Delivers his War Message to Congress, 1941', in Dennis Merrill and Thomas G. Paterson, *Major Problems in American Foreign Relations*, ii. *Since 1914* (Boston: Houghton Mifflin, 2005), 132–3.

13. Leslie Groves, *Now it Can Be Told: The Story of the Manhattan Project* (New York: Harper and Bros., 1962), 265.

14. Sherwin, *A World Destroyed*, pp. xiv, 13; J. Samuel Walker, *Prompt and Utter Destruction: Truman and the Use of Atomic Bombs against Japan* (Chapel Hill, NC: University of North Carolina Press, 1997), 9; Barton J. Bernstein, 'The Atomic Bomb and American Foreign Policy: The Route to Hiroshima', in Barton J. Bernstein, ed., *The Atomic Bomb: The Critical Issues* (Boston: Little, Brown, 1976), 94–7; Groves, *Now it Can Be Told*, 265; Winston S. Churchill, *Triumph and Tragedy* (Boston: Houghton Mifflin, 1953), 639.

15. Wyden, *Day One*, 46–7; Rhodes, *Making of the Atomic Bomb*, 387–9, 398; Compton, *Atomic Quest*, 78.

16. Compton, *Atomic Quest*, 80–2; Rhodes, *Making of the Atomic Bomb*, 399–400.

17. Compton, *Atomic Quest*, 84–5; Wyden, *Day One*, 48; Laura Fermi, *Atoms in the Family: My Life with Enrico Fermi* (Chicago: University of Chicago Press, 1954), 174.

18. For the creation and success of the Met Lab pile, see Compton, *Atomic Quest*, 87–8, 136–45; Wyden, *Day One*, 51–4; Rhodes, *Making of the Atomic Bomb*, 428–42; Fermi, *Atoms in the Family*, 190–8.

19. Herken, *Brotherhood of the Bomb*, 3, 8, 17–19, 26, 33.

20. Ibid. 45, 50; Compton, *Atomic Quest*, 75–7; Rhodes, *Making of the Atomic Bomb*, 487–8.

21. Herken, *Brotherhood of the Bomb*, 10, 12; David. C. Cassidy, *J. Robert Oppenheimer and the American Century* (New York: Pi Press, 2005), 1–2, 11, 16, 63, 83–4, 88–9; Rhodes, *Making of the Atomic Bomb*, 450–1; Alice Kimball Smith and Charles Weiner, eds., *Robert Oppenheimer: Letters and Recollections* (Cambridge, MA: Harvard University Press, 1980), 1–2; Kai Bird and Martin J. Sherwin, *American Prometheus: The Triumph and Tragedy of J. Robert Oppenheimer* (New York: Knopf, 2005), 29, 84.

22. Cassidy, *Oppenheimer*, 91, 94–5, 100–3, 111, 122–3; Bird and Sherwin, *American Prometheus*, 34.

23. Cassidy, *Oppenheimer*, 160–1; Bird and Sherwin, *American Prometheus*, 9–10; Rhodes, *Making of the Atomic Bomb*, 444–5; Herken, *Brotherhood of the Bomb*, 11–15, 32.

24. Cassidy, *Oppenheimer*, 173–80.

25. John Adams and Peter Sellars, comps., *Dr Atomic* (opera); Thomas Powers, 'An American Tragedy', *New York Review of Books*, 22 Sept. 2005, 73–9; Bird and Sherwin, *American Prometheus*, 331–2; Herken, *Brotherhood of the Bomb*, 11; Rhodes, *Making of the Atomic Bomb*, 443–4; id., *Dark Sun: The Making of the Hydrogen Bomb* (New York: Simon and Schuster, 1995), 205. On the revocation of Oppenheimer's security clearance, see Philip M. Stern, with Harold P. Green, *The Oppenheimer Case: Security on Trial* (New York: Harper and Row, 1969); and Priscilla J. McMillan, *The Ruin of J. Robert Oppenheimer and the Birth of the Modern Arms Race* (New York: Viking, 2005).

26. Herken, *Brotherhood of the Bomb*, 29–31; Cassidy, *Oppenheimer*, 185–8; Bird and Sherwin, *American Prometheus*, 135–42.

27. Powers, 'An American Tragedy', 73; Bird and Sherwin, *American Prometheus*, 135–6; Cassidy, *Oppenheimer*, 119, 192–5; Oppenheimer to Francis Fergusson, 17 July 1923, in Smith and Weiner, *Robert Oppenheimer*, 32–3.

28. Groves, *Now it Can Be Told*, 63; Robert S. Norris, *Racing for the Bomb: General Leslie R. Groves, the Manhattan Project's Indispensable Man* (South Royalton, VT: Steerforth Press, 2002), 242.

29. Norris, *Racing for the Bomb*, 176–8; Wyden, *Day One*, 56–7; Groves, *Now it Can Be Told*, 21.

30. Norris, *Racing for the Bomb*, 179–82; Wyden, *Day One*, 57–9; Groves, *Now it Can Be Told*, 36–7.

31. Wyden, *Day One*, 59–60; Compton, *Atomic Quest*, 112–15; Groves, *Now it Can Be Told*, 39–41.

32. Wyden, *Day One*, 60–1.

33. Ibid. 61–2, 66–7; Herken, *Brotherhood of the Bomb*, 71; Cassidy, *Oppenheimer*, 224–6; Bird and Sherwin, *American Prometheus*, 185–7.

34. Wyden, *Day One*, 68–9; Rhodes, *Making of the Atomic Bomb*, 450–2; Fermi, *Atoms in the Family*, 205.

35. Robert Serber, *The Los Alamos Primer: The First Lectures on How to Build an Atomic Bomb*, ed. Richard Rhodes (Berkeley and Los Angeles: University of California Press, 1992), 3–4; Wyden, *Day One*, 67; Cassidy, *Oppenheimer*, 232–3; Groves, *Now it Can Be Told*, 140; Fermi, *Atoms in the Family*, 226; Sherwin, *A World Destroyed*, 58–63.

36. Groves, *Now it Can Be Told*, 180–4; Norris, *Racing for the Bomb*, 326–9.

37. Compton, *Atomic Quest*, 150–2; Groves, *Now it Can Be Told*, 68–9; Rhodes, *Making of the Atomic Bomb*, 486–92.

38. Rhodes, *Making of the Atomic Bomb*, 489–96.

39. Groves, *Now it Can Be Told*, 69; Norris, *Racing for the Bomb*, 214–15.

40. Norris, *Racing for the Bomb*, 221–3; Rhodes, *Making of the Atomic Bomb*, 499; Compton, *Atomic Quest*, 186–7; Groves, *Now it Can Be Told*, 90–3.

41. Norris, *Racing for the Bomb*, 224–6; Rhodes, *Making of the Atomic Bomb*, 497–9, 558–9; Kevles, *The Physicists*, 328–9.

42. Norris, *Racing for the Bomb*, 364–71.

43. Lansing Lamont, *Day of Trinity* (New York: Atheneum, 1965), 47; Robert Jungk, *Brighter than a Thousand Suns: A Personal History of the Atomic Scientists*, trans. James Cleugh (San Diego: Harcourt, 1958), 133–4; Fermi, *Atoms in the Family*, 207.

44. Wyden, *Day One*, 93–4; Fermi, *Atoms in the Family*, 207; Rhodes, *Making of the Atomic Bomb*, 564–7.

45. Groves, *Now it Can Be Told*, 180–4; Norris, *Racing for the Bomb*, 326–9; Gowing, *Britain and Atomic Energy*, 122–3; Sherwin, *A World Destroyed*, 38.

46. Gowing, *Britain and Atomic Energy*, 262, 266–8; Rhodes, *Making of the Atomic Bomb*, 522–3; Fermi, *Atoms in the Family*, 208–9.

47. Henry DeWolf Smyth, *Atomic Energy for Military Purposes: The Official Report on the Development of the Atomic Bomb under the Auspices of the United States Government, 1940–1945* (Stanford, CA: Stanford University Press, 1989 [1945]), 210, 212; Rhodes, *Making of the Atomic Bomb*, 241–9; Wyden, *Day One*, 98–9, 103–5; Groves, *Now it Can Be Told*, 260; Herken, *Brotherhood of the Bomb*, 84.

48. Groves, *Now it Can Be Told*, 151–3; Lamont, *Day of Trinity*, 74–5, 84; Harlow W. Russ, *Project Alberta: The Preparation of the Atomic Bombs for Use in World War II* (Los Alamos, NM: Exceptional Books, 1990), 8; Rhodes, *Making of the Atomic Bomb*, 566–7; Kevles, *The Physicists*, 330; R. R. Wilson, 'A Recruit for Los Alamos', *Bulletin of the Atomic Scientists*, 31/3 (Mar. 1975), 41–7.

49. Jungk, *Brighter than a Thousand Suns*, 201–2; Lamont, *Day of Trinity*, 226; Robert R. Wilson, 'The Conscience of a Physicist', in R. S. Lewis and June Wilson, eds., *Alamogordo plus Twenty-Five Years: The Impact of Atomic Energy on Science, Technology, and World Politics* (New York: Viking Press, 1970), 72–3; Fermi, *Atoms in the Family*, 242.

50. Wyden, *Day One*, 50–1, 207, 212–13; Gerard J. DeGroot, *The Bomb: A History of Hell on Earth* (London: Pimlico, 2005), 58.

51. Gowing, *Britain and Atomic Energy*, 86–7, 104–5; Hewlett and Anderson, *The New World*, 206–7; DeGroot, *The Bomb*, 58; Leslie R. Groves, 'Some Recollections of July 16, 1945', in Lewis and Wilson, *Alamogordo Plus Twenty-Five Years*, 54.

52. Wyden, *Day One*, 16, 98; Interim Committee Minutes, 31 May 1945, in Cantelon, Hewitt, and Williams, *American Atom*, 43; Groves, *Now it Can Be Told*, 269.

53. Gowing, *Britain and Atomic Energy*, 382–6; Hewlett and Anderson, *The New World*, 206–7.

54. Herken, *Brotherhood of the Bomb*, 86–7, 184–5; Lamont, *Day of Trinity*, 85–6.

CHAPTER FIVE. THE UNITED STATES II: USING THE BOMB

1. Robert R. Wilson, 'The Conscience of a Physicist', in Richard S. Lewis and Jane Wilson with Eugene Rabinowitch, eds., *Alamogordo plus Twenty-Five Years: The Impact of Atomic Energy on Science, Technology, and World Politics* (New York: Viking, 1970), 73.
2. Samuel McCrea Cavert to Harry S. Truman, 9 Aug. 1945, and Truman to Cavert, 11 Aug. 1945, in Dennis Merrill, ed., *Documentary History of the Truman Presidency*, i. *The Decision to Drop the Atomic Bomb on Japan* (Washington: University Publications of America, 1995), 213–14.
3. Both quotations, conjoined as if from the same source, appear twice in Gar Alperovitz, *Atomic Diplomacy: Hiroshima and Potsdam* (expanded and updated edn., New York: Penguin, 1985 [1965]), 14, 284–5.
4. Such is the nub of Alperovitz's argument for 'atomic diplomacy'. Note that both Eisenhower statements were made, and thus both recollections came, long after the bombs had been dropped; see Barton J. Bernstein, 'Ike and Hiroshima: Did He Oppose It?', *Journal of Strategic Studies*, 10/3 (Sept. 1987), 377–89.
5. Henry L. Stimson, 'The Decision to Use the Atomic Bomb', *Harper's* (Feb. 1947), 97–107.
6. Michael S. Sherry, *The Rise of American Air Power: The Creation of Armageddon* (New Haven: Yale University Press, 1987), 39; Ronald Schaffer, *Wings of Judgment: American Bombing in World War II* (New York: Oxford University Press, 1985), 36.
7. Sherry, *Rise of American Air Power*, 57–60, 67; Schaffer, *Wings of Judgment*, 32, 36–7; William O'Neill, *A Democracy at War* (Cambridge, MA: Harvard University Press, 1993), 306. There is some evidence that Germans distinguished between American and British bombing strategy early in the war, and had greater regard for the former. See Conrad Crane, *Bombs, Cities, and Civilians: American Airpower Strategy in World War II* (Lawrence, KS: University of Kansas Press, 1993), 11.
8. Schaffer, *Wings of Judgment*, 37–8; Sherry, *Rise of American Air Power*, 100; Tami Davis Biddle, *Rhetoric and Reality in Air Warfare: The Evolution of British and American Ideas about Strategic Bombing, 1914–1945* (Princeton: Princeton University Press, 2002), 208–9.
9. Schaffer, *Wings of Judgment*, 38–9; Sherry, *Rise of American Air Power*, 151.
10. Sherry, *Rise of American Air Power*, 152–4; W. G. Sebald, *On the Natural History of Destruction*, trans. Anthea Bell (New York: Modern Library, 2004), 26–30; Jörg Friedrich, *The Fire: The Bombing of Germany, 1940–1945*, trans. Allison Brown (New York: Columbia University Press, 2006), 167; Richard Rhodes, *The Making of the Atomic Bomb* (New York: Simon and Schuster, 1986), 471–5; A. C. Grayling, *Among the Dead Cities: The History and Moral Legacy of the WWII Bombing of Civilians in Germany and Japan* (New York: Walker, 2006), 271–3.

11. Schaffer, *Wings of Judgment*, 56, 66–8; Sherry, *Rise of American Air Power*, 155–6; Biddle, *Rhetoric and Reality*, 245; Rhodes, *Making of the Atomic Bomb*, 472.

12. Schaffer, *Wings of Judgment*, 97; Sherry, *Rise of American Air Power*, 260–1; Biddle, *Rhetoric and Reality*, 254–6; Rhodes, *Making of the Atomic Bomb*, 592–3; Charles S. Maier, 'Targeting the City: Debates and Silences about the Aerial Bombing of World War II', *International Review of the Red Cross*, 87/859 (Sept. 2005), 429–44; Stephen A. Garrett, *Ethics and Airpower in World War II: The British Bombing of German Cities* (New York: St Martin's, 1993), 138, 206; Frederick Taylor, *Dresden: Tuesday, February 13, 1945* (New York: HarperCollins, 2004), 417. See also Kurt Vonnegut Jr., *Slaughterhouse-Five: Or, the Children's Crusade, a Duty-Dance with Death* (New York: Delacorte Press, 1969).

13. Saburō Ienaga, *The Pacific War, 1931–1945: A Critical Perspective on Japan's Role in World War II* (New York: Pantheon, 1978), 138–9; John W. Dower, *War without Mercy: Race and Power in the Pacific War* (New York: Pantheon, 1986), 104; Ronald H. Spector, *Eagle against the Sun: The American War with Japan* (New York: Free Press, 1985), 148.

14. Spector, *Eagle against the Sun*, 158–63, 166–78, 190–201, 205–14; Ienaga, *Pacific War*, 144.

15. Spector, *Eagle against the Sun*, 502–3.

16. Spector, *Eagle against the Sun*, 532–40; Robert Leckie, *Okinawa: The Last Battle of World War II* (New York: Penguin, 1995), 161; Thomas W. Zeiler, *Unconditional Defeat: Japan, America, and the End of World War II* (Wilmington, DE: Scholarly Resources Press, 2004), 161–73; Minutes of a Meeting on 18 June 1945, in Merrill, *Documentary History*, 92.

17. Richard B. Frank, *Downfall: The End of the Imperial Japanese Empire* (New York: Random House, 1999), 80–1.

18. Sherry, *Rise of American Air Power*, 109, 114, 116, 122–3; Frank, *Downfall*, 54–6.

19. Frank, *Downfall*, 51–7, 62–5; Sherry, *Rise of American Air Power*, 226–7; Schaffer, *Wings of Judgment*, 63; Kenneth P. Werrell, *Blankets of Fire: US Bombers over Japan during World War II* (Washington: Smithsonian Institution Press, 1996), 150–6.

20. Frank, *Downfall*, 65–6; Sherry, *Rise of American Air Power*, 273–4; Crane, *Bombs, Cities, and Civilians*, 132; Werrell, *Blankets of Fire*, 160–3; Gordon Daniels, 'The Great Tokyo Air Raid, 9–10 March 1945', in W. G. Beasley, ed., *Modern Japan: Aspects of History, Literature and Society* (Berkeley and Los Angeles: University of California Press, 1975), 124–6.

21. Daniels, 'Tokyo Air Raid', 119, 121, 123–4; Robert Guillain, *I Saw Tokyo Burning: An Eyewitness Narrative from Pearl Harbor to Hiroshima*, trans. William Byron (Garden City, NY: Doubleday, 1981), 174, 184.

22. Sherry, *Rise of American Air Power*, 277–9; Schaffer, *Wings of Judgment*, 134–6; Guillain, *I Saw Tokyo Burning*, 184–8; Daniels, 'Tokyo Air Raid', 125–9; Frank,

Downfall, 74; Kyoko Selden and Mark Selden, 'Introduction', in Kyoko Selden and Mark Selden, eds., *The Atomic Bomb: Voices from Hiroshima and Nagasaki* (Armonk, NY: M. E. Sharpe, 1989), pp. xiv–xv.

23. Guillain, *I Saw Tokyo Burning*, 184, 187; Daniels, 'Tokyo Air Raid', 129. Guillain gives a figure of 197,000 dead or missing, which seems inflated.

24. Sherry, *Rise of American Air Power*, 275; Guillain, *I Saw Tokyo Burning*, 182.

25. Sherry, *Rise of American Air Power*, 277–8; Schaffer, *Wings of Judgment*, 151–2; Frank, *Downfall*, 48, 67.

26. Quoted in Schaffer, *Wings of Judgment*, 217.

27. James G. Hershberg, *James B. Conant: Harvard to Hiroshima and the Making of the Nuclear Age* (Stanford, CA: Stanford University Press, 1993), 211; Peter Wyden, *Day One: Before Hiroshima and After* (New York: Simon and Schuster, 1984), 140.

28. Rhodes, *Making of the Atomic Bomb*, 524; Leo Szilard, 'Reminiscences', in Donald Fleming and Bernard Bailyn, eds., *The Intellectual Migration: Europe and America, 1930–1960* (Cambridge, MA: Harvard University Press, 1969), 123–5.

29. Szilard, 'Reminiscences', 126–8.

30. Ibid. 128–9; Wyden, *Day One*, 144–5; Robert S. Norris, *Racing for the Bomb: General Leslie R. Groves, the Manhattan Project's Indispensable Man* (South Royalton, VT: Steerforth Press, 2002), 526; Arthur Holly Compton, *Atomic Quest: A Personal Narrative* (New York: Oxford University Press, 1956), 233–5; Gregg Herken, *Brotherhood of the Bomb: The Tangled Lives and Loyalties of Robert Oppenheimer, Ernest Lawrence and Edward Teller* (New York: Henry Holt, 2002), 133.

31. The Franck Committee Report, 11 June 1945, in Michael B. Stoff, Jonathan F. Fanton, and R. Hal Williams, eds., *The Manhattan Project: A Documentary Introduction to the Atomic Age* (New York: McGraw-Hill, 1991), 140–7.

32. Szilard, 'Reminiscences', 130–2; Sherry, *Rise of American Air Power*, 326–7; Martin J. Sherwin, *A World Destroyed: The Atomic Bomb and the Grand Alliance* (New York: Knopf, 1975), 217–19, 305–6.

33. Barton J. Bernstein, 'Truman and the A-Bomb: Targeting Noncombatants, Using the Bomb, and his Defending the "Decision"', *Journal of Military History*, 62/3 (July 1998), 561–2; Sherry, *Rise of American Air Power*, 304–5; Ralph Bard, 'Memorandum on the Use of S-1 Bomb', 27 June 1945, repr. in Sherwin, *A World Destroyed*, 307–8; Fletcher Knebel and Charles W. Bailey II, *No High Ground* (New York: Harper and Row, 1960), 123.

34. Hershberg, *James B. Conant*, 226; Gerhard L. Weinberg, *A World at Arms: A Global History of World War II* (Cambridge: Cambridge University Press, 1994), 885; Sherwin, *A World Destroyed*, 169–70.

35. Sherry, *Rise of American Air Power*, 317; 'Notes of the Interim Committee Meeting, Thursday, May 31, 1945', in Merrill, *Documentary History*, 22–38.

36. Richard G. Hewlett and Oscar E. Anderson Jr., *The New World 1939/1946: Volume I of a History of the United States Atomic Energy Commission* (University

Park, PA: Pennsylvania State University Press, 1962), 358; Compton, *Atomic Quest*, 238–9.

37. In Merrill, *Documentary History*, see 'Notes of the Interim Committee Meeting', 1 June 1945 (pp. 39–48), 21 June 1945 (pp. 94–101), 6 July 1945 (pp. 106–10), 19 July 1945 (pp. 137–44).

38. Rhodes, *Making of the Atomic Bomb*, 618–20.

39. 'Notes of Interim Committee Meeting', 31 May 1945, in Merrill, *Documentary History*, 32–3; Sherwin, *A World Destroyed*, 138, 224, 238.

40. Rhodes, *Making of the Atomic Bomb*, 617–18, 624–5; Knebel and Bailey, *No High Ground*, 74; Norris, *Racing for the Bomb*, 386–8; Sherwin, *A World Destroyed*, 197.

41. Rhodes, *Making of the Atomic Bomb*, 642–3; Sherwin, *A World Destroyed*, 197; J. Samuel Walker, *Prompt and Utter Destruction: Truman and the Use of Atomic Bombs against Japan* (Chapel Hill, NC: University of North Carolina Press, 1997), 61; Sherry, *Rise of American Air Power*, 294; Stimson, 'The Decision to Use the Atomic Bomb'.

42. Bernstein, 'Truman and the A-Bomb', 558–9; Frank, *Downfall*, 258.

43. Lansing Lamont, *Day of Trinity* (New York: Atheneum, 1965), 97–9, 210–11.

44. Sherry, *Rise of American Air Power*, 202–3; Herken, *Brotherhood of the Bomb*, 128–9; Lamont, *Day of Trinity*, 135, 138–41.

45. Lamont, *Day of Trinity*, 168–79; Wyden, *Day One*, 208–12; Rhodes, *Making of the Atomic Bomb*, 663–70.

46. Lamont, *Day of Trinity*, 180–4; Kenneth T. Bainbridge, 'A Foul and Awesome Diplay', *Bulletin of the Atomic Scientists*, 31/5 (May 1975), 40–6; Leslie R. Groves, *Now It Can Be Told: The Story of the Manhattan Project* (New York: Harper and Brothers, 1962), 296–301; 'Groves: Report on Alamogordo Atomic Bomb Test', 18 July 1945, repr. in Sherwin, *A World Destroyed*, 308–14.

47. Lamont, *Day of Trinity*, 187–8, 192–4; 'Groves: Report on Alamogordo', 310.

48. Lamont, *Day of Trinity*, 186, 195; Hershberg, *James B. Conant*, 234; Groves, *Now it Can Be Told*, 298.

49. Walker, *Prompt and Utter Destruction*, 53–4; Tsuyoshi Hasegawa, *Racing the Enemy: Stalin, Truman, and the Surrender of Japan* (Cambridge, MA: Harvard University Press, 2005), 130–3.

50. Walker, *Prompt and Utter Destruction*, 56–8; Hasegawa, *Racing the Enemy*, 136–40; Arnold A. Offner, *Another Such Victory: President Truman and the Cold War, 1945–1953* (Stanford, CA: Stanford University Press, 2002), 72–3.

51. Offner, *Another Such Victory*, 74–6; Walker, *Prompt and Utter Destruction*, 59, 63–4; Hasegawa, *Racing the Enemy*, 138.

52. Hasegawa, *Racing the Enemy*, 154–5; Walker, *Prompt and Utter Destruction*, 67; Ralph E. Weber, ed., *Talking with Harry: Candid Conversations with President Harry S. Truman* (Wilmington, DE: Scholarly Resources Press, 2001), 3.

53. Walker, *Prompt and Utter Destruction*, 69–72; Hasegawa, *Racing the Enemy*, 155–60; Leon V. Sigal, *Fighting to a Finish: The Politics of War Termination in the*

United States and Japan, 1945 (Ithaca, NY: Cornell University Press, 1988), 154–7; 'Proclamation Defining Terms for the Japanese Surrender, July 26, 1945', in Stoff, Fanton, and Williams, *The Manhattan Project*, 215–16.

54. John W. Dower, *War without Mercy: Race and Power in the Pacific War* (New York: Pantheon, 1986), 80–1; Ronald Takaki, *Hiroshima: Why America Dropped the Atomic Bomb* (Boston: Little, Brown, 1995), 71–100; John D. Chappell, *Before the Bomb: How America Approached the End of the Pacific War* (Lexington, KY: University of Kentucky Press, 1997), 16, 18; Sherry, *Rise of American Air Power*, 141.

55. Dower, *War without Mercy*, 79; Chappell, *Before the Bomb*, 27–8, 107; Sherry, *Rise of American Air Power*, 134; E. B. Sledge, *With the Old Breed: At Peleliu and Okinawa* (New York: Oxford University Press, 1990), 120, 152, 155–6, 259. See also Francis B. Catanzaro, *With the 41st Division in the Southwest Pacific: A Foot Soldier's Story* (Bloomington, IN: Indiana University Press, 2002), 50, 88, 129; and Patrick K. O'Donnell, *Into the Rising Sun: In their own Words: World War II's Pacific Veterans Reveal the Heart of Combat* (New York: Free Press, 2002), 113–14, 127–8, 212, 236–7.

56. Takaki, *Hiroshima*, 96; Richard Rhodes, *Dark Sun: The Making of the Hydrogen Bomb* (New York: Simon and Schuster, 1995), 21; Groves, *Now it Can Be Told*, 324; Truman Diary Entry, 25 July 1945, in Merrill, *Documentary History*, 156.

57. See, e.g., Alperovitz, *Atomic Diplomacy*; id., *The Decision to Use the Atomic Bomb and the Architecture of an American Myth* (New York: Knopf, 1995); Kai Bird and Lawrence Lifschultz, 'The Legend of Hiroshima', in Bird and Lifschultz, eds., *Hiroshima's Shadow: Writing on the Denial of History and the Smithsonian Controversy* (Stony Creek, CT: Pamphleteer's Press, 1998), xxxi–lxxvii.

58. Sherwin, *A World Destroyed*, 187, 190–1, 224–5; Alperovitz, *Atomic Diplomacy*, 160; Forrestal Diary Entry, 28 July 1945, in Stoff, Fanton, and Williams, *The Manhattan Project*, 217.

59. Sherwin, *A World Destroyed*, 198; Barton J. Bernstein, 'Roosevelt, Truman, and the Atomic Bomb, 1941–1945: A Reinterpretation', *Political Science Quarterly* (Spring 1975), 23–62; Walker, *Prompt and Utter Destruction*, 94–5; Sherry, *Rise of American Air Power*, 340.

60. Bernstein, 'Roosevelt, Truman, and the Atomic Bomb'; Sigal, *Fighting to a Finish*, 175; Norris, *Racing for the Bomb*, 376.

61. Crane, *Bombs, Cities, and Civilians*, 11, 28–9; Frank, *Downfall*, 46, 257; Sherry, *Rise of American Air Power*, 292–7, 320–3.

62. Chappell, *Before the Bomb*, 80; O'Neill, *Democracy at War*, 414–17; Frank, *Downfall*, 138–45; Minutes of a Meeting held at the White House on June 18, 1945, in Merrill, *Documentary History*, 76–93. For the debate concerning estimates of American casualties on Kyushu, see John Ray Skates, *The Invasion of Japan: Alternatives to the Bomb* (Columbia, SC: University of South Carolina Press, 1994), 76–82; Barton J. Bernstein, 'Reconsidering Truman's Claim of 'Half a Million American Lives' Saved by the Atomic Bomb: The Construction and

Deconstruction of a Myth', *Journal of Strategic Studies*, 22/1 (Mar. 1999), 54–95; D. M. Giangreco, ' "A Score of Bloody Okinawas and Iwo Jimas": President Truman and Casualty Estimates for the Invasion of Japan', *Pacific Historical Review*, 72/1 (Feb. 2003), 93–132; J. Samuel Walker, 'Recent Literature on Truman's Atomic Bomb Decision: A Search for Middle Ground', *Diplomatic History*, 29/2 (Apr. 2005), 311–34.

63. Barton J. Bernstein, 'Understanding the Atomic Bomb and the Japanese Surrender: Missed Opportunities, Little-Known Near Disasters, and Modern Memory', in Michael J. Hogan, ed., *Hiroshima in History and Memory* (Cambridge: Cambridge University Press, 1996), 38–79.

64. Sherry, *Rise of American Air Power*, 73, 300; O'Neill, *Democracy at War*, 316; Paul Boyer, *By the Bomb's Early Light: American Thought and Culture at the Dawn of the Atomic Age* (New York: Pantheon, 1985), 219; Mahatma Gandhi, 'The Atom Bomb and Ahimsa', in Bird and Lifschultz, *Hiroshima's Shadow*, 258–9; Hanson W. Baldwin, 'Atomic Bomb Responsibilities', *New York Times*, 12 Sept. 1945; Schaffer, *Wings of Judgment*, 171–2; Memo by Eben Ayers, 6 Aug. 1951, in Merrill, *Documentary History*, 509; Bernstein, 'Truman and the A-Bomb', 569.

65. David McCullough, *Truman* (New York: Simon and Schuster, 1992), 442.

66. Franck Report, 11 June 1945, in Stoff, Fanton, and Williams, *The Manhattan Project*, 143–4; Bernstein, 'Truman and the A-Bomb', 563; Sherry, *Rise of American Air Power*, 312; Sigal, *Fighting to a Finish*, 164–9; Chappell, *Before the Bomb*, 92–5; Skates, *Invasion of Japan*, 84, 92–7.

67. Sigal, *Fighting to a Finish*, 164–5. Radiation, of course, killed like gas, from the inside out. Despite warnings from the Frisch–Peierls memorandum and clear indications in the Trinity test, policymakers dismissed or denied the extent to which radioactivity was a killing agent of atomic bombs. All that said, as John Ray Skates points out, had it come to an invasion of Japan, the use of gas against ensconced defenders might have been difficult to resist. See Skates, *Invasion of Japan*, 97.

68. Bernstein, 'Truman and the A-Bomb', 562.

69. Knebel and Bailey, *No High Ground*, 130–1.

CHAPTER SIX. JAPAN: THE ATOMIC BOMBS AND WAR'S END

1. John Hersey, *Hiroshima* (New York: Knopf, 1946), 9, 49; Michihiko Hachiya, *Hiroshima Diary: The Journal of a Japanese Physician, August 6–September 30, 1945*, trans. Warner Wells (Chapel Hill, NC: University of North Carolina Press, 1955), 4; Kenzaburō Ōe, *Hiroshima Notes*, trans. David J. Swain and Toshi Yonezawa (New York: Grove Press, 1996 [1965]), 19–20, 175–7.

2. Ronald H. Spector, *Eagle against the Sun: The American War with Japan* (New York: Free Press, 1985), 241–2; Haruko Taya Cook and Theodore F. Cook, *Japan at War: An Oral History* (New York: New Press, 1992), 259, 267–76.

3. Cook and Cook, *Japan at War*, 281–92.
4. Herbert P. Bix, *Hirohito and the Making of Modern Japan* (New York: Harper-Collins, 2000), 484; Cook and Cook, *Japan at War*, 354–63.
5. John W. Dower, ' "NI" and "F": Japan's Wartime Atomic Bomb Research', in John W. Dower, *Japan in War and Peace: Selected Essays* (New York: New Press, 1993), 55–100; Kenji Hall, 'Japan's A-Bomb Goal Still Long Way off in '45', *Japan Times*, 7 Mar. 2003; Peter Wyden, *Day One: Before Hiroshima and After* (New York: Simon and Schuster, 1984), 185–7, 323.
6. Bix, *Hirohito*, 24; Richard B. Frank, *Downfall: The End of the Imperial Japanese Empire* (New York: Random House, 1999), 91–3; Tsuyoshi Hasegawa, *Racing the Enemy: Stalin, Truman, and the Surrender of Japan* (Cambridge, MA: Harvard University Press, 2005), 48–9.
7. Bix, *Hirohito*, 10–15, 424, 437; id., 'Japan's Delayed Surrender: A Reinterpretation', in Michael J. Hogan, ed., *Hiroshima in History and Memory* (Cambridge: Cambridge University Press, 1996), 80–115; Frank, *Downfall*, 87–9.
8. Bix, *Hirohito*, 491–3; Hasegawa, *Racing the Enemy*, 45–8.
9. Frank, *Downfall*, 94–5, 112–15; Hasegawa, *Racing the Enemy*, 91–7.
10. Hasegawa, *Racing the Enemy*, 106–11; Bix, *Hirohito*, 491; John W. Dower, 'Sensational Rumors, Seditious Graffiti, and the Nightmares of the Thought Police', in Dower, *Japan in War and Peace*, 138–45.
11. Frank, *Downfall*, 222–30; Hasegawa, *Racing the Enemy*, 124–6; Bix, *Hirohito*, 493–4.
12. Hasegawa, *Racing the Enemy*, 38; Frank, *Downfall*, 85–6, 164–96; John Ray Skates, *The Invasion of Japan: Alternative to the Bomb* (Columbia, SC: University of South Carolina Press, 1994), 130–2, 148; Bix, *Hirohito*, 480.
13. Skates, *Invasion of Japan*, 190–1; Frank, *Downfall*, 117–18, 194; Bix, *Hirohito*, 496; Fletcher Knebel and Charles W. Bailey II, *No High Ground* (New York: Harper and Row, 1960), 9.
14. Bix, *Hirohito*, 334–5, 364; Cook and Cook, *Japan at War*, 187–92, 199–202; Iris Chang, *The Rape of Nanking* (New York: Basic Books, 1997); Saburō Ienaga, *The Pacific War, 1931–1945: A Critical Perspective on Japan's Role in World War II* (New York: Pantheon, 1978), 187–9.
15. Ienaga, *Pacific War*, 183; Cook and Cook, *Japan at War*, 305–13; Skates, *Invasion of Japan*, 108–10.
16. Robert H. Ferrell, ed., *Dear Bess: The Letters from Harry to Bess Truman, 1910–1959* (New York: W. W. Norton, 1983), 519; id., ed., *Off the Record: The Private Papers of Harry S. Truman* (New York: Harper and Row, 1980), 54; Wyden, *Day One*, 236–7.
17. Richard Rhodes, *The Making of the Atomic Bomb* (New York: Simon and Schuster, 1986), 583–6; Charles W. Sweeney, with James A. Antonucci and Marion K. Antonucci, *War's End: An Eyewitness Account of America's Last Atomic Mission* (New York: Avon Books, 1997), 94–9.

18. Rhodes, *Making of the Atomic Bomb*, 638–9; Wyden, *Day One*, 192, 237; William Bradford Huie, *The Hiroshima Pilot* (New York: G. P. Putnam's Sons, 1964), 21–2; Harlow W. Russ, *Project Alberta: The Preparation of Atomic Bombs for Use in World War II* (Los Alamos, NM: Exceptional Books, 1990), 48, 52.

19. The foregoing paragraphs are based on Wyden, *Day One*, 237–47; Rhodes, *Making of the Atomic Bomb*, 699–711; Knebel and Bailey, *No High Ground*, 146–74, 205–6; Huie, *Hiroshima Pilot*, 21–4; Russ, *Project Alberta*, 62; Hanson W. Baldwin, 'Hiroshima Decision', in *Hiroshima Plus 20,* prepared by *New York Times*, intro. John W. Finney (New York: Delacorte Press, 1962), 40–1; Norman F. Ramsey, 'August 1945: The B-29 Flight Logs', *Bulletin of the Atomic Scientists*, 38/10 (Dec. 1982), 33–5.

20. Knebel and Bailey, *No High Ground*, 210–12.

21. Knebel and Bailey, *No High Ground*, 2–3, 229; Wyden, *Day One*, 286–9; Robert S. Norris, *Racing for the Bomb: General Leslie R. Groves, the Manhattan Project's Indispensable Man* (South Royalton, VT: Steerforth Press, 2002), 418–19.

22. Knebel and Bailey, *No High Ground*, 39–40; US Strategic Bombing Survey (USSBS), *The Effects of Atomic Bombs on Hiroshima and Nagasaki* (Washington: US Government Printing Office, 1946), 6; Pacific War Research Society (PWRS), *The Day Man Lost: Hiroshima, 6 August 1945* (Palo Alto: Kodansha International, 1972), 220–1.

23. Knebel and Bailey, *No High Ground*, 41, 180; USSBS, *Effects of Atomic Bombs*, 6; Wyden, *Day One*, 274; Committee for the Compilation of Materials on Damage Caused by the Atomic Bombs, *Hiroshima and Nagasaki: The Physical, Medical, and Social Effects of the Atomic Bombings*, trans. Eisei Ishikawa and David L. Swain (New York: Basic Books, 1981), 461, 468–9, 475–83.

24. Knebel and Bailey, *No High Ground*, 41, 180; Robert J. Lifton, *Death in Life: Survivors of Hiroshima* (New York: Simon and Schuster, 1967), 17–18.

25. Lifton, *Death in Life*, 16–17; Wyden, *Day One*, 201; PWRS, *The Day Man Lost*, 220–1.

26. Lifton, *Death in Life*, 19; Knebel and Bailey, *No High Ground*, 180–1; PWRS, *The Day Man Lost*, 252; Hachiya, *Hiroshima Diary*, 1; Toyofumi Ogura, *Letters from the End of the World: A Firsthand Account of the Bombing of Hiroshima*, trans. Kisaburo Murakami and Shigeru Fujii (Tokyo: Kodansha International, 1997), 15–17; Hersey, *Hiroshima*, 78–9; Cook and Cook, *Japan at War*, 382–3; Arata Osada, ed., *Children of Hiroshima* (Tokyo: Publishing Committee for Children of Hiroshima, 1980), 14, 127.

27. Kyoko Selden and Mark Selden, eds., *The Atomic Bomb: Voices from Hiroshima and Nagasaki* (Armonk, NY: M. E. Sharpe, 1989), p. xix; Knebel and Bailey, *No High Ground*, 183; *Hiroshima and Nagasaki*, 80–1; Kenzaburo Ōe, *Hiroshima Notes*, 171–2; Ogura, *Letters*, 73; Rhodes, *Making of the Atomic Bomb*, 715; Osada, *Children of Hiroshima*, 176; Lifton, *Death in Life*, 27.

28. Osada, *Children of Hiroshima*, 179–80; Ogura, *Letters*, 65, 67; Hersey, *Hiroshima*, 54; PWRS, *The Day Man Lost*, 275.
29. USSBS, *Effects of Atomic Bombs*, 6; Ogura, *Letters*, 71, 142–3; Lifton, *Death in Life*, 58–9.
30. Hachiya, *Hiroshima Diary*, *passim*; Wyden, *Day One*, 273.
31. Cook and Cook, *Japan at War*, 387–91.
32. Osada, *Children of Hiroshima*, 127–30.
33. Wyden, *Day One*, 279–81.
34. Hachiya, *Hiroshima Diary*, 3, 52; Lifton, *Death in Life*, 50–3; Ogura, *Letters*, 10–11; Selden and Selden, *Atomic Bomb*, pp. xx–xxi.
35. Lifton, *Death in Life*, 28, 31; Ogura, *Letters*, 41, 54. There were exceptions to this emotional numbness: see Katsuzo Oda, 'Human Ashes', in Kenzaburō Ōe, ed., *The Crazy Iris and Other Stories of the Atomic Aftermath* (New York: Grove Press, 1995), 71–2.
36. *Hiroshima and Nagasaki: The Physical, Medical, and Social Effects*, 106–7.
37. Hersey, *Hiroshima*, 30; Wyden, *Day One*, 253, 267; Ogura, *Letters*, 148–9.
38. Michael S. Sherry, *The Rise of American Air Power: The Creation of Armageddon* (New Haven: Yale University Press, 1987), 344; Lifton, *Death in Life*, 22–; Hachiya, *Hiroshima Diary*, 114–15, 208.
39. Hersey, *Hiroshima*, 91; *Hiroshima and Nagasaki: The Physical, Medical, and Social Effects*, 86.
40. Knebel and Bailey, *No High Ground*, 188–93, 198–9; Hasegawa, *Racing the Enemy*, 184; Frank, *Downfall*, 268–9. In his diary that day, however, Anami acknowledged the likelihood that an atomic bomb had been used on Hiroshima.
41. Knebel and Bailey, *No High Ground*; Hasegawa, *Racing the Enemy*, 185; Frank, *Downfall*, 271–2.
42. Hasegawa, *Racing the Enemy*, 185–6; Frank, *Downfall*, 271–2; Bix, *Hirohito*, 502–3; Leon V. Sigal, *Fighting to a Finish: The Politics of War Termination in the United States and Japan, 1945* (Ithaca, NY: Cornell University Press, 1988), 225.
43. Hasegawa, *Racing the Enemy*, 189–91, 195–6; David Holloway, *Stalin and the Bomb: The Soviet Union and Atomic Energy, 1939–1956* (New Haven: Yale University Press, 1994), 127–8.
44. Hasegawa, *Racing the Enemy*, 197–201, 203–4; Frank, *Downfall*, 288–91; Bix, *Hirohito*, 512; Sigal, *Fighting to a Finish*, 226–7.
45. Frank, *Downfall*, 284; Sweeney, *War's End*, 179, 185–9, 200; Russ, *Project Alberta*, 68.
46. Frank, *Downfall*, 284–7; Sweeney, *War's End*, 203–26; John W. Dower, *War without Mercy: Race and Power in the Pacific War* (New York: Pantheon, 1986), 298; Rhodes, *Making of the Atomic Bomb*, 739–42; Ramsey, 'August 1945', 35; Terai Sumie, 'White Nagasaki: A Haiku Sequence', in Lequita Vance-Watkins and Aratani Mariko, eds. and trans., *White Flash, Black Rain: Women of Japan Relive the Bomb* (Minneapolis, MN: Milkweed Editions, 1995), 13.

47. This account of the Japanese debate over the terms of surrender is based on Robert J. C. Butow, *Japan's Decision to Surrender* (Stanford, CA: Stanford University Press, 1954), 166–88; Edwin P. Hoyt, *Hirohito: The Emperor and the Man* (New York: Praeger, 1992), 139–45; Bix, *Hirohito*, 511–18; Hasegawa, *Racing the Enemy*, 203–14; Frank, *Downfall*, 288–96.

48. Hasegawa, *Racing the Enemy*, 217–27; Frank, *Downfall*, 300–3; Sigal, *Fighting to a Finish*, 249–52; Walter LaFeber, *The Clash: US–Japanese Relations throughout History* (New York: W. W. Norton, 1997), 252–3; Diary of Henry Wallace, 10 Aug. 1945, in Michael B. Stoff, Jonathan F. Fanton, and R. Hal Williams, *The Manhattan Project: A Documentary Introduction to the Atomic Age* (New York: McGraw-Hill, 1991), 245.

49. This account of the Japanese decision to surrender is based on Butow, *Japan's Decision to Surrender*, 189–227; Hasegawa, *Racing the Enemy*, 227–51; Frank, *Downfall*, 308–21; Bix, *Hirohito*, 519–28; Dower, *War without Mercy*, 300–1; Sigal, *Fighting to a Finish*, 252–81; Robert Guillain, *I Saw Tokyo Burning: An Eyewitness Narrative from Pearl Harbor to Hiroshima*, trans. William Byron (Garden City, NY: Doubleday, 1981), 257–69.

50. Frank claims that the Emperor also made explicit reference to the atomic bomb at this meeting. Hasegawa is doubtful, pointing out that only one of the six accounts of Hirohito's statement mentioned the bomb, and that one was second-hand. See Frank, *Downfall*, 295–6, and Hasegawa, *Racing the Enemy*, 346 n. 90.

51. Hasegawa, *Racing the Enemy*, 240, 242, 249; Frank, *Downfall*, 295–6, 315, 320; John W. Dower, *Embracing Defeat: Japan in the Wake of World War II* (New York: W. W. Norton, 1999), 36.

52. Wyden, *Day One*, 309; Sigal, *Fighting to a Finish*, 279; Bix, *Hirohito*, 509; USSBS, *Effects of Atomic Bombs*, 23.

53. Wyden, *Day One*, 298–9, 302–3, 307; Robert Jungk, *Brighter than a Thousand Suns: A Personal History of the Atomic Scientists*, trans. James Cleugh (San Diego: Harcourt, 1958), 210–14; John W. Dower, 'The Bombed: Hiroshimas and Nagasakis in Japanese Memory', in Hogan, *Hiroshima in History and Memory*, 119.

54. Wyden, *Day One*, 321–5, 345; Norris, *Racing for the Bomb*, 438–41; Sherry, *Rise of American Air Power*, 346; Hersey, *Hiroshima*, 95–7.

55. Hachiya, *Hiroshima Diary*, 139–40.

56. USSBS, *Effects of Atomic Bombs*, 15, 19; *Hiroshima and Nagasaki: The Physical, Medical, and Social Effects*, 217–23, 260, 270, 449–50; Hiroshima International Council for Medical Care of the Radiation-Exposed, *Effects of A-Bomb Radiation on the Human Body* (Chur, Switzerland: Harwood Academic Publishers, 1995), 16–20; Lifton, *Death in Life*, 103–5.

57. Frank, *Downfall*, 285–7; Dower, *War without Mercy*, 298; *Effects of A-Bomb Radiation*, 8.

58. Lifton, *Death in Life*, 69; Monica Braw, *The Atomic Bomb Suppressed: American Censorship in Japan, 1945–1949* (Lund, Sweden: Liber, 1986); Richard H. Minear,

ed. and trans., *Hiroshima: Three Witnesses* (Princeton: Princeton University Press, 1990), 36, 138–42; Dower, *Embracing Defeat*, 413–15.

59. Dower, 'The Bombed', 128; Lifton, *Death in Life*, 329; Wyden, *Day One*, 327–8.

60. Lifton, *Death in Life*, 80–1, 97, 319–21; Hersey, *Hiroshima*, 117; Ōe, *Hiroshima Notes*, 9; Hachiya, *Hiroshima Diary*, 87; Ogura, *Letters*, 121; Dower, *Embracing Defeat*, 493.

61. Yōkō Ōta, 'Residues of Squalor', in Selden and Selden, *The Atomic Bomb*, 55–85.

62. Selden and Selden, *The Atomic Bomb*, 143, 147.

63. Eisaku Yoneda, 'Standing in the Rains', in Lifton, *Death in Life*, 446.

64. Kurihara Sadako, 'Ruins', in Kurihara Sadako, *When We Say 'Hiroshima': Selected Poems*, trans. with an intro. by Richard H. Minear (Ann Arbor: Center for Japanese Studies, University of Michigan, 1999), 16–17.

65. Wyden, *Day One*, 335.

66. Osada, *Children of Hiroshima*, 35–6.

67. Ogura, *Letters*, 109–10.

68. Hanson W. Baldwin, 'The Atomic Bomb: The Penalty of Expediency', in Barton J. Bernstein, ed., *The Atomic Bomb: The Critical Issues* (Boston: Little Brown, 1976), 33–40.

CHAPTER SEVEN. THE SOVIET UNION: THE BOMB AN THE COLD WAR

1. Prue Torney-Parlicki, ' "Whatever the Thing May Be Called": The Australian News Media and the Atomic Bombing of Hiroshima and Nagasaki', *Australian Historical Studies*, 31/114 (Apr. 2000), 55–6; 'Atom Bomb, Red Move, Seen Ending War Soon', *Shanghai Evening Post*, 10 Aug. 1945; 'La Bombe atomique, engin de guerre ou de paix?' *L'Autorité*, 18 Aug. 1945; 'Britons Awed by Atomic Bomb', *Rhodesia Herald*, 11 Aug.1945; 'A New Age', *Palestine Post*, 8 Aug. 1945; Regis Cabral, 'The Mexican Reactions to the Hiroshima and Nagasaki Tragedies of 1945', *Quipu*, 4/1 (Jan.–Apr. 1987), 88; 'Heard Round the World', *New York Times*, 7 Aug. 1945; Paul Boyer, *By the Bomb's Early Light: American Thought and Culture at the Dawn of the Atomic Age* (New York: Pantheon, 1985), 6.

2. Pascal, 'La Part du Canada dans la bombe atomique', *L'Autorité*, 11 Aug. 1945; 'Désintégration', *Le Populaire*, 14 Aug. 1945; 'Ce que dissent les journaux', *La Croix*, 16 Aug. 1945; Stuart Gelder, 'The Bomb is a Menace to Humanity's Future', *Statesman*, 13 Aug. 1945; 'Britons Awed by Atomic Bomb', *Rhodesia Herald*, 11 Aug. 1945; 'World Hopes Atomic Bomb Is not a Frankenstein', *Trinidad Guardian*, 8 Aug. 1945; 'Controlling the New Power', *Sydney Morning Herald*, 9 Aug. 1945.

3. 'La Bombe atomique', *Montreal-Matin*, 8 Aug. 1945; 'Unbelievable Force Let Loose', *Albertan*, 8 Aug. 1945; 'A New Age', *Palestine Post*, 8 Aug. 1945; Hanson W. Baldwin, 'The Atomic Weapon', *New York Times*, 7 Aug. 1945; 'Eternal Enemy of Humanity', *Hong Kong News*, 9 Aug. 1945; 'Japan Submits', *Free Press Journal*, 13 Aug. 1945; E. L. De Saint-Just, 'La Bombe atomique met entre les mains de l'homme une force qui peut le détruire', *La Patrie du Dimanche*, 12 Aug. 1945; 'World Hopes Atomic Bomb Is not a Frankenstein', *Trinidad Guardian*, 8 Aug. 1945.

4. Harry S. Truman to Richard B. Russell, 9 Aug. 1945, in Dennis Merrill, ed., *Documentary History of the Truman Presidency*, i. *The Decision to Drop the Atomic Bomb on Japan* (Washington: University Publications of America, 1995), 210; 'Everyman', *New York Times*, 18 Aug. 1945; *The Complete War Memoirs of Charles de Gaulle*, iii. *Salvation 1944–1946*, trans. Richard Howard (New York: Simon and Schuster, 1968), 926.

5. Cabral, 'Mexican Reactions', 82; Robert J. Lifton, *Death in Life: Survivors of Hiroshima* (New York: Simon and Schuster, 1967), 73; *Rhodesia Herald*, 8 Aug. 1945; 'World Hopes', *Trinidad Guardian*, 8 Aug. 1945; 'The 'Jap-atomiser', *Pretoria News*, 8 Aug. 1945.

6. Lifton, *Death in Life*, 29. Mary McCarthy criticized John Hersey's writing on Hiroshima for representing the bombing as a 'natural catastrophe'. Quoted in Boyer, *Bomb's Early Light*, 206.

7. Gregg Herken, *The Winning Weapon: The Atomic Bomb in the Cold War 1945–1950* (New York: Random House, 1981), 23, 48; Henry L. Stimson, 'Memorandum for the President', 11 Sept. 1945, in Merrill, *Documentary History*, 222–7; Richard Rhodes, *Dark Sun: The Making of the Hydrogen Bomb* (New York: Simon and Schuster, 1995), 205; Henry A. Wallace, Diary, 10 Aug. 1945, in Michael B. Stoff, Jonathan F. Fanton, and R. Hal Williams, eds., *The Manhattan Project: A Documentary Introduction to the Atomic Age* (New York: McGraw-Hill, 1991), 245.

8. William D. Leahy, *I Was There: The Personal Story of the Chief of Staff to Presidents Roosevelt and Truman, Based on his Notes and Diaries Made at the Time* (New York: McGraw-Hill, 1950), 441–2; Gar Alperovitz, *Atomic Diplomacy: Hiroshima and Potsdam* (expanded and updated edn., New York: Penguin, 1985 [1965]), 1; Boyer, *Bomb's Early Light*, 314–15; Rhodes, *Dark Sun*, 21–2; John W. Dower, *Embracing Defeat: Japan in the Wake of World War II* (New York: W. W. Norton, 1999), 375.

9. Rhodes, *Dark Sun*, 205–6; Boyer, *Bomb's Early Light*, 138, 212; Robert Jungk, *Brighter than a Thousand Suns: A Personal History of the Atomic Scientists*, trans. James Cleugh (San Diego: Harcourt, 1958), 227; 'Truman is Urged to Bar Atom Bomb', *New York Times*, 20 Aug. 1945.

10. Morris L. Kaplan, 'Atom Bomb Fails to Excite Savants', *New York Times*, 25 Aug. 1945; Gregg Herken, *Brotherhood of the Bomb: The Tangled Lives and Loyalties of Robert Oppenheimer, Ernest Lawrence, and Edward Teller* (New York:

Henry Holt, 2002), 153; Boyer, *Bomb's Early Light*, 116; Allan M. Winkler, *Life under a Cloud: American Anxiety about the Atom* (New York: Oxford University Press, 1993), 28; Daniel J. Kevles, *The Physicists: The History of a Scientific Community in Modern America* (Cambridge, MA: Harvard University Press, 1995 [1971]), 368–70.

11. Kevles, *The Physicists*, 369, 376.

12. Boyer, *Bomb's Early Light*, 10–13, 182–4; Winkler, *Life under a Cloud*, 27–8.

13. Winkler, *Life under a Cloud*, 67; Herken, *Winning Weapon*, 98–9, 230–2; Joseph Albright and Marcia Kunstel, *Bombshell: The Secret Story of America's Unknown Atomic Spy Conspiracy* (New York: Times Books, 1997), p. xiii.

14. Arnold Kramish, *Atomic Energy in the Soviet Union* (Stanford, CA: Stanford University Press, 1959), 4–6, 19; Thomas B. Cochrane, Robert S. Norris, and Oleg A. Bukharin, *Making the Russian Bomb: From Stalin to Yeltsin* (Boulder, CO: Westview Press, 1995), 2–4; David Holloway, *Stalin and the Bomb: The Soviet Union and Atomic Energy, 1939–1956* (New Haven: Yale University Press, 1994), 8–48.

15. Kramish, *Atomic Energy*, 22–32; Holloway, *Stalin and the Bomb*, 49–75.

16. Kramish, *Atomic Energy*, 35, 40–1; J. W. Boag, P. E. Rubinin, and D. Shoenberg, eds., *Kapitza in Cambridge and Moscow: Life and Letters of a Russian Physicist* (Amsterdam: North-Holland, 1990), 351–3; Holloway, *Stalin and the Bomb*, 82–4, 89–95.

17. Holloway, *Stalin and the Bomb*, 82–3; John Earl Haynes and Harvey Klehr, *Venona: Decoding Soviet Espionage in America* (New Haven: Yale University Press, 1999), 1–7.

18. *Webster's Deluxe Unabridged Dictionary*, 2nd edn. (New York: Simon and Schuster, 1979), 511, 1439.

19. Jerrold Schecter and Leona Schecter, *Sacred Secrets: How Soviet Intelligence Operations Changed American History* (Washington: Brassey's, 2002), 52; Rhodes, *Dark Sun*, 55, 118, 137–8; Albright and Kunstel, *Bombshell*, 6, 63, 66, 76; Allen Weinstein and Alexander Vassiliev, *The Haunted Wood: Soviet Espionage in America: The Stalin Era* (New York: Random House, 1999), 195, 199–200.

20. Rhodes, *Dark Sun*, 153; Albright and Kunstel, *Bombshell*, 119–23; Weinstein and Vassiliev, *Haunted Wood*, 195–6; Nigel West, *Venona: The Greatest Secret of the Cold War* (London: HarperCollins, 1999), 124–8. Two other atomic spies, codenamed Fogel and Quantum, are implicated by Venona but have never been identified; see Haynes and Klehr, *Venona*, 16.

21. Albright and Kunstel, *Bombshell*, 124–6; Cochrane, Norris, and Bukharin, *Making the Russian Bomb*, 15; Schecter and Schecter, *Sacred Secrets*, 78; Alexander Feklisov and Sergei Kostin, *The Man behind the Rosenbergs* (New York: Enigma Books, 2001), 201. Kurchatov did not think that Fuchs's information helped the Soviets build a hydrogen bomb, though that is often alleged; see James G. Hershberg, *James B. Conant: Harvard to Hiroshima and the Making of the Nuclear Age* (Stanford, CA: Stanford University Press, 1993), 878 n. 104.

22. Christopher Andrew and Oleg Gordievsky, *KGB: The Inside Story of its Foreign Operations from Lenin to Gorbachev* (New York: HarperCollins, 1990), 378; Holloway, *Stalin and the Bomb*, 221–2; Yuli Khariton and Yuri Smirnov, 'The Khariton Version', *Bulletin of the Atomic Scientists*, 49/4 (May 1993). The story about Stalin and the plutonium comes from Andrew and Gordievsky. Holloway has the incident occurring in 1949, at the chemical separation plant at Chelynbinsk-40, and between different parties altogether; see his *Stalin and the Bomb*, 203.

23. Kramish, *Atomic Energy*, 40–1; Holloway, *Stalin and the Bomb*, 220–2; Rhodes, *Dark Sun*, 215–17; Haynes and Klehr, *Venona*, 321–2.

24. Holloway, *Stalin and the Bomb*, 222–3; Khariton and Smirnov, 'The Khariton Version'.

25. Holloway, *Stalin and the Bomb*, 117, 128–9, 132; Tsuyoshi Hasegawa, *Racing the Enemy: Stalin, Truman, and the Surrender of Japan* (Cambridge, MA: Harvard University Press, 2005), 44; Cochran, Norris, and Bukharin, *Making the Russian Bomb*, 10.

26. Rhodes, *Dark Sun*, 213, 223; Andrew and Gordievsky, *KGB*, 376; Kaptisa to J. V. Stalin, 25 Nov. 1945, in Boag, Rubinin, and Shoenberg, *Kapitza in Cambridge and Moscow*, 372; Holloway, *Stalin and the Bomb*, 138–42, 147–9.

27. Rhodes, *Dark Sun*, 214, 314–17, 331–2; Holloway, *Stalin and the Bomb*, 176–7, 180–3, 186–9.

28. Kramish, *Atomic Energy*, 60; Rhodes, *Dark Sun*, 364–7; Holloway, *Stalin and the Bomb*, 196–201, 213–17.

29. Rhodes, *Dark Sun*, 367–8; Holloway, *Stalin and the Bomb*, 217–18.

30. Thomas G. Paterson, *On Every Front: The Making and Unmaking of the Cold War*, rev. edn. (New York: Norton, 1992), 63–4; Walter LaFeber, *America, Russia, and the Cold War, 1945–2000*, 9th edn. (Boston: McGraw-Hill, 2002), 42–4.

31. Gar Alperovitz and Kai Bird, 'The Centrality of the Bomb', *Foreign Policy* (Spring 1994), 3–18; Holloway, *Stalin and the Bomb*, 253, 258–63.

32. Herken, *Winning Weapon*, 99; Daniel Yergin, *Shattered Peace: The Origins of the Cold War* (New York: Penguin, 1990 [1977]), 123, 135–7.

33. Dean Acheson, *Present at the Creation: My Years in the State Department* (New York: W. W. Norton, 1969), 151–4; Herken, *Winning Weapon*, 98, 153–8; Melvyn P. Leffler, *A Preponderance of Power: National Security, the Truman Administration, and the Cold War* (Stanford, CA: Stanford University Press, 1992), 114.

34. Acheson, *Present at the Creation*, 154–6; Herken, *Winning Weapon*, 158–91, 224–5; Leffler, *Preponderance of Power*, 114–16; Yergin, *Shattered Peace*, 237–1; Rhodes, *Dark Sun*, 261–2; James Chace, 'Sharing the Atomic Bomb', *Foreign Affairs*, 75/1 (Jan.–Feb. 1996), 129–44.

35. Rhodes, *Dark Sun*, 320–1; Chace, 'Sharing the Atomic Bomb', 142.

36. Holloway, *Stalin and the Bomb*, 225–7; Hershberg, *James B. Conant*, 253–6.

37. Herken, *Winning Weapon*, 219; Holloway, *Stalin and the Bomb*, 132–3.

38. Rhodes, *Dark Sun*, 287; Hershberg, *James B. Conant*, 253; Holloway, *Stalin and the Bomb*, 133; Khariton and Smirnov, 'The Khariton Version'.

39. Rhodes, *Dark Sun*, 371–4; Kai Bird and Martin J. Sherwin, *American Prometheus: The Triumph and Tragedy of J. Robert Oppenheimer* (New York: Knopf, 2005), 416–17.

40. Gerard J. DeGroot, *The Bomb: A History of Hell on Earth* (London: Pimlico, 2005), 116–17, 147; Rhodes, *Dark Sun*, 377–8; Herken, *Brotherhood of the Bomb*, 200–1.

41. Rhodes, *Dark Sun*, 246–9; Herken, *Brotherhood of the Bomb*, 86–7; DeGroot, *The Bomb*, 162–3.

42. Herken, *Brotherhood of the Bomb*, 86, 152–5; Bird and Sherwin, *American Prometheus*, 418.

43. Herken, *Brotherhood of the Bomb*, 202–4, 211; Bird and Sherwin, *American Prometheus*, 417–19; Hershberg, *James B. Conant*, 468–72; Rhodes, *Dark Sun*, 386–8.

44. Herken, *Brotherhood of the Bomb*, 206–10; Hershberg, *James B. Conant*, 473–8; Bird and Sherwin, *American Prometheus*, 420–3; Rhodes, *Dark Sun*, 395–403.

45. Rhodes, *Dark Sun*, 404–5; Bird and Sherwin, *American Prometheus*, 423–4; Acheson, *Present at the Creation*, 348.

46. Rhodes, *Dark Sun*, 406–7; Arnold Offner, *Another Such Victory: President Truman and the Cold War, 1945–1953* (Stanford, CA: Stanford University Press, 2002), 363; Herken, *Winning Weapon*, 320–1; Acheson, *Present at the Creation*, 349; Harry S. Truman, *Memoirs: Years of Trial and Hope* (Garden City, NY: Doubleday and Co., 1956), 309.

47. Rhodes, *Dark Sun*, 416–19; Herken, *Brotherhood of the Bomb*, 222–3.

48. Holloway, *Stalin and the Bomb*, 296–7; Rhodes, *Dark Sun*, 256–7.

49. Holloway, *Stalin and the Bomb*, 297–8; Rhodes, *Dark Sun*, 332–3; Andrei Sakharov, *Memoirs*, trans. Richard Lourie (New York: Random House, 1990), 96–8.

50. Holloway, *Stalin and the Bomb*, 298–9; Rhodes, *Dark Sun*, 334–5; DeGroot, *The Bomb*, 167, 171; Herken, *Brotherhood of the Bomb*, 173, 186; Sakharov, *Memoirs*, 92, 102–6.

51. Rhodes, *Dark Sun*, 463, 478, 498–510; Herken, *Brotherhood of the Bomb*, 222–4; Holloway, *Stalin and the Bomb*, 302–3; DeGroot, *The Bomb*, 174–6.

52. Vladislav Zubok and Constantine Pleshakov, *Inside the Kremlin's Cold War: From Stalin to Khrushchev* (Cambridge, MA: Harvard University Press, 1996), 151–2; Sakharov, *Memoirs*, 166–7; Holloway, *Stalin and the Bomb*, 303–7; Khariton and Smirnov, 'The Khariton Version'.

53. Sakharov, *Memoirs*, 188–93; DeGroot, *The Bomb*, 194–9; Holloway, *Stalin and the Bomb*, 303.

54. Gerhard L. Weinberg, *A World at Arms: A Global History of World War II* (Cambridge: Cambridge University Press, 1994), 562–3; Robert A. Divine,

Blowing on the Wind: The Nuclear Test Ban Debate 1954–1960 (New York: Oxford University Press, 1978), 169–70.

55. Michael R. Beschloss, *Mayday: Eisenhower, Khrushchev and the U-2 Affair* (New York: Harper and Row, 1986), 148; John H. Barton and Lawrence D. Weiler, eds., *International Arms Control: Issues and Agreements* (Stanford, CA: Stanford University Press, 1976), 54–5.

56. Barton and Weiler, *International Arms Control*, 55–6.

57. Zubok and Pleshakov, *Inside the Kremlin's Cold War*, 192; Gareth Porter, *Perils of Dominance: Imbalance of Power and the Road to War in Vietnam* (Berkeley and Los Angeles: University of California Press, 2005), 3–7.

58. William Taubman, *Khrushchev: The Man and his Era* (New York: W. W. Norton, 2003), 359, 380, 404–5, 504–6.

59. On the missile crisis, see Taubman, *Khrushchev*, 529–77; Graham Allison and Philip Zelikow, *Essence of Decision: Explaining the Cuban Missile Crisis*, 2nd edn. (New York: Longman, 1999); Sheldon M. Stern, *Averting 'The Final Failure': John F. Kennedy and the Secret Cuban Missile Crisis Meetings* (Stanford, CA: Stanford University Press, 2003); James G. Blight and Philip Brenner, *Sad and Luminous Days: Cuba's Struggle with the Superpowers after the Missile Crisis* (Lanham, MD: Rowman and Littlefield, 2002), 1–31.

60. Taubman, *Khrushchev*, 578–9, 602; Barton and Weiler, *International Arms Control*, 106–8.

CHAPTER EIGHT. THE WORLD'S BOMB

1. Robert Gilpin, *American Scientists and Nuclear Weapons Policy* (Princeton: Princeton University Press, 1962), 65; Robert Jungk, *Brighter than a Thousand Suns: A Personal History of the Atomic Scientists*, trans. James Cleugh (San Diego: Harcourt, 1958), 244; Memorandum to Members of the Advisory Committee on Human Radiation Experiments from Advisory Committee Staff, 5 Apr. 1995, http://www.gwu.edu/nsarchiv/radiation, accessed 13 Dec. 2006.

2. Daniel J. Kevles, *The Physicists: The History of a Scientific Community in Modern America* (Cambridge, MA: Harvard University Press, 1995 [1971]), 379; Laura Fermi, *Atoms for the World: United States Participation in the Conference on the Peaceful Uses of Atomic Energy* (Chicago: University of Chicago Press, 1957), 1; Paul Boyer, *By the Bomb's Early Light: American Thought and Culture at the Dawn of the Atomic Age* (New York: Pantheon, 1985), 80; Leo Szilard, 'The Mined Cities', *Bulletin of the Atomic Scientists*, 17/10 (Dec. 1961), 407–12; Niels Bohr, 'For an Open World', *Bulletin of the Atomic Scientists*, 6/7 (July 1950), 213–19; Richard Rhodes, *The Making of the Atomic Bomb* (New York: Simon and Schuster, 1986), 784–8.

3. Robert A. Divine, *Blowing on the Wind: The Nuclear Test Ban Debate 1954–1960* (New York: Oxford University Press, 1978), 90; id., *Eisenhower and the*

NOTES

337

Cold War (New York: Oxford University Press, 1981), 112–13; 'Atomic Bomb Shudders', *New York Times*, 8 Aug. 1945.

4. Three books by Margaret Gowing are authoritative; see *Britain and Atomic Energy 1939–1945* (New York: St Martin's, 1964); *Independence and Deterrence: Britain and Atomic Energy, 1945–1952*, i. *Policy Making*, ii. *Policy Execution* (London: Macmillan, 1974). Also valuable is Brian Cathcart, *Test of Greatness: Britain's Struggle for the Atom Bomb* (London: John Murray, 1994). See also C. P. Snow, *The New Men* (London: Macmillan, 1960 [1954]); E. M. Fitzgerald, 'Allison, Attlee and the Bomb: Views on the 1947 British Decision to Build an Atom Bomb', *Journal of the Royal United Services Institute for Defence Studies*, 122/1 (1977), 49–56; Graham Spinardi, 'Aldermaston and British Nuclear Weapons Development: Testing the "Zuckerman Thesis"', *Social Studies of Science*, 27 (1997), 547–82. Regarding wartime collaboration between Britain and the United States, see Martin J. Sherwin, *A World Destroyed: The Atomic Bomb and the Grand Alliance* (New York: Knopf, 1975), 67–89, 108–14; Gregg Herken, *The Winning Weapon: The Atomic Bomb in the Cold War 1945–1950* (New York: Random House, 1981), 147; Richard G. Hewlett and Oscar Anderson Jr., *The New World 1939/1946*, i. *A History of the United States Atomic Energy Commission* (University Park, PA: Pennsylvania State University Press, 1962), 458.

5. This account is based on Bertrand Goldschmidt, *Atomic Rivals*, trans. Georges M. Temmer (New Brunswick, NJ: Rutgers University Press, 1990); Spencer R. Weart, *Scientists in Power* (Cambridge, MA: Harvard University Press, 1979), esp. 191–267; Jules Guéron, 'Atomic Energy in Continental Western Europe', in Richard S. Lewis and Jane Wilson, with Eugene Rabinowitch, eds., *Alamogordo plus Twenty-Five Years: The Impact of Atomic Energy on Science, Technology, and World Politics* (New York: Viking, 1970), 140–3; Jungk, *Brighter than a Thousand Suns*, 159; CIA, 'Current Intelligence Bulletin', 29 May 1957, http://www.gwu.edu/nsarchiv/NSAEBB/NSAEBB184/FR09.pdf, accessed 7 June 2007; CIA, 'Current Intelligence Weekly Summary', 28 Jan. 1960, http://www.gwu.edu/nsarchiv/NSAEBB/NSAEBB184/FR12.pdf, accessed 7 June 2007.

6. This account is based almost entirely on Avner Cohen's *Israel and the Bomb* (New York: Columbia University Press, 1998). See also Meirion Jones, 'Britain's Dirty Secret', *New Statesman*, 13 Mar. 2006, and Howard Kohn and Barbara Newman, 'How Israel Got the Bomb', *Rolling Stone*, 12 Jan. 1977. For US policy towards Israel and the Middle East, see Douglas Little, *American Orientalism: The United States and the Middle East since 1945* (Chapel Hill, NC: University of North Carolina Press, 2002), and Peter L. Hahn, *Trapped in the Middle East: US Policy toward the Arab–Israeli Conflict, 1945–1961* (Chapel Hill, NC: University of North Carolina Press, 2004). I am grateful to Daniel Bertrand Monk for the story of the Davidka mortar.

7. Sources on the South African nuclear program include J. D. L. Moore, *South Africa and Nuclear Proliferation: South Africa's Nuclear Capabilities and Intentions in the Context of International Non-Proliferation Policies* (New York: St Martin's, 1987); Barbara Rogers and Zdenek Cervenka, *The Nuclear Axis: Secret Collaboration between West Germany and South Africa* (New York: Times Books, 1978); Waldo Stumpf, 'Birth and Death of the South African Nuclear Weapons Programme', http://www.fas.org/nuke/guide/rsa/nuke/stumpf.htm, accessed 19 Dec. 2006; David Albright, 'South Africa and the Affordable Bomb', *Bulletin of the Atomic Scientists*, 50/4 (July–Aug. 1994), 37–47; id., 'South Africa's Nuclear Weapons Program', 14 Mar. 2001, http://web.mit.edu/seminars/wed_archives_01spring/albright.htm, accessed 19 Dec. 2006; Thomas B. Cochran, 'Highly Enriched Uranium Production for South African Nuclear Weapons', *Science and Global Security*, 4 (1994), 161–76.

8. This section is based principally on John Wilson Lewis and Xue Litai, *China Builds the Bomb* (Stanford, CA: Stanford University Press, 1988). For specialized subjects, see also Ming Zhang, *China's Changing Nuclear Posture: Reactions to the South Asian Nuclear Tests* (Washington: Carnegie Endowment for International Peace, 1999), 2–7; Rana Mitter, *A Bitter Revolution: China's Struggle with the Modern World* (Oxford: Oxford University Press, 2004), 194–8; Divine, *Eisenhower and the Cold War*, 55–66; William Taubman, *Khrushchev: The Man and his Era* (New York: W. W. Norton, 2003), 391–2; Mark Oliphant, 'Over Pots of Tea: Excerpts from a Diary of a Visit to China', *Bulletin of the Atomic Scientists*, 22/5 (May 1966), 36–43.

9. This section relies heavily on George Perkovich, *India's Nuclear Bomb: The Impact on Global Proliferation* (Berkeley and Los Angeles: University of California Press, 1999). See also Itty Abraham, *The Making of the Indian Atomic Bomb: Science, Security, and the Postcolonial State* (London: Zed Books, 1998); Karsten Frey, *India's Nuclear Bomb and National Security* (London: Routledge, 2006); Pratap Bhanu Mehta, 'India: The Nuclear Politics of Self-Esteem', *Current History* (Dec. 1998), 403–6; Andrew J. Rotter, *Comrades at Odds: The United States and India, 1947–1964* (Ithaca, NY: Cornell University Press, 2000), 287–90; Ashok Kapur, *India's Nuclear Option: Atomic Diplomacy and Decision Making* (New York: Praeger, 1976); Spencer R. Weart, *Nuclear Fear: A History of Images* (Cambridge, MA: Harvard University Press, 1988), 211.

10. Michael Walzer, *Just and Unjust Wars: A Moral Argument with Historical Illustrations* (New York: Basic Books, 1977), 263; Lansing Lamont, *Day of Trinity* (New York: Atheneum, 1965), 225–30; Jungk, *Brighter than a Thousand Suns*, 288; Gregg Herken, *Brotherhood of the Bomb: The Tangled Lives and Loyalties of Robert Oppenheimer, Ernest Lawrence, and Edward Teller* (New York: Henry Holt, 2002), 151; Boyer, *Bomb's Early Light*, 219; Dwight Macdonald, 'The Decline to Barbarism', in Kai Bird and Lawrence Lifschultz, eds., *Hiroshima's Shadow: Writings on the Denial of History and the Smithsonian Controversy* (Stony Creek, CT: Pamphleteer's Press, 1998), 264.

11. Lawrence S. Wittner, *The Struggle against the Bomb*, i. *One World or None: A History of the World Nuclear Disarmament Movement through 1953* (Stanford, CA: Stanford University Press, 1993), 82, 105; P. M. S. Blackett, 'The Decision to Use the Bombs', in Bird and Lifschultz, *Hiroshima's Shadow*, 78–89; *The Collected Philosophical Papers of G. E. M. Anscombe*, iii. *Ethics, Religion, and Politics* (Minneapolis, MN: University of Minnesota Press, 1981), 58–65; Wilfred Burchett, 'The First Nuclear War', in Bird and Lifschultz, *Hiroshima's Shadow*, 63–77; Mahatma Gandhi, 'The Atom Bomb and Ahimsa', in ibid. 258–9.

12. Albert Camus, 'Between Hell and Reason', in Bird and Lifschultz, *Hiroshima's Shadow*, 260–1; Wittner, *One World or None*, 108–54.

13. Lawrence S. Wittner, *The Struggle against the Bomb*, ii. *Resisting the Bomb: A History of the World Nuclear Disarmament Movement 1954–1970* (Stanford, CA: Stanford University Press, 1997); iii. *Toward Nuclear Abolition: A History of the World Nuclear Disarmament Movement 1971 to the Present* (Stanford, CA: Stanford University Press, 2003).

EPILOGUE: NIGHTMARES AND HOPES

1. William J. Broad and David E. Sanger, 'With Eye on Iran, Rivals Also Want Nuclear Power', *New York Times*, 15 Apr. 2007.

2. Richard Sale (UPI), 'Israel Finds Radiological Backpack Bomb', 14 Oct. 2001, http://www.papillonsartpalace.com/israelf.htm, accessed 14 Apr. 2007; Abby Goodnough and Matthew L. Wald, 'Marshals Shoot and Kill Passenger in Bomb Threat', *New York Times*, 8 Dec. 2005.

3. 'Board Statement: 5 Minutes to Midnight', *Bulletin Online*, 17 Jan. 2007; http://www.thebulletin.org/minutes-to-midnight/board-statements.html, accessed 23 Apr. 2007. See also Walter Pincus, 'Pentagon Revises Nuclear Strike Plan', *Washington Post*, 11 Sept. 2005, online, accessed 17 Apr. 2007.

4. Stuart Jeffries, 'Fanning the Flames', *Guardian*, 23 Dec. 2006.

Bibliographical Essay

This book hopes to recast somewhat the strident debate over the use of the atomic bomb by placing the issue in a broadly global context. But it relies for its material largely on the published scholarship. Happily, there is a good deal of this, and much is of excellent quality. Start with three collections of documents on the bomb and particularly the decisions to build and use it: Dennis Merrill, ed., *Documentary History of the Truman Presidency*, i. *The Decision to Drop the Atomic Bomb on Japan* (Washington: University Publications of America, 1995); Philip L. Cantelon, Richard G. Hewlett, and Robert C. Williams, eds., *The American Atom: A Documentary History of Nuclear Policies from the Discovery of Fission to the Present*, 2nd edn. (Philadelphia, PA: University of Pennsylvania Press, 1991); and Michael B. Stoff, Jonathan F. Fanton, and R. Hal Williams, eds., *The Manhattan Project: A Documentary Introduction to the Atomic Age* (New York: McGraw-Hill, 1991). After 6 August 1945, newspapers and magazines were filled with stories and comment about the bombing of Hiroshima; the *New York Times* had thoughtful coverage of the event and its implications, while the *Bulletin of the Atomic Scientists*, founded in December 1945, carries to this day some of the best writing, commentary, and reminiscence on the issue, often by nuclear scientists.

Speaking of reminiscence, useful memoirs by scientists and those close to them include Arthur Holly Compton, *Atomic Quest: A Personal Narrative* (New York: Oxford University Press, 1956); two books by Laura Fermi, *Atoms in the Family: My Life with Enrico Fermi* (Chicago: University of Chicago Press, 1954), and *Atoms for the World: United States Participation in the Conference on the Peaceful Uses of Atomic Energy* (Chicago: University of Chicago Press, 1957); Otto Hahn, *My Life: The Autobiography of a Scientist*, trans. Ernst Kaiser and Eithne Wilkins (New York: Herder and Herder, 1970); Rudolf E. Peierls's collected *Atomic Histories* (Woodbury, NY: American Institute of Physics, 1997); a summary of five lectures given at Los Alamos by Robert Serber—*The Los Alamos Primer: The First Lectures on How to Build an Atomic Bomb*, ed. with an introduction by Richard Rhodes (Berkeley and Los Angeles: University of California Press, 1992); and Spencer R. Weart and Gertrud Weiss Szilard, eds., *Leo Szilard: His Version of the Facts: Selected Recollections and Correspondence* (Cambridge, MA: MIT Press, 1978). Two collections that include scientists' reminiscences are *Hiroshima Plus 20*, prepared by the *New York Times* and introduced by John W. Finney (New York: Delacorte Press, 1962), and

Richard S. Lewis and Jane Wilson, with Eugene Rabinowitch, eds., *Alamogordo plus Twenty-Five Years: The Impact of Atomic Energy on Science, Technology, and World Politics* (New York: Viking, 1970). Memoirs by political or military figures involved in the Manhattan Project and postwar atomic issues include Leslie R. Groves, *Now it Can Be Told: The Story of the Manhattan Project* (New York: Harper and Brothers, 1962); Harry S. Truman, *Memoirs*, i. *Year of Decisions* (Garden City, NY: Doubleday and Co., 1955), and ii. *Years of Trial and Hope* (Garden City, NY: Doubleday and Co., 1956); William D. Leahy, *I Was There: The Personal Story of the Chief of Staff to Presidents Roosevelt and Truman, Based on his Notes and Diaries Made at the Time* (New York: McGraw-Hill, 1950); Henry L. Stimson and McGeorge Bundy, *On Active Service in Peace and War* (New York: Harper and Brothers, 1947); and Dean Acheson, *Present at the Creation: My Years in the State Department* (New York: W. W. Norton, 1969).

Several books on the atomic bomb generally have greatly informed and enriched this study. Richard Rhodes has been criticized by some historians for not fully consulting the documentary record, but, if Rhodes's books are perhaps not definitive concerning atomic-bomb decisionmaking, they are nevertheless clear on the physics of the bomb, compelling in their sweep and scope, and superb sources of information about the men and women who imagined and built and used the bombs, and I have relied on them heavily: see his *The Making of the Atomic Bomb* (New York: Simon and Schuster, 1986) and *Dark Sun: The Making of the Hydrogen Bomb* (New York: Simon and Schuster, 1995). Other fine general studies of the bomb are Fletcher Knebel and Charles W. Bailey II, *No High Ground* (New York: Harper and Row, 1960); Peter Wyden, *Day One: Before Hiroshima and After* (New York: Simon and Schuster, 1984); Robert Jungk, *Brighter than a Thousand Suns: A Personal History of the Atomic Scientists*, trans. James Cleugh (San Diego: Harcourt, 1958); Ronald W. Clark, *The Greatest Power on Earth: The International Race for Nuclear Supremacy* (New York: Harper and Row, 1980); and Gerard J. DeGroot, *The Bomb: A History of Hell on Earth* (London: Pimlico, 2005). All five of these books are written with exceptional flair and vividness, and are likely to captivate general readers.

CHAPTER ONE. THE WORLD'S ATOM

On the quest to understand the structure of the atom, see, in addition to Rhodes, *Making of the Atomic Bomb*, Fermi, *Atoms in the Family*, Serber, *The Los Alamos Primer* and Jungk, *Brighter than a Thousand Suns*, J. Bronowski, 'The ABC of the Atom', in *Hiroshima Plus 20*; George Gamow, *Atomic Energy in Cosmic and Human Life: Fifty Years of Radioactivity* (New York: Macmillan, 1946); Margaret Gowing, *Britain and Atomic Energy 1939–1945* (New York: St Martin's, 1964); and Daniel J. Kevles, *The Physicists: The History of a Scientific Community in Modern America* (Cambridge, MA: Harvard University Press, 1995 [1971]). The use of poison gas on the battlefield during the First World War is covered by participant observers in

Victor Lefebure, *The Riddle of the Rhine: Chemical Strategy in Peace and War* (New York: Chemical Foundation, 1923); Amos A. Fries and Clarence J. West, *Chemical Warfare* (New York: McGraw-Hill, 1921); and Hahn, *My Life*. Scholarly works on gas include L. F. Haber, *The Poisonous Cloud: Chemical Warfare in the First World War* (Oxford: Oxford University Press, 1986); and Edward M. Spiers, *Chemical Warfare* (Urbana, IL: University of Illinois Press, 1986). On the role played by the state in the pursuit of science, see various essays in Etel Solingen, ed., *Scientists and the State: Domestic Structures and the International Context* (Ann Arbor: University of Michigan Press, 1994). The evolution of Soviet nuclear science is covered brilliantly in David Holloway, *Stalin and the Bomb: The Soviet Union and Atomic Energy, 1939–1956* (New Haven: Yale University Press, 1994); for the story in the United States, see, along with Kevles, *The Physicists*, Robert Gilpin, *American Scientists and Nuclear Weapons Policy* (Princeton: Princeton University Press, 1962). As for the morality of using certain types of weapons against certain types of populations, see Charles R. Beitz, Marshall Cohen, Thomas Scanlon, and A. John Simmons, eds., *International Ethics* (Princeton: Princeton University Press, 1985); Darrell J. Fasching and Dell deChant, *Comparative Religious Ethics: A Narrative Approach* (Malden, MA: Blackwell Publishers, 2001); and the classic Michael Walzer, *Just and Unjust Wars: A Moral Argument with Historical Illustrations* (New York: Basic Books, 1977).

CHAPTER TWO. GREAT BRITAIN: REFUGEES, AIR POWER, AND THE POSSIBILITY OF THE BOMB

H. G. Wells, *The World Set Free* (Leipzig: Bernhard Tauchnitz, 1914), is commonly (and properly) cited as the work of fiction that most scarily predicts the atomic bomb. But see also the weirdly appealing *The Coming Race* (London: G. Routledge and Sons, 1874) by Edward Bulwer-Lytton, and Harold Nicolson's cringe-inducing (but funny) *Public Faces* (Boston and New York: Houghton Mifflin, 1933). On the refugee scientists, Jungk, *Brighter than a Thousand Suns*, and Rhodes, *Making of the Atomic Bomb*, are good; see also Donald Fleming and Bernard Bailyn, eds., *The Intellectual Migration: Europe and America, 1930–1960* (Cambridge, MA: Harvard University Press, 1969); Jean Medawar and David Pyke, *Hitler's Gift: Scientists who Fled Nazi Germany* (London: Piatkus, 2000); and, especially on Klaus Fuchs, the appealing Lansing Lamont, *Day of Trinity* (New York: Atheneum, 1965).

The literature on the development of bombing strategy prior to the Second World War tends to repeat itself, but outstanding exceptions are, on the United States especially, Michael S. Sherry, *The Rise of American Air Power: The Creation of Armageddon* (New Haven: Yale University Press, 1987), and Ronald Schaffer, *Wings of Judgment: American Bombing in World War II* (New York: Oxford University Press, 1985), and, more generally, Tami Davis Biddle, *Rhetoric and Reality in Air Warfare: The Evolution of British and American Ideas about Strategic Bombing,*

1914–1945 (Princeton: Princeton University Press, 2002), and Priya Satia, 'The Defense of Inhumanity: Air Control and the British Idea of Arabia', *American Historical Review*, III/I (Feb. 2006), 16–51. See also Robin Neillands, *The Bomber War: The Allied Air Offensive against Nazi Germany* (Woodstock and New York: Overlook Press, 2001), and David R. Mets, *The Air Campaign: John Warden and the Classical Airpower Theorists* (Maxwell Air Force Base, AL: Air University Press, 1999). On Hugh Trenchard, see Andrew Boyle, *Trenchard* (London: Collins, 1962). On Arthur Harris, see Charles Messenger, *'Bomber' Harris and the Strategic Bombing Offensive, 1939–1945* (New York: St Martin's, 1984), Dudley Saward, *Bomber Harris: The Story of Arthur Harris* (Garden City, NY: Doubleday and Co., 1985), and Sir Arthur T. Harris, *Bomber Offensive* (New York: Macmillan, 1947), and *Despatch on War Operations, 23rd February, 1942, to 8th May, 1945* (London: Frank Cass, 1995).

CHAPTER THREE. JAPAN AND GERMANY: PATHS NOT TAKEN

Apart from histories of the atomic-bomb projects generally, four books were useful on the discovery, mining, and properties of uranium: Robert D. Nininger, *Minerals for Atomic Energy: A Guide to Exploration for Uranium, Thorium, and Beryllium* (New York: D. Van Nostrand and Co., 1954); Martin Lynch, *Mining in World History* (London: Reaktion Books, 2002); Robert Laxalt, *A Private War: An American Code Officer in the Belgian Congo* (Reno and Las Vegas: University of Nevada Press, 1998); and Lennard Bickel, *The Deadly Element: The Story of Uranium* (New York: Stein and Day, 1979). Sources on the Japanese atomic project are limited. The best of them are John W. Dower, ' "NI" and "F": Japan's Wartime Atomic Bomb Research', in John W. Dower, *Japan in War and Peace: Selected Essays* (New York: New Press, 1993), 55–100, and Walter E. Grunden, *Secret Weapons and World War II: Japan in the Shadow of Big Science* (Lawrence, KS: University Press of Kansas, 2005); see also Kenji Hall, 'Japan's A-Bomb Goal Still Long Way off in '45', *Japan Times*, 7 Mar. 2003. German atomic-bomb research is treated best in Thomas Powers, *Heisenberg's War: The Secret History of the German Bomb* (New York: Knopf, 1993); despite serious reservations about the author, David Irving, *The German Atomic Bomb: The History of Nuclear Research in Nazi Germany* (New York: Simon and Schuster, 1967); David C. Cassidy, *Uncertainty: The Life and Science of Werner Heisenberg* (New York: W. H. Freeman, 1992); Mark Walker, *Nazi Science: Myth, Truth, and the German Atomic Bomb* (New York: Plenum Press, 1995); Paul Lawrence Rose, *Heisenberg and the Nazi Atomic Bomb Project: A Study in German Culture* (Berkeley and Los Angeles: University of California Press, 1998); the memoir by Albert Speer, *Inside the Third Reich*, trans. Richard and Clara Winston (New York: Macmillan, 1970); and Jeremy Bernstein, *Hitler's Uranium Club: The Secret Recordings at Farm Hall* (Woodbury, NY: American Institute of Physics, 1996), with a useful introduction by Cassidy. After digesting the history, readers will enjoy Michael Frayn's provocative play *Copenhagen* (London: Methuen, 1998). And the curious

story of a former major league baseball player and spy extraordinaire is told by
Nicholas Dawidoff, *The Catcher Was a Spy: The Mysterious Life of Moe Berg* (New
York: Pantheon, 1994).

On Leo Szilard's approach to Albert Einstein and Alexander Sachs, and on much
else besides, the best source remains Martin J. Sherwin, *A World Destroyed: The
Atomic Bomb and the Grand Alliance* (New York: Knopf, 1975).

CHAPTER FOUR. THE UNITED STATES I: IMAGINING AND BUILDING THE BOMB

Rhodes, *Making of the Atomic Bomb*, Wyden, *Day One*, Gowing, *Britain and Atomic
Energy*, Sherwin, *A World Destroyed*, Jungk, *Brighter than a Thousand Suns*, Kevles,
The Physicists, and Lamont, *The Physicists*, tell the American story, from a variety
of perspectives. See also the memoirs: Weart and Szilard, *Leo Szilard*, Compton,
Atomic Quest, and Groves, *Now it Can Be Told*, and a less exalted but interesting
one by Harlow W. Russ, *Project Alberta: The Preparation of the Atomic Bombs
for Use in World War II* (Los Alamos, NM: Exceptional Books, 1990). Rather
technical, but nevertheless very valuable, are Richard G. Hewlett and Oscar E.
Anderson Jr., *The New World, 1939–1946*, vol. 1 of *A History of the United States
Atomic Energy Commission* (University Park, PA: Pennsylvania State University
Press, 1962); and Henry DeWolf Smyth, *Atomic Energy for Military Purposes: The
Official Report on the Development of the Atomic Bomb under the Auspices of the
United States Government, 1940–1945* (Stanford, CA: Stanford University Press,
1989 [1945]).

On James Conant's key role in the bomb project, James G. Hershberg, *James
B. Conant: Harvard to Hiroshima and the Making of the Nuclear Age* (Stanford, CA:
Stanford University Press, 1993), is authoritative and indispensable; for a marvelous
study of three leading players in the nuclear weapons' drama, see Gregg Herken,
*Brotherhood of the Bomb: The Tangled Lives and Loyalties of Robert Oppenheimer, Ernest
Lawrence, and Edward Teller* (New York: Henry Holt, 2002). Oppenheimer alone has
inspired several thoughtful treatments, including most recently David C. Cassidy,
J. Robert Oppenheimer and the American Century (New York: Pi Press, 2005); Kai
Bird and Martin J. Sherwin, *American Prometheus: The Triumph and Tragedy of J.
Robert Oppenheimer* (New York: Knopf, 2005); and a Thomas Powers review essay,
'An American Tragedy', *New York Review of Books*, 22 Sept. 2005, 73–9. Some
of Oppenheimer's correspondence is available in Alice Kimball Smith and Charles
Weiner, eds., *Robert Oppenheimer: Letters and Recollections* (Cambridge, MA: Harvard
University Press, 1980). For the unhappy denouement of Oppenheimer's career,
consult Philip M. Stern, with Harold P. Green, *The Oppenheimer Case: Security on
Trial* (New York: Harper and Row, 1969); Richard Polenberg, ed., *In the Matter of J.
Robert Oppenheimer: The Security Clearance Hearing* (Ithaca, NY: Cornell University
Press, 2002) ; and especially Priscilla J. McMillan, *The Ruin of J. Robert Oppenheimer*

and the Birth of the Modern Arms Race (New York: Viking, 2005). And see (and hear) the opera *Dr Atomic*, composed by John Adams and Peter Sellars. On Leslie Groves's story, told by someone a good deal less absorbed with Groves than the general himself, the book is Robert S. Norris, *Racing for the Bomb: General Leslie R. Groves, the Manhattan Project's Indispensable Man* (South Royalton, VT: Steerforth Press, 2002).

CHAPTER FIVE. THE UNITED STATES II: USING THE BOMB

While maintaining its determination to narrate the history of the atomic bomb, this chapter nevertheless finds itself engaged with the longstanding and bitter scholarly dispute over the reasons for its use. There is simply no avoiding it. The best recent summary of the argument, judicious and perceptive, is J. Samuel Walker, 'Recent Literature on Truman's Atomic Bomb Decision: A Search for Middle Ground', *Diplomatic History*, 29/2 (Apr. 2005), 311–34. Walker has also told the story himself, with economy and grace, in *Prompt and Utter Destruction: Truman and the Use of Atomic Bombs against Japan* (Chapel Hill, NC: University of North Carolina Press, 1997). The controversy, broadly speaking, has divided those who believe the atomic bombs were dropped for good and sufficient cause—that is, to save American and even Japanese lives—and those who claim that the bombs were unnecessary given Japan's ruined state by the summer of 1945 and Japan's willingness to surrender on reasonable terms, or that the bombs were less an effort to end the war than to intimidate the Soviet Union, or simply immoral weapons given their singular power and radioactive products. The 'orthodox' interpretation of the bombings has followed Henry L. Stimson's essay 'The Decision to Use the Atomic Bomb', *Harper's* (Feb. 1947), 97–107, in which the former Secretary of War defended Truman's decision. Atomic-bomb 'revisionism', generally to do with the theory that the bomb was directed more against the Russians than the beaten Japanese, began as early as 1946, with the publication of an essay by Norman Cousins and Thomas K. Finletter, entitled 'A Beginning for Sanity', *Saturday Review of Literature*, 15 June 1946, 5–9, and a book published the following year by the British physicist P. M. S. Blackett: *War and the Bomb: Military and Political Consequences of Atomic Energy* (New York: McGraw-Hill, 1947). Submerged for a time, revisionism resurfaced fully in 1965 with the publication of Gar Alperovitz's *Atomic Diplomacy: Hiroshima and Potsdam* (expanded and updated edn., New York: Penguin, 1985 [1965])—the most comprehensive argument to that date that Truman, James Byrnes, and key US policymakers saw the bomb as a diplomatic rather than a military tool. Alperovitz updated his argument and added some evidence in *The Decision to Use the Atomic Bomb and the Architecture of an American Myth* (New York: Knopf, 1995). The revisionist thesis received support from several quarters, including Robert Jay Lifton and Greg Mitchell, *Hiroshima in America: Fifty Years of Denial* (New York: G. P. Putnam's Sons, 1995); and the introductory essay, written by the editors, to the useful collection of Kai Bird and Lawrence Lifschultz, eds., *Hiroshima's Shadow: Writings on the Denial of History and the Smithsonian Controversy* (Stony Creek, CT: Pamphleteer's Press, 1998). Ronald Takaki argues, in *Hiroshima: Why America Dropped the Atomic Bomb* (Boston: Little, Brown, 1995), that white American racism and Truman's desire to prove himself tough explain the decision.

The backlash against the revisionists' claims was almost immediate. Historians and other commentators, many of them with military experience, criticized Alperovitz for what they said was his selective use of evidence and tendentious arguments. 'Thank God for the Atomic Bomb' was the title of Paul Fussell's 1991 article for the *New Republic*, repr. in Bird and Lifschultz, *Hiroshima's Shadow*, 211–22; Fussell had fought in Europe, and his division was scheduled to invade Honshu in early 1946. Other debunking efforts were Robert James Maddox, *Weapons for Victory: The Hiroshima Decision Fifty Years Later* (Columbia, MO: University of Missouri Press, 1995), and Robert P. Newman, *Truman and the Hiroshima Cult* (East Lansing, MI: Michigan State University Press, 1995).

The result of this polemic, as is often the case, was a postrevisionist 'middle ground' (as J. Samuel Walker has termed it) in which scholars found a more nuanced position between the extremes. Walker's *Prompt and Utter Destruction* is perhaps the best example of this. But see also the multiple and insightful essays by Barton J. Bernstein. Two—'The Atomic Bomb and American Foreign Policy: The Route to Hiroshima' and 'Atomic Diplomacy and the Cold War—are printed in Bernstein's edited volume *The Atomic Bomb: The Critical Issues* (Boston: Little, Brown, 1976), 94–120, 129–35. Other revealing essays by Bernstein include 'Why We Didn't Use Poison Gas in World War II', *American Heritage*, 36 (Aug.–Sept. 1985), 40–5; 'America's Biological Warfare Program in the Second World War', *Journal of Strategic Studies*, 11/3 (Sept. 1988), 306–17; 'Ike and Hiroshima: Did He Oppose It?' *Journal of Strategic Studies*, 10/3 (Sept. 1987), 377–89; 'Writing, Righting, or Wronging the Historical Record: President Truman's Letter on his Atomic Bomb Decision', *Diplomatic History*, 16/4 (Winter 1992), 163–73; 'Compelling Japan's Surrender without the A-Bomb, Soviet Entry, or Invasion: Reconsidering the US Bombing Survey's Early Surrender Conclusions', *Journal of Strategic Studies*, 18/2 (June 1995), 101–48; 'Seizing the Contested Terrain of Early Nuclear History', repr. in Bird and Lifschultz, *Hiroshima's Shadow*, 163–96; 'Truman and the A-Bomb: Targeting Noncombatants, Using the Bomb, and his Defending the "Decision"', *Journal of Military History*, 62/3 (July 1998), 547–70; and 'The Alarming Japanese Buildup on Southern Kyushu, Growing US Fears, and Counterfactual Analysis: Would the Planned November 1945 Invasion of Southern Kyushu Have Occurred?' *Pacific Historical Review*, 68/4 (Nov. 1999), 561–609. Sherwin, *A World Destroyed*, rests comfortably on the middle ground. Also there, if shaded slightly toward the orthodox pole, is Richard B. Frank's deeply informed *Downfall: The End of the Imperial Japanese Empire* (New York: Random House, 1999).

The Second World War is well handled—it cannot be altogether covered—in Gerhard L. Weinberg, *A World at Arms: A Global History of World War II* (Cambridge: Cambridge University Press, 1994). See also William O'Neill, *A Democracy at War* (Cambridge, MA: Harvard University Press, 1993). The Pacific Theater is treated in Saburō Ienaga, *The Pacific War, 1931–1945: A Critical Perspective on Japan's Role in World War II* (New York: Pantheon, 1978); John W. Dower, *War without Mercy: Race and Power in the Pacific War* (New York: Pantheon, 1986); and Ronald H. Spector, *Eagle against the Sun: The American War with Japan* (New York: Free Press, 1985); eyewitness accounts include E. B. Sledge, *With the Old Breed: At Peleliu and Okinawa* (New York: Oxford University Press, 1990); Francis B. Catanzaro, *With the 41st Division in the Southwest Pacific: A Foot Soldier's Story* (Bloomington, IN: Indiana University Press, 2002); and Patrick K. O'Donnell, *Into the Rising Sun: In their own Words, World War II's Pacific Veterans Reveal the Heart of Combat* (New York: Free Press, 2002). For the strategic bombing of Germany and Japan, see, in addition to titles by Sherry, Biddle, and Schaffer, General Curtis E. LeMay, with MacKinley Cantor, *Mission with LeMay: My Story* (Garden City, NY: Doubleday and Co., 1965); Conrad Crane, *Bombs, Cities, and Civilians: American Airpower Strategy in World War II* (Lawrence, KS: University of Kansas Press, 1993); W. G. Sebald, *On the Natural History of Destruction*, trans. Anthea Bell (New York: Modern Library, 2004); Jörg Friedrich, *The Fire: The Bombing of Germany, 1940–1945*, trans. Allison Brown (New York: Columbia University Press, 2006); A. C. Grayling, *Among the Dead Cities: The History and Moral Legacy of the WWII Bombing of Civilians in Germany and Japan* (New York: Walker, 2006); Stephen A. Garrett, *Ethics and Airpower in World War II: The British Bombing of German Cities* (New York: St Martin's, 1993; and Charles S. Maier, 'Targeting the City: Debates and Silences about the Aerial Bombing of World War II', *International Review of the Red Cross*, 87/859 (Sept. 2005). On Hamburg, see Hans Erich Nossack, *The End: Hamburg 1943*, trans. Joel Agee (Chicago: University of Chicago Press, 2004); for Dresden, see Kurt Vonnegut Jr., *Slaughterhouse-Five: Or, the Children's Crusade, a Duty-Dance with Death* (New York: Delacorte Press, 1969); and Frederick Taylor, *Dresden: Tuesday, February 13, 1945* (New York: HarperCollins, 2004). On the bombing of Tokyo, see the harrowing account of Robert Guillain, *I Saw Tokyo Burning: An Eyewitness Narrative from Pearl Harbor to Hiroshima*, trans. William Byron (Garden City, NY: Doubleday, 1981); Kenneth P. Werrell, *Blankets of Fire: US Bombers over Japan during World War II* (Washington: Smithsonian Institution Press, 1996); and Gordon Daniels, 'The Great Tokyo Air Raid, 9–10 March 1945', in W. G. Beasley, ed., *Modern Japan: Aspects of History, Literature and Society* (Berkeley and Los Angeles: University of California Press, 1975). On the endgame of the Pacific War, consult, in addition to Frank, *Downfall*, Robert Leckie, *Okinawa: The Last Battle of World War II* (New York: Penguin, 1995); Thomas W. Zeiler, *Unconditional Defeat: Japan, America, and the End of World War II* (Wilmington, DE: Scholarly Resources Press, 2004); John Ray Skates, *The Invasion of Japan: Alternatives to the Bomb* (Columbia, SC: University of South Carolina Press, 1994);

John D. Chappell, *Before the Bomb: How America Approached the End of the Pacific War* (Lexington, KY: University of Kentucky Press, 1997); Leon V. Sigal, *Fighting to a Finish: The Politics of War Termination in the United States and Japan, 1945* (Ithaca, NY: Cornell University Press, 1988); and especially the prize-winning volume by Tsuyoshi Hasegawa, *Racing the Enemy: Stalin, Truman, and the Surrender of Japan* (Cambridge, MA: Harvard University Press, 2005). The question of how many Americans would die in a planned invasion of Japan, set to begin in November of 1946, is debated, on the one side, by Barton J. Bernstein in 'Understanding the Atomic Bomb and the Japanese Surrender: Missed Opportunities, Little-Known Near Disasters, and Modern Memory', in Michael J. Hogan, ed., *Hiroshima in History and Memory* (Cambridge: Cambridge University Press, 1996), 38–79, and 'Reconsidering Truman's Claim of "Half a Million American Lives" Saved by the Atomic Bomb: The Construction and Deconstruction of a Myth', *Journal of Strategic Studies*, 22/1 (Mar. 1999), 54–95; and, on the other, by D. M. Giangreco, ' "A Score of Bloody Okinawas and Iwo Jimas": President Truman and Casualty Estimates for the Invasion of Japan', *Pacific Historical Review*, 72/1 (Feb. 2003), 93–132, and Michael Kort, 'Casualty Projections for the Invasion of Japan, Phantom Estimates, and the Math of Barton Bernstein', *Passport*, 34/3 (Dec. 2003), 4–12.

Biographers have sought to analyze Truman's thinking with regard to the atomic bomb. Three biographies that come out in two different places are David McCullough, *Truman* (New York: Simon and Schuster, 1992), and Robert H. Ferrell, *Harry S. Truman: A Life* (Columbia, MO: University of Missouri Press, 1994), both of which argue that Truman had virtually no choice but to drop the bombs; and the far more critical Arnold Offner, *Another Such Victory: President Truman and the Cold War, 1945–1953* (Stanford, CA: Stanford University Press, 2002). Some of what Truman said himself is collected in Ralph E. Weber, ed., *Talking with Harry: Candid Conversations with President Harry S. Truman* (Wilmington, DE: Scholarly Resources Press, 2001); and three volumes edited by Robert H. Ferrell: *Off the Record: The Private Papers of Harry S. Truman* (New York: Harper and Row, 1980), *Dear Bess: The Letters from Harry to Bess Truman, 1910–1959* (New York: W. W. Norton, 1983), and *Truman in the White House: The Diary of Eben A. Ayers* (Columbia, MO: University of Missouri Press, 1991).

CHAPTER SIX. JAPAN: THE ATOMIC BOMBS AND WAR'S END

Dramatic stories of the atomic bombings themselves are told in Rhodes, *Making of the Atomic Bomb*, Wyden, *Day One*, Knebel and Bailey, *No High Ground*, Russ, *Project Alberta*, and Charles W. Sweeney, with James A. Antonucci and Marion K. Antonucci, *War's End: An Eyewitness Account of America's Last Atomic Mission* (New York: Avon Books, 1997); Norman Polmar, *Enola Gay: The B-29 that Dropped the Atomic Bomb on Hiroshima* (Washington: Brassey's, 2004); Gordon Thomas and Max

Morgan Witts, *Enola Gay* (New York: Stein and Day, 1977); Merle Miller and Abe Spitzer, *We Dropped the A-Bomb* (New York: Thomas Y. Crowell, 1946); William Bradford Huie, *The Hiroshima Pilot* (New York: G. P. Putnam's and Sons, 1964); Hanson W. Baldwin, 'Hiroshima Decision', in *Hiroshima Plus 20*; and Norman F. Ramsey, 'August 1945: The B-29 Flight Logs', *Bulletin of the Atomic Scientists*, 38/10 (Dec. 1982), 33–5.

John Hersey's *Hiroshima*, serialized in the *New Yorker* then published in 1946 (New York: Knopf, 1946), broke the silence of the survivors of the Hiroshima bombing. It is an arresting account. Interested readers should see also Michihiko Hachiya, *Hiroshima Diary: The Journal of a Japanese Physician, August 6–September 30, 1945*, trans. Warner Wells (Chapel Hill, NC: University of North Carolina Press, 1955); Kenzaburō Ōe, *Hiroshima Notes*, trans. David J. Swain and Toshi Yonezawa (New York: Grove Press, 1996 [1965]); Kenzaburō Ōe, ed., *The Crazy Iris and Other Stories of the Atomic Aftermath* (New York: Grove Press, 1995); Robert J. Lifton, *Death in Life: Survivors of Hiroshima* (New York: Simon and Schuster, 1967); Toyofumi Ogura, *Letters from the End of the World: A Firsthand Account of the Bombing of Hiroshima*, trans. Kisaburo Murakami and Shigeru Fujii (Tokyo: Kodansha International, 1997); Arata Osada, ed., *Children of Hiroshima* (Tokyo: Publishing Committee for Children of Hiroshima, 1980); Japanese Broadcasting Corporation ed., *Unforgettable Fire: Pictures Drawn by Atomic Bomb Survivors*, ed. (New York: Pantheon, 1977); Pacific War Research Society (PWRS), *The Day Man Lost: Hiroshima, 6 August 1945* (Palo Alto: Kodansha International, 1972); Lequita Vance-Watkins and Aratani Mariko, eds. and trans., *White Flash, Black Rain: Women of Japan Relive the Bomb* (Minneapolis, MN: Milkweed Editions, 1995); Richard H. Minear, ed. and trans., *Hiroshima: Three Witnesses* (Princeton: Princeton University Press, 1990); John W. Dower, 'The Bombed: Hiroshimas and Nagasakis in Japanese Memory', in Hogan, *Hiroshima in History and Memory*, 116–42; John Whittier Treat, *Writing Ground Zero: Japanese Literature and the Atomic Bomb* (Chicago: University of Chicago Press, 1995); James N. Yamazaki, with Louis B. Fleming, *Children of the Atomic Bomb: An American Physician's Memoir of Nagasaki, Hiroshima, and the Marshall Islands* (Durham, NC: Duke University Press, 1995); Kyoko Selden and Mark Selden, eds., *The Atomic Bomb: Voices from Hiroshima and Nagasaki* (Armonk, NY: M. E. Sharpe, 1989); and Kurihara Sadako, *When We Say 'Hiroshima': Selected Poems*, trans. with an intro. by Richard H. Minear (Ann Arbor: Center for Japanese Studies, University of Michigan, 1999).

For a superb historical context for the American–Japanese relationship, see Walter LaFeber, *The Clash: US–Japanese Relations throughout History* (New York: W. W. Norton, 1997). A vital source for the response to the war's end of the Japanese generally is Haruko Taya Cook and Theodore F. Cook, *Japan at War: An Oral History* (New York: New Press, 1992).

The Emperor Hirohito, his advisers, his War Cabinet, and the so-called Big Six decisionmakers had an anguished debate over whether to surrender after

6 August, and on what terms. Robert J. C. Butow, *Japan's Decision to Surrender* (Stanford, CA: Stanford University Press, 1954), does not get it all right, but holds up remarkably well given the limited sources available to Butow in the early 1950s. More authoritative is Herbert P. Bix, *Hirohito and the Making of Modern Japan* (New York: HarperCollins, 2000), and his essay 'Japan's Delayed Surrender: A Reinterpretation', in Hogan, *Hiroshima in History and Memory*, 80–115. See also Tsuyoshi Hasegawa, ed., *The End of the Pacific War: Reappraisals* (Stanford: Stanford University Press, 2007), including state-of-the-art essays by Hasegawa, Bernstein, Frank, and others; Edwin P. Hoyt, *Hirohito: The Emperor and the Man* (New York: Praeger, 1992); Sadao Asada, 'The Shock of the Atomic Bomb and Japan's Decision to Surrender: A Reconsideration', *Pacific Historical Review*, 68/4 (Nov. 1998), 477–512; Pacific War Research Society, *Japan's Longest Day* (Tokyo: Kodansha International, 1980); Yukiko Koshiro, 'Eurasian Eclipse: Japan's End Game in World War II', *American Historical Review*, 109/2 (Apr. 2004), 417–44; and books by Hasegawa, Frank, and Sigal.

Statistical information about the victims of the atomic bombs is contained in the US Strategic Bombing Survey (USSBS), *The Effects of Atomic Bombs on Hiroshima and Nagasaki* (Washington: US Government Printing Office, 1946); Ashley W. Oughterson and Shields Warren, eds. *Medical Effects of the Atomic Bomb in Japan* (New York: McGraw Hill, 1956); Committee for the Compilation of Materials on Damage Caused by the Atomic Bombs, *Hiroshima and Nagasaki: The Physical, Medical, and Social Effects of the Atomic Bombings*, trans. Eisei Ishikawa and David L. Swain (New York: Basic Books, 1981); and I. Shigematsu, C. Ito, N. Kamada, M. Akiyama, and H. Sasaki, *Effects of A-Bomb Radiation on the Human Body*, trans. B. Harrison (Chur, Switzerland: Harwood Academic Publishers, 1995).

Regarding the management of memory of the bomb (and the war) in occupied Japan, see Monica Braw, *The Atomic Bomb Suppressed: American Censorship in Japan, 1945–1949* (Lund, Sweden: Liber, 1986); John W. Dower, *Embracing Defeat: Japan in the Wake of World War II* (New York: W. W. Norton, 1999); Yoshikuni Igarashi, *Bodies of Memory: Narratives of War in Postwar Japanese Culture, 1945–1970* (Princeton: Princeton University Press, 2000); and Naoko Shibusawa, *America's Geisha Ally: Reimagining the Japanese Enemy* (Cambridge, MA: Harvard University Press, 2006).

CHAPTER SEVEN: THE SOVIET UNION: THE BOMB AND THE COLD WAR

The impact of nuclear weapons on American culture is assessed in Paul Boyer, *By the Bomb's Early Light: American Thought and Culture at the Dawn of the Atomic Age* (New York: Pantheon, 1985); Spencer R. Weart, *Nuclear Fear: A History of Images* (Cambridge, MA: Harvard University Press, 1988); Stephen J. Whitfield, *The Culture of the Cold War*, 2nd edn. (Baltimore: Johns Hopkins University Press,

1996 [1991]); and Allan M. Winkler, *Life under a Cloud: American Anxiety about the Atom* (New York: Oxford University Press, 1993). For the international reaction to the bombings and their aftermath, the pickings are rather slimmer; consult national newspapers. Australia is covered in Prue Torney-Parlicki, ' "Whatever the Thing May Be Called": The Australian News Media and the Atomic Bombing of Hiroshima and Nagasaki', *Australian Historical Studies*, 31/114 (Apr. 2000), 49–66; for Mexico, see Regis Cabral, 'The Mexican Reactions to the Hiroshima and Nagasaki Tragedies of 1945', *Quipu*, 4/1 (Jan.–Apr. 1987), 81–118; a short but instructive piece on France is E. L. De Saint-Just, 'La Bombe atomique met entre les mains de l'homme une force qui peut le détruire', *La Patrie du Dimanche*, 12 Aug. 1945.

The literature on the Cold War generally deserves a bibliography of its own. For a quick primer, with reference to the atomic bomb, see John Lewis Gaddis, *Strategies of Containment: A Critical Appraisal of Postwar American National Security Policy* (New York: Oxford University Press, 1982); Daniel Yergin, *Shattered Peace: The Origins of the Cold War* (New York: Penguin, 1990 [1977]); Thomas Paterson, *On Every Front: The Making and Unmaking of the Cold War*, rev. edn. (New York: Norton, 1992); Melvyn P. Leffler, *A Preponderance of Power: National Security, the Truman Administration, and the Cold War* (Stanford, CA: Stanford University Press, 1992); Vladislav Zubok and Constantine Pleshakov, *Inside the Kremlin's Cold War: From Stalin to Khrushchev* Cambridge, MA: Harvard University Press, 1996); and Walter LaFeber, *America, Russia, and the Cold War, 1945–2000*, 9th edn. (Boston: McGraw-Hill, 2002). The bomb, and what to do with it, is the centerpiece of Gregg Herken's superb *The Winning Weapon: The Atomic Bomb and the Cold War 1945–1950* (New York: Random House, 1981). Gar Alperovitz and Kai Bird, 'The Centrality of the Bomb', *Foreign Policy* (Spring 1994), 3–18, make a provocative case for their essay's title. See also memoirs by Truman, Acheson, Leahy, Groves, and Compton.

In the early 1990s the Russians briefly opened archives to scholars, with the result being the publication soon afterwards of a number of impressive books on Soviet policy, atomic and otherwise. Study of the Soviet bomb project begins and practically ends with Holloway's *Stalin and the Bomb*. Rhodes's *Dark Sun* came out in 1995; Rhodes acknowledged a significant debt to Holloway's book, but added much detail, particularly concerning the role of the atomic spies who contributed to the Soviet project. Also useful on this subject are Arnold Kramish, *Atomic Energy in the Soviet Union* (Stanford, CA: Stanford University Press, 1959); Thomas B. Cochrane, Robert S. Norris, and Oleg A. Bukharin, *Making the Russian Bomb: From Stalin to Yeltsin* (Boulder, CO: Westview Press, 1995); J. W. Boag, P. E. Rubinin, and D. Shoenberg, eds., *Kapitza in Cambridge and Moscow: Life and Letters of a Russian Physicist* (Amsterdam: North-Holland, 1990); Andrei Sakharov, *Memoirs*, trans. Richard Lourie (New York: Random House, 1990); and Yuli Khariton and Yuri Smirnov, 'The Khariton Version', *Bulletin of the Atomic Scientists*, 49/4 (May 1993), 20–31.

The same brief opening of Soviet-era records produced a flurry of studies of espionage, many of them fetishistic in their obsessions and ambitious, in several cases reckless, in scope. The best of these include Allen Weinstein and Alexander Vassiliev, *The Haunted Wood: Soviet Espionage in America: The Stalin Era* (New York: Random House, 1999); John Earl Haynes and Harvey Klehr, *Venona: Decoding Soviet Espionage in America* (New Haven: Yale University Press, 1999); Nigel West, *Venona: The Greatest Secret of the Cold War* (London: HarperCollins, 1999); and Joshua Rubenstein and Alexander Gribanov, *The KGB File of Andrei Sakharov* (New Haven: Yale University Press, 2005). See also Christopher Andrew and Oleg Gordievsky, *KGB: The Inside Story of its Foreign Operations from Lenin to Gorbachev* (New York: HarperCollins, 1990); Pavel Sudoplatov and Anatoli Sudoplatov, with Jerrold L. and Leona P. Schecter, *Special Tasks: The Memoirs of an Unwanted Witness: A Soviet Spymaster* (Boston: Little, Brown, 1994); Joseph Albright and Marcia Kunstel, *Bombshell: The Secret Story of America's Unknown Atomic Spy Conspiracy* (New York: Times Books, 1997); Alexander Feklisov and Sergei Kostin, *The Man behind the Rosenbergs* (New York: Enigma Books, 2001); Jerrold Schecter and Leona Schecter, *Sacred Secrets: How Soviet Intelligence Operations Changed American History* (Washington: Brassey's, 2002).

The development of the arms race between the Cold War superpowers is the subject of James Chace, 'Sharing the Atomic Bomb', *Foreign Affairs*, 75/1 (Jan./Feb. 1996), 129–44; John H. Barton and Lawrence D. Weiler, eds., *International Arms Control: Issues and Agreements* (Stanford, CA: Stanford University Press, 1976); Gerard H. Clarfield and William M. Wiecek, *Nuclear America: Military and Civilian Nuclear Power in the United States, 1940–1980* (New York: Harper and Row, 1984); John B. Harris and Eric Markusen, eds., *Nuclear Weapons and the Threat of Nuclear War* (San Diego: Harcourt, Brace, Jovanovich, 1986); David E. Lilienthal, *Change, Hope, and the Bomb* (Princeton: Princeton University Press, 1963); and Hans A. Bethe, *The Road from Los Alamos* (New York: American Institute of Physics, 1991). On nuclear testing, see Robert Divine, *Blowing on the Wind: The Nuclear Test Ban Debate 1954–1960* (New York: Oxford University Press, 1978); John G. Fuller, *The Day We Bombed Utah: America's Most Lethal Secret* (New York: New American Library, 1984); and Howard Ball, *Justice Downwind: America's Atomic Testing Program in the 1950s* (New York: Oxford University Press, 1986). For Sputnik and the U-2 incident, see Michael Beschloss, *Mayday: Eisenhower, Khrushchev and the U-2 Affair* (New York: Harper and Row, 1986).

The Cuban Missile Crisis stand ignobly at the summit of postwar nuclear threats and counterthreats. Among the leading sources are Alexander Fursenko and Timothy Naftali, *'One Hell of a Gamble': Khrushchev, Castro, and Kennedy, 1958–1964* (New York: W. W. Norton, 1997); Graham Allison and Philip Zelikow, *Essence of Decision: Explaining the Cuban Missile Crisis*, 2nd edn. (New York: Longman, 1999); James G. Blight and Philip Brenner, *Sad and Luminous Days: Cuba's Struggle with the Superpowers after the Missile Crisis* (Lanham, MD: Rowman and Littlefield,

2002); Sheldon M. Stern, *Averting 'The Final Failure': John F. Kennedy and Secret Cuban Missile Crisis Meetings* (Stanford, CA: Stanford University Press, 2003); and William Taubman's wonderful biography *Khrushchev: The Man and his Era* (New York: W. W. Norton, 2003).

CHAPTER EIGHT. THE WORLD'S BOMB

Scientists' hopes to re-establish their pre-war republic find voice in Rhodes, *Making of the Atomic Bomb*; Kevles, *The Physicists*; Fermi, *Atoms for the World*; Abraham Pais, *Niels Bohr's Times: In Physics, Philosophy, and Polity* (Oxford: Oxford University Press, 1991); and especially Niels Bohr, 'For an Open World', *Bulletin of the Atomic Scientists*, 6/7 (July 1950), 213–19.

On the British bomb project, see three impressive books by Margaret Gowing, the historian of Britain's Atomic Energy Authority: *Britain and Atomic Energy 1939–1945* and (New York: St Martin's, 1964), *Independence and Deterrence: Britain and Atomic Energy, 1945–1952*, i. *Policy Making*, and ii. *Policy Execution* (London: Macmillan, 1974). Also helpful are Brian Cathcart, *Test of Greatness: Britain's Struggle for the Atom Bomb* (London: John Murray, 1994); E. M. Fitzgerald, 'Allison, Attlee and the Bomb: Views of the 1947 British Decision to Build an Atom Bomb', *Journal of the Royal United Services Institute for Defence Studies*, 122/1 (1977), 49–56; Graham Spinardi, 'Aldermaston and British Nuclear Weapons Development: Testing the "Zuckerman Thesis"', *Social Studies of Science*, 27 (1997), 547–82; and C. P. Snow, *The New Men* (London: Macmillan, 1960 [1954]).

The French story is told most thoroughly and entertainingly by Bertrand Goldschmidt in *Atomic Rivals*, trans. by Georges M. Temmer (New Brunswick, NJ: Rutgers University Press, 1990). See also Spencer R. Weart, *Scientists in Power* (Cambridge, MA: Harvard University Press, 1979), and Jules Guéron, 'Atomic Energy in Continental Western Europe', Lewis and Wilson, with Rabinowitch, in *Alamogordo plus Twenty-Five Years*, 140–58.

The definitive study of Israel's quest for the bomb is Avner Cohen, *Israel and the Bomb* (New York: Columbia University Press, 1998). See also Meirion Jones, 'Britain's Dirty Secret', *New Statesman*, 13 Mar. 2006, and Howard Kohn and Barbara Newman, 'How Israel Got the Bomb', *Rolling Stone*, 12 Jan. 1977. Much of the context for Israeli decisionmaking—US policy toward the Middle East—is provided by Douglas Little, *American Orientalism: The United States and the Middle East since 1945* (Chapel Hill, NC: University of North Carolina Press, 2002), and Peter L. Hahn, *Trapped in the Middle East: US Policy toward the Arab–Israeli Conflict, 1945–1961* (Chapel Hill, NC: University of North Carolina Press, 2004).

Sources on the South African nuclear program include J. D. L. Moore, *South Africa and Nuclear Proliferation: South Africa's Nuclear Capabilities and Intentions in the Context of International Non-Proliferation Policies* (New York: St Martin's,

1987); Barbara Rogers and Zdenek Cervenka, *The Nuclear Axis: Secret Collaboration between West Germany and South Africa* (New York: Times Books, 1978); Thomas B. Cochran, 'Highly Enriched Uranium Production for South African Nuclear Weapons', *Science and Global Security*, 4 (1994), 161–74; Waldo Stumpf, 'Birth and Death of the South African Nuclear Weapons Programme', http://www.fas.org/nuke/guide/rsa/nuke/stumpf. htm; David Albright, 'South Africa and the Affordable Bomb', *Bulletin of the Atomic Scientists*, 50/4 (July–Aug. 1994), 37–47; id. 'South Africa's Nuclear Weapons Program' 14 Mar. 2001, http://web.mit.edu/seminars/ wed_archives_01spring/albright.htm.

China's nuclear project gets judicious treatment in John Wilson Lewis and Xue Litai, *China Builds the Bomb* (Stanford, CA: Stanford University Press, 1988). Other sources include Ming Zhang, *China's Changing Nuclear Posture: Reaction to the South Asian Nuclear Tests* (Washington: Carnegie Endowment for International Peace, 1999); Rana Mitter, *A Bitter Revolution: China's Struggle with the Modern World* (Oxford: Oxford University Press, 2004); and Mark Oliphant, 'Over Pots of Tea: Excerpts from a Diary of a Visit to China', *Bulletin of the Atomic Scientists*, 22/5 (May 1966), 36–43.

The book to know on India's (and South Asia's) atomic aspirations is George Perkovich, *India's Nuclear Bomb: The Impact on Global Proliferation* (Berkeley and Los Angeles: University of California Press, 1999). Supplement Perkovich with Itty Abraham, *The Making of the Indian Atomic Bomb: Science, Security, and the Postcolonial State* (London: Zed Books, 1998); Karsten Frey, *India's Nuclear Bomb and National Security* (London: Routledge, 2006); Andrew J. Rotter, *Comrades at Odds: The United States and India, 1947–1964* (Ithaca, NY: Cornell University Press, 2000); Ashok Kapur, *India's Nuclear Option: Atomic Diplomacy and Decision Making* (New York: Praeger, 1976); and Pratap Bhanu Mehta, 'India: The Nuclear Politics of Self-Esteem', *Current History* (Dec. 1998), 403–6.

The worldwide movement against nuclear weapons is thoroughly chronicled in Lawrence S. Wittner's three-volume study *The Struggle against the Bomb*, published by Stanford University Press: i. *One World or None*, takes the story through 1953 (published 1993); ii. *Resisting the Bomb*, covers the period 1954–1970 (1997); and iii. *Toward Nuclear Abolition*, runs from 1971 to 2002 (2003). See also Frances B. McCrea and Gerald E. Markle, *Minutes to Midnight: Nuclear Weapons Protest in America* (Newberry Park, CA: Sage Publications, 1989). Essays by Mohandas Gandhi, Wilfred Burchett, Albert Camus, and other opponents of nuclear weapons and the arms race are included in Bird and Lifschultz, *Hiroshima's Shadow*. On the morality of atomic weapons, consult Walzer, *Just and Unjust Wars*, and *The Collected Philosophical Papers of G. E. M. Anscombe*, iii. *Ethics, Religion, and Politics* (Minneapolis, MN: University of Minnesota Press, 1981).

Finally, a few good collections of writing on the bomb. In addition to the Bird and Lifschultz, Bernstein, Hasegawa, and Hogan volumes cited above, see Shane J. Maddock, ed. *The Nuclear Age* (Boston: Houghton-Mifflin, 2001); Laura Hein and Mark Selden, eds. *Living with the Bomb: American and Japanese Cultural Conflicts in the Nuclear Age* (Armonk, NY: M. E. Sharpe, 1997); and, with emphasis on the ill-starred 1995 Smithsonian exhibition on the atomic bomb, Edward T. Linenthal and Tom Englehardt, eds., *History Wars: The 'Enola Gay' and Other Battles for the American Past* (New York: Henry Holt, 1996).

Credits

IMAGES

Brookhaven National Laboratory: 8; Corbis: 1, 3, 13, 14; Empics: 12; Weimar Archive/Mary Evans Picture Library: 2; AFP/Getty Images: 11; Getty Images: 9; Hulton Archive/Getty Images: 5; Time Life Pictures/Getty Images: 7, 16; Los Alamos National Laboratory: 10; Marilyn Silverstone/Magnum: 18; National Archives/Double Delta Industries, Inc.: 4; The Harry Charles Kelly Papers, Special Collections Research Center, North Carolina State University Libraries: 6; A. lu Semenov: 17; Joe O'Donnell/Vanderbilt University Press: 15.

POETRY

Haiku by Genshi Fujikawa, Nobuyuki Okada, and Isami Sasaki from *The Atomic Bomb: Voices from Hiroshima and Nagasaki* edited by Kyoko & Mark Selden (M E Sharpe, Armonk NY, 1989), reprinted by permission of the publishers.

Sadako Kurihara: 'Ruins' from *When We Say 'Hiroshima' Selected Poems* by Kurihara Sadako translated by Richard H Minear (Center for Japanese Studies, University of Michigan, Ann Arbor, 1999), reprinted by permission of the publishers.

Terai Sumie: 'White Nagasaki: A Haiku Sequence' from *White Flash/Black Rain: Women of Japan Revive the Bomb* edited and translated by Lequita Vance-Watkins and Aratani Mariko (Milkweed Editions, 1995).

Eisaku Yoneda: 'Standing in the Rains' from *Death in Life* by Robert Jay Lifton (Touchstone, 1967).

We have tried to trace and contact all copyright holders before publication. If notified, the publishers will be pleased to rectify any errors or omissions at the earliest opportunity.

Index

X-rays 8

Yamamoto (Lieutenant General) 197
Yamamoto, Isoroku (Admiral) 67
Yamashiro, Kikuko 196
Yamauchi, Takeo 178
Yasuda, Takeo 67
Yonai, Mitsumasa
    Big Six 207
    settlement favored 180
    Soviet war declaration 208

surrender 219
surrender terms 209, 212, 215
Yoneda, Eisaku 225
York, Herbert 262
Yoshihiro, Kimura 196, 201
Yukawa, Hideki 64
Yutaka, Yokota 186–7

Zeldovich, Yakov 237, 243, 260, 263
Zhou Enlai 294, 295
Zoe reactor (France) 284